HIS MOTHER
HER SISTER MARY AND
MARY MAGDALENE

JESUS
HIS MOTHER
HER SISTER MARY AND
MARY MAGDALENE

The Gnostic Background
to the Gospel of John

ROBERT CROTTY

DAVID LOVELL PUBLISHING
MELBOURNE AUSTRALIA

Published in 2016 by

David Lovell Publishing
PO Box 44, Kew East
Victoria 3102 Australia
tel/fax +61 3 9859 0000
publisher@davidlovellpublishing.com

Front cover image: 'John of Patmos', illuminated page from the Waldburg
Prayer Book, Württembergische Landes Library, Stuttgart, Breviary codex 12,
folio 34v, 1486; courtesy Wikimedia Commons.
Typeset in 9.5/14 Garth Graphic
Printed in Australia by Griffin Digital

National Library of Australia Cataloguing-in-Publication data

Crotty, R., 1937 - author.
Jesus, his mother, her sister Mary and Mary Magdalene : the gnostic
background to the gospel of John /Robert Crotty.
  ISBN: 978 1 86355 159 5 (paperback)
  Jesus Christ – History of doctrines.
  Bible. John – Criticism, interpretation etc.
  Church history – Primitive and early church, approximately 30-600.
  Christianity. Gnosticism.
226.5

FOREWORD

THE GOSPEL OF JOHN has long been recognised as being different in structure, language and orientation to the other three gospels. Robert Crotty, however, demonstrates by means of historical-critical and literary research that John's Gospel is radically different, grounded not only in early Christian traditions but also in non-canonical Gnostic writings that were never officially recognised by the Christian church.

Crotty completes a brilliant analysis of these ancient writings and challenges us to face the reality that John's Gospel is not an expression of 'absolute historical truth'. He holds that a scientific historical approach must be complemented by research into the cultural context of the writing, especially the religious cultural context.

Significant and challenging is Crotty's analysis of early Christian Gnosticism, which involved several historical movements. The texts from Nag Hammadi, for example, include alternative myths of creation and salvation, the human soul, the feminine divine principle and accounts of the sayings and deeds of Jesus. These accounts included the *Gospel of Mary* and the *Gospel of Judas*.

A complex Gnostic cosmology lies behind the structure and formulation of the Gospel of John, according to Crotty. The Gospel of John has incorporated seven independent Gnostic treatises as well as a Book of Seven Signs. The first of the treatises is a Hymn to the Word (*Logos*) (1:1-18), which incorporates classic Gnostic terms such as *Logos*, Beginning, Only Son, Light, Life, Fullness, The World, and so on. This cluster of terms, argues Crotty, only makes sense when interpreted in the light of its Gnostic cosmology. These treatises are also full of surprises, including the discovery that Judas is not the betrayer of Jesus and that Jesus married his Mother at Cana.

Crotty's work challenges most current understandings of the Gospel of John. By tracing the Gospel's complex history, Crotty has highlighted diverse historical, cultural and religious developments, some of which are suggested by the enigmatic title of his book. However, in time the Gnosticism of John was muted and over-written by Roman Christianity.

Thanks to Robert Crotty, however, we are confronted by an early stream of thought that demonstrates that our Christian heritage is complex, controversial and mystical.

His book is a bold, brilliant unearthing of the religious roots of the Gospel of John.

Dr Norman Habel

Editor of *The Earth Bible Project*

Professorial Fellow at Flinders University of South Australia

CONTENTS

To the three important
women in my life

Marie – my wife
Miriam – my daughter
Matilda– my granddaughter

INTRODUCTION

THIS IS A STUDY OF THE GOSPEL OF JOHN as a piece of literature, and very fine literature at that. It concentrates mainly on the background and the literary structure of the gospel and tries to conjecture, with substantiation, how it came to be in the shape that it is.

The title of the book (*Jesus, His Mother, Her Sister Mary and Mary Magdalene*) underlies the challenge that the book sets out to answer. Who is Jesus in the Gospel of John? At times he seems human, at times he seems divine. Who is his Mother? At two crucial points in the narrative she appears and in both instances her presence has caused grave difficulties for the interpreter. Who is the Sister? Did the Mother of Jesus have a sister never noted in the other gospels? And there is Mary Magdalene. She plays a major role in the narrative of the Resurrection of Jesus. But who is she? The Gospel of John has long been seen by its readers as different from the other canonical gospels (the four gospels that have been recognized by the Christian Church since the fourth century CE as belonging to the official list of Christian Scriptures, as suitable to be used in its liturgies, as deriving from the apostolic age and as handing on accurate Christian teaching and practice). These other gospels are Matthew, Mark and Luke, called the Synoptics because they can be seen 'from the same viewpoint'.[1]

These three are similar in language (sometimes actually overlapping, word for word), in their chronological sequence for the life and ministry of Jesus and in their theological outlook. However, while there are some significant differences between them, there are far more notable differences between the Synoptics and John: in events, in geography, chronology, language, literary style and theological viewpoints.

---

[1] We acknowledge that the authorship of the four gospels is unknown. The names of Matthew, Mark, Luke and John appended to the canonical gospels are later additions. When reference is made to the four evangelists by name ('Mark writes...', 'Luke recounts...') then it simply refers to the final edition of the writings that bear their name.

John was, from quite ancient times, called 'The Spiritual Gospel' because of the beauty and expansiveness of its discourse. This can never be denied. Its emphasis on spiritual knowledge, on love, on unity has inspired many subsequent Christian writers down through the ages. It reads at times like a mystical treatise. Some have even seen parallels between it and that earlier classic, *The Bhagavad Gita*, one of the sacred Hindu writings full of the language of compassionate love.

However, in the Christian history of thought, the Gospel of John has caused problems. In places, it indicates that the Father is greater than the Son, that a Paraclete will come to replace Jesus, that the World is a despicable place, that some humans will never find salvation despite their efforts. It also contains new disciples unmentioned in the three Synoptics: Nathanael, Nicodemus, the 'Beloved Disciple' (identity not revealed). Other disciples play new roles compared to their namesakes in the Synoptics – Simon Peter, Thomas, Philip, Mary Magdalene. On the other hand, the Virgin Mary is not mentioned by name or her virginity; there is only reference to 'the Mother of Jesus'. There is a clear disapproval of Baptism as understood in the Synoptics, and there is no text instituting the Eucharist.

A new Johannine vocabulary came into vogue. Some of its terminology overlapped in meaning with the Synoptics, but much did not. What do The Word, Sign, Son of Man, Knowledge, Truth, Eternal Life, The Hour, the World, Judgement, Paraclete, the Spirit (and various combinations of these) mean in the context of John's gospel?

Scholars have also puzzled over the literary structure of John. What should be the basis for any structure? Many have claimed that the structure should be based on its chronology: there are at least four separate visits by Jesus to Jerusalem to celebrate a variety of Festivals (Passover, Booths, Dedication and an unnamed Festival) and it was thought that perhaps the gospel could be ordered around each celebration. It has also been suggested that the sequence of the Jewish yearly liturgy might have been used as a structure. Others see the enigmatic reference to Signs (*semeia*) as the key to an underlying structure. In fact, what seems to be the original conclusion in 20:30-31 would indicate that these Signs are indeed the secret to the book's structure.

> [30] Now Jesus did many other Signs in the presence of his disciples, which are not written in this book. [31]But these are written so that you may come to believe that Jesus is the Messiah, the Son of God, and that through believing you may have Life in his Name.

But, if this is so, we are still left wondering how many of these Signs there actually are and how they form an underlying literary template. The Cana event and the cure of the Official's Son are clearly called Signs in the text. But where are the other Signs, not specifically named? And what is the structure of the non-Sign material that lies between them?

Many years ago I was a student in Rome under one of the great Johannine scholars, Ignace de la Potterie, now deceased. He was a Belgian Jesuit, a friendly man. He taught a semester course just on chapters 18-19 of John. We pored over the Greek text, word by word. I loved every minute of it and would return home from the university ready to continue my own analysis. I learned much about the peculiar terminology in John's gospel, much about literary analysis, much about finding links in the very language of John. There were always some niggling questions in my mind about the text. In many ways this book is the result of my own musings over decades since that introduction by De la Potterie to the analysis of John.

De la Potterie also introduced us to the Hebrew Scriptures' allusions in John's gospel. We compared Hebrew texts with Greek texts. He also indicated where the Dead Sea Scrolls were relevant to understanding the text. At that time, few recognized the importance of the Dead Sea Scrolls. Later, the Gnostic texts from Nag Hammadi, which were only coming into the public domain in De la Potterie's era, provided the same sort of challenge. I now see these latter texts as of paramount importance. They are the reason for this book being written.

These matters will all be food for thought in this book. Where did the Gospel of John come from? How should it be structured? What is it saying?

There are certain things that must be made clear. This study will engage with the four canonical gospels. More, it will equally engage with non-canonical writings and traditions, never recognized by the Christian Church as being guaranteed teachings, particularly the Gnostic writings from the first centuries. All such items of literature will be given their requisite status as historical and literary openings to that interesting period of Christian beginnings. It must be stated that this book is not written from the vantage point of the Christian Church which differentiates between canonical biblical writings (inspired and inerrant) and those writings outside the canon.

In fact, this book is written from an historical and literary point of view and it uses the methods of historical research and literary criticism. No outcome is *a priori* excluded from its argument (because, for example, an outcome contradicts a Creed or an official Church position) and no conclusion needs to answer to any other authority than the secular historical and literary Academe. Of course, if it were otherwise and if the gospels, for example, were held to be inerrant and divinely inspired, then what is said about the Gospel of John would have to be reconciled with the other gospels and all of them with some absolute historical truth; any seeming discrepancies would have, by definition, to be explained away. If the Gnostic gospels are considered heretical and erroneous by the Christian Church, as they are, and this book was in accord with authoritative Christian teaching, then it would not be worth considering them. I recognize that there are many modern Christian writers, apart from myself, who do not think in this absolutist way.

Finally, at the risk of being repetitive, I do not consider the four canonical gospels to be inerrant and I do not consider the Gnostic gospels to be anything less than variant presentations written mostly by Christian communities different to those responsible for the canonical writings. These writings are given equal hearing in this book. I am beholden only to the canons of history and literature. On the other hand, if the contrary to what I will conclude can be reasonably proved by others on academic grounds, then, as a reasonable historian and literary critic, I will be quite willing to admit my error and change my opinion.

IMPORTANT NOTE

In all cases that follow the biblical text will be English. This will be basically the New Revised Standard Version (NRSV) as found in The Harper-Collins Study Bible. The following acknowledgement is made:

> The Scripture quotations contained herein are from the New Revised Version Bible, copyright © 1989 by the Division of Christian Education of the National Council of the Churches of Christ in the USA. Used by permission. All rights reserved.

However, on occasions the NRSV has been edited to highlight any significant words by using upper case and, in a few instances, by amending the translation where it is felt that the translation of the Greek has been betrayed. What are considered expansions (additions, corrections, explanations) to the original text are indicated by the use of italics.

All quotes from the Gnostic Scriptures are taken from J. M. Robinson ed. (1978), *The Nag Hammadi Library in English*, HarperSanFrancisco: San Francisco. As with the NRSV text, where important keywords have not been translated from the Coptic there is an insertion explaining this fact.

— 1 —
SOME PRELIMINARIES

SOME PRELIMINARY PRINCIPLES must be stated at the onset. These will inform the book from this point onwards.

The first principle regards History and the Bible. To what extent can the study of the Bible be described as an historical search? The second principle regards Religion. Did religion fall from the heavens? Or is it an explicable phenomenon within the ambit of human development?

HISTORY AND THE BIBLE

Since the nineteenth century there has been an emphasis in the Western world as concerns the science of history. History is a social science; it has its own field of discipline, its own methodology. The historian collects, organizes and then presents past data. First, this collected data must be accurate and could be the result of the archaeologist's discoveries, of a literary scholar's search through past manuscripts or books, of a social scientist's surveys, of the analyst's oral interviews of people involved in events and so on. But the tabulation of 'facts', factual data, is not yet history. The historian must go further and interpret this data in a narrative. The narrative should attempt to explain the sequence of events and identify the causes and effects in that sequence; the narrative is 'history'. Generations of historians have done this; their narrative interpretations have been, of course, affected by the differing time and place of their history-writing. Historians, who agree over the admissibility of data, will often differ over the line of interpretation. A new cultural situation will inevitably give rise to a new interpretive perspective. There will never be a final history of any sequence of facts.

In the nineteenth century, history was lauded as superior to religious tradition, but some distinctions were made. Data from the past, such as the history of Rome derived from the writings of Livy, had once been seen as containing an incontrovertible sequence of 'facts'. Livy had handed on the exact facts. Scholars of the nineteenth century acknowledged the importance of the data but they also recognized that those recorded 'facts' were often portrayed from the social and political point of view of an interested Roman writer and not from the standpoint of 'objectivity'. These historians wanted to stand back from the data and to write 'true' history, a history that was not beholden in its line of interpretation to any authority or convention. They thought of it as the final historical project. It was a noble endeavour, but quite unattainable.

As might have been expected, these historians very soon showed interest in the Bible, both the Hebrew Scriptures[2] and the Christian Scriptures.[3] Certainly the Bible seemed to contain credible data, but its need for historical analysis and interpretation was just too obvious. So the historians asked: what might be a history of Israel, written by working on the facts related in the Hebrew Scriptures but with much more suspicion and caution? What actually happened historically when Moses ordered the Sea to part? More to the point, what would be the history of Jesus, using the Christian Scriptures, and particularly the gospels, from the point of the objective literary critic and historian? Was he biologically born of a virgin? Did Jesus physically walk on water? Did he, after his death, literally come out of a tomb? This gave rise at that time to a search for an historical Jesus.

---

[2] The collection of Hebrew Scriptures contains, in its present layout, three major sections.

　　1. The first section is usually called the *Torah* (its Hebrew title, usually translated as 'Law') or the Pentateuch (which means 'five scrolls' or a 'five-part book' in Greek). These five books are: Genesis, Exodus, Leviticus, Numbers and Deuteronomy.

　　2. The second section of the Hebrew Scriptures, the *Nevi'im* or Prophets, include the following books: Joshua, Judges, 1 and 2 Samuel, 1 and 2 Kings, Isaiah, Jeremiah, Ezekiel and The Twelve Prophets. Not all of these would make up what is commonly understood as 'prophetic' books.

　　3. The third section of the Hebrew Scriptures, the *Kethuvim* or Writings include the following books: Psalms, Proverbs, Job, Song of Solomon, Ruth, Lamentations, Ecclesiastes, Esther, Daniel, Ezra-Nehemiah and 1 and 2 Chronicles.

[3] The Christian Scriptures had been gathered into a definitive and official collection, or canon, only by the end of the fourth century CE. There were twenty-seven books in all. These were composed of the following: the four gospels of Matthew, Mark, Luke and John; the Acts of the Apostles; fourteen letters of Paul, although there was always doubt about his authorship of at least one of them (the Letter to the Hebrews) and today there is widespread agreement that seven of the Letters were composed by Paul, while six are not from his hand; the Catholic letters, so-called because they were presumed to be not addressed to particular communities but to the universal (in Latin, *catholica*) church – the letter of James, two letters of Peter, three letters of John, one letter of Jude; finally, the book of Revelation.

The resolution to sift out the history of Israel and the biography of Jesus has continued to the present day. It has coloured a great deal of biblical research, both on the Hebrew Scriptures and the Christian Scriptures. As pointed out above, it would be unlikely that any one history or biography would be the final version, but there are some biblical critics who claim just that.

Our first principle is that a scientific historical approach is only one approach to these writings. But an analysis of religion in a social context, as will follow, would give cause for hesitation in seeing this historical endeavour as the aim of all biblical research. In fact, it will become clear that the search for historicity blights much of the academic scrutiny and interpretation of both the Hebrew Scriptures and the Christian Scriptures.

There is need, therefore, to look at the broader subject of our enquiry which so far has been blithely taken for granted – religion in its social context.

RELIGION AND CULTURE

We need to clarify what can be understood as religion. We begin with the idea of human culture.

Human Culture

We are surrounded by secular culture in everyday life. Culture consists of the organized ways of thinking, acting and valuing proper to a group of humans. Secular culture allows human beings to find order amid common human experience, to explain historical events, to solve problems regarding their own identity. We are able to walk down the street of a city, to pass certain people by and to greet others in conversation, to share a meal and to achieve a day's work because we share a common culture with these people. We feel comfortable in our own cultural setting (whereas we may not feel comfortable in a North African one, strolling down a street, conversing, eating or working).

However, there are times when people find themselves faced with profound ignorance that does not provide easy answers, or with the experience of suffering (friends, relatives and even we ourselves may experience physical and mental problems), or with the death of loved ones, or with the problem of evil (why are children abused? why do innocent people suffer and die? why are there tsunamis?). These things can threaten an ordered, cultural world, where people feel at home and safe.

Culture and Religion

At this point, where secular culture cannot cope, there is an urgent need for something more – a religious culture. A 'religious culture' could include the living world religions, indigenous religions such as the many Aboriginal Australian religions, New Religious Movements, Marxism, Humanism and so on. Conventionally, some of these would not be acknowledged as religions. The broadly religious person, by means of such a religious culture, can make sense of the world, of others and of self in terms of Ultimacy.

Ultimacy is ultimate order, where everything fits in perfectly, as against everyday order, where most everyday things fit into some order, but there are exceptions. A religious culture provides us with a focus by which we can see everything in relationship with Ultimacy. Whereas we can manage, with our secular culture, to get by day-to-day, there are times when we need to see the Big Picture. All humans, who are capable of independent thought and are not mentally handicapped to any significant degree, have the inborn capacity to do this. All human persons should therefore be designated as 'religious persons', although the 'religion' of some of these people might not necessarily be recognized as a religion in anything like the conventional sense. Someone might follow Humanism with a mixture of Buddhist meditation and Christian belief in an afterlife – and it might work.

Humans feel that there is a great gulf between themselves and the Ultimacy of which we have spoken earlier. Religion is about bridging that gulf. But, which religion or religions achieve this bridging?

With everyday culture (say Chinese culture or European culture) there is always the possibility of ethnocentrism, the idea that *my* culture, with its particular ways of thinking and acting and valuing is the only true culture. In fact, it is normal to affirm that the way *I* think and do things is the right way. There can be many intermediate steps until we put aside this ethnocentrism and come to multiculturalism, where we recognize that all human cultures are true, despite being different. It is something the same with religion.

There are three main highpoints in the scale, with possibilities in between, when we examine the attitudes of humans towards religious culture.

Exclusivism, an analogue of ethnocentrism, is the attitude that only one particular religious culture is valid, all others are mistaken.

Inclusivism describes the view that one religious culture is certainly valid, but that other religious cultures, but not all, may share – completely, partially, even perhaps inadequately – the truth of the one valid religious culture.

Pluralism, an analogue of multiculturalism, would maintain that all religious cultures are acceptable. They all can achieve the same purpose of putting a group into contact with Ultimacy, ultimate meaning. Why choose one rather than another? This choice would be because of the family into which the person was born, societal pressure, subsequent education, the chance events of a person's life story.

Analysis of Religion

We need now to analyse this religious culture, religion, in broader detail. As was said above, religion is about bridging the gulf between a human group and Ultimacy. We now state that the central phenomenon of any religion is not its sacred text (if it should be a literate society), nor its ethical system, nor its doctrinal teaching, but its religious experience, the quality of human reaction that is aroused by a deep-felt moment of making contact with Ultimacy.

To confirm this priority of religious experience, we could take the example of Islam. Its sacred story (not necessarily an historical story!) recounts that at a certain moment Muhammad, while deep in meditation on a hill outside Mecca, was enabled to contact what he interpreted as Ultimacy. On this occasion he identified Ultimacy by means of *al 'ilah*, 'The God' or Allah. For him *al 'ilah* became a new religious focus that gave him access to Ultimacy. By means of *al 'ilah* he was able to understand life and self through the focus of Ultimacy. He described this experience as *islam*, absolute submission and an awareness of human frailty in the presence of Allah. He thereby achieved an ultimate order in his life. Muhammad's religion is the religion of *islam* or 'submission' and its adherents are *muslims* or 'people submitted' to Allah.

Whether the sacred story is historically true is of no importance. What is important is the religious experience it has generated.

But Muhammad might have died without revealing how he had achieved his personal contact with Ultimacy; he might have kept it as a personal secret. In that case, there would have been no followers and no Islam. However, he left a body of myths (or sacred stories, not to be confused with the popular use of the term meaning untruths) and accounts of rituals (or religious ceremonies) which could allow his followers to bring the same ultimate meaning and direction into their own lives. Islamic myth and ritual are the principal means by which a Muslim can contact *al 'ilah*, as he did.

A similar process can be identified with all religions. Religious experience is effected by sacred myth or story and ritual. In the first place, myth is the way religious people speak and communicate with each other. All religious traditions have a fund of such stories. Importantly, though, sacred stories are not necessarily historical stories.

This mythical story is a metaphor that conveys the most profound spiritual truth, a truth not communicable by everyday language. It provides the essential features of a religious culture in story-form. But myth does more than recount facts about life. It recreates, for those who will listen, the original 'world' of the 'time of the beginnings', in which the way of life of a human group, the fund of its common understandings and its principal values, were established.

Myths convey information to the group about how the world came to be ('creation' or beginning-stories), about how humans were separated from Ultimacy (stories about a First Fall or a cosmic tragedy), about the possibility that the group can regain contact with Ultimacy (for example, the sacred stories of Founders of religions and stories of Atonement), about the possibility of final reconciliation with Ultimacy (eschatological myths).

In the second place, myth or sacred story is organically connected with religious ritual. Ritual is a ceremony, a sacred drama. Rather than recounting the deepest truths, the persons involved in ritual act out these truths. A core ritual is the re-enactment of that past event, when contact was initially made between a Founder or founding group and Ultimacy. But ritual, like myth, can only be understood when it is acknowledged to be essentially and inextricably connected with religious experience.

For example, the Jewish Passover is the dramatic, ritual-portrayal of the story of the Exodus out of Egypt, not as an historical event but as recounted in the sacred book of Exodus. This was achieved, Jews believe, by the God of Israel, known by the personal name of Yahweh.[4] Performing the ritual of

---

4   The Hebrew Scriptures has a number of names for 'God'. *'Elohim*, usually translated as 'God', is a plural form of 'god' in Hebrew. It is a generic term. 'Yahweh', usually translated as 'LORD' in the NRSV, is the personal name of the God of Israel. Its origin and meaning is disputed. The older Hebrew text of the Bible has only consonants with some markers for vowels. In the Christian period, from the seventh century, vowels were added to the consonants. Because the Jews did not pronounce this name of Yahweh in their religious services, the text left only the Hebrew consonants for Yahweh (Y-H-W-H). In those religious services, instead of 'Yahweh' the reader would substitute *'Adonai*, translated as 'My Lord', and so the vowels of 'Adonai were linked with the consonants of Yahweh to give the impossible word 'Jehovah'. Yahweh and YHWH are therefore alternate writings for the divine name, although the precise vowels of Yahweh are still disputed. We will use 'Yahweh' in this book.

Passover brings the past Exodus-event, as described in its tradition, into the present for the believing group. It is as if a particular group of Jews, gathered in the home on the festival of Passover, eating unleavened bread and drinking wine, becomes part of the story of the Moses-group and the Passover people and personally experiences the saving, guiding, comforting presence of the God of Israel, Yahweh. That Exodus-experience was considered to be the founding experience of Judaism, and celebrating Passover brings the experience of the past event into the present. Yahweh becomes their focus on Ultimacy.

Likewise for Roman Christians, the celebration of the sacrament of Baptism is the dramatic, ritual re-enactment of being incorporated into the community that is ruled by Jesus. Jesus as the envoy of The Father[5] came to establish a believing group. In the ritual of Baptism the Christian undergoes the initiation of passing through the waters of the Sea of Reeds, as the Israelites did at the beginning of the Exodus, and the Christian also experiences the passing through of the waters of Jordan, as the Israelites did to enter the Land of Promise. But, more, the Christian is inducted into participation in Jesus and his community. According to this way of thinking, the baptized become members of the people of the full promise: the Christians. The Father, as revealed by Jesus, becomes their focus on Ultimacy.

Myth, together with ritual, provide the context for a religion's particular experience; that experience is the moment of contact; the experience reveals that the group has made contact with Ultimacy. It provides ultimate meaning and gives ultimate direction to the participants. That is why humans have religions.

Religious Succession

Let us return to one point made in the earlier Muhammad example. Muhammad, Islam claims, underwent a profound religious experience that allowed him to see everything in ultimate perspective. He found *al 'ilah*

---

[5]   While the God of Israel was occasionally addressed as 'Father', the term was taken on by the early Christians as their particular name for their God (not seen as in any way distinct from Yahweh). Possibly the original form was Aramaic *'abba*. The meaning of *'abba* can be 'Daddy', but there is debate as to whether this was the meaning given to it by early Christians. When Aramaic *'abba* was translated into Greek, it became *pater*. To confuse the matter further, the Christian statement on the Trinity refers to the Divinity, in which the 'Father' or *pater* is one element. The Trinity is a later construction that was motivated by Greek philosophical analysis and a rather protracted acrimonious political debate. In what follows, 'Father' refers to the Christian identification of Yahweh.

and through that focus he contacted Ultimacy. Imbued with the religious experience of submissiveness, *islam*, he was satisfied, but the question was left open, as was pointed out earlier, as to whether his experience could be repeated by others. If not, then Muhammad's new, individual religious culture, personally satisfying as it undoubtedly was, would be spontaneously aborted. There would have been a Muhammad, but not an Islam.

This is the vital point about the establishment of a religion. Can the founding religious experience be replicated by others? Can the Founder, who has already experienced Ultimacy, have successors? 'Founders' are like great artists. Most people have at some time deep experiences of nature and human relationships in their lifetime. These experiences are usually occasional and indescribable. The artist is that rare, gifted individual who is able to use a medium – words, paint, musical sound – to communicate and share a deep, personal experience with others.

Similarly, the religious 'Founder' is the person (or sometimes a group or a human construction) who has undergone a personal contact with Ultimacy, but is thereafter also able to construct a system which can convey the ability to achieve this original religious experience to others. That system would consist basically of a collection of myths and rituals, sometimes linked to a sacred text in literate societies. The system can be called an intermediary system, because it brings about mediation between a human group and Ultimacy. A religious intermediary system is something analogous to a great work of art. Religious believers are analogous to art-lovers surrounding a superb painting or music-lovers listening to a Beethoven symphony, enthralled in the experience of the moment.

This intermediary system organizes other religious phenomena. Its driving mechanism, the recital of myths and performance of rituals, produces a profound religious experience, considered to be a replica of the founder's own original experience. (Whether it is or not is of no importance). The same mechanism also establishes a social-structure, a group of like-minded people who share more or less the same experience and, like all societies, its members will be graded into different religious roles (leaders/followers, teachers/learners, dominant/submissive and so on). The group learns what is expected as far as ethical behaviour and thinking are concerned; it is controlled by a compulsory list of essential beliefs, by the interpretation of essential symbols and usually, in literate societies, by a sacred text.

We can now outline the main facets of this intermediary system. Mediation, linking a human group to Ultimacy, allows that group to see life from an ultimate perspective. Depending upon the group's culture and world view, the gulf between the ultimate order of things and the human group will be perceived as more or less wide. From the side of Ultimacy, the gulf can be partially bridged by Other-worldly Intermediaries such as divine children and divine messengers; from the side of the human group it can be bridged by This-worldly Intermediaries such as sacred persons, kings, priests, prophets or heroes. The two sides of the system are intended to ensure that the human group makes contact with the sacred focus. This focus then allows the group to come into contact with Ultimacy.

All of this can be entered into a schematic model:

Focus on Ultimacy

↓

Other-worldly Intermediaries

(Contact Achieved)

This-worldly Intermediaries

↑

Religious Group

The focus on Ultimacy is usually, but not always, depicted as a High God, creator of the cosmos and determiner of human destiny. However, the focus can also be a group of gods or a more indistinct god-like structure.

But the identification of This-worldly and Other-worldly Intermediaries is not the only way that humans make contact with Ultimacy. In mystical religions there can be a more direct approach. For example, in Theravada Buddhism or, as we will see, Gnosticism, where devotees enter into divine space by personal meditation or secret knowledge, Ultimacy can be attained without the need for Intermediaries from either side. The system has been short-circuited.

Focus on Ultimacy

↓

(Contact Achieved)

↑

Mystical Religious Group

In short, religion is the means by which humans make contact with Ultimacy, either through Intermediaries or directly. The way they depict their focus on Ultimacy (symbolized as a God like Allah for Islam, a pantheon of gods for the ancient Greeks, a great world-soul or Brahman for the Hindus, Dreamtime Beings for Aboriginal Australians, the ideal of Humanity-within-a-Good-World-Order for Humanists) differs from one religion to another.

We can now more clearly ask the question posed earlier: is one particular depiction of a focus on Ultimacy the only right one for everyone (exclusivism), or is one focus certainly right and some others are close enough (inclusivism) or are all foci on Ultimacy, which presumably work, right and it is just a matter of personal preference which is chosen (pluralism)? This book will not be deciding on that question, interesting as it is.

As far as the readership of this book is concerned, there will be room for exclusivists, inclusivists and pluralists to feel at home.

When a religious group does make contact with Ultimacy, via its focus, then there is a religious experience (of submission or *islam* for Islam, of loving-kindness and 'chosenness' for the Jews, of *agape* or love of God and others for Christians, of enlightenment for Buddhists). That religious experience is generated by the religious group's myth and religious ritual leading to the identification of the Other-worldly Intermediary (or Intermediaries) by which the group achieves its focus and makes contact with Ultimacy; in mystical religions, the experience is achieved by the group, and its individuals singularly, making direct contact.

The important point that must be made is that, if a religion is to be successful and put the human group into contact with Ultimacy, then that experience will be believed to be the replication of what the Founder or Founders experienced. However, for a religious system to survive there has to be not only replication but also succession. Succession is the vital component for the perpetuation of a religion.

Returning one more time to Islam, we know that the focus on Ultimacy was symbolized as *al 'ilah* or Allah. Allah, it is firmly believed in Islam, produced the sacred book of the Qur'an. Its words were Allah's words (which goes a step further than the notion of Inspiration of the humanly-composed Scriptures in Judaism and Christianity) and were originally written on gold plates still preserved in the heavenly region. So the structure of Islam emerges:

Focus on Ultimacy: Allah

Other-worldly Intermediary:
the Divine Qur'an

(Contact Achieved)

This-worldly Intermediary:
Muhammad and the successors of Muhammad
who interpret the Divine Qur'an

Community of Islam

Dissension within Islam is not over Muhammad, but over the identification of the successors of Muhammad.[6]

This theory applies to all religion.

What we now want to see is how, first in Judaism and then in Christianity, there came about an established Sacred Story which expanded on the type of structure detailed above and validated first a religious way of life and secondly religious successors.

NOTES

The material in this Introduction depends on many sources, both old and new. I have found that the works of Clifford Geertz and John Hick, perhaps dated, have been invaluable. Both have many publications, only the key ones are included here. J. J. Smolicz, once Professor Education at the University of Adelaide, stimulated my thinking greatly, although his interest was more in Education.

D'Costa, G. (1966), 'The impossibility of a pluralism view of religion', *Religious Studies,* 32, pp. 223-232.

Geertz, C (1984), 'Distinguished lecture: anti anti-relativism', *American Anthropologist,* 86, 263-278.

Geertz, C. (1973), *The interpretation of cultures,* Basic Books: New York.

Hanson, F. A. (1979), 'Does God have a body? Truth, reality and cultural relativism', *Man* NS 14, 515-529.

Harari, Y. N. (2011), *Sapiens: A Brief History of Humankind,* Harvill Secker: London.

Hick, J. (1989), *An interpretation of religion: human responses to the transcendent.* Macmillan: London.

---

[6] The differences between Shia Islam and the Sunnis are based on this very point.

Loughlin, G. (1987), 'Noumenon and phenomenon.' *Religious Studies* 23, 495-508.

Lumsden, C. & Wilson, E. (1981), *Genes, mind and culture*, Harvard University Press: Cambridge, Mass.

Silver, L. (2006), *Challenging Nature: The Clash of Science and Spirituality at the New Frontiers of Life*, HarperCollins: New York.

Smolicz, J. (1984,) 'Multiculturalism and an overarching framework of values: some educational responses to assimilation, interaction and separatism in ethnically plural societies.' *European Journal of Education* 2, 2-24.

Smolicz, J. (1988), 'Tradition, core values and intercultural development.' *Ethnic and Racial Studies* 11, 384-410.

Spiro, M. (1978), 'Culture and human nature', in G Spindler (ed), *The making of psychological anthropology*, University of California Press: Berkeley.

Wilson, E.O. (2014), *The Meaning of Human Existence*, Liveright Publishing Corporation: New York and London.

— 2 —
STUDYING THE JEWISH BACKGROUND

THE JEWISH BACKGROUND IS ESSENTIAL for understanding the Christian literature that followed from the first century CE. It is also essential for understanding the Gospel of John. What follows is a literary and historical approach to Judaism and Ancient Israel that may be at odds with many other presentations.

JUDAISM AND THE ANCIENT NEAR EAST

Most books on the history of Judaism, even up to the present day, include as more or less historical fact some or even most of the following biblical stories:

- Creation by Yahweh, and Sin-stories (Adam and Eve, Cain and Abel, the Flood Generation, the Tower of Babel);
- The Ancestors: Abraham and Sarah, Isaac and Rebekah, Jacob/Israel and his four wives from whom are born twelve sons who establish the Twelve Tribes of Israel;
- Moses and the Exodus of the Twelve Tribes out of Egypt, Meeting of People of Israel with the God of Israel, Yahweh, on Sinai;
- The Taking of the Land of Canaan;
- Judges, usually self-appointed guerrilla leaders, rule the Land;
- David becomes King and captures Jerusalem as the capital of a great Kingdom. He is succeeded by his son, Solomon, who builds the First Temple to Yahweh;
- This united Kingdom divides into two separate kingdoms, Israel in the north and Judah in the south, each with a separate line of kings. Israel has its capital in Samaria (eventually) and Judah has its capital in Jerusalem;

- Northern Israel is destroyed by the Assyrians;

- Jerusalem in the south is destroyed by the Babylonians together with its First Temple;

- The people of Jerusalem and Judah are exiled to Mesopotamia;

- The Persians, succeeding the Babylonians, allow the people to return to rebuild the Second Temple of Yahweh. The Persians are later overcome by the Greeks;

- The Hasmoneans, successors to the Maccabee family, who rebelled against the Greeks, retake possession of Jerusalem and Judah. They cleanse the Second Temple and reassert Jewish independence.

The primary source for this narration of events has always been the Hebrew Scriptures, supplemented by the secular history of Josephus[7], some Roman histories and archaeological finds.

Earlier Approaches

We have already seen that, until the nineteenth century, these events, as related in the Hebrew Scriptures, had been generally considered as deriving from a Golden Age. They were regarded as reliable reports from an era when life was radically different to what modern people know, a time when wondrous natural events, miracles and bodily cures wrought by divine intervention were commonplace, when angels and demons openly roamed the world.

But there was rethinking from the nineteenth century. Historians were not satisfied with a naive recital of the events in the Hebrew Scriptures. There was first the recognition that the Hebrew Scriptures were based on pre-existing sources. The stories of creation and the early generations of humans in the book of Genesis were found to have parallels in the myths of other ancient literatures. The stories of the Ancestors, the Exodus, the Taking of the Land were found to contain duplications and discrepancies that pointed to the combination of several earlier documents or traditions. This uncovering of previous sources was devastating news to many practising

---

[7] Flavius Josephus (37-100 CE) was a Jew, regarded by fellow Jews as a renegade because in the struggle against Rome he went over to the Roman side. He became the protégé of the Roman general, Vespasian. When Vespasian became Emperor in 69 CE he adopted Josephus and Josephus took on the family name of the dynasty, Flavius. Josephus then wrote in Greek two principal books: *The Jewish War* in about 75 CE and *The Antiquities of the Jews* in about 94 CE. His works can be found in Whiston, W. (trans.) (1987), *The Works of Josephus*, Hendrickson Publishers Inc: Peabody, MA. Whiston can be accessed online.

Jews and Christians who had long claimed that these were inspired words handed on by divine dictation to outstanding people like Moses, David and Solomon. Much re-thinking was required.

There followed an important acknowledgement that the Hebrew Scriptures had made use of literary forms other than history. There were for example stories that were similar to myth, legend, fable, poetry, wisdom-writing and occasionally, but not always, history. These literary forms were also found in other ancient Near Eastern literatures. Of vital importance, it was claimed that the texts needed to be understood according to these particular literary forms, which were not always familiar to readers in modern times. Poetry could not be read as scientific discourse; legends could not be read as history. It was decided that the process of writing and re-writing of the Hebrew Scriptures, their transmission, had to be charted in order for the meaning to be extracted.

There have been desperate attempts, even in the recent past, to prove that at least the historical outline of events in the Hebrew Scriptures was trustworthy, even if some details might be questioned. Archaeology and non-biblical historical records were engaged to give fuller descriptions and dates to the Ancestors, the Exodus, the building of the two Temples, the reigns of the kings of Judah and Israel, the destruction of Jerusalem and the Exile of some of its citizens into Mesopotamia. However, historical sources and archaeology could not always provide this information. It was still maintained nevertheless that, while there might be debate over some historical issues and dates, the main events themselves were sacrosanct, real and historical events which had occurred more or less as outlined in the Hebrew Scriptures.

But in time even these pivotal events fell under scrutiny. The archaeology of Jericho, whose walls were said to have tumbled when Joshua's soldiers blew the sacred trumpets in the book of Joshua, did not seem to indicate any destruction at the time proposed for the end of the Exodus; in fact, there was no Egyptian evidence for an Exodus which must have been a massive enterprise; there was little or no evidence for any grandiose kingdom of David and Solomon or the building of a magnificent Temple of Yahweh in Jerusalem. By the middle of the twentieth century there was a move away from the emphasis on the past events of Judaism as being themselves bearers of meaning and teaching, to a stress on the biblical text itself as the bearer of meaning. The question was asked: what do the Hebrew Scriptures, with their literary forms and rhetorical structure, tell us? Whatever might or might not historically have taken place in the past became less and less important.

As a result, there was to be a new development, as the twentieth century came to its end. It depended on the text-based approach just described above. It was a minimalist theory that recognized only a small amount of history in the biblical texts and placed the writing of biblical scrolls, which were to be eventually incorporated into the Hebrew Scriptures, quite late.

A Text-based Approach

Previously, it had been strongly maintained that texts incorporating the earliest forms of the Hebrew Scriptures, the forerunners of the Hebrew Bible, could be dated back at least to the time of David and Solomon. Texts were said to be almost contemporary with the earliest events themselves and certainly contemporary with later ones. The description of the Exodus out of Egypt was attributed to writers in the time of David, around 1000 BCE, and the writings of the great prophets were attributed to those very people such as Amos and Isaiah, with additions and corrections added not long after their time. These primary texts, it was said, were then edited time and again but the template remained the ancient text. The Psalms were mostly dated at that time to the song practices in the first Temple of Jerusalem.

The new minimalist approach has questioned most of this dating and certainly questioned more than ever the historicity of the Hebrew Scriptures. As a result, this minimalist theory also requires the establishment of the religion of Judaism to be dated much later than had previously been accepted. According to the minimalists, Judaism did not begin with Abraham, not even with Moses or David, not with the writing prophets. On the contrary, they have dated Judaism as a specific and identifiable religion to around the second century BCE, during the time of the Hasmonean kings who succeeded the Maccabee warriors.[8]

I will make use of the terminology that I have developed elsewhere to describe what I see as the three facets of this approach: Literary Israel (The Jewish sacred Story), Historical Israel and Biblical Israel.[9]

Literary Israel

There is first and most importantly a Literary Israel, the Jewish sacred Story, contained within the amalgam of stories in the Hebrew Scriptures. Literary Israel is a sacred story that has its own chronology and its own succession of

---

[8] I will not put down the argument for this new approach here, although on the basis of evidence I am most sympathetic towards it.

[9] See my book, *Three Revolutions: Three Drastic Changes in Interpreting the Bible,* ATF Press: Hindmarsh, 2012, particularly chapter 14.

events, as chronicled in the earlier description of 'historical events' above. The Jewish Story includes its own sacred and non-sacred characters, who successively appear from Adam via Moses to Ezra, and it concludes its tale in the Greek period prior to Christian beginnings. That is important. Literary Israel looks very much like the 'history' described at the beginning of this chapter.

Beneath its surface is a structure, such as we saw in the earlier chapter.

Like all religions, Judaism also required a replication and a succession. The Story of Israel described the great moment when the original contact was made with the God of Israel, Yahweh. Not always did Yahweh appear directly; there were sometimes references to the Word-action of Yahweh which had to be interpreted; at other times there was the Spirit of Yahweh, causing detectable change; at other times he sent an Angel or messenger. Sometimes the Story told of Abraham meeting Yahweh; at other times Moses met Yahweh on Sinai. At least in its final written form, the Story centred on Moses as the This-worldly Intermediary. This ensured replication.

Focus on Ultimacy: Yahweh

Other-worldly Intermediaries:
Word of Yahweh, the Spirit of Yahweh,
the Angel of Yahweh (and others)

(Contact Achieved)

This-worldly Intermediary: 'Moses'

The People of Israel

The Sinai Story was the tradition describing the original moment of contact with Yahweh. How could this moment be replicated? In the first place, it had to be achieved by 'Moses'. But more than that, like Muhammad at a later date, Moses had to have successors. So Moses (who had earlier been foreshadowed by Abraham in the literature) was said in the tradition to have handed on his role to Joshua, the hero of yet another version of the Story. From Joshua the role passed to the Kings, with David the greatest of them, and also prophets like Elijah and Elisha. Whether any of this succession is historical is not important. What is important is that it was firmly believed that there had been a succession.

The big question was: who is 'Moses' today? Or, again, will 'Moses' come in the future as another Prophet, a Messiah[10] or some other God-sent being?

We will see later that there were Jews in the pre-Christian period who were despairing of their Intermediaries. They managed to find a short-circuited system whereby they re-interprted the Jewish story. There will be more about them in the section on Jewish Gnosticism.

We must distinguish, however, this Sacred Story from Historical Israel.

Historical Israel

We can also distinguish an Historical Israel. It is the orderly description and explanation of the sequence of people and events in the areas later known as Judah and Israel (and their neighbours), reliably reconstructed from various historical documents and inscriptions (not including the Bible without double-checking), and archaeology.

Hence, we know from inscriptions that there were northern kings called Omri and Menahem and that they ruled from a city called Samaria. We know virtually nothing about their ethnic origins or their impact on world events. We know that the city of Samaria was destroyed by the Assyrians in the eighth century BCE, and that the city of Jerusalem was destroyed by the Babylonians in the sixth century BCE.

This historical account, Historical Israel, would define an ancient entity called 'Israel' (since there are inscriptions naming it) and other neighbouring kingdoms, of which we possess only a vague knowledge. From the early Iron Age, around 1200 BCE, this 'Israel' may have been the name of a geographical area or it may have been applied to a particular group of people. Certainly, in the highlands to the north, a loosely-aligned kingdom called Israel eventually developed and was destroyed by the Assyrians in 722 BCE. That date is historically verified by documents, not the Bible. Perhaps the biblical writers had more sources on hand than we do (they did not however have archaeological information), but they would have overlaid any sources with their own particular religious thought.

Outside of this northern 'Israel', what could be concluded historically about Judah in the southern area around Jerusalem? There were certainly a few overlaps between written record and biblical story: the Assyrian king

---

[10] We will see that 'Messiah' had a variety of meanings both in Judaism and, later, in Christianity. Its basic etymology is 'The Anointed One' and this principally referred to a king. Various forms of Deliverer, sent to the People of Israel by their God, were subsumed under the title. The topic will be dealt with further in the book.

Sennacherib's siege of Jerusalem when Hezekiah was king is well attested in both Assyrian documents and the book of Kings; the Lachish *ostraca*, broken pottery on which inscriptions were written, tell of the Babylonian invasion into Judah in the sixth century BCE (that invasion is also in the Book of Kings); an historical reference to the exiled Judean king, Jehoiachin (mentioned in the same biblical book), being given rations in the Babylonian court. These are all references to an Historical Judah but in its later times.

What about the Ancestors, Moses, the Exodus out of Egypt, the Judges? We have no historical evidence whatsoever. What about the earlier foundation of Jerusalem as the great Judean capital by King David and his son Solomon, who built a grandiose Temple of Yahweh, a capital that ruled a mighty empire in the Near East? There is one passing and uncertain inscription mentioning the 'House of David' in the south, but nothing as regards a kingdom in any inscriptions. The inscription is uncertain; it could even refer to another David or to a David who was a local chieftain not a king. The united kingdom of David and Solomon, covering an area of vast geographical proportions, as reported in the biblical text, exists only in Literary Israel not in Historical Israel.

While there is a presumption that at least one Temple would have been established in Jerusalem (since cities invariably had a temple or temples), there is no evidence for it apart from some small furnishings, certainly no evidence of a grandiose Temple specifically to Yahweh. There is no historical evidence that the northern kingdom ever broke away from the south, as the biblical text narrates. In fact, the extra-biblical evidence points to the fact that southern Judah did not even exist at the period that 'Israel' did in the north. Archaeology affirms that there was nothing like an independent administrative state or empire in the southern area until the eighth century BCE.

Jerusalem certainly became the capital of this southern kingdom by the eighth century, although the archaeology of early Jerusalem is uncertain as to its earlier populations and history. Possibly, Judah and Jerusalem increased in size as a result of the Assyrian destruction in the north. By the seventh century Judah may have included a sizeable northern Israelite population who had fled from their homeland destruction. Matters would remain so until the attacks by the Babylonians destroyed Jerusalem in 586 BCE.

But this is all historical reconstruction, based on some evidence and educated interpretation. Historical Israel is very scrappy and incomplete. Writing a history of those times is fraught with problems.

This historical study will be continued below with an objective attempt to explain how Literary Israel emerged from its setting in Historical Israel.

Biblical Israel

Finally, there is a Biblical Israel, the construct brought about by inserting Historical Israel into Literary Israel to produce a hybrid.

Biblical Israel enthusiasts would explain the Burning Bush that was never consumed, seen by Moses in the desert according to the book of Exodus, as ignited natural gas escaping from the soil. The manna provided as food in the desert journey was a natural excrescence growing on certain plants. The phenomena of thunder and lightning that accompanied Yahweh's appearance on Mount Sinai, described in Exodus and Deuteronomy, were attributed to the rumblings and emissions of a volcanic area. Biblical Israel accounts would carefully chart the route of the Israelites during the Exodus, in order to put order into the events in the text. It would describe the Taking of the Land in the book of Joshua with the precision of an historian documenting the Normandy landings. Biblical Israel would give precise dates for all the kings of Israel and Judah who are mentioned in the books of Kings.

Going further and even stretching the imagination further, the Ten Plagues mentioned in the book of Exodus have provided a playground for the Biblical Israel cohort. The Nile being turned to blood in the First Plague is explained as red algae which poisoned fish life. The Tenth and final plague, the Death of the Firstborn, has been attributed to Egyptian children eating polluted grain, rendered damp by the hail of the Seventh Plague and then contaminated by locust faeces from the Eighth Plague and the grain being stored during the several days of Darkness from the Ninth Plague, which was caused by a sandstorm.

Some accommodations were made to reconcile text and archaeology. The stories of The Ancestors are dated to around the seventeenth century BCE and they mention camels. But archaeology shows that camels were not domesticated until the late tenth century BCE at the earliest. Therefore, it is claimed, a later hand must have inserted a mention of camels into a much earlier historically sound text.

Even well-trained archaeologists, whose aim should be the presentation of Historical Israel, get involved instead in Biblical Israel.[11] Remnants of a building uncovered recently in Jerusalem were promptly dated to the tenth century and immediately attributed to David despite the absence of any inscription or other evidence. David is presumed to have lived in Jerusalem in the tenth century BCE, and this site is presumed to have been the palace of

---

[11] Scholars who would not contemplate some of the absurdities cited, but still remained committed to Biblical Israel and its methodology, would have been William Foxwell Albright, John Bright, Martin Noth, George Mendenhall and their academic heirs.

David, and the presumptions go further. Biblical Israel presumes that from the open top of this palace, David would have been able to see, across the ravine, the nude Bathsheba bathing in the evening on her house-top, as a lurid story in 1 Kings relates; they presume that the same building's extensions should be attributed to Solomon, because the account of a Solomonic extension is in the text of Kings.

So it goes on. Inferences from archaeology and inscriptions are inserted into the biblical text by Biblical Israel scholars and the combination is a heady one. This scholarly activity expands the usually dull archaeological reports; at the same time it considers itself to be substantiating the historicity of the Story in the Hebrew Scriptures. In fact, there are many competing versions of this Biblical Israel and some of the great scholars of the twentieth century have produced their own, often at odds with each other. It is a flawed endeavour and there is no advantage in producing a Biblical Israel.

For historians the study of Historical Israel, not Biblical Israel, should be the sole aim. The principal aim of students of religion and religious development (as against historians of religion) has to be the study of Literary Israel, although they may need to consult Historical Israel in their research.

To find out how Literary Israel, as contained in the Hebrew Bible, came into existence it is valid to interrogate history. This is an interesting question; it is not a matter of inserting history into the Story, but explaining the development of the Story by reference to the historical context. What we want to know is – at what stage or stages could such a large body of written material as the Hebrew Scriptures have come into being?

THE INTERSECTION OF THE LITERARY AND HISTORICAL ISRAELS

For a long time, any claim that Moses wrote still-extant documents, that the historians in the court of David wrote still-extant documents, that Solomon wrote wisdom-literature or that Prophets wrote still-extant texts has been challenged. The biblical writing shows a much later provenance. In fact, a case can be made that the biblical text originated after the Exile in the sixth century BCE and was completed only much later in the second century. We turn now to Historical Israel in the Persian and Greek periods, based on historical sources and historical reasoning (not on biblical texts as such), as it can be reconstructed in that later period. Primarily, the aim of this section is not to write history, but to see where the elements of Literary Israel may have originated.

Judah in the Persian Period

The numbers of Jerusalem citizens (and others living around the city) involved in the Exile into Mesopotamia after the destruction of the city by the Babylonians in 586 BCE could not have been as extensive and drastic as depicted in Literary Israel. The removal of almost an entire population to the East would have been logistically an impossible task. In reality, the majority of people must have been left where they were – in Jerusalem and its surrounds. Archaeology indicates that this was exactly the case; houses and towns continued to be occupied.

However, the ancient Near East changed. In 539 BCE the Babylonian Empire was taken over by the Persians who had moved inexorably towards the West, taking all in their path. During the fifth century BCE, it would seem that there had been transfers of population in the opposite direction to that taken by the exiles – from Mesopotamia to Judah, now known as the Persian satrapy or province of Yehud. This administrative area of Yehud had been constructed as a satrapy, comprising Jerusalem and the area adjacent to it, militarily under the control of the Persians.[12] The Persians, according to accepted colonial practice, next transplanted a new population into Yehud with a mandate to build a Temple and rebuild the city. These immigrants might or might not have had genealogical descent from the earlier exiled groups taken from the same area by the Babylonians.

It would seem that the latter hypothesis – they did not have genealogical descent – has the stronger case. Yehud shows an increase (by 25 per cent!) of newly occupied settlements, in the form of un-walled villages, around this time. This archaeological data points to new settlers not of the same stock as the earlier exiles; former residents on their return would have been expected to go back to where they came from.

Most of these new villages had not been inhabited during the time of the monarchy and a quarter of them had never been occupied at all previously. It is clear enough that a new population was being resettled. The colonists would have been transported specifically to promote the economic and political purposes of the Persians in Yehud. They would then have been settled into collectives, which became convenient units for Persian taxation and the promotion of farming units.

---

[12] From what we can gather the name of the area around Jerusalem from the eighth century BCE was called Judah. The Babylonians translated the Hebrew name into Aramaic as *Yehud Medinata* ('the province of Judah') or simply *Yehud* and made it a new Babylonian province. Under the Greeks *Yehud* was translated as Judaea and this was taken over by the Romans. After the Jewish rebellion of 135 CE, the Romans renamed the area as *Syria Palaestina* or simply Palestine. The area described by these land titles differed to some extent in the different periods.

At this point, historical speculation, certainly based on historical sources and archaeology, should be allowed its head. These new social groupings in Yehud, which had developed greatly by about 400 BCE, could well have given rise to the idea of the 'Twelve Tribes of Israel' who took over the Land, an event not therefore in the Iron Age (after 1200 BCE), but in the Persian period in the fifth century BCE. The new immigrant population had not descended from 'Jacob/Israel' but from the new Persian arrangements for settling and controlling Yehud.

However that question might be decided, the newly-settled immigrants would have been required to make the land of Yehud their own; their purpose was to carry out Persian directives and to ensure that the native population, who had largely never left the land, concurred. This undoubtedly set up conflict between the presumably more urban immigrants and the native, more rural population of Judah. The immigrants would have had instructions from the Persians to establish themselves as a social enclave, setting up a Temple, temple authorities, local managers, tax collectors and entrepreneurs. Importantly, the immigrant group would have included some literate people to maintain records.

Yahweh the High God

Within the city of Jerusalem, restored for their use, the newcomers from Persia must have established the cult of a new High God, Yahweh. There is an important, and possibly to some people a disturbing, distinction to be made here. Previously, there would have been several cults in both Israel and Judah dedicated to the fertility and war god of the same name, Yahweh. The earlier religion of Yahweh, a fertility and war god, which can be reconstructed from archaeological remains, appears as a normal development from Canaanite religion and the worship of 'El. Yahweh was another form of the Canaanite god 'El and had a consort, Asherah. Historical Israel can verify that there would have been a number of other cults not dedicated to Yahweh (for example the worship of 'El himself, Ba'al and Hadad) and a number of other religious practices.

But this Yahweh of the earlier towns and villages was not the exclusive High God that came from the East, who was the creator of heaven and earth. What was the origin of this High God?

In this regard the question of the rebuilding of the so-called Second Temple of Yahweh in Jerusalem, so prominent in the story of Literary Israel, becomes important. There was a particular form of 'temple' promoted by the Persians, common in the ancient Near East but difficult to understand if religion is seen as a separate institution within society (a common supposition today where Church and State are sedulously divided). A temple was in ancient times not solely a religious foundation. It was an institution that linked landowners and official temple personnel with the ruling elite. The ancient Near Eastern temple had been a common religious form, combining architecture, personnel (both sacred and secular in our terms) and practice. Thus it became the proprietor of public lands that were attributed to the deity as owner, and it performed the function of a treasury for the god's city. The king held his position and power by appointment from the temple deity and his claim to public lands and financial income depended on the deity's benevolence. Hence, control of the temple meant control of the economy and regulation of the social and legal structures as well as supervision of religious ritual. Royalty and temple administration combined as the joint controllers of ancient Near Eastern society.

The Society of Yehud

It would seem that the Jerusalem Temple, built by command of the Persians in about 515 BCE, was constructed hastily and without ornamentation. It was functional. By this stage any remaining archaeological outline of a building or buildings, the so-called First Temple of Solomon in Literary Israel, supposedly destroyed by the Babylonians some seventy years earlier, would have been conjectural.[13] We have no idea of the First Temple's footprint, whether there was one Temple or more, nor what took place within its or their confines. However, the 'Second Temple', in Literary Israel, was accepted as replacing an earlier magnificent First Temple of Yahweh built by Solomon. There is no historical evidence for this.

In short, Persia had a strategic policy that included: first, resettling peoples in new locations; next, either the building or restoration of temples; third, setting up a system of military defence, agriculture, taxation and administration based on the temple; and, finally, the establishment of law-codes considered to have been provided by the temple deity. Perhaps, in Yehud, by the end of the sixth century BCE, the economic and agricultural renewal was successfully under way, and this would have been followed by a military restructure in the mid-fifth century BCE. This renewal and restructuring would have been accompanied by some legal and constitutional establishment. This legal establishment, the Law of Yahweh would have

---

[13] There would certainly have been one or more temples in Jerusalem, prior to the Babylonian destruction. That one or more would have been dedicated to the fertility and war god, Yahweh, would be expected. Their location, structure and ritual is historically unknown.

been compiled side by side with the economic and agricultural changes and incorporate case-law, some past law codes and new legal initiatives. All of this social activity had its centre in the Temple of Yahweh.

However, the new society, with its mixed population, would have been in a state of confusion. Persian political rule meant that any earlier social class system was defunct or at least defective. There would have been noticeable social differences between the privileged newly-arrived immigrants (about five per cent of the population), dispatched by the Persians, and the locals left there in Yehud by the Babylonian and Persian conquerors. There would have been tensions between these two strata of society, as well as between the very parochial culture of the one and a more cosmopolitan culture of the other, between urban dwellers and rural people, between those who accepted the High God Yahweh and those who still followed local cults (even perhaps that of the fertility form of the god, Yahweh). Yahweh the High God, as an unattached male with no consort and sole creator of the world, was more similar to the High Gods in the East – such as Sin (Akkadia), Marduk (Babylonia), Ahura Mazda (Persia) – than the fertility god, Yahweh, known in earlier times in the Palestinian region.

The Persians and the new immigrants both wanted the same thing: that the immigrants should take over the land as their own, and manage it efficiently for the benefit of their Persian overlords. The immigrants had come with funds to build a new Temple and to begin the process of indigenization. Their first step, unusual to our way of thinking, would have been to give a priority to scribal activity in a Temple context. They needed to counter any presumption on the part of those who had been left behind in the land that it was theirs, even though that presumption might well have had the most solid foundation. If this 'people of the land' wanted to be part of Yehud or a new 'Judah' under the High God Yahweh, they must conform to a new definition of god, of society and of ethnicity.[14]

As the Persian political control became the order of the day, the following Temple institutions were set up: a priesthood, a sacrificial system, a caste system, a charter of holiness and a scribal centre. This is not to say that religion, as a separate entity, dominated the life of the populace. Politics and economics dominated; religion was enmeshed in them and served their purposes. And explicit religion was mainly a preoccupation of the elite.

---

[14] The Samaritans in the north, who had used the name of 'Israel' for their land and were Yahweh-worshippers, were on the other hand removed from participation in this new Israel because of their alleged moral and racial lapses in integrity. They developed separately and were later regarded by the people of the south with great suspicion.

Scribal Activity

Court scribes, tutored in this environment, wrote a 'history' (a 'story' in our terms) of Yehud, which created for the newcomers an identity that went back to an earlier 'People of Israel' and its antecedents. This Story must have been based not only on the new Persian ideology but on some local living memories and traditions within the local scene (about the Ancestors, about particular kings, about prophets, their activities and even their discourses), and some archival materials such as king-lists. In the main, though, in constructing their Story, the scribes followed the line of argument provided by their Persian masters. The discourse explained the status of the community of that time, and verified the rights and privileges of the immigrant elite within that society.

Importantly, into this new Story there were inserted Exile-like events in which an immigrant group would take over a land and rule its previous inhabitants by divine mandate: the tradition regarding Abraham leaving Ur at the call of Yahweh and coming to Canaan, where his sons eventually flourished; traditions about a suffering group's Exodus out of Egypt (where they had been imprisoned by the Egyptians) by Moses; and the Taking of the Land of Canaan by Joshua. These traditions were cleverly combined into a fluent Story. In each case the local existing inhabitants of the new land were described as 'the Canaanites', or as other related ethnic groups who were strangers to the conquerors.

In the case of the Abraham Story, the newly arrived group from Persia identified itself with the true Israel, descended from an Ancestor, the son of Abraham and Sarah – Isaac (who was the Father of Jacob/Israel). They were the People of the High God, Yahweh. The 'people of the land', who had remained in Yehud and were depicted as the Canaanites, were descended from the other son of Abraham (but by the secondary wife, Hagar) Ishmael. The 'Canaanites' had to be subdued. In the case of the Moses Story the newly arrived group, consisting of the Twelve Tribes descended from Jacob/Israel, also found a Land occupied by the Canaanites. The Taking of the Land incorporated a new leader, Joshua, and a more complete account of the division of the Land among the victorious People of Israel.

This was the beginning, the first draft as it were, of Literary Israel. But it was certainly not yet Literary Israel. It was primarily a Persian document speaking to the right of settlement and rule.

The existence of a scribal school presumes that its members had dedicated time, the resources, sufficient access to archives and motivation to write. They would have been professionals, paid and supported either by the Temple or by the Persian administration directly. The scribes were seen as an important part of the society; they did not write for leisure; there was purpose in their labour. Commercial records controlled the economy; archiving controlled the past or responded to antiquarian interests; 'history' or story-writing recreated a preferred past that gave precedence to the newcomers; prophetic texts could critique both the past and the present and point to a future, without involving the actual anonymous writers in any responsibility; wisdom writing described and maintained the social status and mores of the elite.

This growing body of literature was close to what we would know today as the Hebrew Scriptures, Literary Israel, not complete though and not so organized as they would be. The texts would have been found in many manuscripts, some filed together, some in multiple copies. There would be continued scribal activity to redact and to combine them. Nascent Literary Israel would perhaps in tone not have been what we like to call religious literature. The next phase of world history, however, would see the literature of the Persian elite become Jewish Scripture.

Hellenization

Following the collapse of the largely benevolent Persian Empire in the fourth century BCE, the Greeks moved eastwards and endeavoured to spread Hellenistic culture and religion in the Near East in a belligerent fashion. The Judeans (or Judahites), the descendants from the mixed and assimilated population of earlier Yehud, retaliated by reinforcing their nationalism. Circumcision, the avoidance of pork and other dietary rules, the observance of the Sabbath and the cult of the High God Yahweh became stabilising features; they marked off the Judean person from any others. The written scrolls from their immediate past, produced under the aegis of the Persian immigrants, became part of both their cultural and national identity.

The distinction between the immigrants sent by the Persians and those left in the land was becoming blurred and inconsequential.

What is being said is that at some time in the Greek period, the Hebrew scrolls underwent a great change in understanding and authority. They became the sacred symbol of a people and its culture and its religion. One text from the collection would now be used to interpret or even correct another; texts from the past could be used to scrutinise the future. Certain teacher-figures in the community would have been trusted to interpret the texts. There was a movement away from regarding the scrolls as human constructions controlling nationalistic history to regarding the scrolls as divine and everlasting truth inspired by Yahweh, controlling a particular form of religious life. This was the real beginning of Literary Israel as a separate sacred text that provided its adherents with meaning. Literary Israel was a story, compounded by commentary, song and wisdom writings. We can now speak in a more complete fashion of the Hebrew Scriptures, the Bible, as the matrix of Literary Israel.

Now comes the big question: when can these dramatic developments bringing about Literary Israel from the ear\ier Persian texts be placed in an historical sequence? The only answer that allows any credibility is – the time of the Hasmonean dynasty. To justify this claim, it is first necessary to understand more clearly the history of these Hasmoneans.

The Hasmoneans

We can never be sure of the exact details, but the later Jewish tradition related that in a rural area of Judah the simmering local revolt against the foreign Greek military and cultural incursion ignited in the early second century BCE. According to a tradition, almost certainly not historical but indicative, it was in Modein, a town north west of Jerusalem that a village priest called Mattathias refused to offer a pig-sacrifice to Zeus when so ordered. A bystander offered to sacrifice in his stead, and Mattathias killed both the Jewish renegade and the Syrian commander. Then Mattathias, his five sons and some loyal followers, fled into the wilderness. From there they waged guerrilla warfare on the Greeks. Whether the details are correct or not, the main line of the story reflects the opposition of the people of what was now Judaea to the Greeks.

Mattathias died soon after but he was succeeded by his eldest son, Judas, known as *Maccabeus*.[15] Father and son were regarded as the eponymous heads of a line that would become known as the Hasmoneans, probably because Mattathias' grandfather had been named Asamonaeus. Within that Hasmonean house, Judas and his four brothers would become known as The Maccabees. Filled with religious zeal, Judas and his growing group of local discontents managed to defeat rather dispirited Greek forces. They soon retook Jerusalem and demolished the Greek altar set up by the Greek king and restored the Second Temple ritual. This cleansing of the Temple was to be commemorated by the establishment of a feast called *Hanukkah* or the Feast of Dedication.

One by one, the Maccabee brothers led the little state and were then

---

[15] We are unsure what the name meant, possibly 'The Hammer'.

succeeded by another. The Hasmoneans would remain in place almost to the Christian period, until the Romans arrived with their superior military force. In the meantime, the Hasmonean State saw itself as the successor to the great traditions of David and Solomon, and earlier than them of the Ancestors and the Exodus generation. They claimed to be the fulfilment of all that the people of Judah had sought. This Hasmonean State adopted the Hebrew Scriptures, the Story and its accompaniments first composed under the Persians, and inserted its own order into the stories by means of a chronology.

It is only at this point that we can talk about Judaism as a religion. It began as the official religion of the Hasmoneans of Judah. Its charter text was the Hebrew Scriptures, originally produced by the scribes attached to the Temple built under Persian control but developed under the later Judeans and the Hasmonean dynasty itself. These writings were seen by the Hasmoneans as a sacred phenomenon produced under the control of their god, Yahweh. The focal point of Judaism was the Temple, built by the Persians it was true, but now the Temple was a Hasmonean possession, cleansed by them of Greek defilement. The sacred Story of the Hasmoneans, formed now into a single Book, was Literary Israel.

The scrolls taken over by the Hasmoneans were edited so as to include an overall chronology of dates to show clearly that the cleansing of the Temple event was the high-point of all human history. The Hasmoneans saw themselves as the fulfilment of Literary Israel.

By simply counting the figures given in the biblical text, the period from creation until the Exodus from Egypt is 2666 years. This is two-thirds of 4000 years, a period regarded as a world epoch in the thinking of that time. The coincidence is obvious. The full cycle of 4000 years would end with the glorious re-dedication of the Temple under Judas Maccabeus in 164 BCE:

Creation ⇨ Exodus: 2666 years
Creation ⇨ Re-dedication of Temple: 4000 years

Within these parameters the Jewish Story was given its own chronology:

Exodus ⇨ Building of First Temple: 480 years
Building of First Temple ⇨ Building of Second Temple: 480 years

Why 480? Probably it was the sum of 12 (for the Twelve Tribes) multiplied by the universal number of 40. However, we may never clearly understand the arithmetical system on which the biblical dates have been based. It is sufficient to say that they were not intended to be historical reference points; they are symbolic numbers pointing to the Hasmoneans as the high-point of Literary Israel.

We have now arrived in this review to the cusp of the millennium. Judaism was seen at this time as the religion of the Judean people who had resisted the Greeks. Just as the immigrants sent by Persia had established a Story to give themselves validity, so did the Hasmoneans. They simply adapted the earlier Story composed under the Persians. The Story would outlive them all. It was the Story of a suffering people who were led by their treaty with the High God, Yahweh, and who found a Land which they could inhabit in peaceful security. It was a Good Land. There, these once downtrodden people could be themselves and find fulfilment living in a Kingdom of God.

NOTES

Some of this material and various other general matters pertaining to the Hebrew Scriptures (and the Christian Scriptures) have been published in a different form in my book *The Jesus Question: The Historical Search* (HarperCollins Religious: Melbourne, 1996).

Other materials pertaining to both the Hebrew Scriptures and Christian Scriptures were covered in my subsequent book *Beyond the Jesus Question; Confronting the Historical Jesus* (PostPressed, Flaxton, Qld, 2003).

I have taken the liberty of reproducing some of the text from my more recent book, *Three Revolutions: Three Drastic Changes in Biblical Interpretation* (ATF Press, 2012).

The bibliographies in the three books above would lay a good foundation for what has been written in this chapter.

Much of my thinking on the Hebrew Scriptures in this chapter has been particularly affected by the work of Philip Davies and Thomas Thompson.

Davies, Philip (1992), *In Search of 'Ancient Israel'*, Sheffield Academic Press: London and New York.

Davies, Philip (1998), *Scribes and Schools: The Canonization of the Hebrew Scriptures,* Westminster John Knox Press: Louisville

Thompson, Thomas (2000), *The Bible in History: How writers create a past,* Pimlico: London.

Thompson, Thomas and Verenna, Thomas (2012), *'Is this not the Carpenter?' The Question of the Historicity of the Figure of Jesus,* Acumen Publishing: Durham.

Davies makes use of the terminology: Historical Israel, Biblical Israel and Ancient Israel. I have adapted this.

— 3 —
STUDYING THE CHRISTIAN CONTEXT

A SIMILAR TYPOLOGY AS THAT APPLIED to the study of Judaism (Historical Israel, Literary Israel, Biblical Israel), can also be applied to the study of Christianity. We have seen that the importance of the basic structure of an ongoing religion is Succession. This also becomes a prime issue in Christianity. The problem is that there were too many Successors.

THE STUDY OF JESUS

What we have seen in the previous chapter about Judaism provides the necessary background for describing the literary context of Christianity. By the time of Jesus there was widespread dissatisfaction with the Judaism established earlier by the Hasmoneans (even though Jews of that time would consider their Jewish origins to have gone much further back in the past). Decades of Roman rule had devastated the rural economy; the Temple in Jerusalem seemed to be ruled by self-seeking High Priests and their underlings. As a result, there were many claimants to the role of a new 'Moses' within the Judaism of that time. These claimants would offer to usher in a new world for Jews.

From Judaism, there emerged a new religion, a sect of Judaism that would eventually be called Christianity. It was one of the attempts at renewal. We want to analyse it. The terminology I have devised, in line with the analysis of the Israel phenomenon, relates to a Literary Jesus, an Historical Jesus and a Biblical Jesus.

Literary Israel, as described earlier, is essentially required as background to explain how the Literary Jesus came to be and to explain the contexts and understandings within that Story. The Literary Jesus is the Story of a Jesus as it is contained in the Christian Scriptures, almost exclusively the four canonical gospels.

From the outset, it should be made clear that there was certainly an Historical Jesus, a person whom historians can identify in the early part of the first millennium CE. He was mentioned in non-biblical documentation quite specifically.

The Biblical Jesus is the insertion of the Historical Jesus into the Literary Jesus. Like Biblical Israel, it has produced a hybrid that never existed and has no purpose.

We begin with the Literary Jesus.

Literary Jesus

The Literary Jesus is the Jesus of the four canonical gospels. In fact, there are four Literary Jesus-es in those gospels. They have their own versions of the Story (admittedly with significant overlaps) and they have their own line of argument. We have no idea regarding the authorship of the four canonical gospels and can only date them with hesitation.

We will take the Literary Jesus in Mark's gospel as a first example. The gospel is structured as follows in order to present that Literary Jesus:

Prologue　　1:1-13

　　　　　　　　John the Baptist – the Forerunner who announces Jesus' coming

　　　　　　　　Jesus is baptized as the Messiah

　　　　　　　　Jesus begins a Testing, a battle with Satan in the desert

1　　　　　　1:14-8:30

　　　　　　　　Mark shows by means of stories, sayings and disputes that Jesus is the Messiah

　　　　　　　　A Blind Man is healed.

　　　　　　　　The first disciples confess: 'You are the Messiah!'

2　　　　　　8:31-10:52

　　　　　　　　Mark shows that following Jesus the Messiah entails suffering and self-giving

　　　　　　　　A Blind Man is healed

　　　　　　　　The first disciples decide to follow the Messiah to Jerusalem

3　　　　　　11:1-16:8

　　　　　　　　Mark describes the death and resurrection of the Messiah

　　　　　　　　End of gospel

The Prologue identifies Jesus as the Messiah, succeeding to the prophet-like John the Baptist, a most austere man of the desert, who had come to confront evil in the world and save his Jewish brethren from the end of times. Earlier, we made passing mention of the term 'Messiah'. Messiah means the 'anointed one' in Hebrew (the Greek is *Christos* or Christ). There was a variety of expectations about an Anointed One who would come to save the Jews. Some thought that the Messiah would be belligerent; others thought he would be peaceful; some thought there would be one; others thought there would be two or more. Jews would not have considered the Messiah to be divine; there was, after all, only one God, Yahweh. The Prologue then describes a final battle between Jesus and Satan (the leader of evil demons and perpetrator of Evil in the world) that takes place in a desert, the scene of the Exodus. This sets the context for the role of Jesus as Messiah. He has come to conquer Evil.

Following the Prologue, Mark describes the ministry of the Messiah in Galilee, even though his own followers have not yet realized that he is the Messiah. Jesus performs the works expected of a Messiah: he gathers followers and makes them into a 'Twelve', a New Israel; he teaches, heals, casts out demons and debates with religious opponents in the manner expected of the Messiah and consistently he is met with hostility and rejection.

The Literary Jesus calls for The Twelve to make an affirmation of faith in him as the Messiah. After the cure of a blind man, the disciples make the affirmation through Peter. Together, Jesus and these disciples make a final journey to Jerusalem where he will fulfill the role of the Messiah by dying and rising from the dead.

Jesus prepares them to accompany him on what is called The Way. This is no ordinary journey; it will lead to Jerusalem, the hub of the world, the place where history is to come to its high-point with the death and resurrection of the Messiah. Before they can confront this last stage another blind man is cured. The repeated cure of a blind man is one of the rhetorical devices included in the Markan story.

Mark would seem to be the first written gospel in the canon, dating from at least 65 CE (and probably later), some thirty years after the death of Jesus. Whether that 65 CE gospel was exactly the same as the gospel we have today is unlikely.

Matthew would have been written within the next decade or decades, around the same time as Luke. His gospel used some form of Mark's gospel and also a collection of sayings and stories attributed to Jesus (which were not in Mark). Luke also used Mark and this same collection of sayings and stories, although he put them into different contexts compared to Matthew.

Scholars have referred to this collection of sayings and stories – the overlap (sometimes verbatim) in Matthew and Luke which does not occur in Mark – as 'Q', which is short for *Quelle*, German for 'source'. Today, many prefer to use the title 'Sayings Gospel Q'. There is a supposition that this was a separate gospel (even though no separate manuscript has ever been found), used by church members even prior to the time of the four canonical gospels. I do not find the arguments for a separate Sayings Gospel Q convincing. Matthew would have had access to the Jesus Sayings he used in the amorphous Jesus-Tradition.

The Jesus-Tradition is the tradition about Jesus that remained from the time immediately after his death. This Jesus-Tradition would have only gradually reached any sort of regular shape; it would have been expanded, corrected and amended over time after the death of Jesus. In the first place, it would seem that the earliest followers of Jesus incorporated only pivotal Jesus events, elaborated as the years passed, in their first formulations of Jesus: his Last Meal, his death by crucifixion, his Visions to disciples after his death. Further details would have been supplied to fill out the events particularly by reflection on the Hebrew Scriptures' prophecies and thought-patterns (for example, the Virgin Birth and the details of the crucifixion taken from the Psalms and Isaiah). The belief that the Jesus events had been foretold in the Hebrew Scriptures was a very early presumption.

Second, there would have been input into the narratives of the Jesus events by comparing those events with much later Christian communities and their troubles. It was presumed that the events of Jesus were a paradigm for what would follow for his disciples. This produced the memory of Jesus sayings: some remembered, some constructed on the idea of 'what Jesus might have said, had he been confronted with this situation'. At some stage there would have been the gathering of such sayings of Jesus (such as the early Greek text of sayings attributed to the apostle Thomas, various collections of parables) and the collection of 'events' such as miracle stories, cures, exorcisms.

These sayings and events would have developed within a catechetical life-situation of the early Jesus movements, where there was a need to instruct both newcomers and more mature members. Some of these collections may have been oral, diligently remembered by memory; some may have been written.

Such amorphous groups of traditions, oral and written, constituted what we mean by the Jesus-Tradition and we can identify certain elements in it:

- A pool of Jesus Sayings, formed into a number of collections including the parables
- The Greek Gospel of Thomas
- Birth Stories of Jesus
- Collections of Jesus Miracle Stories
- Passion, Death and Burial Story of Jesus
- Visions of Jesus after his death; Empty Tomb stories were later appended to these.

Not all of these would have existed side by side in any one place. Not all of them would have had only one format. They were a large and growing Tradition about Jesus, his sayings and narratives concerning the events of his life, which would have tended to move further and further away from what we would call history or *ipsissima verba*, the actual words of Jesus.

In the Sayings used by Matthew, Jesus explains his role as a healer and exorcist in Galilee. What he is achieving by clearing the world of demons, and removing their impact on sickness and ignorance, is the Kingdom of God or the Reign of God. This is a worldly haven where the inhabitants who have accepted the principles of Yahweh, the God of Israel, can live. There is safety therein. Jesus promises that, in these new times, safety and food will be readily available for those who trust God.

However, only the Jews are regarded as being part of this promise. The Literary Jesus shows that he is continuing in the path of his onetime leader, John the Baptist, but he is more relaxed and more open and gentle than the ascetic John.

We become aware that there were a number of groups who had been stimulated and aroused by the Jesus event. These can be named as Jesus-movements. Most were Jews but they had not yet realized that others of their number, also motivated by Jesus, were focusing on a mission to the outsiders, the Gentiles. Who would have composed and used the Sayings used by Matthew? Most probably some of these very early Jesus-movement groups after the death of Jesus who still expected their movement to remain within Judaism.

The Jesus Sayings cannot be considered a transcript of what Jesus may have said or preached. They would have belonged to a remembered collection of texts, undoubtedly undergoing editing and pruning as time went on. However, the Sayings would have pre-dated the four canonical gospels, although not necessarily in any one collection.

Matthew adopted and combined the Jesus Sayings in his possession with his version of Mark. Matthew was commissioned by a community that included Gentiles but was still within the Palestinian area. Gradually it became the most popular gospel and its text was spread in later times as far as Egypt and was extensively used by early Christian scholars.

Matthew's Literary Jesus is presented as a Moses-like Messiah in a highly structured writing which follows that of Mark but makes significant changes to allow for the insertion of the Sayings.

Thus, Matthew's gospel begins with a Jesus infancy-narrative, peppered with references to Moses taken from the Hebrew Scriptures. Jesus is given the sacred name of Immanuel ('God with Us'). Jesus' public ministry in Matthew, reusing the material from Mark and also from the Jesus Sayings, is divided into five books of Stories/Sayings, parallel to the Five Books of Moses in the Hebrew Scriptures:

1:1-2:23 Prologue: Genealogy and the Infancy Story of Jesus the Messiah and New Moses.

1 **3:1-4:25 Story: The beginning of the messianic ministry of Jesus**

5:1-7:29 Sayings: the key attitudes of the Jesus-community (Sermon on the Mount)

2 **8:1-10:4 Story: Jesus' messianic activity in Galilee**

10:5-11:1 Sayings: The need and struggle to enlist new members (Mission Discourse)

3 **11:2-12:50 Story: Jesus' rejection**

13:1-53 Sayings: The loss of members (Parables)

4 **13:54-17:27 Story: Jesus establishes a new group**

18:1-19:2 Sayings: Internal group divisions (Community Discourse)

5 **19:3-23:39 Story: Jesus' final journey to Jerusalem**

24:1-26:2 Sayings: Woes on the Jews and Gentiles (Eschatological Sermon)

26:3-28:10 Epilogue: The Suffering, Death and Resurrection of the Messiah

Later additions to Epilogue:

28: 11-15 The Story of the lying guards

28: 16-20: The Great Commission

The Five Books culminate with the ministry of Jesus in Jerusalem and the account of his death, more or less parallel with what Matthew would have received from his main source, Mark. His death is the death of a Suffering Messiah.

Matthew's resurrection consists of the combination of a Vision from Jesus, returned from the dead in Galilee, and the story of the empty tomb in Jerusalem. Jesus' final exhortation is: 'I am with you'. It corresponds to the title of Immanuel ('God-with-us') used as the sacred name for Jesus in the opening infancy-narrative and intended to form an *inclusio*, a connection between the beginning of the gospel and its end.

Luke's gospel also combines Mark and the Jesus Sayings already contained in Matthew. Luke's use of some form of Matthew would explain his usage of the Jesus Sayings just as well as any conjecturing on a Sayings Gospel Q. He also seemed to have had access to the older Jesus-Tradition, outside of its usage in Matthew. The gospel's structure is continued into a second volume (although each part had a different author), the Acts of the Apostles. The Literary Jesus of Luke's gospel is, as with Matthew, a Messiah but Luke has depicted his Messiah-Jesus in the manner of a Prophet announcing that the End Times are near.

Luke's Prologue 1:1-4

1. **1:5-2:52 The Infancy Story: Jesus is declared to be the Prophet-Messiah**
2. **3:1-4:13 Preparations for the ministry of Jesus, the Prophet-Messiah**
3. **4:14- 9:50 The Ministry in Galilee of Jesus, the Prophet-Messiah**
4. **9:51-19:27 The Prophet-Messiah journeys to Jerusalem: the travelogue**
5. **19:28-21:38 Jerusalem Rejects Jesus, the Prophet-Messiah**
6. **22:1-23:56 The sacrificial Death of Jesus, the Prophet-Messiah**
7. **24:1-53 The Resurrection, Appearances and Ascension of Jesus, the Prophet-Messiah**

The Prophet-Messiah prepares the first stage of his ministry in Galilee. Then the gospel describes a remarkable and very extensive journey to Jerusalem, replete with sayings, stories (many taken from the Jesus Sayings) and good works. It covers some ten of Luke's twenty-four chapters in length, a veritable travelogue. At the culmination of the journey Jesus reaches Jerusalem, where he is rejected by mainstream Judaism and condemned to death.

Tellingly, as Jesus dies on the cross in Luke's gospel, a Gentile centurion announces: 'Truly this man was a Just One'. Luke's Literary Jesus is interpreted as a Just One (in Hebrew, a *zaddik*). Among the Jews, the Just Ones were thought to be holy prophet-like men who lived ascetic lives. They intervened on the part of the people and every generation required one or more of them. They were able to pray for the people to God in hard times, to protect them, to heal their ills. For particular groups, a Just One could become their Intermediary.

Luke has a more extended resurrection section with appearances to women, then to two disciples on the road to Emmaus and finally to the group of disciples. The gospel concludes with a rather physical Ascension-into-Heaven story.

Mark, Matthew and Luke – we recall that they are called the 'Synoptics' – had substantially the same Literary Jesus, but with some important variations. In each case Jesus was the Just One and Messiah, but the experience of the group associated with a particular gospel must have coloured the presentation of each of these Literary Jesus-es.

It is obvious that the Literary Jesus of the Synoptics is an interesting topic. However, this book will be primarily concerned with the Literary Jesus in John. It will be seen that this latter Literary Jesus is drastically different from the overriding view of Jesus in the three Synoptics. As far as the four canonical gospels are concerned, the main contrast is between the Literary Jesus of the Synoptics and the Literary Jesus of John.

We can describe the Literary Jesus of the Synoptics in this way, although each evangelist will expand on the elements:

YHWH/Now known as Father

**Word of Yahweh, the Wisdom of Yahweh,
the Spirit of Yahweh**

(Contact achieved)

Jesus as a dead and risen *zaddik*/Son of God/*mashiah*

Jesus-movement

We can now turn to the Historical Jesus, the history of Jesus that can be constructed from historical sources by the historical method.

Historical Jesus

What do we know historically of Jesus?

If we were to put down the historical certainties, this would be a very short piece. Josephus and Roman sources affirm his birth. Where he was born is open to question. Where he was brought up is equally contentious. What took place during his lifetime has to be conjectured. Obviously he died, but the circumstances of his death have also to be conjectured.

We have the possibility that the Historical Jesus was recognized by his contemporaries as a Just One, a *zaddik*, and was also given the titles of the Messiah and Son of God (not necessarily divine but a Godly-man) by later followers after his death. In other words, he was first identified as a local saint, a Just One, in rural Galilee, an advocate of the people before their God. If this is granted then he would have been seen as dedicated to the overturn of evil. As an individual Just One his ministry of healing, of miracle working and table fellowship would have been recalled as a prolonged ritual that dramatized as well as effected God's progressive victory over the forces of evil. Evil was being conquered and human barriers were being dismantled. The Reign of God in the world was imminent. The sequence sounds plausible but all of this history is based on very little evidence.

We might go a step further. Perhaps, Jesus wanted to revitalize the local Galilean community, to restore the values of a way of life fully in tune with the ideals of Judaism and to bring about for them the Reign of God. He revealed no intention of moving out of Judaism, of founding another religious group. He probably did not foresee that he would have a successor or even needed one. For him, as a Just One, any succession would have been in the hands of Yahweh who himself designated Just Ones.

This is all in the realm of possibility. We know very little indeed about an Historical Jesus. With certainty we can say that he was born and that he died by Roman execution.

Biblical Jesus

Scholars dedicated to the Biblical Jesus insert the findings about the Historical Jesus (including a great deal that is far more conjectural than what was stated above) into the stories of the Literary Jesus. Most proponents would maintain that they are thereby presenting another and better, more expansive, Historical Jesus. They are not. They are mixing Story and History, Literary Jesus and Historical Jesus, in a highly inappropriate fashion.

Biblical Jesus followers claim that the Historical Jesus actually and physically worked some of the miracles and cures. Some are unsure of the nature miracles, where Jesus stops storms and causes a fig-tree to wither, but they are more certain of the cure of bodily ills. They temper their claims by introducing modern medical ideas regarding recognized forms of hysteria to show that sometimes Jesus may have simply supplied a placebo effect to mentally-challenged people; he persuaded people to cure themselves, they claim. What of the cured lepers? They point out that 'leprosy' covered a wide range of serious and not so serious skin ailments from Hansen's disease to psoriasis and eczema. Further, some claim that Jesus simply changed people's attitudes to these unsightly conditions, considered to render the sick ritually unclean; he did not physically cure the medical conditions themselves. Some Biblical Jesus scholars say that this change in onlookers' bias was the 'cure'. Likewise, these scholars compare Jesus' exorcisms, the casting out of demons, with modern-day exorcisms, although they may be willing to count some of the gospel demon-possessions as based on mental illness.

It can be annoying to follow their tracks. The Biblical Jesus scholars are willing to construct an exact, almost daily, chronology of Jesus events from the material in the four gospels, disregarding the place of a particular story in its gospel structure and disregarding the fact that the gospel writers had their own agenda, made their own selection of material and created at will. They reconcile obvious discrepancies by ingenuous means. The Birth Narrative in Matthew is combined with the quite different Birth Narrative in Luke. The Passion stories in the four gospels are combined to produce a running account that could be submitted to legal scrutiny in Jesus' favour. There are seven Last Words on the cross, despite the fact that no one gospel has all seven.

Without going further, I need to say that this Biblical Jesus, like Biblical Israel, never existed; the exercise has no purpose in the Christian religion, in literature or in history.

Succession and the Literary Jesus

We now return to the Literary Jesus, the only really recoverable item. What was its prime purpose? It was meant to replace other forms of an Intermediary, derived from the Hebrew Scriptures. Jesus was the This-worldly Intermediary. But, who would be his successor? That is what the variant forms of the Literary Jesus are involved in explaining.

Succession, we have seen, is of vital importance. There is no continuation for a religion without succession. Peter was never named in the Sayings gathered by Matthew and Luke, but by the time of the Synoptic gospels and their Literary Jesus, at least some decades later, he was clearly proposed in their circles as the successor to Jesus. He was first mentioned in the list of The Twelve by Mark and became the official spokesman for the disciples at the very centre of the gospel where he makes his profession of faith. His successor role was confirmed in Matthew and Luke, although Acts wanted to propose Paul as an early replacement for Peter.

We will see that, in John, the matter is not so clear and in fact is confusing. There were, it seems, a number of contenders for the successor of Jesus in John: Peter, but there are also Mary Magdalene and the 'Beloved Disciple'. This question of succession will be a major point in our discussion of the Gospel of John. The Synoptics' Literary Jesus, however, leaves room for no doubt: Peter was the first successor. The question decided by the Synoptic gospels is not so much who Jesus was, but whom he left as his chosen successor.

We now need to return to our historical research and examine the early events of the time after Jesus and how succession operated in an historical mode. This was the time of the Jesus-movements. From this investigation we hope to extract more information on the torturous question of the succession to Jesus.

This study of the Jesus-movements is essential to understanding what will follow in the analysis of the Gospel of John.

THE SUCCESSORS OF JESUS IN PALESTINE

A reading between the lines of early Christian literature soon reveals that the establishment of an early 'Christian church' was not a simple or a harmonious affair. Even the canonical literature such as the Acts of the Apostles indicates, beneath the surface, the complexity of the Church's formation. After Jesus, there was no one established church; there were a number of quite separate Jesus-movement groups each of which had been stimulated by the events surrounding the life and death of the Historical Jesus.

We will follow the evidence for these separate Jesus-movements.

James the Brother of the Lord

The rather grudging admission, in the Acts of the Apostles, that James was a significant leader, perhaps the chief leader in Jerusalem, immediately raised problems for any seamless description of the founding days of Christianity. It would seem that the sequence in Acts (Jesus was succeeded by James, Peter and John and then, at a later time, Paul) needs to be questioned. We will eventually see in more detail that Acts gives us a particular version of events, a story intended for church members, which would reach its logical sequence in the writings of Clement of Alexandria, an early Greek Christian theologian who wrote around the turn of the third century.

> To James the Just and John and Peter, the Lord after the resurrection transmitted the *gnosis* (knowledge); they transmitted it to the other apostles and the other apostles, to the seventy, one of whom was Barnabas. (*Hypotyposeis* in *Historia Ecclesiastica* 2.1. 3-5)

Acts and Clement both wanted to depict an orderly transmission from Jesus to Peter and the Twelve, incorporating Acts' hero, Paul, and thence to the world. James is manoeuvred more and more out of the equation.

However, the *First Apocalypse of James*, a Gnostic document[16] written between 180 and 250 CE, did the opposite; it exalted the position of James and played down the role of the Twelve. It has been called a 'revelation dialogue' and consists of a discussion between Jesus and James in which it is James who receives the revelation of the Saviour. In the text, James rebukes the Twelve and associates them with the evil god, Achamoth; they have not achieved full *gnosis* or saving knowledge.

The text explains the seeming enigma of the delay between the death of Jesus and the destruction of Jerusalem as being because of the fact that the death of Jesus and the martyrdom of James are complementary events. This parallel treatment of the two brothers is important. After the completion of the second event, the fall of Jerusalem would take place. The disparity between the Acts of the Apostles and the *First Apocalypse of James* demonstrates clearly that there were important conflicting interpretations of the role of James in the early Christian centuries.

In some way it is necessary to delve beneath these texts and establish the roles played by the key players: James the 'Brother of the Lord' and the Brothers, Peter and the Twelve, Stephen and the Hellenists. Eventually, we will deal with Paul of Tarsus and John.

The character whose position is most difficult to assess within the above list is James, clearly attested as leader of a Jesus-movement group in Jerusalem and known as the 'Brother of the Lord'. One of the letters of the Christian Scriptures, the Letter of James, was attributed to him. After he is fleetingly identified in the Synoptics as the brother of Jesus and, like the rest of the family, as one who does not support his brother, Jesus, he suddenly appears in Acts as the leader of the Brothers of the Lord, a Jesus-movement group. It is quite clear that something has been glossed over.

---

[16] Gnosticism and *gnosis* will be explained in ch. 4.

In Acts 12:17 Peter, on leaving Jerusalem, gives orders that a message be taken to him and his group, who obviously live somewhere else in Jerusalem.

> He described for them how the Lord had brought him out of the prison.
> And he added, 'Tell this to James and to the Brothers.'

Why the plural 'Brothers'? Why, later, must Paul reckon with him? There is no account of how he came to acquire his substantial position in Jerusalem or of his later fate in the canonical scriptures. We need to use our sources to identify James more precisely.

First, there is Josephus and also the fourth century *Ecclesiastical History* of Eusebius (260-340), which has preserved earlier material derived from Clement of Alexandria's *Hypotyposeis,* and from Hegesippus' *Hypomnemata.* There is also *The Gospel according to the Hebrews* which survives fragmentarily in Jerome's writings and a document about the Jerusalem episcopal succession. A passing but important reference is found in the Gnostic *Gospel of Thomas* and further material in the fourth century Pseudo-Clementine *Homilies* and *Recognitions.* Finally, there is the text, also from the fourth century, of the writer Epiphanius (367-404), the *Panarion* (the 'Medicine Chest'). Epiphanius had been brought up in Palestine during the reign of Constantine and had been taught in Tiberias by a Jewish Christian called Joseph.

What do these sources reveal to us about James? James, the brother of the Lord, was known as 'James the Just' (*zaddik* in Hebrew, the same term that we saw applied to Jesus) by some of these early Christian writers. The title is never explicitly applied in the canonical writings, but certainly appears in reference to James in Hegesippus (as cited in Eusebius, of which more below), the *Gospel of the Hebrews* (cited by Jerome and cited below) and the *Gospel of Thomas*. The latter Gnostic gospel from the early centuries states:

> The disciples said to Jesus, 'We know that you will depart from us.
> Who is to be our leader?'
> Jesus said to them, 'Wherever you are, you are to go to James the
> Righteous [*zaddik*], for whose sake heaven and earth came into being.'
> (logion 12)

We will need to explore the role of James further.

There was a solid tradition of a post-mortem Vision granted to James at a meal, as has been handed on in the *Gospel according to the Hebrews.*

> And when the Lord had given the linen cloth to the servant of the
> priest, he went to James and appeared to him. For James had sworn that
> he would not eat bread from that hour in which he had drunk the cup

of the Lord until he should see him risen from among them that sleep. And shortly thereafter the Lord said: Bring a table and bread! And immediately it is added: He took the bread, blessed it and broke it and gave it to James the Just and said to him: My brother, eat thy bread, for the Son of man is risen from among them that sleep. (cited in Jerome, *De viris illustribus* 2)

Within the Christian Scriptures there are one and possibly two oblique references to this revelation. The text of 1 Corinthians 15 gives a disordered list of those who received Jesus Visions. James is accounted as one among many. However, this text was added later to 1 Corinthians and is not from the hand of Paul. The other more questionable reference is the Emmaus story in Luke 24:13-35. It refers to a 'breaking of bread' event involving a Cleopas and an unnamed disciple. It would be reasonable to conjecture that the unnamed person at the Emmaus meal was James and that a more original version of the tradition is that recorded in the *Gospel according to the Hebrews*. It was adapted by Luke. It could well be that this was the Last Supper of the James' community which took place after the death of Jesus, not before.

James, the Brother of the Lord, succeeded Jesus after Jesus died according to the thinking of a significant Jesus-movement group. He was next in line in the Jesus family. There is sufficient precedent in the Judaism of the time for such brotherly succession, as seen in the Maccabee brothers, but beneath the surface of the canonical Christian texts it is possible to perceive significant opposition to dynastic succession. The Synoptic and, as we will see, Johannine sources were adamant that the 'family of Jesus' had viewed his public activities with jaundiced eyes and had never been his followers.

In fact this led to the denial on the part of the Synoptics' Jesus that he wanted to retain such blood relationships, preferring to establish spiritual relationships.

[31]Then his mother and his brothers came; and standing outside, they sent to him and called him. [32]A crowd was sitting around him; and they said to him, 'Your mother and your brothers and sisters are outside, asking for you.' [33]And he replied, 'Who are my mother and my brothers?' [34]And looking at those who sat around him, he said, 'Here are my mother and my brothers! [35]Whoever does the will of God is my brother and sister and mother.' (Mark 3:31-35)

However, it must be remembered that such texts are coloured by events of a period some decades after the death of Jesus. By this stage the succession of the Brothers had become an embarrassment, something to be explained away by a convenient Jesus-story.

It does raise the possibility that James, and Jesus' other brothers, could have been established in Jerusalem earlier than the final visit of Jesus. Jesus would have remained in Galilee and his sphere of activity was established there. The Family would already have gained adherents in Jerusalem. An earlier establishment might explain how James was so well set up in Jerusalem at the time of the death of Jesus. It had been his base for some time.

We can surmise that the blood brothers of Jesus formed the nucleus of a group known as the 'Brothers of the Lord' which may have been originally led by Jesus, but was taken over by James. It could be that this group was also known as the 'Christos' or The Messiah group. Paul refers to such a 'Christ' group in 1 Corinthians 1:12.

> What I mean is that each of you says, 'I belong to Paul', or 'I belong to Apollos', or 'I belong to Cephas', or 'I belong to *Christos*.' Has *Christos* been divided?

The texts show that there are several Jesus-movement groups in existence, including that of Cephas, the Aramaic form of 'Peter'. Acts, some years later, would try to harmonize the groups in retrospect. It placed the Brothers of the Lord in close proximity with the Twelve as part of the 120 original disciples (Acts 1:14). This number is a symbolic composite of twelve (i.e. The Twelve tribes) multiplied by ten. Acts thereby constructed a hypothetical Jerusalem 'group' formed of several components, one of which was the Brothers of the Lord.

More information on James can be found in Eusebius' *Ecclesiastical History* when he repeats the memoirs of the Christian writer Hegesippus' account, dated from around 170 CE, of the trial and execution of James. Hegesippus was a Christian who looked to both Corinth and Rome as substantiating his teaching. He did not come from the Jerusalem Jesus-movement as such, but had been formed in the later and more developed Roman Christian tradition. However, he did have privileged access to memories from the first century CE in Palestine.

His five-volume work *The Memoirs of the Acts of the Church* claimed to contain the oral traditions of the first century Jerusalem Jesus-movement group as well as those of the Gnostic heretics in the area. His account of the death of James would seem to be the most original of those Christian writers who described James' martyrdom.

Hegesippus' description of the execution of James maintains that 'all the people' were expecting Jesus to return as the Messiah, and the Jewish leaders were afraid. James was challenged by 'scribes and Pharisees'[17] to explain what he meant when he referred to the term 'the door of Jesus'. The term is enigmatic to us and may be garbled or it may mean something like Jesus' claim in John to be the Gate of the sheepfold. This interrogation took place while James was set up on the Temple parapet. He did not answer the question directly but used terms reminiscent of Acts' account of the inter- rogation of Stephen. He was then thrown down and they began to stone him, before he was finally dispatched by a fuller's club.

Hegesippus includes a further and disconcerting item of information. He states that James wore priestly vestments and had the right to enter the Holy of Holies of the Temple.

> To James alone it was permitted to enter the sanctuary for he did not wear wool but linen. He entered the shrine alone and was found there kneeling and begging forgiveness for the people. (In Eusebius *Hist Eccl* 2. 23. 6; 78:13; see Jerome *De Viris Ill* 2)

This is substantiated by Epiphanius' *Panarion*, which hands on the statement of Epiphanius' teacher, Joseph, that James had been accepted by the Jewish leaders as the High Priest prior to the destruction of Jerusalem. Epiphanius also recounts that James entered the Holy of Holies and wore the High Priestly *to petalon* on his forehead. This was a thin gold plate, laced to the High Priest's turban and inscribed with the text 'holy to Yahweh'.

None of this makes sense. James was not of priestly lineage and it does not seem that such a person as he could function as a priest, certainly not as High Priest. In the Pseudo-Clementine *Recognitions* 1: 43-44, we are told that Jesus 'ordained (James) bishop in the church of the Lord that was consti- tuted in Jerusalem'. There is consequently a claim that, from the foundation of the church, James was the 'bishop of Jerusalem'. Later, Chrysostom at the end of the fourth century CE writes:

> The Lord is said to have himself ordained his brother James, and made him bishop [*episkopos*] of Jerusalem in the first days. (Homily 38:4)

There is no doubt that James is the unchallenged leader in Jerusalem, when we analyse the Pseudo-Clementine texts from the fourth century. Peter's missionary commission comes from James, and Peter is required to make a yearly report to James (*Homilies* 1.20; *Recognitions* 1.17); all Chris-

---

[17] 'Scribes and Pharisees' is a strange combination found in several places of early Christian writings. 'Scribes' did not form a sect of Judaism, like Pharisees or Sadducees. They were a class of scholars responsible for the authoritative interpretation of Jewish law. Most scribes were probably Pharisees. Perhaps in the course of time the distinction was blurred.

tian teachers must have the 'testimonial of James' (*Recognitions* 4.25); in the *Homilies* we find James acclaimed as 'bishop of bishops who rules the churches everywhere' and also the 'prince of priests'. In other words, early Christian tradition recognized him as the undisputed leader, the High Priest.

But if he was not historically the High Priest, yet is said to have access to the Holy of Holies, who was he? I put forward the historical conjecture that he was considered within the Jerusalem Jesus-movement as the Priestly Messiah, the Brother of Jesus, who was the Davidic Messiah. The reference to an 'ordination' to the role of *episkopos* of Jerusalem could be a reference to a tradition of Jesus' appointment of James as the Priestly Messiah. He thus claimed to supplant the High Priest of Jerusalem. When Christianity drifted away from its Jewish roots, the idea of James being High Priest was unacceptable; he became a bishop.

It would seem that both Jesus and James in their constituencies were regarded as *zaddikim*, Just Ones. They fulfilled a role in Jewish life and they fulfilled a role in the Jesus-movement that remained in the East. At some stage Jesus was acknowledged as the Davidic Messiah, but this would have been after his death. In this community, James was seen as his successor, having his own Vision story to consolidate the appointment. At some time, presumably during his lifetime but after the death of Jesus, he was acknowledged as the Priestly Messiah, a legitimate alternate High Priest of the Jesus-movement.

Why his execution? One possible scenario would be the following. In the early 60s the war clouds were already gathering, and nationalism would have pressured Jesus-movement people in Jerusalem and its environs to acknowledge that there was need for another Davidic Messiah rather than a Jesus who had departed and showed no signs of any immediate return. James, regarded by the Jesus-movement as their leader and as a Priestly Messiah, stood firmly by the Jewish Jesus-movement position on Jesus' ongoing Davidic Messiahship[18] and would have been seen thereby to have endangered the broad Jewish political position. For this reason he was killed. It was a political assassination.

However, there was widespread indignation at his death and so his position in support of the coming return of Jesus must have had popular support. The subsequent destruction of Jerusalem and the Temple was attributed to his death, the martyrdom of a *zaddik*.

Successors after the death of James

We now turn to the aftermath of the death of James. Eusebius, relying on

---

[18] This may have been the meaning of James' assertion of 'the door of Jesus', an assertion that led to his death.

Hegesippus' text, once again claims that the successor of James in Jerusalem was Simeon, the son of Clopas, the head of the *desposyni*, literally the 'family of the Lord' *(Hist Eccl* 3.11.1).

> After the martyrdom of James and the capture of Jerusalem which instantly followed, there is a firm tradition that those of the apostles and disciples of the Lord who were still alive assembled from all parts together with those who, humanly speaking, were kinsmen [*desposyni*] of the Lord – for most of them were still living. Then they all discussed together whom they should choose as a fit person to succeed James, and voted unanimously that Simeon, son of the Clopas mentioned in the gospel narrative, was a fit person to occupy the throne of the Jerusalem See.

This Simeon may have been the cousin of Jesus. That at least was Eusebius' opinion:

It is clear that Hegesippus believed that as long as the church was led by one of the *desposyni*, the faith would be kept safe:

> Consequently they came and presided over every church, as being martyrs and members of the Lord's family, and since profound peace came to every church they survived until the reign of Trajan Caesar ... *(Hist Eccl* 3. 32)

Eusebius compiled a list of these group leaders related to Jesus up to the dispersion of Jews from Jerusalem. Two other pieces of evidence need to be considered.

One is the description, again by Hegesippus (In *Hist Eccl* 3. 19. 1-3.20.7), of a search by Domitian, who ruled as emperor from 81 CE until his assassination in 96, for descendants of the house of David. Although Hegesippus' text could hardly relate to fact, it does claim that Domitian discovered descendants of Jesus who were subsequently dismissed by Domitian as harmless peasants. We do know that Domitian looked unfavourably on Christians in Rome and there was a limited period of persecution during his reign, but the personal search by a Roman emperor in Palestine for miscreants does not fit into any known historical scenario. The important point highlighted by the tradition is that it seems that blood descent from Jesus was recalled and esteemed.

The other piece of evidence is a reference by the second century historian and chronographer, Julius Africanus (in *Hist Eccl* 1.7.14), that in the east Jordan area there were still Christians descended from the bloodline of the Saviour. Obviously, such a matter was of sufficient esteem and importance to be recorded.

These items indicate that there was an emphasis on blood descent from Jesus, a dynastic succession as some have seen it. Hegesippus makes it clear that it is not only a matter of blood descent from Jesus, but also blood descent from David. We are dealing here with a Davidic dynasty. Jesus was considered to be the Davidic Messiah who would eventually return to establish his earthly kingdom. His time on earth coincided with the reign of the Priestly Messiah, James. In the interim, after his death, his fellow Davidic blood successors remained behind to uphold his rule. This is the implication of the tumult aroused by the 'many who were convinced and gloried in James' testimony' when James was apprehended, and the fact that the House of David was considered to continue. For Hegesippus, the death of the last blood relative, together with the death of The Apostles, was therefore an important moment, a fall from grace for the early church. Until then, he claims, the church had remained 'a pure and uncorrupted virgin'.

We now need to identify these Jewish Jesus-movement people, who followed their leaders James and the blood relatives of Jesus, more precisely. Epiphanius mentions the *Nazaraioi* which, Tertullian tells us, was an early name for Christians (*Adv Marc* 4:8)[19] and there is later mention in Jewish sources of the *Nozrim*. This group seems to be identical to the *Nasarenoi or Nazoarei*. Epiphanius links the *Nazaraioi* to another group, the *Iessaioi* (*Panarion* 29,1,3-9; 4.9) and ventured the opinion that this latter term derived from the name of Jesus. This is most unlikely. The etymological derivation is certainly to have been from the messianic term 'Jesse' in Isaiah 11: 1.

A shoot shall come out from the stump of Jesse,
and a branch [*nezer*] shall grow out of his roots.
The Spirit of Yahweh shall rest on him. (Isaiah 11:1-2)

That being so, the derivation of the Nazaraioi could well be from the term 'branch' or *nezer* in Hebrew since it occurs in the same context. Hence, it could be that the Messianic family, headed by the brothers of Jesus, was known as the *Nazaraioi* or the *Iessaioi*. We will see that this could have given rise to a mistaken impression that Jesus' earlier years had been spent in Nazareth (which is similar in spelling).

Theodoret, the bishop of Cyrrhus (c.393-466) throws some more light on this discussion. While together with Epiphanius he states that the *Nazaraioi* are Jews ('rather Jews and nothing else' *Panarion* 29.91), he goes on to state

---

[19] In Acts 24:5 Tertullus, a lawyer prosecuting Paul before the High Priest in Caesarea, refers to his adversary as 'a leader of the party of Nazarenes (*nazaraioi*)'.

that they honour Jesus, as a Just One or as Jesus the Just (*Haereticorum Fabularum compendium, PG* 83, 389). In short, they acknowledge him to be a *zaddik*.

The followers of James were the original Jesus-movement group, the *Nazaraioi* or Nazarenes. They were Jews and remained Jews. They did acknowledge that Jesus was a *zaddik* and a member of the Messianic Family but still a Jew. Jesus was Jesus the Nazarene and they were the *Nazaraioi*. After the assault by the Romans on Jerusalem and the land, some returned to Jerusalem while others settled in the eastern area of the Jordan until the second Jewish revolt in 135 CE. They would have practised the essential Jewish rituals: maintenance of the Torah, circumcision, the dietary rules and observance of the Sabbath.

But they were rejected by the mainstream Jews. Their refusal to support Bar Kochba in his revolt against Rome would have confirmed this impression. This growing exclusion meant that they were included in the heretics' list, the *mimim*, by other Jews.

In another important text, Epiphanius in 29.3.1 argues that the royal line of succession in Judah had passed 'from its fleshly dwelling of Judah and Israel' to the Church. The Church exercised this authority from 'two aspects, both royal and High Priestly'. While the royal aspect was carried on by Jesus, because of his descent from David, the priestly aspect fell to James. The Epiphanius text reads:

> He who is High Priest and chief of High Priests afterwards was
> installed as the first bishop: James, called apostle and brother of the
> Lord. (3.9)

At the point we can sum up the state of the question on James, the Brother of the Lord, and Jesus, with due caution and a readiness to reconsider the answer.

In a time of colonial repression and general despoliation of the population in Galilee, a family of five brothers stood up and were counted as a Family. They were seen as and probably self-identified with the Maccabee brothers who, for a short time at the inauguration of the Hasmonean dynasty, had restored the fortunes of the people of Judah. There would have been a sense in which this family would have claimed the attributes of a Messianic group, not that any one of them would have been identified as Messiah.

The Brothers, without Jesus who had launched his own movement, must have translocated to Jerusalem and established themselves there under

James. The group regarded James as a *zaddik*, who was a bitter critic of the Jewish establishment and particularly of the Temple personnel.

Jesus-movement groups, after his death, claimed that they were the authentic followers of Jesus, who was now acclaimed as the Davidic Messiah. Talk of the Messiah became rampant. The Brothers, led by James, saw the trend and claimed Jesus as their own. Their leader's brother, they said, had been the Davidic Messiah; their brother James, also a *zaddik,* was acclaimed as a Priestly Messiah. A Vision was related in a meal context that gave James pre-eminence. He claimed to be the legitimate successor to Jesus. Thus, The Brothers became a Jesus-movement group, centred in Jerusalem, composed only of Jewish followers and following Jewish ritual.

But The Brothers' claim was by no means the only one to the succession of Jesus.

Peter and The Twelve

Another group, according to the Literary Jesus, was led by Peter and included 'The Twelve'. What do we know of Peter? Presumably Peter would have held a position of some responsibility within Jesus' own Galilee group as distinct from Jesus' position within his family. He would have been Jesus' lieutenant, at least in the period after the break with the Baptist.

As regards The Twelve, while we are certain that the lists in the canonical gospels contain precisely twelve names, we are uncertain as to the exact Twelve. The lists run as follows:

Mark	Matthew	Luke	Acts
Simon Peter	Simon Peter	Simon Peter	Peter
James of Zebedee	Andrew	Andrew	John
John of Zebedee	James of Zebedee	James of Zebedee	James of Zebedee
Andrew	John of Zebedee	John of Zebedee	Andrew
Philip	Philip	Philip	Philip
Bartholomew	Bartholomew	Bartholomew	Thomas
Matthew	Thomas	Matthew	Bartholomew
Thomas	Matthew	Thomas	Matthew
James of Alphaeus	James of Alphaeus	James of Alphaeus	James of Alphaeus
Thaddaeus	Thaddaeus	Simon the Zealot	Simon the Zealot
Simon the Cananean	Simon the Cananean	Jude of James	Jude of James
Judas Iscariot	Judas Iscariot	Judas Iscariot	Judas Iscariot, but then replaced by Matthias

Whether there was any such historical group of The Twelve during the lifetime of Jesus is doubtful, although some scholars argue strongly for its historicity. There is only one mention of them in the Letters of Paul, in 1 Corinthians 15:5 ('he appeared to Cephas [Simon Peter], then to The Twelve'). The text, as we will see later, had been added later by a Roman editor; it has no independent force. They receive minor recognition in the early part of Acts; they then disappear.

A conjectural reconstruction could hold that Peter assumed the leadership of a Jesus-movement group after Jesus' death. It could have been that this group then formed a Council of The Twelve. The Council of The Twelve, based on the Twelve Tribes of Israel, did not function for long but its memory was perpetuated in Roman theology.

Around 43-44 CE, Acts recounts that Herod Agrippa I executed James of Zebedee[20] and arrested Peter. These moves, if substantiated, were political, perhaps religio-political; the Peter Jesus-movement had become messianic, but by that very fact it was also political and it was seen to be in confrontation with the Roman occupation. Herod Agrippa owed his appointment to the Romans and he would have been seen by this Jesus-movement as a usurper, perhaps even as an impediment to the return of Jesus. Reports of executions at the time, which may or may not have been historically reliable, would give rise in turn to the myth of widespread early Jewish persecution of the Jesus-movement and provide the impression that there was a stark Jew versus Christian confrontation in the first century CE.

Peter and the Twelve lived on in Roman Christianity. At this point we need to go back to the Jerusalem context.

Stephen and the Hellenists

In Acts 6 we are introduced to a Jesus-movement group known as the 'Hellenists', who stand in contradistinction to the 'Hebrews'. These separate categories do not make immediate sense. Hebrews or Jews were living in a Hellenistic setting and Greek speakers were often committed to Judaism. Perhaps the reference is to separate Jewish synagogues[21] or meeting places.

---

[20] There is confusion over these names. We will later see that James of Zebedee becomes confused with James the Brother of the Lord; John of Zebedee becomes confused with John of Patmos. This causes enormous problems in trying to identify the 'James, Peter and John' who were said to reside in Jerusalem.

[21] This would mean that the synagogues of Jerusalem and elsewhere, whatever format they took, were faced with the decision to accept or reject one or other Jesus ideology in circulation after his death. In other words some synagogues admitted Jesus-movement people, some did not. 'Hellenists' and 'Hebrews' would have been two such synagogues that did accept them. This system of

The Hellenists were said to have been led by Stephen, who was supported by a council of The Seven. This Jesus-movement would seem to have had radical Jewish views that spoke against particularistic interpretations of Jewish history. If any of his 'speech' in Acts is to be trusted as reflecting his views or those of his following, he maintained that the Jesus-movement involved the complete abrogation of Mosaic custom and signalled the end of the Temple and its sacrificial worship. He named a series of messengers: Joseph, Moses, the Prophets and 'the Just One', who was Jesus. The Jews, according to the Stephen speech, had not recognized the abrogation of the Law of Moses, and hence rejected Jesus. Acts is the only source for these suggestions.

This Hellenist position would have meant the virtual rejection of the authority of the Torah and the abandonment of the Jewish Temple cult. Because of this stance, Stephen was deemed to have spoken against the sanctity of the Temple, an offence over which the Sanhedrin still had jurisdiction. Rightly or wrongly, therefore, he and his group were seen, in the circumstances, as subversives.

Stephen's execution (the details in Acts were probably based on traditions about the execution of James the Just such as we have found in Josephus) would have come as a warning to other Jewish Jesus-movement groups in Jerusalem to be cautious. It would have caused a swing towards conservatism. This Hellenist group was subsequently led by a Philip, who began a mission in Samaria. It is possible that the execution of Stephen had forced the whole of the Hellenist group out of Jerusalem. They went to the Jews of the Diaspora in the Hellenistic cities along the Palestinian coast. Acts indicates that Samaritans, including Simon Magus, were attracted to their following.

> But when they [the people of Samaria] believed Philip, who was proclaiming the good news about the Reign of God and the name of Jesus Christ, they were baptized, both men and women. Even Simon himself believed. After being baptized, he stayed constantly with Philip and was amazed when he saw the signs and great miracles that took place. (Acts 8: 12-13)

According to the Acts' text, Philip moved from Samaria to Gaza and then to Caesarea. There is no further mention of Philip or the Hellenists until Acts 21:8-9 when Paul meets him in Caesarea with his four prophet-daughters .

synagogues supporting both mainstream Jews and Jesus-movement people would have eventually collapsed, as it did in Rome.

> The next day we left and came to Caesarea; and we went into the house
> of Philip the Evangelist, one of The Seven, and stayed with him. He had
> four unmarried daughters who had the gift of prophecy.

We will see that at a still later date Nicolaus, named as one of The
Seven, was identified very unfavourably as the eponymous ancestor of the
'Nicolaitans', as mentioned in Revelation 2:6,15.

> Yet this is to your credit: you hate the works of the Nicolaitans, which I
> also hate.

They are also mentioned in Irenaeus' text of *Adversus Haereses*. Irenaeus was the bishop of Lugdunun (Lyons) in France during the second
century CE (he died around 202 CE). He wrote a massive work on all the
heresies known up to his time and concentrated on Gnostics, whom he
abhorred.

> The Nicolaitans are the followers of that Nicolaus who was one of The
> Seven first ordained to the diaconate by the apostles. They lead lives
> of unrestrained indulgence. The character of these men is very plainly
> pointed out in the Apocalypse of John, [when they are represented] as
> teaching that it is a matter of indifference to practise adultery, and to
> eat things sacrificed to idols. Wherefore the Word has also spoken of
> them thus: But this you have, that you hate the deeds of the Nicolaitans,
> which I also hate. (1.26)

The Nicolaitans would have been a remnant of the Hellenists. At some
stage they had morphed into a Gnostic group which (if Irenaeus' polemic
can be believed) disdained the flesh and allowed followers to use it at will.

Acts tried to normalize this aberrant Jesus-movement group, who disdained its Jewish roots and tended towards Gnosticism. However, we are
probably at too far a distance now and have so few reliable sources that we
cannot reconstruct with any certainty the history of this and the other early
Jesus movement groups.

Conclusion

What we have seen is that historically we can trace a number of Jesus-
movement groups in the Palestinian area. We have only vague information
on their origins and development. The Brothers group, the Peter group and
the Hellenists must all have lived separate community lives, with the stimu-
lus of the Jesus-event their only real commonality.

We can attempt to reconstruct the common Literary Jesus within these
groups:

YHWH/Now known as Father

Jesus as Son of God, Son of Man, Messiah

(Contact achieved)

'The Twelve', Successors of James, Stephen's successors,

Jesus-movements

However, these attempts at explaining the variety of Jesus-movements require that attention be given to two important Christian movements: Christian Gnostic communities beginning in Palestine and a separate and powerful Jesus-movement group existing in Rome from the first century CE. Without due consideration of these two factors, what has been achieved so far means nothing, and our conclusions on the Gospel of John will be unclear. We now turn first to the Gnostics and second to the Roman Christians.

NOTES

On the question of the religious successors of Jesus, see my own article and its bibliography, on which I have drawn for this chapter: Crotty, R (1996), 'James the Just in the History of Early Christianity', *Australian Biblical Review*, 44, pp. 42-52.

There is a good collection of relevant articles in Byrne R. & McNary-Zak, B. eds. (2009), *Resurrecting the Brother of Jesus: The James Ossuary Controversy and the Quest for Religious Relics*, University of South Carolina Press: Chapel Hill.

I have also drawn on another of my books, *Peter the Rock: What the Roman Papacy Was and What It Might Become*, Spectrum Publications: Melbourne, 2015, for material on Peter and The Twelve and John of Zebedee. It deals with the origins of the notion of papacy in the Roman Church.

— 4 —
INTRODUCING CHRISTIAN GNOSTICISM

WE NOW COME TO ONE OF THE MOST VITAL ASPECTS of Early Christianity. There were a number of Jesus-movements that developed – some flourished and some declined. However, it was the Gnostic Jesus-movement groups that were air-brushed out of the Church Story. In the end, they could not be incorporated into a Story suitable for orthodox Church members.

However, in more recent times, we have by chance re-found the Gnostic writings and are able to chart their thinking and their practice.

What follows is an attempt to describe the thought-world of Christian Gnosticism using the relatively new texts.

JEWISH PROTO-GNOSTICISM

In order to follow the path that led to the early Christian Gnostics, we need to go back as far as the Greek philosophers who followed Plato and continued to do so even after the dramatic change in thinking introduced by Aristotle. In modern times this trend has been called Neo-Platonism. We then need to see how this Greek philosophy affected Judaism which had, as seen above, only been established in the Hasmonean period.

This was the time of a Hellenistic world where Greek philosophy and its world-view predominated.

The Platonic Background

Plato challenged the belief that the material world is real. It is, he claimed, only an image of the Real World. What lies behind the seemingly established world are Forms. These are archetypes which are reflected in the many types of things. Behind the Form of Stone there are many stones; behind the Form of Beauty are the many beautiful things. The material world is always in a state of flux; the World of Forms is eternal and unchanging.

Humans must not be satisfied with a phenomenal world of ever-changing images.

True knowledge consists of the mental apprehension of the unchanging Forms. Humans should seek to abstract themselves from the ever-changing material world and seek the Forms and thereby acquire true knowledge.

This philosophy continued to attract followers. Its followers saw clearly that they did not acquire saving knowledge by means of worldly experience or tradition that had been handed on. In some way they must achieve contact with the very Forms themselves, particularly the Form of Goodness, The One, which could be renamed 'God'. We can follow Platonic thought further.

What of this changing material world and its humans? All material things, including humans, have derived ultimately from The One. In fact, The One continually emits a force from itself, the Emanations, and produces things (without itself being in any way diminished). The Emanations are derived from The One, and they were meant eventually to return to The One. The One is at the centre of concentric circles of Emanations, each moving out from The One, and each diminishing in its degree of divinity the further that Emanation departs from its source. Each concentric circle is dependent on an earlier one and all of them tend towards reunion with The One. On this basic concept, the cosmology of the Platonists was built.

The first concentric circle is The Nous (reason and intelligence as against sense perception). As the first Emanation, it perfectly mirrors The One and simultaneously prefigures all being that will proceed subsequently. The Nous is the Demiurge (the craftsperson or creator) who organizes all subsequent being. Then, from the Nous there comes The Spirit, the World-Soul. There is an analogous relationship between Nous/Demiurge and Spirit as there is between The One and the Nous.

From the Spirit derives the world which includes humans who carry the spark of the Nous in their inner soul. This world and its human occupants are shadowy images of the heavenly world of Nous and Spirit. By the practice of virtue and by ascetic living, humans can re-find in themselves the true divinity from which they once came. More importantly, by thinking outside self, in the manner of an ecstatic lost in contemplation, it is possible for the human to transcend all and reach to The One here and now. This knowledge (which importantly is translated from the Greek *gnosis*) is not achieved by the personal effort of human persons. However, aided by the divinity, humans can passively become the recipients of *gnosis* and find reunion with The One, with God.

This *gnosis* is a state of utter happiness, of unity with all others who have made the same journey. God becomes Light and Life to the passive individual who has achieved it. This is salvation for the individual.

In Greek philosophy, the *Logos* (or Word) had become a very important idea from an early date and it had a variety of meanings. It was drawn into the realm of Platonism. The *Logos* for Platonists was the invisible principle that permeated all of reality. It was a universal divine Reason, to be found in the World but transcending all the imperfections of the World. It was the unchanging truth beneath the variety of change and oppositions in the World.

It was this Platonic thinking that infiltrated the world-view of some Jews in the period prior to the Christian era. Because of Greek occupation of their land, they were confronted, sometimes unwillingly, with the process of Hellenization, acquiring Greek culture in all its forms of thinking, religious observance, art, architecture, town planning. Jewish Platonists adopted the thinking as regards Forms, as regards a cosmology of Emanations, as regards the *Logos* and Spirit. Next, they interpreted their own Jewish texts in the light of Platonism. Thus, they produced new texts, adapting Platonic thought to Jewish religious imagery.

While this exercise might not have produced an immediate contact with Ultmacy for them, it did transform the Intermediaries in the Jewish religious mediation. For this reason we can talk of Jewish Proto-Gnosticism. The traditional structure was changed and it was headed towards the immediate structure of Gnosticism.

New Other-worldly Intermediaries

We can catalogue some of the new Intermediaries. They included among others the *dabar Yahweh* (the Word of God), *ruah Yahweh* (the Spirit of Yahweh), *hokmah* (Wisdom), Michael (or another angel), Melchizedek and Enoch. Each Intermediary had its own religio-social history and obviously no particular group within pre-Christian Israel would have utilized all the Intermediaries. In fact, no one group would have even known them all. It would have been similar to Roman Catholic groups with their insistence on a focus on The Virgin Mary (under a number of local guises such as Our Lady of Guadalupe, Our Lady of Fatima), The Holy Spirit, The Sacred Heart, Saint Francis and so on.

For these Jews, the *dabar Yahweh* depicted graphically an aspect of the activity of Yahweh in his dealings with the world. Speech in an official Jewish context, such as the verdict of a judge or the statement of a contract, was considered to have immediate and binding effect. Yahweh's speech, or the *dabar Yahweh*, likewise had its immediate effect in the world order. However, in the Greek mode of thinking the *dabar Yahweh* slowly acquired its own personality, separate from that of Yahweh, although not in opposition to him. By the time of Wisdom 18 the *dabar* was a separate entity with its own role in the Exodus from Egypt.

> For while gentle silence
> enveloped all things,
> and night in its swift course was
> now half gone,
> Your all-powerful word [*dabar*] leaped
> from heaven, from the royal throne
> into the midst of the land that was doomed. (Wisdom 18:14-15)

There is no single English word that translates the Hebrew *ruah*, 'breath' or 'wind' or 'spirit'. There is, however, a single meaning from which a number of applications derive according to the context. It can signify 'breath' as a principle of life and vital activity, or the movement of air when the breath of Yahweh becomes a wind and hence an agent of significant power. And it can be The Spirit of Yahweh inasmuch as it is the force that effects the works of Yahweh.

This spiritual force of The Spirit was made into an Intermediary as a substantial source of activity and a creative power in its own right. It became a divine, dynamic entity by which Yahweh accomplished his purposes. This is obvious in the late creation story in Genesis 1.

> In the beginning when God created the heavens and the earth, [3] the
> earth was a formless void and darkness covered the face of the deep,
> while a wind [*ruah*] from God swept over the face of the waters.

By the time of the Wisdom literature, the *ruah Yahweh* had become the pervading divine presence, the Holy Spirit of Yahweh which guided Israel.

> [7] Because the spirit [*ruah*] of Yahweh has filled the world,
> and that which holds all things together knows what is said,
> [8] therefore those who utter unrighteous things will not escape notice,
> and justice, when it punishes, will not pass them by.

The same was true of *hokmah* or Wisdom. It gradually achieved separate status and by the time of the redaction of Proverbs 8: 22-23, it too assumed pre-existence with Yahweh.

> [22] Yahweh created me [*hokmah*] at the beginning of his work,
> the first of his acts of long ago.
> [23] Ages ago I was set up,
> at the first, before the beginning of the earth.

Hokmah or Wisdom was also accounted as having a major role both in creation and the Exodus and its form as an Intermediary became even more established in the book of Wisdom chapters 10-11 where it is shown to have directed the entire sacred history of Israel.

Michael and other angelic beings possibly entered the Jewish mindset from Persia, which was not surprising. By the time of the writing of Daniel 12:1 Michael had become 'The Great Prince, the Protector of your people'. He had become the special divine angel of Israel just as divine angels were known in Persia. In the Qumran writings we are told of the 'Dominion of Michael', a world of good angels.

> He [Yahweh] has sent everlasting aid
> to the lot redeemed
> by the power of the majestic angel
> for the dominion [*blank*] of Michael
> in everlasting light. (1 QM 17:6)

In other late Jewish texts such as the *Testament of Levi* 5:6-7, a part of the *Testament of the Twelve Patriarchs,* Michael is depicted in his role as Intermediary. This Jewish text was never included in the canonical list of Hebrew Scriptures but it was influential. In its final form the book would have been written in the second century CE. However, its ideas would have been in circulation much earlier.

> And I said to him [Michael]: I pray you, O Lord, tell me Thy name, that
> I may call upon you in a day of tribulation. And he said: I am the angel
> who intercedes for the nation of Israel that they may not be smitten
> utterly, for every evil spirit attacks it. And after these things I woke,
> and blessed the Most High, and the angel who intercedes for the nation
> of Israel and for all the righteous.

What these texts about Michael describe is precisely the role expected of an Other-worldly Intermediary.

There are two other Other-worldly Intermediary figures. Melchizedek and Enoch were once biblical characters who had progressed beyond their original context in the sacred stories and taken on supernatural form. Enoch, great-grandfather of Noah, was said to have been 'taken by God' and a later tradition interpreted this as meaning that he had not died and would return. He was to become the Eschatological Judge in this later line of thinking. In 1 Enoch 13-14 he is seen to have the function of mediating between Yahweh and the 'Watchers of Heaven', the fallen angels, as the command of Yahweh to come to his side makes clear:

> Come near to me, Enoch, and to my holy Word. (1 Enoch 14:24)

In 3 Enoch 12: 3-5, Enoch is transformed into the angel Metatron, who is crowned by God and known as the 'Lesser Yahweh'.

> He set it [a crown] upon my head and he called me 'The Lesser Yahweh' in the presence of his whole household in the heights as it is written, 'My name is in him.' (3 Enoch 12:5)

Melchizedek, from his shadowy literary mention as a wandering warrior-king in Genesis 14, was accorded a miraculous birth in 2 Enoch 71; at Qumran he was elevated to a divine form, both 'el and 'elohim being his titles, and he was described as a heavenly deliverer.

> 'Your 'Elohim' is Melchizedek, who will free [them] from the hand of Belial. (11Q Melchizedek II.24-25)

Still within the Qumran literature, Melchizedek resists the other evil spirits and Belial in order to protect God's people, as does Michael.

In short, at least in some intellectual Jewish circles the Other-worldly Intermediaries were becoming the equivalent of the divine. Word, Spirit, Wisdom, Michael, Melchizedek, Enoch became the means by which Yahweh, and so Ultimacy, could be attained. Sometimes, these Intermediaries could lead directly to Ultimacy. This was the incipient form of Jewish Gnosticism that arose because the established channels of divine contact, within the Jewish ritual framework, were not considered active.

New This-worldly Intermediaries

On the other side of the structural equation, the principal This-worldly Intermediary had long been identified as 'Moses'. 'Moses', as the mediator between Yahweh and the group, hearkened back to the figure of the biblical Moses, who spoke face to face with Yahweh and brought the *torah* from him to the people in the text of Exodus. But from that point the mediatorial symbol lived its own life

'Moses', as a structural symbol, overlapped the Jerusalemite king or line of kings. There was quasi-identification of Moses and David, considered to be the Ur-King of Israel.

David as King gave rise to the idea of an ongoing leader and defender of Israel, the Anointed One or *mashiah*, as already discussed. In the Second Temple period, *mashiah* was not used as a distinctive title; it covered a number of different models: priest/teacher, prophet/teacher and 'son of God' (in the sense of an exceptional human being, as in the usage of Sirach 4:10, 'a son of the Most High'). The term was used for the Davidic king, and in the *Psalms of Solomon* the term is used specifically of a Davidic king who is expected in the future.

> And their king is the Messiah [*mashiah*] of the Lord. (17:32)

However, no crystallization of this messianic expectation into a specific figure can be witnessed before a text of Daniel 9:25 makes it explicit ('to the coming of the *mashiah*, the prince'). This was a definite figure expected in the future. The expectation of a single specific Messiah was to be continued in Judaism. At Qumran, the literature is able to designate the royal Messiah as the 'Branch of David', 'Prince of the Congregation' and perhaps 'Son of God'.

This royal theology was almost certainly taken up in subsequent poetic texts such as the following from Isaiah 9:

> [6] For a child has been born for us,
> a son given to us;
> authority rests upon his shoulders;
> and he is named
> Wonderful Counsellor, Mighty God,
> Everlasting Father, Prince of Peace.
> [7] His authority shall grow continually,
> and there shall be endless peace
> for the throne of David and his kingdom.
> He will establish and uphold it
> with justice and with righteousness
> from this time onwards and for evermore.
> The zeal of Yahweh of The Armies[22] will do this.

However, messianic expectation was neither uniform nor universal in Judaism in the pre-Christian period. In general, it can be said that in those Jewish circles where there was an unacceptable socio-religious and politico-religious situation, together with a fervent expectation that an ideal future was possible, then messianism bridged the gulf between the *now* and the *then*. Messianism portrayed that particular initiative by God which would marshal the forces within the group in order to achieve the objective of amelioration. The group's depiction of the Messiah and the Messiah's redemptive activity would obviously reflect the values and assumptions of the group.

Thus, where political independence was the future ideal, then a political, Davidic Messiah would be employed. Where a purified cultic system in

---

[22] 'Yahweh of the Armies' is a literal translation of *Yahweh Saba'oth*. This title of Yahweh may have referred to the earlier time when Yahweh was seen as a war deity.

which religious independence could be enjoyed was the goal, then a priestly, Aaronic Messiah was called for. These two aspects, political and priestly, could be linked in a dual Messiah or in the person of the priest-king. For example, David was depicted as both king and priest, controlling both the political and religious domains.

Where a radical transformation of a suffering human situation leading to a New Age and a new 'Land' was the final objective then a Messiah in the style of the Mosaic Prophet rather than the Davidic king was needed. In the post-Exilic period, this messianic expectation, when it was realized, sometimes took the form of a diarchy, a lay leader in the style of a Moses or David, accompanied by a priestly leader in the style of an Aaron.

The reason for this diarchy was to be found in the prevailing politico-social form realized after the post-Exilic resettlement. Any hope of a restitution of an independent monarchy in Judah had been soon quelled. Instead, the religious leadership of the High Priest became the set pattern. Ezekiel 37 had given an outline of a restoration by a diarchy of a Davidic prince and a Zadokite priest.

> [24] My servant David shall be king over them; and they shall all have one shepherd. They shall follow my ordinances and be careful to observe my statutes. [25] They shall live in the land that I gave to my servant Jacob, in which your ancestors lived; they and their children and their children's children shall live there for ever; and my servant David shall be their prince for ever. [26] I will make a covenant of peace with them; it shall be an everlasting covenant with them; and I will bless them and multiply them, and will set my sanctuary among them for evermore. [27] My dwelling-place shall be with them; and I will be their God, and they shall be my people. [28] Then the nations shall know that I Yahweh sanctify Israel, when my sanctuary is among them for evermore.

At a later point this was taken up by the prophet Zechariah who had been stimulated by the hopes raised by the local prince, Zerubbabel, and Joshua the High Priest to see that a future diarchy could be the decisive turning point in Jewish history. His depiction of two olive trees and the anointing of two figures looks towards the implementation of an ideal future age (4:1-14).

> [1] The angel who talked with me came again, and wakened me, as one is wakened from sleep. [2] He said to me, 'What do you see?' And I said, 'I see a lampstand all of gold, with a bowl on the top of it; there are seven lamps on it, with seven lips on each of the lamps that are on the top of it. [3] And by it there are two olive trees, one on the right of the bowl and the other on its left.' [4] I said to the angel who talked with me, 'What are these, my lord?' [5] Then the angel who talked with me answered me,

'Do you not know what these are?' I said, 'No, my lord.' [6] He said to me, 'This is the word of Yahweh to Zerubbabel: Not by might, nor by power, but by my spirit, says Yahweh of hosts. [7] What are you, O Great Mountain? Before Zerubbabel you shall become a plain; and he shall bring out the top stone amid shouts of "Grace, grace to it!" '

[8] Moreover, the word of Yahweh came to me, saying, [9] 'The hands of Zerubbabel have laid the foundation of this house; his hands shall also complete it. Then you will know that Yahweh of hosts has sent me to you. [10] For whoever has despised the day of small things shall rejoice, and shall see the plummet in the hand of Zerubbabel.

'These seven are the eyes of Yahweh, which range through the whole earth.' [11] Then I said to him, 'What are these two olive trees on the right and the left of the lampstand?' [12] And a second time I said to him, 'What are these two branches of the olive trees, which pour out the oil through the two golden pipes?' [13] He said to me, 'Do you not know what these are?' I said, 'No, my lord.' [14]Then he said, 'These are the two anointed ones [*mashiakim*] who stand by Yahweh of the whole earth.'

This dual messianic expectation, while not universal and not set in its agenda, was prominent in certain Jewish groups, as was also reflected in their writings and the Qumran literature.

For many the expectation would be fulfilled by the Hasmoneans when they assumed the High Priesthood. The identification of Jesus with the Davidic Messiah and his brother James with the Priestly Messiah can also be explained.

Qumran and Proto-Gnosticism

The Qumran literature is a good example of what the process was about.[23] There are references to the dual messianic expectations identifying a diarchic expectation in the form of a Mosaic lay Messiah and a priestly Messiah. There are several references to the anointed twins of Israel and Aaron. Some of the Qumran texts indicate that a *yahad* ('the unity') or community group, presumably a group related to the Scrolls and Qumran, reflected the messianic future in its own structure of government with a Priest and a Supervisor. There is no reason to suspect that a Jesus-movement could not have been similarly affected by this diarchic expectation.

The phenomenological structure of pre-Christian Judaism was never static. There were a number of ascent and descent patterns intertwined.

---

[23] There is ample bibliography on the Dead Sea Scrolls in the Notes at the end of this chapter.

Either an Other-worldly Intermediary would descend as a pre-existing figure to offer mediation to the people, or a human figure would be elevated to the role of a This-worldly Intermediary.

The religious structure of Judaism was under stress, as is revealed in its literature. It was being manipulated as a religious population sought contact with Ultimacy. It is only at this point we can understand Jewish Gnosticism. There was a closer and closer link between the Focus on Ultimacy and the Religious Community. For a number of reasons, the trust in any of the existing mediatorial systems was collapsing. Instead there were those who sought an immediate union.

The Dead Sea Scrolls give evidence of this process. In some parts, the Scrolls relate their own symbolic universe. It was based on dualism: Light and Darkness, Truth and Lie, Spirit and Flesh. This religio-cultural World was ruled by Darkness and Lie. The Ruler of the World was the Angel of Darkness, also known as the Devil. This is Gnostic language derived from a Hellenistic way of thinking being applied to Jewish thought.

The *Community Rule* explains this symbolic universe in detail:

> He has created man to govern the world, and has appointed for him two spirits in which to walk unto the time of his visitation: the spirits of truth and injustice.
>
> Those born of truth spring from a fountain of light, but those born of injustice spring from a source of darkness. All the children of righteousness are ruled by the Prince of Light and walk in the ways of light, but all the children of injustice are ruled by the Angel of Darkness and walk in the ways of darkness. The Angel of Darkness leads all the children of righteousness astray, and until his end, all their sin, iniquities, wickedness, and all their unlawful deeds are caused by his dominion in accordance with the mysteries of God. Every one of their chastisements, and every one of the seasons of their distress, shall be brought about by the rule of his persecution; for all his allotted spirits seek the overthrow of the Sons of Light.
>
> But the God of Israel and his Angel of Truth will succour all the Sons of Light. For it is he who created the Spirits of Light and Darkness and founded every action upon them and established every deed [upon] their [ways]. And he loves the one everlastingly and delights in its works for ever; but the counsel of the other He loathes and forever hates its ways. (1QS 3: 18-4:1)

The stark Dualism of the two Spirits and Light/Darkness is only too clear. Disdain for the World with its Angel of Darkness as against the Prince of Light is also clear. Those who will find salvation are the Sons of Light, who walk in the Light. There is less need of any Intermediary.

There is evidence that within the Judaism of the late Greek period there was a deterioration in the commitment to established Intermediaries. New Intermediaries were being trialled. But there would also have been some more adventurous thinkers who moved to an immediate structure. There was no need for new Intermediaries; there was no need for any Intermediary.

Conclusion

This is what we can call Proto-Gnosticism. We will see that 'Gnostic' and 'Gnosticism' are modern terms used by academics to cover an important religious spectrum. The trend towards immediate union was basically widespread in human thought, the contention that the human intellect can make direct contact with the Infinite, the Ultimate. Judaism was on the verge of producing a full-blown Gnostic tradition.

From here we can turn to Christian Gnosticism or Jesus-movement Gnosticism.

CHRISTIAN GNOSTICISM

There were rival successors to Jesus. We have seen some of them, headed by James the Just and the Brothers, Peter and the Twelve and Stephen. However, we can also document Mary Magdalene, Thomas, Philip, Judas Iscariot esteemed as leaders by some Christian communities. Where did these communities fit into the pattern?

They were the Christian Gnostics, many of them heirs of the proto-Gnosticism of the pre-Christian movement within Judaism.

There was never anything like a recognizable and single 'Gnostic Jesus-movement'. There were many Gnostic Jesus-movement groups and they had a plethora of beliefs, of terminologies, of practices. Some Gnostic groups dissociated themselves from other Gnostic groups and they wrote bitterly about each other. However, it is convenient to subsume them under a title like 'Gnosticism', as they did have essential characteristics in common. At the time, this similarity might not have been visible to the proponents; possibly the sameness among the groups was more apparent to the orthodox opponents.

The Christian Gnostic communities had to define themselves as against those who were outside their boundaries. There were, first of all, rival Gnostic groups who had different teachings and practices, including different sexual practices. For example, the *Testimony of Truth*, written probably at the end of the second century in Alexandria, singles out other specific

Gnostic groups – those led by Valentinus, those led by Basilides and his son and the Simonians. Speaking of a wayward Gnostic, it reads:

> He completed the course of Valentinus. He himself speaks about the Ogdoad, and his disciples resemble the disciples of Valentinus. They on their part, moreover, [...] leave the good, but they have worship of the idols ...
> ... [8 lines unrecoverable]... he has spoken many words, and he has written many books [...] words ...
> ... [lines 16 through end-of-page unrecoverable]
> ... they are manifest from the confusion in which they are, in the deceit of the world. For they go to that place, together with their knowledge, which is vain. (56-57)

Second, and more importantly, the Christian Gnostics had to define themselves against the mainstream Jews, including the Pharisees and the scribes. These latter were regarded as outsiders who followed their own Law, the Torah. They are decried by Gnostics in the *Second Treatise of the Great Seth* by a Jesus-statement:

> Moses, a faithful servant, was a laughingstock, having been named 'the Friend,' since they perversely bore witness concerning him who never knew me. Neither he nor those before him, from Adam to Moses and John the Baptist, none of them knew me nor my brothers.
> For they had a doctrine of angels to observe dietary laws and bitter slavery, since they never knew truth, nor will they know it. For there is a great deception upon their soul, making it impossible for them ever to find a Nous of freedom in order to know him, until they come to know the Son of Man. (63-64)

Finally there were the other non-Gnostic mainstream Christians, with a variety of leaders, who also had to be dispatched to the role of outsider. They had not achieved full *gnosis* or divine knowledge according to the Gnostics. In the *Second Treatise of the Great Seth* these incomplete Christians are described by the Gnostic Jesus:

> I did not refuse them even to become a Christ, but I did not reveal myself to them in the love which was coming forth from me. I revealed that I am a stranger to the regions below. (52)

The mainstream Jesus-movement groups (most of all, the Roman Christians) retained, according to the Gnostic view, incomplete teachings. In the *Second Treatise of the Great Seth,* one such teaching is revealed – 'It is slavery that we shall die with Christ'. Such a teaching about Jesus' atoning death is rejected as incompatible with Gnostic teaching.

At this point, having introduced Christian Gnosticism, we need to explain how it is that at the present moment we know more about the Gnostics than at any time previously. We will trace this modern interest in Gnosticism and its outcomes.

The Texts from Nag Hammadi

Up until relatively recently, Christian Gnosticism was known to the academic world only by the writings of early century heresy-hunters who quoted their foe with acrimony, disdain and misunderstanding. There had been a few stray discoveries of Gnostic texts but not enough to fill out the thought-world of Gnosticism. That situation changed in the twentieth century.

In December 1945 there was a fortuitous find. It took place in Upper Egypt in a district known as Nag Hammadi. Two peasant farmers were bagging fertilizer from the numerous caves along a rugged cliff face when one of them, Muhammad 'Ali al-samman, came upon a reddish earthenware jar. Being Muslim, he feared there might be a *djinn* or evil spirit inside but he still smashed it open with a mattock and found a collection of codices. These were books of papyrus leaves with writing, each bound in leather-covered wooden boards. The writing was Coptic.

Because of the fact that the brothers were being investigated for a family revenge murder and because of protracted bureaucratic dealings and bargaining over the codices, the texts were not comprehensively studied until the 1960s. There were twelve bound codices or books and the loose leaves of another. Altogether 53 separate texts have been identified in the codices (five of them in duplicate; one in triplicate). Most certainly others have been lost forever since Muhammad confided that his mother used some papyrus sheets as fire-starters.

The texts from Nag Hammadi have been dated to about 350-400 CE (mainly by the fact that some had leather covers padded with datable commercial receipts), but they are, for the most part, copies of Greek originals (fragments of which had been actually found or cited in antiquity) which go back perhaps to the second century CE or even, some maintain, to the first century CE. They had been probably deposited at Nag Hammadi by Christian monks from a nearby Coptic monastery of Saint Pachomius. The contents of the texts explain why they would have been hidden; their Jesus was very much contrary to the canonical Jesus, the Literary Jesus of the four gospels. The monastic community, who presumably made use of the texts, was afraid that Roman soldiers in the fourth century CE might come to take the texts and punish the readers. Possibly the monks hoped for more peaceful days when they could dig up their hoard. That day did not come.

The list of texts from Nag Hammadi, under broad themes, is as follows:

Alternative myths of Creation and Salvation: *The Apocryphon of John* (three copies, two long and one short plus an earlier copy of the short version); *The Hypostasis of the Archons*; *On the Origin of the World* (two copies); *The Apocalypse of Adam*; *The Paraphrase of Shem*; *Trimorphic Protennoia*.

Gnostic Teachings (the world, the human soul, life in the World): *The Gospel of Truth* (two copies); *The Treatise on the Resurrection*; *The Tripartite Tractate*; *Eugnostos the Blessed* (two copies); *The Second Treatise of the Great Seth*; *The Teachings of Silvanus*; *The Testimony of Truth*.

The Gnostic liturgies: *The Discourse on the Eighth and Ninth*; *The Prayer of Thanksgiving*; *A Valentinian Exposition*; *The Three Steles of Seth*; *The Prayer of the Apostle Paul*; *On the Anointing*; *On Baptism*; *On the Eucharist*.

The Feminine Divine Principle: *The Thunder, Perfect Mind*; *The Thought of Norea*; *The Sophia of Jesus Christ*; *The Exegesis on the Soul*.

Gnostic Apostolic Writings:: *The Apocalypse of Peter*; *The Letter of Peter to Philip*; *The Acts of Peter and the Twelve Apostles*; *The (First) Apocalypse of James*; *The (Second) Apocalypse of James*; *The Apocalypse of Paul*.

Gospel accounts of the Sayings and Deeds of Jesus: *The Dialogue of the Saviour*; *The Book of Thomas the Contender*; *The Apocryphon of James*; *The Gospel of Philip*; *The Gospel of Thomas*.

Not easily classified under the above headings: *The Prayer of the Apostle Paul*; *The Gospel of the Egyptians* (two copies); *The Apocalypse of Adam*; *Authoritative Teaching*; *The Concept of Our Great Power*; *Plato, Republic*; *the Prayer of Thanksgiving*; *Asclepius 21-29*; *Zostrianos*; *Melchizedek*; *Marsanes*; *The Interpretation of Knowledge*; *Allogenes*; *Hypsiphrone*; *The Sentences of Sextus*; *Fragments*.

Because of these texts we now have a much better idea of the meaning of Gnosticism in the early Christian centuries and the ideas that circulated in these Christian circles about a Gnostic Jesus. It must be stressed yet again that while there are commonalities among the Gnostic library, there are certainly also contradictions and differences. We now know that there was often only a blurred line that divided ideas and forms of orthodox Christianity from the Gnostics. Later, we will be referring specifically to some of these texts.

There were also two important texts that had been discovered earlier in Egypt but were not part of the cache found at Nag Hammadi: *The Gospel of Mary [Magdalene]* and *The Gospel of Judas.*

We will look at these key texts found outside Nag Hammadi, since they will both have significant relevance to the Gospel of John.

The Gospel of Mary

In The Gospel of Mary, discovered earlier in the nineteenth century unfortunately in fragmentary form, Mary Magdalene reveals to the other disciples that she has received special teachings from Jesus that were transmitted to her through visionary experience. She assumes the role of leader of the believers, reassuring the male apostles who live in fear of arrest and death. The other apostles react vigorously and ask why the Saviour would have chosen a woman to be the recipient of his special and secret teachings. The most outspoken is Peter, and he is soundly rebuked by Levi:

> Levi answered, speaking to Peter, 'Peter, you have always been a wrathful person. Now I see you contending against the woman like the Adversaries. For if the Saviour made her worthy, who are you then for your part to reject her? Assuredly the Saviour's knowledge of her is completely reliable. That is why he loved her more than us.
> Rather we should be ashamed. We should clothe ourselves with the perfect Human, acquire it for ourselves as he commanded us, and announce the good news, not laying down any other rule or law that differs from what the Saviour said.' (18)

The designation of Mary as the one whom 'he loved more than us' has caused scholars to consider the identity of the Beloved Disciple in John. This friction between Mary and Peter probably reflects the divisions between orthodox Roman Christians and Gnostics in the second century. The text of the *Gospel of Mary* appears to have been written in Greek some time in that century.

The Gospel of Judas

The newly discovered Gnostic *Gospel of Judas,* only made public in the 1990s, depicts Judas not as a traitor but as that follower who receives Jesus' most profound revelation and who hands Jesus over for his crucifixion only at the specific request of Jesus. Jesus needed Judas' help to be freed from his earthly body of Flesh which retained his divine Spirit.

The actual codex of the Gospel of Judas has been well scrutinized. Five separate samples from the papyri sheets have been carbon-dated to 220-340 CE. The ink has been analysed and proves to be an ancient mixture (iron gall and soot). The Coptic text appears genuine to linguistic scholars and indicates, by its particular structures, that it is translating a Greek original. Scholars are confident that what we have is a Coptic manuscript dating from about the fourth century CE and that it is a translation of a Greek text which could have circulated quite early.

There was a mention of a *Gospel of Judas* by the Christian bishop Irenaeus in about 180 CE. His second century CE book *Adversus Haereses* has been mentioned already. He referred to a Greek text used by a group who revered Judas Iscariot and with great disdain he called this text a 'fictitious history'. Irenaeus, as we have seen, was bishop of Lugdunun in Roman Gaul and wrote his *Adversus Haereses*, particularly against the Gnostics in that city. In turn, the Gnostics looked down upon Irenaeus since they regarded all bishops of the mainstream churches as 'waterless canals', a term used in the *Gospel of Philip* (written in the second half of the third century CE). The *Gospel of Judas* was attributed by Irenaeus to such a Gnostic group.

At this point an important statement needs to be made. The Nag Hammadi texts, in their present copies, were dated mainly to the fourth century. On the basis of style, language and content they have subsequently been dated to earlier originals in the second and third centuries. When comparing them to the Christian Scriptures, it is too easy to state that these were written earlier and that the Gnostic texts simply incorporated their ideas and language but in a different idiom.

It is most unlikely that the Christian Scriptures were actually written much earlier or any earlier. We will see that some texts of the Christian Scriptures have had a long transmission. When it is confidently said that the gospel of Mark was written around 65 CE, it means that it was possible that the process resulting in the Markan gospel might have begun around that date. Its final composition would not have taken place until some time in the second century CE. This is comparable to many Gnostic texts. Where there are parallels between Christian Scriptures and Gnostic texts, direct dependence of one on the other should never be an automatic conclusion.

So much for a review of the writings revered by the Christian Gnostics. What can be said of the communities themselves?

Christian Gnostic Communities

From an early period in the Christian era there must have been Gnostic groups, some of whose members would have had contact with the changing tides in Judaism. Christian Gnostics did not emerge from nowhere. We have seen above that there had already been a Gnostic tradition within Judaism, growing stronger as the Christian era approached, and this would seem to have been the origin of Christian Gnosticism.

Christian Gnosticism seems to have flourished mostly among hermits and ascetic monks, living an austere life in desert regions, particularly in Egypt. However, other Gnostic groups may well have attracted the more general urban populace. They were regarded by many of the Roman Church group in particular as The Enemy. They would be effectively wiped out (but never completely eradicated) by the Roman military in the fourth century CE. These Gnostic groups, as recorded in their own writings, looked back to a variety of founders (who had acquired *gnosis* and could then hand it on to others) such as Mary Magdalene, Thomas, Philip, Judas Iscariot. There is no historical proof that these characters were actually leaders, but then there is little or no historical proof for any Christian founder. Although the Gnostics had their own rituals, they demanded that adherents should individually achieve their salvation by experiencing the depth of knowledge or *gnosis* in themselves. Their sacred rituals acknowledged the progress towards full *gnosis* and salvation; they did not create that progress.

They saw themselves as liminal groups, waiting on the threshold in the period between the Heavenly Home, which had been disrupted by the creation of the World, and the World in which they lived. They awaited the return of the chosen ones to Heaven. They saw themselves as strangers or 'passers-by' (as the *Gospel of Thomas* logion 42 puts it) in this World. They had been awakened from their ignorance and darkness and allowed to achieve *gnosis*. This attainment, in their terms, was the state of being 'born again' or entering the Bridal Chamber.

The Gnostic writings, belonging to a number of diverse groups, viewed many of the characters in the canonical gospels of Roman Christianity in a very different fashion. Thomas was not a dim-witted person; he was rather the chosen one to whom secret knowledge was confided by Jesus. Mary Magdalene was not just a distinguished follower of Jesus (and less so a prostitute!) who saw him after he was risen from the dead; she was, at least for some Gnostics, the recipient of Jesus' full revelation and his true successor. Peter was a different character in the *Apocalypse of Peter* from the Peter of the canonical gospels, as was James the brother of The Lord in the *Gospel of Thomas*.

Gnosticism must have been a fully-fledged movement in the early period of Christianity, even if there were a number of quite separate Gnostic communities with differing beliefs, differing practices and different sacred texts. They clearly posed a threat to other Jesus-movements. By the time of Constantine, Gnostic teaching was seen by Roman Christians as the abject corruption of the valid teaching of Jesus. Gnostic writings on the divine realm were derided by mainstream Christians for their confusion, despite the fact that there was equal confusion in the interminable arguments on the divinity of Jesus and the Trinity in the pre-Nicene period (and indeed, afterwards).

It followed that Gnosticism was denounced as a heresy from an early stage of the Jesus-movements in Palestine, and Gnostics were viewed as religious deviants. Eventually, when the orthodox bishops gained complete power in Egypt, particularly after the fourth century, and were backed by the Roman army, the Gnostics were purged and their sacred books burned.

Ever since then, Christian Gnosticism has been the elephant in the room as far as any history of the early Church was concerned. It was obvious that it was there. Why else would the earlier orthodox writers have fulminated with such zeal against it unless it threatened them? Why would their fulsome lists of heresies have concentrated on it? However, it has been too often consigned to a footnote or passing reference in the emergence of the Christian Church.

It is true that the Christian Gnostics became the losers. They succumbed to the superior political (and military) power of the mainstream Roman Church by the fourth century CE. But they left their impression and, we will see, their influence must be understood in order to interpret the Gospel of John.

The Christian Gnostic Myth

At this point we need to concentrate on the thought-world of these Gnostic Jesus-movement people, who like the Jewish Gnostics, saw no need for elaborate hierarchical structures (in the Christian case, leadership under bishops, elders and deacons; a series of key rituals said to have derived from Jesus himself; a canon of sacred writings) that were being developed in other areas at that time.

While we admit fully that there was no one thing called Gnosticism, and there is little need to go into the complex spread of trends (such as the Sethian and Valentinian), there are common features to the movements that can readily be dubbed 'Gnostic'. What was their common Myth (intended in the strict sense dealt with earlier)?

We will use illustrative texts from a variety of Gnostic sources. Not all of these have the same teaching, but there are enough common features to get the main thrust of Gnosticism.

Gnosis

In the first place, the Christian Gnostic Myth (like all Gnosticism) stressed the need for *gnosis*, a special knowledge, experience or illumination. The Myth claimed that salvation was only possible through such a secret and profound intellectual experience which was reserved for the chosen few. Jesus, in the Christian version of events, came into the World to teach the elect how to achieve that intellectual experience. But *gnosis* presumed a previous scaffolding of religious thought.

The *gnosis* encompassed a saving insight into the divinity and the heavenly environs from the Beginning, an insight into the reality of Self, living in the World. This included a knowledge of where the Self came from, its divine nature, its possibility of salvation.

The Great Invisible Spirit

Gnosis reveals to the believer, in the first instance, the eternal, unknowable divinity, the Monad or Oneness. This Godhead was infinite, beyond anything that could be described. The Godhead had many names: The Great Invisible Spirit, The Father, The All (*pleroma*), Our Great Power, The Light. In *The Apocryphon of John* (must be dated before the time it was condemned by Irenaeus in 185 CE), John questions his personal Revealer about these sacred mysteries:

> And I asked to know it, and he said to me, 'The Monad is a monarchy
> with nothing above it. It is he who exists as God and Father of
> everything, the Invisible One who is above everything, who exists as
> Incorruption, which is in the pure Light into which no eye can look.' (2)

From this eternal and unknowable Godhead there came a series of Emanations of other divinities. This idea of Emanation was also common to all forms of Gnosticism and, like *gnosis*, had its roots in Platonic thought.

In fact, some Gnostics had a sort of Trinity. From The Divine Father there emanated a Mother, called Barbelo[24] in some texts. She became the

---

[24] Barbelo is an unusual name and its Hebrew etymology is contested. It has been suggested that it should be transcribed as *b'arba-'El* or 'in the four [letters of YHWH], there is God'.

Female Consort of The Father. Then from The Father and Barbelo came The Child. The Child was also known as Autogenes, the Self-Generated One, who emerged by his own initiative.[25] In some Gnostic texts, this derivation of The Child is made more complicated with descriptions of a spiritual intercourse between The Father and Barbelo, as also described in the *Apocryphon of John.*

> And he looked at Barbelo with the pure light which surrounds the invisible Spirit, and [with] his spark, and she conceived from him. He begot a spark of light with a light resembling blessedness. But it does not equal his greatness. This was an only-begotten child of the Mother-Father which had come forth; it is the only offspring, the only-begotten one of the Father, the pure Light. (6)

Hence, there was, in the Beginning, The Father and Barbelo; from the two of them there emanated by self-generation the Child, a Son, Autogenes. Autogenes also became known as the *Logos* or Word. The Divine Child or Son had come on earth for the salvation of the *pneumatikoi* or 'the Spirit-filled ones', those capable of perceiving the divine spark within themselves.

> And the Holy Spirit completed the divine Autogenes, his son, together with Barbelo, that he may attend the mighty and invisible, virginal Spirit as the divine Autogenes, the Christ whom he had honoured with a mighty voice. He came forth through the forethought. And the invisible, virginal Spirit placed the divine Autogenes of truth over everything. And he subjected to him every authority, and the truth which is in him, that he may know the All which had been called with a name exalted above every name. For that name will be mentioned to those who are worthy of it. (7)

In the *Trimorphic Protennoia* (the Three Forms of the First Thought), which was written about the same time as the *Apocryphon of John,* we read:

> Then the Son who is perfect in every respect – that is, the Word who originated through that Voice; who proceeded from the height; who has within him the Name; who is a Light – he revealed the everlasting things, and all the unknowns were known. And those things difficult to interpret and secret, he revealed. And as for those who dwell in Silence with the First Thought, he preached to them. And he revealed himself to those who dwell in darkness, and he showed himself to those who dwell in the abyss, and to those who dwell in the hidden treasuries, he told ineffable mysteries, and he taught unrepeatable doctrines to all those who became Sons of the Light. (37)

---

[25] Autogenes, in other Christian groups, would become known as Monogenes or Only-begotten.

The Divine Child is the Son of the Father and The Word and will become the One sent to preach to the World. Importantly, as we will see in dealing with the gospel of John, the Child is the Son of The Mother.

From this Gnostic Trinity there began a series of further Emanations, of Luminaries, Angels and Aeons. The Gnostic writings give many complex accounts of the variety of these and their order (the question was asked: should they be tabulated as 'sons' or 'numbers' or 'sounds'?).

Adam and Eve

At this point, we need to back-track and explain the origin of Adam. There was one divine being, from the Emanation process, who was the ideal Form of Humanity, the archetypal Human in Platonic thinking, who was close to The Invisible Spirit. He was given the name of Adamas. The human Adam was patterned on this heavenly Adamas, as the *Apocryphon of John* explains:

> And from the foreknowledge of the perfect mind, through the revelation of the will of the invisible Spirit and the will of the Autogenes, [the] Perfect Man [appeared], the first revelation, and the truth. It is he whom the virginal Spirit called Pigera-Adamas, and he placed him over the first Aeon with the mighty one, the Autogenes, the Christ, by the first light Armozel; and with him are his powers. And the invisible one gave him a spiritual, invincible power. And he spoke and glorified and praised the invisible Spirit, saying, 'It is for thy sake that everything has come into being and everything will return to thee. I shall praise and glorify thee and the Autogenes and the Aeons, the three: the Father, the Mother, and the Son, the perfect power.' (8-9)

There was also Divine Wisdom, Sophia, who had emanated from the Great Spirit. She was known by many names, but she was The Mother. She was identical to the Wisdom of Jewish Gnostic thought mentioned in a number of texts.[26] She became a This-worldly Intermediary for some Proto-Gnostic Jewish groups, equal to and sometimes confused with *Logos*, The Word.

But, in the more developed Gnostic world, it was Sophia who, without permission, gave rise to the Emanation of the Demiurge. This was a cosmic error, a divine fall of unimaginable outcome. For the Gnostics, the Demiurge was a deformed, ignorant divinity, evil because of the error of his origin. To him a number of names were given in various Gnostic texts, such as: Demiurge, Nebro, 'Elohim and Yaldabaoth ('child of chaos'). He

---

[26] Sophia had become a personal figure in Jewish thought towards the time of the Christian period. She is found in the Book of Proverbs, the Wisdom of Solomon and Sirach as personified Wisdom.

was sometimes accompanied by another defective divinity called ⟨ ('The Fool', no doubt a title bestowed by opponents), and sometimes he was identified with Saklas. The Demiurge was the defective god who created the world and humanity. It was a terrible outcome. The creation of humanity and the material world was therefore the result of a mistake in Gnostic eyes.

And it was a mistake of cosmic proportion. As a result, in some texts Sophia is called 'Corruptible Sophia'. This abysmal act is described in the *Apocryphon of John*:

> And the Sophia of the Epinoia [The First Thought], being an Aeon, conceived a thought from herself and the conception of the invisible Spirit and foreknowledge. She wanted to bring forth a likeness out of herself without the consent of the Spirit, – he had not approved – and without her consort, and without his consideration. And though the person of her maleness had not approved, and she had not found her agreement, and she had thought without the consent of the Spirit and the knowledge of her agreement, [yet] she brought forth. And because of the invincible power which is in her, her thought did not remain idle, and something came out of her which was imperfect and different from her appearance, because she had created it without her consort. And it was dissimilar to the likeness of its mother, for it has another form.
>
> And when she saw [the consequences of] her desire, it changed into a form of a lion-faced serpent. And its eyes were like lightning fires which flash. She cast it away from her, outside that place, that no one of the immortal ones might see it, for she had created it in ignorance. And she surrounded it with a luminous cloud, and she placed a throne in the middle of the cloud that no one might see it except the Holy Spirit who is called the mother of the living. And she called his name Yaltabaoth.[27] (9-10)

The human Adam was part of this defective creation. In a similar fashion, the human Eve shares traits with Sophia, Divine Wisdom; in fact, the Gnostic texts sometimes indulge in a deliberate ambiguity as to whether they are dealing with Sophia or Eve. Like her forebear, Sophia, who had transgressed in the divine order, Eve proposes that Adam eat the fruit of the tree of *gnosis* of good and evil. Eve transgressed in the phenomenal world just as Sophia had transgressed in the divine order.

This close link between Sophia, The Mother, and Eve will be important for our later considerations.

The Gnostic Jesus

It is only at this point in the Gnostic Myth that Jesus enters. Amidst the

---

[27] Yaltabaoth is an alternative spelling for Yaldabaoth.

heavenly Emanations, there is, in the Gnostic writings, a variety of descriptions identifying the place of Jesus, prior to his manifestation in the World. Sometimes he is described simply as the Son or as the Word or *Logos* – one of the heavenly characters. The *Logos* was the aspect of God that could act in the World. At other times the divine Jesus is one manifestation of a heavenly character. The divine Jesus came into the World to deliver the saving experience of *gnosis*. But why?

The first answer is that he came to release Sophia from her error. Another clear teaching on this Emanation from The Father can be seen in the *Valentinian Exposition*. The text that we have at our disposal was copied around 350 CE. However, the original could date from the later second century CE. It describes the descent of the Son into the World:

> Since it is a perfect Form that should ascend into the Pleroma, he did not at all want to consent to the suffering, but he was detained [...] him by Limit, that is, by the syzygy, since her correction will not occur through anyone except her own Son, who alone is the fullness of divinity. He willed within himself bodily to leave the powers and he descended. (33)

He descended because of 'the syzygy'. This is a male/female pairing of the Emanations from The Father. The Greek word means a 'yoking together'. Jesus was in a syzygy with his Mother, Sophia.[28] Jesus was intimately connected with Sophia because Corruptible Sophia could only be restored to full status in the Pleroma of divinity when Light amongst humans had been restored. The Gnostic Jesus brought Light into the World, struggling in Darkness. Jesus came into the world to restore Sophia (also known as The Mother and Barbelo).

But that was not the sole purpose of Jesus' descent into the world. There was a complementary role. He came also to offer salvation to those humans who would believe in the Truth, who would take on *gnosis*.

There is variety of thought on the Jesus who descends. In some Gnostic thinking there was overlap between Autogenes, the Divine Child, the *Logos* behind all phenomenal things, and Adamas, the Perfect Man. Adamas is interestingly described in the *Gospel of Judas*:

> And after the founding of the world, Saklas said to his angels, 'I, I am a jealous god, and apart from me nothing has come into being,' since he ⁻usted in his nature.
> ⁻hen a voice came from on high, saying, 'The Man exists, and

---

ʾzygy' was proper to only some forms of Gnosticism, particular Valentinus who moved from Asia Minor to Rome.

the Son of the Man.' Because of the descent of the image above,
which is like its voice in the height of the image which has looked
out through the looking out of the image above, the first creature was
formed.

Then, from Adamas, The Man, there comes the human Adam, the Son
of Man, as we read in the *Gospel of the Egyptians*. This Gnostic gospel is of
uncertain date and probably contains some Christian interpolations.

> Then, the great *Logos*, the divine Autogenes, and the incorruptible
> man Adamas gave praise, [and] they asked for a power and eternal
> strength for the Autogenes, for the completion of the four aeons,
> in order that, through them, there may appear [...] the glory and
> the power of the invisible Father of the holy men of the great light
> which will come to the world, which is the image of the night. The
> incorruptible man Adamas asked for them a son out of himself,
> in order that he [the son] may become father of the immovable,
> incorruptible race, so that, through it [the race], the silence and the
> voice may appear, and, through it, the dead aeon may raise itself, so
> that it may dissolve. (49)

In other words, Adam is the Son of Man who has descended from Adamas, the Prototype of Humanity. But, from Adam and Eve the sinfulness of
the transgression is transferred to their sons, Cain and Abel. Both sons come
to unfortunate ends. Then, from Adam but by 'a different seed', there comes
Seth. The *Gospel of the Egyptians* actually narrates a life of Seth describing
how Seth, in the Gnostic interpretation, was incarnated as Jesus in order to
offer salvation to those in the evil prison of creation.

Seth re-finds the divine spark of his parents. He is known as Allogenes,
'The Stranger' to the World, and we find texts identifying him as Christ. He
belongs to the world of the Spirit and gives rise to the Generation of Seth,
divine beings in human form, culminating in Enoch.

This is a challenging image. It is not always told with clarity or with
the same characters. In short, there is The Mother who has erred. From her
there emanates a Son, Autogenes, the Logos and also Adamas, the prototype
of all humanity.

In the pivotal story of Adam and Eve, Eve is the representation of The
Mother and Adam is the Son of Man, the representation of Adamas. They
hand on the sinfulness of The Mother to humans. However, there is a tan-
gent: Adam creates a divine being in human form, Seth, and this generation
ends in the divine Enoch.

The importance of Seth cannot be underestimated. There was a human Seth, but there had always been a divine Seth. The divine Seth was

the son of Adamas, and Adamas had been connected with Autogenes.

In the *Gospel of Judas*, Jesus explains to Judas that the Generation of Seth is from the heavenly realm:

> 'And then the image of the great generation of Adam will be exalted, for
> prior to heaven, earth, and the angels, that generation, which is from
> the eternal realms, exists. Look, you have been told everything. Lift
> up your eyes and look at the cloud and the light within it and the stars
> surrounding it. The star that leads the way is your star.'

More importantly, Seth Allogenes (The Stranger) is also Christ, as a re-markable line in the *Gospel of Judas* informs us when recounting the Angels of the World:

> The first is [S]eth, who is called Christ.
> The [second] is Harmathoth, who is [...].
> The [third] is Galila.
> The fourth is Yobel.
> The fifth [is] Adonaios.
> These are the five who ruled over the underworld, and first of all over
>   chaos. (52)

Seth was the divine Christ, but he would also take on the role of Jesus by assuming Flesh. Seth was clothed with the 'Living Jesus' and Jesus became The Saviour. In other words, Jesus is Seth the Allogenes, the Christ who has taken on Flesh.

Jesus is the Son, the Autogenes (called Monogenes in John), Adamas and also The Son of Man (like Adam, since both took on the veil of humanity).

Therefore Jesus is described as coming from the divine order. He was not really incarnated, since the Gnostics considered all flesh and matter to be inferior and evil, and he could not have died a real death since he did not have a real body, and therefore did not undergo a physical resurrection. The *Logos* was taken from the cross and returned to the heavenly realms. In short, the Gnostic Jesus did not have a human beginning (conception and birth) or a human end (death).

Jesus takes the form of a human being. In a wide variety of Gnostic de-scriptions, he was said to have put on a 'garment', or to have put on a 'form', which enabled him to mix with humans, to communicate with them and, on occasions, to hide himself from his enemies. This garment or form is also The Flesh. There is confusion as to whether taking on Flesh required human parents (plus the divine parenthood) or perhaps one parent (whose womb returned to its virginal state) or no human agency.

But, putting on this garment of Flesh does not equal a real dwelling of

The Word in Flesh but an 'appearance' as the *Gospel of Thomas* makes clear. The text reads:

> Jesus said, 'I took my place in the midst of the world, and I appeared to them in Flesh. I found all of them intoxicated; I found none of them thirsty. And my soul became afflicted for the sons of men, because they are blind in their hearts and do not have sight; for empty they came into the world, and empty too they seek to leave the world. But for the moment they are intoxicated. When they shake off their wine, then they will repent.' (logion 28)

This Gnostic Jesus, divine not human except in appearance, has come into the World. He comes as a Revealer not a Redeemer. He does not have a human body; he cannot undergo any blood sacrifice for the redemption of sinfulness.

The last events in the life of Jesus are described in a Gnostic manner by the *Apocalypse of Peter.* Three revelations are made to Peter and then they are interpreted to him by Jesus. The first regards persecution. It probably refers obliquely to persecution of the Gnostics by the mainstream Christian church. Jesus reveals it is not real persecution; the persecutors are blind and floundering. The second deals with the crucifixion (which is not regarded in the text as a real event); Jesus explains that he is the 'living Jesus' who looks on at the crucifixion activities and laughs. The third explains what is meant by the resurrection, the final glorification of the divine Jesus:

> And I saw someone about to approach us resembling him, even him who was laughing on the tree. And he was [filled] with a Holy Spirit, and he is the Savior. And there was a great, ineffable light around them, and the multitude of ineffable and invisible angels blessing them. And when I looked at him, the one who gives praise was revealed. (82)

We now need to look more closely into that Gnostic World to which Jesus was sent by the Father.

The Gnostic World

Some Gnostics were able to distinguish four Ages from the creation of the World:

- The Age of Adam
- The Age of Seth
- The Age of the Sethian Generation ending with Enoch
- The Present Time

Humans, the Gnostics believed, who presently live in The Present Time have been estranged from their divine beginnings. True, some do have the spark of the divinity in them, breathed by the Demiurge or Yaldabaoth, who in turn had received it from Sophia. But the only way out of the impasse caused by the disastrous creation would be for humans to realize (by *gnosis*) that they do have this spark of divinity within them. It is hidden and confused by their bodiliness, the Flesh. They must realize that their body, sexuality and gender are not to be esteemed; they must search for the light in the darkness, the bread in the wilderness, the water of life. They must find true *gnosis*.

The *Trimorphic Protennoia* explains this further. Protennoia, the First Thought, explains her divine origin. As the *Logos* of the Thought, she takes on a human appearance to restore the faithful humans.

> As for me, I put on Jesus. I bore him from the cursed wood, and established him in the dwelling places of his Father. And those who watch over their dwelling places did not recognize me. For I, I am unrestrainable, together with my seed; and my seed, which is mine, I shall place into the holy Light within an incomprehensible Silence. Amen. (50)

We have seen that the Gnostic World has been imperfectly created; it was a mistake, formed by Yaldabaoth or The Demiurge. *The Gospel of Philip* explains:

> The world came about through a mistake. For he who created it wanted to create it imperishable and immortal. He fell short of attaining his desire. For the world never was imperishable, nor, for that matter, was he who made the world. For things are not imperishable, but sons are. Nothing will be able to receive imperishability if it does not first become a son. But he who has not the ability to receive, how much more will he be unable to give? (75)

This World is the domain of evil powers and, for humans to be saved, it must be dismantled in their regard.

Jesus came into this World. He came as a Revealer and Saviour to those humans ready for him. His essential Form was spiritual and eternal. However, he necessarily donned the Form of Flesh so that he could actually enter a World that was governed by the Archons, the leaders of the World. The Archons belong to Yaldabaoth. In the World, Jesus was confronted by a host of enemies who wanted to see the end of him.

But not all were enemies. The *Tripartite Tractate* is a revision of Gnostic teaching, probably revised because of bad press deriving from early Church

Fathers. It is provisionally placed in the period 200-250 CE. The *Tripartite Tractate* divides humans into three categories: the spiritual *(pneumatikoi)*, the psychics *(psychoi)* and the material (the *hylikoi)*.

> The spiritual race [*pneumatikoi*, 'Spirit-filled beings'], being like light from light and like spirit from spirit, when its head appeared, it ran toward him immediately. It immediately became a body of its head. It suddenly received knowledge in the revelation. Within the spiritual ones, there are 'seeds' left by Sophia, when the mistake occurred.
>
> The psychic race [*psychoi*, 'spiritual beings'] is like light from a fire, since it hesitated to accept knowledge of him who appeared to it. (It hesitated) even more to run toward him in faith. Rather, through a voice it was instructed, and this was sufficient, since it is not far from the hope according to the promise, since it received, so to speak as a pledge, the assurance of the things which were to be.
>
> The material race [*hylikoi*, 'material beings'], however, is alien in every way; since it is dark, it shuns the shining of the light, because its appearance destroys it. And since it has not received its unity, it is something excessive and hateful toward the Lord at his revelation.
>
> The spiritual race will receive complete salvation in every way. The material will receive destruction in every way, just as one who resists him. The psychic race, since it is in the middle when it is brought forth and also when it is created, is double according to its determination for both good and evil. It takes its appointed departure suddenly and its complete escape to those who are good. (119)

It is the 'material race', the *hylikoi*, who were responsible for the persecution and death of Jesus. *The Tripartite Tractate* continues:

> Those, however, who are from the thought of lust for power, who have come into being from the blow of those who fight against him, those whom the thought brought forth, from these, since they are mixed, they will receive their end suddenly. Those who will be brought forth from the lust for power which is given to them for a time and for certain periods, and who will give glory to the Lord of glory, and who will relinquish their wrath, they will receive the reward for their humility, which is to remain forever. Those, however, who are proud because of the desire of ambition, and who love temporary glory, and who forget that it was only for certain periods and times which they have that they were entrusted with power, and for this reason did not acknowledge that the Son of God is the Lord of all and Saviour, and were not brought out of wrath and the resemblance to the evil ones, they will receive judgment for their ignorance and their senselessness, which is suffering, along with those who went astray, anyone of them who turned away; and even more [for] wickedness in doing to the Lord things which were not fitting, which the powers of the left did to him, even including his death. They persevered saying, 'We shall become rulers of the universe, if the one who has been proclaimed king of the universe is slain,' [they

said this] when they laboured to do this, namely the men and angels who are not from the good disposition of the right ones but from the mixture. (120-121)

Amongst these *hylikoi* are the Archons or Leaders of The World, led by Yaldabaoth. They are all 'robbers'. Twelve of them live in Jerusalem. In Gnostic writings the list of enemies continues with Pharisees, Scribes, Jews, Priests and People. These are all types of the Archons. In the *First Apocalypse of James* there is further explanation:

> The Lord said, 'James, do not be concerned for me or for this people. I am he who was within me. Never have I suffered in any way, nor have I been distressed. And this people has done me no harm. But this [people] existed as a type of the archons, and it deserved to be destroyed through them. (31)

Although they are seemingly responsible for the suffering and death of Jesus, the very opposite is true: Jesus did not suffer or die. *The Gospel of Philip* explains:

> Christ came to ransom some, to save others, to redeem others. He ransomed those who were strangers and made them his own. And he set his own apart, those whom he gave as a pledge according to his plan. It was not only when he appeared that he voluntarily laid down his life, but he voluntarily laid down his life from the very day the world came into being. Then he came first in order to take it, since it had been given as a pledge. It fell into the hands of robbers and was taken captive, but he saved it. He redeemed the good people in the world as well as the evil. (53)

The Gnostic Jesus had a 'history' in the evil World formed by Yaldabaoth as a result of the error of Sophia. He came into the World and sought out those who still searched for the spark of divinity within themselves. He seemed to live as a human among them, to be crucified and die and then to be resurrected. This was not the true 'history'.

What Jesus essentially did was to offer the *pneumatokoi* salvation.

Gnostic Salvation

We need to go deeper into the Gnostic teaching of salvation. The elect few of the Gnostics, haters of the world and its attractions, were called to the intellectual experience of *gnosis*, and that knowledge led them to see and find the living, eternal Jesus within themselves. They realized their own divinity and became like Jesus. That was the Gnostic intellectual experience, their deep secret; it was the secret teaching that Jesus entrusted only to a few.

The true Gnostic became Another Jesus and really understood the divine mysteries and thus found redemption even before death. Judas Didymos Thomas, to whom the Gospel of Thomas was attributed, was known as 'Judas the Twin' (*Didymos* is Greek and *Thomas* is Aramaic for 'twin'). He was not called this on the basis of any physical fact (since the Gnostic Jesus had neither birth nor body, he could not have a twin), but because he had reached equality with the Divine Jesus through the Gnostic intellectual experience.

The Gnostic *Gospel of Judas* also describes the state of one saved by *gnosis*. In its text, Jesus, speaking to his disciples, calls for the 'Perfect Human' to stand before him. Only Judas can step forward. Judas then states:

> I know who you are and where you have come from. You are from the
> immortal realm of Barbelo. And I am not worthy to utter the name of
> the one who has sent you.

Judas found salvation. For others, during the time of his being Flesh, Jesus revealed the divine *gnosis* and offered them a like salvation. Some followed him and some did not.

The Departure of Jesus

So, Jesus left the World. This is described by the analogies of 'taking off the Flesh' or 'changing garments'. Usually, his departure is seen in the context of the Archons of the World thinking that they have succeeded only to find that they have failed. Jesus has escaped them. His departure is described in various ways. Usually the disposal of the Flesh is a struggle, but Jesus remains in control. Sometimes, a note of humiliation or of real suffering is introduced. On the other hand, we have seen that *The Apocalypse of Peter* describes how Jesus views the Archons crucifying the 'son of their glory', a pseudonymous person. Jesus looks on and laughs.

For some time after Jesus has disposed of the Flesh, he remained to finalize his teaching. In fact, a majority of the Nag Hammadi documents situate Jesus in this liminal stage before he returns to the divine *pleroma*.

The description of what occurs after his return to the divinity is also subject to variant description. Usually, in some way it is clearly stated that his place is taken by The Spirit or The Paraclete. In a few places in the total Gnostic documentation there is still talk of his final return in a *parousia*, a final manifestation.

What should be stressed again is that there is no single statement on Christian Gnosticism. It is not like defining the official belief system of

Western Christians after the Councils of Nicaea and Chalcedon. There were many versions of Gnosticism and the above statement of the Myth has combined many of these in trying to get to the core.

In the next section we will try and extract an outline of a fluent Christian Gnostic belief, stressing its commonalities and glossing over its many differences.

A Gnostic Creed

In early Christianity there was no one Gnostic Jesus-movement, but there was an alternative Gnostic way of thinking. This is its Creed, although it would not have been accepted by any one Gnostic group, perhaps by none in its entirety.

> In the Beginning is The Great Invisible Spirit, The Monad, the Father, The All
>
> The Gnostic Triad is The Father (= The Invisible Spirit), Barbelo (= The Mother or Sophia) and The Child
>
> The Child, Autogenes the Self-Generated (or Monogenes, the Only-Begotten), is the Word or *Logos* of God
>
> Within the Pleroma ('fullness' in Greek and Coptic), or divine realm, there is the Gnostic Triad as above, Adamas, Seth and the Luminaries and Angels and many other Emanations.
>
> Some say these are formed into syzygies or pairings such as: Father of All/Invisible Spirit and Sophia; Christ and the Holy Spirit; Jesus/Seth and Mary Magdalene/also Sophia (= The Bridegroom and the Bride).
>
> Sophia, Divine Wisdom, errs and emanates Yaldabaoth without permission of the Great Invisible Spirit.
>
> Yaldabaoth, The Arrogant One, sometimes called Saklas, the Demiurge, creates the world and humans (including Adam and Eve).
>
> The World is therefore evil and misshapen.
>
> Humans are divided into the spiritual *(pneumatikoi)*, the psychics *(psychoi)* and the material (the *hylikoi*). These levels correspond to their levels of the acquisition of *gnosis*. This *gnosis* is the knowledge or experience of the divinity, of self in the World and of salvation.
>
> 'By a separate seed' there comes the human Seth, who is the partner of the divine Seth, Allogenes, The Stranger. The divine Seth is identified with Autogenes.

The World is a place ruled by Yaldabaoth, evil Archons and Authorities.

The Divine Seth takes on Flesh and becomes Jesus.

Jesus (the Divine Seth clothed in Flesh) is sent into the World by The Father as Teacher of *gnosis* and thereby becomes the Saviour of the World.

Jesus departs from The World, having divested himself of The Flesh in the crucifixion, but sends the Holy Spirit or The Paraclete to take his place as an invisible and spiritual Jesus.

Those *pneumatikoi,* who have attained full *gnosis,* have already found salvation (among others: Thomas the Twin of Jesus, Mary Magdalene, James the Brother of the Lord) and only need to divest themselves of Flesh to be reinstated in the Pleroma of which they retain sparks; those who do not achieve *gnosis,* retain The Flesh and presumably are re-engaged in the World.

A Glossary of Gnostic Terms

To expand on the Creed, we now append a Glossary of Gnostic terms. The Glossary attempts to convey a general understanding of what composed the broad Christian Gnostic thought-world. This Glossary can be referred to in the course of the analysis of John's gospel as it is presented piece by piece.

Above and Below Gnostics followed the Platonic mentality which saw the World as essentially dual – good and bad, spiritual and material, soul or spirit and body. This dualism could be summed up as 'Above and Below'. Above was the heavenly realms of the divine; Below was The World and its evil excesses. It was the task of the Christian Gnostics, living within this thought-world, to resolve the Dualism by *gnosis* and plan their lives accordingly. Situated Below, they had to find The Above.

The Above or the Pleroma ('Fullness') was also the divine dwelling place. This was the true homeland and was sometimes described as 'someone's homeland' (in Greek, *eis ta idia*) or 'people of the homeland' (in Greek, *hoi idioi*).

Aeon The Emanations from the Triad of the Great, Invisible Spirit, Barbelo and Child are Aeons, beings of light and immateriality. These are also known as Angels. They perform the same work as Angels in the Judaeo-Christian thought-world: they attend on the divinity, they are messengers. Not all Gnostic Angels were upright; after Yaldabaoth had created

The World, some of the Aeons/Angels were also included in the material and evil World.

Archon, Ruler of the World The word Archon comes from *arche*, the 'beginning'. Archons are spiritual beings who have been around since The Beginning and were formed by Emanations. Yaldabaoth was an Archon and was looked upon as the evil Ruler of the World, the equivalent of Satan or the Evil One in later Jewish thought. Other Archons joined him in ruling The World. In this guise, Archons were also looked upon as Demons. The Archons and Aeons overlap.

The Beginning As with Archon, the term comes from *arche*. It refers to The Beginning before the creation of time and space. The term is used in the Hymn that opens the Creation story in Genesis and the Prologue of John's Gospel ('In the Beginning [*arche*] ...'). Both there and in Christian Gnosticism generally, it refers to the time before time began, before the phenomenal creation took place, before the error that caused the world was committed, when there were only Emanations.

Blindness *See Light.*

Blood In the normal parlance of Jewish expression, blood was the distinct property of life, the vitality of being alive; hence 'flesh and blood' is a figure for living humanity. However, for some Christian Gnostics, blood was seen as the life-giving property of Jesus' teaching. To 'drink his blood' was to assimilate the vital message of his teaching. It was also used as a symbol for the Holy Spirit. Blood was not a normal symbol in Gnostic usage.

Bread The symbol of bread had already been well established in Jewish religious terminology. It referred to the bread that was made available to the Israelites in the Exodus story, first in the Passover story and then in the manna in the desert. This bread included an image of God feeding the Israelites with his care and direction and it eventually became a symbol of the divine self-revelation of Yahweh.

Bread was used in a new context by the Christian Gnostics. Bread became the *gnosis* that derived from The Invisible Spirit. It was brought into The World by Jesus, in fact Jesus was the very Bread of God or the Bread of Life.

Christ In the Jewish tradition the *christos* or Anointed One was a future figure constructed on the example of some anointed kings of Jerusalem, primarily David, as their forebear. Then, the meaning of Christ in the Christian Scriptures, as applied to Jesus, underwent a number of changes including Paul's reference to 'Christ, the Wisdom of God' in 1 Corinthians 1:24.

This latter instance reflected a Christian Gnostic development, which acknowledged 'Christ' as one of the Emanations.

Commandment *See Grace*

Darkness *See Light*

Death *See Light*

Demon *See Angel*

Eternal Life Briefly, the Gnostic doctrine of Emanations is founded on a spiritual universe, the realm of the divine, the Pleroma. The Emanations were not created separately by God but were parts of God. Sparks of the divine were encased in later humans when they subsequently fell into matter and became clothed with The Flesh. Because these divine sparks had once found their abode in the heavenly state, on earth humans still retained a portion of divinity and yearned to return to the divine. But they would only attain this by *gnosis*.

Christian Gnostics believed that the true destiny of the human was to return to the spiritual realms by a process termed 'the resurrection', which was demonstrated by Jesus. Thereby, the sparks of the divine would regain Eternal Life ('the life of the Aeon') or a return to the Aeon in the sense of the Age of Glory.

Faith (and Belief) Having faith or believing had a long Jewish tradition. It was not a cerebral activity but the active decision to belong and to be involved with Yahweh and his People. Jews who 'believed' were part of the community of Israel and observed its Yahweh-derived ordinances.

In the Christian Gnostic community, believing or faith had much the same meaning and indicated that Gnostics had committed themselves to adhere to Jesus who was the manifestation of the Divine in the clothing of Flesh.

To refuse such a commitment, in Gnostic terms, was 'to hate'. To accept this commitment was to 'love and be loved'.

The Flesh In Hebrew parlance flesh (*basar* in Hebrew or *sarx* in Greek) was one way of looking at the human being. From this vantage point, the human was considered to be part of this world-order, immersed in created things. There were other ways of defining humanity but this was an essential one.

The Christian Gnostics went further. They used the term Flesh in order to describe the evil medium in which the divine spark, that came unintentionally from the breath of Yaldabaoth, was entrapped. The spark of divinity was enclosed in carnal Flesh, which was evil, a by-product of the creation of Yaldabaoth. The Gnostic must escape from The Flesh and The World. This would mean becoming free, achieved only by *gnosis*.

Jesus took on the appearance of Flesh in order to become present among and communicate with humans. He divested this appearance in his Death.

Fullness The Invisible Spirit, linked with the Mother, Barbelo, produced the Child; from thence there were Emanations of the divine until Fullness was achieved. This was the *pleroma*. The *pleroma* lived in the heavenly dwelling of the homeland, *ta idia*. The aim of the Christian Gnostics was to return to the *pleroma* from which their divine spark had originated.

Glory The manifestation of the fullness of Yahweh was known to the Jews as glory or *kabod*. In Isaiah 6 the prophet is depicted as having a vision in the Temple of Jerusalem and, in an ecstatic state, sees the *kabod* or the holiness of Yahweh and he hears the angelic statement of the seraphs:

> Seraphs were in attendance above him; each had six wings: with two they covered their faces, and with two they covered their feet, and with two they flew. [3]And one called to another and said:'Holy, holy, holy is Yahweh of the Armies; the whole earth is full of his glory.'
> [4]The pivots on the thresholds shook at the voices of those who called, and the house filled with smoke. [5]And I said: 'Woe is me! I am lost, for I am a man of unclean lips, and I live among a people of unclean lips; yet my eyes have seen the King, Yahweh of the Armies!'

For Christian Gnostics the *kabod* (*doxa* in Greek) could be perceived by all those who had gained *gnosis*. Certain human events or Signs, in which the divine Jesus was implicated, could reveal the *kabod* to believers, in much the same way as Isaiah had penetrated to the core of the Temple event.

Grace Grace was a term used in Hebrew thought meaning 'being highly favoured' because Yahweh showed divine favour by bestowing The Torah with its Covenant to guide the Jews. In Christian Gnostic terms it was used to imply that the Great Invisible Spirit gave humans the right to understand and participate in the divine *Logos* by gaining *gnosis*. Thus, 'Grace upon Grace' implies, a New Gnostic Covenant to replace the former Covenant. The Torah has been replaced by the divine Jesus who brings full *gnosis*.

Hatred *See Faith*

Holy Spirit In mainstream Hebrew thought, Holy Spirit (*ruah*, Hebrew for 'breath' or 'wind') was literally the Spirit of Holiness (that is, 'of Yahweh'). The term simply referred to Yahweh in his capacity to act decisively (like a breath blown to stimulate action or like a wind that stirred things up) in human affairs.

In later Jewish Proto-Gnosticism, The Holy Spirit became an hypostatization, a separate divine Being, who could act as an Other-worldly Intermediary. Then, in Christian Gnosticism, The Holy Spirit became a description of Barbelo, the Mother and Virgin. Since Barbelo was also characterized as Wisdom, then Holy Spirit and Wisdom overlapped.

Hylikoi See *pneumatikoi*

Judgement To the Gnostic mind, Judgement is the opposite of Salvation. It is not, as in its forensic meaning, a judgement declaring a charged person as innocent or guilty. It is a condemnatory sentence: to 'judge' is to condemn.

While mainstream Jewish and Christian thought tended towards the idea of a Judgement at the end of time, in the forensic sense of a final discriminating between good and evil persons, the Christian Gnostics claimed that Judgement was achieved here and now. It was effected immediately by the choice of the individual to seek *gnosis* or not.

Knowledge (*gnosis*) Gnostic knowledge (*gnosis*) is at the centre of religious achievement. The Gnostics eventually became broadly known by the term *gnostikoi* or 'the knowers'. Gnosis is not the same as the intellectual act; it could not be achieved by the personal effort of human persons. Passively, aided by the divinity, humans could become the recipients of *gnosis* and find reunion with The One, with the Godhead. This Gnostic searching is more akin to experience, whereby the Gnostic is aware of the dualism in the World, their rather dire place in the World, and the divine plan to extricate humans from it.

Law *See New Commandment.*

Light The image of Light is used commonly by Gnostics to express the fullness of divinity. The Great Invisible Spirit, the author of all things, is defined as being Light itself. Hence, The Light's opposite is The Darkness, which can be applied to the Demiurge and his followers in The World.

Those who do not perceive, amid The Darkness, the Light in the World are therefore blind and ignorant. Death is the state of those who are Ignorant. Those who do not participate in the Light and gain *gnosis* are already dead.

Logos *Logos* is Greek for 'word'. At the core of mainstream Jewish thinking there was the 'word of God', *dabar* in Hebrew. This signified that Yahweh spoke and his utterance was effected. He acted in the world by means of his word. The Jewish prophets maintained that the 'word of Yahweh' had come to them and enlightened them as regards heavenly things. Greek philosophy used the term in the sense of a grounding principle of order and knowledge in the world. For the Jewish Proto-Gnostics the term was extended to a self-sufficient being; the *Logos* had emanated from God. Through the *Logos*, Yahweh brought about change in the world.

The Christian Gnostics made the *Logos*/Word into that aspect of The Father which had dealings with The World. The *Logos* was God or more exactly the reasoning within the divinity.

Love *See Faith*

Messiah *See Christ*

Mother Mother had a number of derivations for Christian Gnostics and they do not imply discriminatory sexual overtones. Barbelo was the Divine Mother, even though Barbelo was not sexually differentiated. Likewise Sophia became the Mother of All the Living through the error in emanating without permission. Strangely enough for us, 'Mother' in Gnostic thought does not have a specifically feminine meaning.

New Commandment The Torah was, in Jewish terms, called The Commandment. It was considered a rule of life to be followed, particularly in its ritual requirements regarding diet, circumcision, Sabbath observance.

However, the Christian Gnostic Jesus was said to bring a 'New Commandment' based on the Gnostic vision and *gnosis*.

Oneness At Qumran, where Jewish Proto-Gnosticism flourished, the community that was described in the sectarian texts was known as The Unity, the *yahad*. The Christian Gnostic goal of merging, or being united with the divine, aimed at finding union or unity in a community of believers. For the Gnostics, knowledge and wisdom gave entry to a united community which would lead to eternal life, while ignorance, the absence of *gnosis*, left the person outside the unity or Oneness.

Only Son (Monogenes) This term, Monogenes, the Only-Begotten, is ambivalent. In the first instance it was used in mainstream Judaism to identify the only son of Abraham and Sarah – Isaac. Abraham was asked to sacrifice this Only Son and, at the last moment, the child was delivered by divine intervention. In Jewish tradition, Abraham thereafter became the Father of Faith, because he carried out the demand of Yahweh, while Isaac became the symbol of the True Israel, who was (almost) sacrificed for his people.

Gradually, as we approach the Christian period, the Jews switched the emphasis on the Abraham and Isaac story from Abraham to Isaac. Isaac was seen as a (near) martyr and the fact that he had not been sacrificed was overlooked. He became the symbol of a suffering people who would overcome their situation.

Roman Christians, confronted by this Jewish symbol of Isaac the Martyr who suffered on behalf of his people, made a significant change in their thinking. They declared that there had been a new Isaac. He was Jesus. Jesus had been sent by the Father as his Monogenes, the Only Begotten, to give his life for others by crucifixion. A new Christian vocabulary emerged: Jesus the High Priest (who offered the sacrifice of himself), Jesus the Victim, the bloody sacrifice, the precious blood, Christians being washed in the blood of the sacrificed Lamb of God.

However, this was the vocabulary of Roman Christianity, not Gnosticism where Jesus could not die. In Christian Gnostic thought generally, there had been the Divine Child who came from The Great Invisible Spirit and Barbelo. The Child was known as *Autogenes* or 'Self-generated'. This designation overlapped with Monogenes or 'Only-Begotten'. There was no reference to Isaac in Gnostic thinking.

Paraclete Paraclete comes from the Greek *parakalein*, 'to call to the side of', or 'to encourage, give comfort'. It refers to someone called to another's side such as a Court Assistant, or someone who bestows help and guidance to another. In Judaism there was talk of a divine This-worldly Intermediary who would act as a Paraclete.

In Christian Gnosticism it could also mean that Jesus' place would be taken by a Paraclete. This Paraclete is also known as the Spirit of Truth. The Spirit is, like Jesus, an Emanation but not now with the human form of Flesh, as in the case of Jesus. This Spirit will still bring divine knowledge to believers. She ('spirit' in Hebrew is feminine) will remain with believers from this point onwards. For subsequent believers, after the departure of Jesus, the Paraclete or Spirit becomes the paramount factor in mediation.

Peace The main search of the Gnostic mind was for *gnosis*. This was the deep knowledge of the fact of dualism in the world, that beneath appearances, there is Good and Evil and that Good must be sought and Evil rejected. For this reason the Gnostic sought a re-birth, into the world of Goodness and Divinity. The new state that was achieved by this effort was described as Peace *(eirene)*. Peace was the state of fulfilment after achieving *gnosis*. Some Gnostics even made Peace into one of the Emanations from the Divine.

Pleroma *See Fullness.*

Pneumatikoi The *Tripartite Tractate* divides humans into three categories: the spiritual *(pneumatikoi or the 'Spirit-filled ones')*, the psychics *(psychoi or the 'spiritual ones')* and the material (the *hylikoi or the 'material ones')*.

> The *pneumatikoi* will receive complete salvation in every way. The *hylikoi* will receive destruction in every way, just as one who resists him. The *psychoi*, since it is in the middle when it is brought forth and also when it is created, is double according to its determination for both good and evil. It takes its appointed departure suddenly and its complete escape to those who are good. (119)

It is the *hylikoi*, who were responsible for the persecution and death of Jesus. Amongst these *hylikoi* are the Archons or Leaders of The World, among whom is numbered Yaldabaoth. In Gnostic writings the list of enemies continues with Pharisees, Scribes, Jews, Priests and People. The *pneumatakoi* have already attained *gnosis*; they are responsible for guiding the *psychoi*; the *hylikoi* are beyond hope.

Psychoi See pneumatikoi

Resurrection Resurrection is a common term in both Judaism, in the time close to the Christian period, and in early Christian thought. In Judaism it became one of the ways in which justice could be enabled. Those who were righteous in this life, even though they might have died young after suffering or fighting for their faith, would be resurrected in a future divine intervention.

However, there was a Proto-Gnostic Jewish idea that, instead of waiting for a future resurrection, the action took place immediately. Those who were martyred for the faith, and indeed all the just, went immediately into the divine realm at death.

Christian Gnostics took over the notion. Gnostics who attained the fullness of *gnosis* were already resurrected from the dead; they had already achieved the fullness of life.

Sign A Sign (*semeion*) was already in use in Jewish thinking as an indication of what God was achieving in the world, but in Christian Gnostic thinking it signified a this-worldly activity of Jesus that could be interpreted only by disciples who had Faith, who thus adhered to Jesus and had to ability to interpret by *gnosis*. Reflecting on the event, the Gnostic disciples could perceive, because of their faith, the Glory of God in the Jesus-event.

Son of God In Hebrew terminology, Son of God simply referred to a dedicated follower of Yahweh, a Godly person. Good kings and prophets could be called 'sons of God'. The term had no pretention to divinity. In mainstream Christianity, the term was readily applied to Jesus and, at some stage, it acquired a divine overtone in the canonical gospels.

In Gnostic parlance, it referred to the process of eternal Emanation. The Son of God derived from that process. Where Jesus is referred to, in Gnostic terms, as Son of God then it does have a divine meaning. He has emerged as a divine being from his Emanation from the Father.

Son of Man *The Apocryphon of John* explains:

'And a voice came forth from the exalted aeon-heaven: 'The Man exists and the Son of Man.' (14)

Whereas, in Hebrew or Aramaic, 'Son of Man' simply means a 'human being', the term acquired new connotations among the Jews. In pre-Christian Judaism it could refer to a mysterious figure from the divine realm who came to earth to save humanity. It was used in this way in the Book of Daniel. The Son of Man was a divine figure, but only in some Jewish apocalyptic contexts.

In Christian Gnosticism, such as the *Apocryphon of John* above, it referred to an Emanation from the divine androgynous Perfect Man, Adamas. This was the divine Adam and Jesus was seen as another form, Seth.

Testimony The term 'testimony' is taken from the forensic situation within the Jewish context. The legal system depended on charges being laid against the defendant, who had the right to self-defence but, more importantly, to witnesses. The statements of witnesses were Testimony. The Law in Deuteronomy 17:6 had stated that two or three witnesses were required for testimony in any capital case.

On the evidence of two or three witnesses the death sentence shall be executed; a person must not be put to death on the evidence of only one witness.

The Christian Gnostics used the term to describe the evidence that various parties gave positively to the divinity of Jesus.

The Father Sometimes 'Father' was used in Judaism as a title for Yahweh. The early Christians adopted the title, possibly in its Aramaic form, *'abba*, which might have had a diminutive connotation. Later, Christian theologians used the term to designate the first *persona* of the Trinity.

For Gnostics, The Great Invisible Spirit, when defined as the partner of Barbelo, the Mother, was also named The Father.

The Way The Way is the pathway that pneumatic humans can take in order to find ultimate meaning, the divinity within themselves. That Way is very simply summed up as Jesus himself. He is the Way, first because he is Truth. He by his very revelation of The Truth has revealed the meaning of The Father, Ultimate Divinity. Someone reading the events of Jesus, his Signs, understands this Truth. He is also, as a consequence, The Life. The Way to the Father is by means of that *gnosis* brought into the World by Jesus which is The Truth and which brings believers to Eternal Life. The Way is opened for believers from The World to The Above. Hence the oft-misquoted text in John's gospel: I am the Way, the Truth and the Life.

Truth This word already had a history in Jewish thought. It is the translation of the Hebrew *'emeth*, which also has the connotation of 'mystery'. By the time of the Jewish Gnostic writings, it had acquired the meaning of the divine reality itself, but only insofar as it could be apprehended by humans. It designates the divine plan within the divine reality. Jesus brings that Truth into The World; he actually becomes Truth for humanity. The Spirit of Truth is simply the Spirit who performs the same role as Jesus, making present the Truth in material circumstances so that disciples can believe. To be 'on the side of Truth' is to have begun and made progress in deciphering the role of divinity in the world order.

Washing Washing with, or steeping in, water is a symbolic ritual in many religions. In Judaism, the story of Moses leading the people of Israel through the Sea of Reeds in the Exodus and Joshua leading the people through the Jordan in the entry into The Land, offered the way to construct a water-ritual. Later *goyyim* or non-Israelites who requested to become Jews were required to undergo a water-ritual to signify that they had participated in the two great events, even thought they were not symbolically present in the original ones. Minor water washing was also used as a ritual for purification in Judaism.

By the time of the Qumran population, baptism or immersion in water was a ritual of entry not into the People of Israel but into the *yahad*, the particular Jewish community that was responsible for some of the scrolls. This entry would lead to salvation.

It could be that the Gnostics had a ritual of foot-washing.

Water Water had long been symbolic in Judaism. God's revelation to humans was well described as Yahweh giving his people water to drink. The Christian Gnostic had a similar notion except that the water was the *gnosis* brought into the World by Jesus. In the Gnostic *Gospel of Thomas*, Jesus says, 'Whoever drinks from my mouth will become like me; I myself shall become that person, and the hidden things will be revealed to that person.'
See also Washing

Wisdom In the Hebrew Scriptures wisdom (*hokmah*) describes the essential knowledge of life. Sailors have 'wisdom' when they know the skills of navigation. However, by the pre-Christian period there was the belief that Yahweh ruled the world by his *hokmah*. Like 'Word', in Jewish Proto-Gnosticism, Wisdom became a personification and then a separate hypostatization. In Greek *hokmah* was translated as *sophia* and, in pre-Christian Judaism, Sophia was lauded as a personalized aspect of the divinity.

In Christian Gnosticism, Sophia became a feminine power, The Mother, who sought to bring about an Emanation from herself without due permission and she produced the deformed Yaldabaoth.

Word *See Logos*

World The World (*kosmos*) is of much importance to the Gnostic worldview. The World is the created entity which has derived from Yaldabaoth through the error of Sophia. It is basically evil and irredeemable. Gnostics shun The World and, usually, this would lead to the avoidance of material excess and sex.

Yaldabaoth Sophia or Wisdom erred. She produced by Emanation another Aeon without the consent of her superior partner, her consort, the Invisible Spirit. So Yaldabaoth (probably 'child of chaos') came to be. He was the Platonic Demiurge.

Yaldabaoth was a deformed, ignorant divinity. He was accompanied by another defective divinity called Saklas ('The Fool'), sometimes identified with him. He was the defective god who created the World and humanity. It was a terrible outcome. The creation of humanity and the material World was therefore the result of a mistake in Gnostic eyes. And it was a mistake of cosmic proportion. Therefore, in some texts Sophia is called 'Corruptible Sophia'.

Conclusion

Already, parallels between the gospel of John (as against the Synoptics) and Gnosticism can be glimpsed. They raise the problems of interpreting John.

It will be important to acknowledge the fact that Christianity began with a number of discrete Jesus-movement groups. We can document some of them, but we are in ignorance about a great deal of their history. Likewise, we are very ignorant about the life of an Historical Jesus. We are primarily dealing with a number of Literary Jesus-es. There were mainstream Jewish Palestinian groups, each of whom struggled with their Literary Jesus, hoping to find a new Intermediary in his memory. There were also the Gnostic Jesus-movements. Their ideas had come from a rich past heritage.

But Palestinian Jesus-movements and Gnostic Christians occupying much the same areas do not provide the whole picture of the situation in early Christianity.

We must now turn to the other major Jesus-movement group: Roman Christianity.

NOTES

On Proto-Gnosticism in Judaism there is a great deal written with respect to the Dead Sea Scrolls:

First of all, there are a variety of good translations. Two can be recommended for the general reader:

Martinez, F. G. & Tigcheklaan, E. (1997-98), *The Dead Sea Scrolls* (in two volumes), Brill: Leiden and Eerdmans: Grand Rapids.
Vermes, G. (1997), *The Complete Dead Sea Scrolls in English* (complete edition), Allen Lane Penguin: London.

There are also some general introductions that fill in much of the background. They differ in their quality and some should only be used with caution:

Baigent, M. & Leigh, R. (1992), *The Dead Sea Scrolls Deception*, Corgi Books: London.
De Vaux, R. (1973), *Archaeology and the Dead Sea Scrolls*, OUP: London.

Eisenman, R. (1983), *Maccabees, Zadokites, Christians and Qumran*, E. J. Brill: Leiden.

Fitzmyer, J. (2009), *The Impact of the Dead Sea Scrolls*, Paulist Press: New York.

Golb, N. (1995), *Who Wrote the Dead Sea Scrolls?: The Search for the Secret of Qumran*, BCA: London, New York, Sydney, Toronto

Schiffman, L. H. (2010), *Qumran and Jerusalem: Studies in the Dead Sea Scrolls and the History of Judaism*, William B. Eerdermans: Grand Rapids.

Schuller, E.M. (2006), *The Dead Sea Scrolls: What have we learned?*, Westminster John Knox Press: New York

Shanks, H. (1992), *Understanding the Dead Sea Scrolls*, Random House: New York

Vanderkam, J. (rev. ed. 2010), *The Dead Sea Scrolls Today*, William B. Eerdemans: Grand Rapids.

Yadin, Y. (1957), *The Message of the Scrolls*, Weidenfeld & Nicolson: London.

The Gnostic texts, as found in this chapter and elsewhere in this book, are taken from J. M. Robinson ed. (1978), *The Nag Hammadi Library in English*, HarperSanFrancisco: San Francisco.

The text and a commentary on the Gospel of Judas is to be found in Kasser, R., Meyer, M. & Wurst G. eds (2006), *The Gospel of Judas*, National Geographic: Washington.

There is a good introduction to the Gospel of Judas in Krosney, H. (2006), *The Lost Gospel: The Quest for the Gospel of Judas Iscariot*, National Geographic: Washington.

For an introduction to the Gnostic writings and their thought a good start can be made with some of the prolific work of Elaine Pagels

Elaine Pagels (1975), *The Gnostic Paul*, Fortress Press: Minneapolis

Elaine Pagels (1979), *The Gnostic Gospels*, Weidenfeld & Nicholson: London,

Elaine Pagels (1988), *Adam, Eve and the Serpent*, Weidenfeld & Nicholson: London

Elaine Pagels (1989), *The Johannine Gospel in Gnostic Exegesis*, Scholars Press: Atlanta.

Elaine Pagels (1995), *The Origin of Satan*, Random House: New York.

Also recommended is King, K. (2003), *What is Gnosticism?*, Harvard University Press: Harvard.

For readers seeking greater depth I am indebted to the following publications by Professor Majella Franzmann of Curtin University, both of which have been used in this book:

Franzmann, M. (2001), *Jesus in the Nag Hammadi Writings*, T. and T. Clark: Edinburgh.

Franzmann, M. (2011). 'Gnostic Portraits of Jesus', in *The Blackwell Companion to Jesus*, ed. Delbert Burkett, pp. 160-175. Blackwell Publishing: London.

ROMAN CHRISTIANITY

ROMAN CHRISTIANITY WAS FOUNDED by unnamed Jews in the world capital of the time. It was a Jesus-movement similar to those in the East.

The first Jewish arrivals in Rome can probably be dated to the mid-second century BCE. The Jews formed a foreign enclave in the city, mainly in *Trans Tiberim*, the area on the other side of the Tiber, still today known as Trastevere. Next, in the first century BCE numerous Jewish slaves were brought to Rome as a result of Pompey the Great's conquests in the East, and so the Jewish population in Rome increased. It is assumed that, as time went on, still other Palestinian Jews saw new business opportunities in the capital and migrated to Rome as free merchants.

Somewhere, amidst the Jewish synagogues of Rome, Roman Christianity took its rise. It would be a different entity to any of the Jesus-movements we have examined up to this point.

THE FOUNDING OF ROMAN CHRISTIANITY

Immigrant Jews during the second century BCE were integrated in some ways into the Roman culture and adopted Roman ways. The family, so crucial to Roman culture, became in turn all important to the Roman Jews. Although these Roman Jews have left behind hundreds of unmarked grave sites, or sites marked only by crude and sometimes grammatically inaccurate scratches, there were also some fine tomb inscriptions. These inscriptions reveal that over time there was less and less use of Hebrew or Aramaic and more of the Roman languages, Greek and Latin. However, there is enough evidence to show that the Jewish population of Rome retained its own Jewish identity in the face of adapting to Roman culture; they retained Jewish symbols, such as the menorah, on their grave sites, for example. Still, no doubt the Romans regarded them as foreign and different, particularly because of their unusual religious practices such as circumcision, Sabbath observance and abstinence from pork.

These Jews in Rome did have some advantages. They had been granted privileges for politically supporting Julius Caesar, including exemption
from military service, permission to collect and to send back to Jerusalem a
Temple tax and freedom of worship. Their religion was regarded as a lawful
one, a *religio licita*. This meant that they could set up and administer their
own synagogues without further authorization.

And so, for the most part, when we refer to Jews in Rome in the first
century CE we are referring to a population of about 20,000 that was composed of Greek-speaking, poor non-citizens, often slaves or ex-slaves as
well as merchants and lower-class citizens. Most would have been living in
overcrowded *insulae*, multi-storey buildings, in *Trans Tiberim*, under most
insanitary conditions. They would have been organized around about
eleven local autonomous synagogues in Rome, each of them independent,
with a 'synagogue ruler' as the leader. However, not all Jews attended the
synagogue; the family was the more important focus for their Jewish religious practice in Rome.

Who would have brought the Jesus-movement to the Roman synagogues
and *Trans Tiberim*? It was never suggested that it was Peter. Paul had written to certain already existing Jesus-movement members in Rome. He even
acknowledged in his Letter to the Romans that the Roman church was 'someone else's foundation' (15:20) and that he had wanted to visit the Christian
group in Rome for many years. We will see later that Paul was probably
writing only to a limited number of Roman Christians in his Letter.

We can only speculate that either Jews (whether they were merchant
immigrants, prisoners of war or slaves) who had somehow come into contact
with the Jesus-movements in Palestine went to Rome or that Roman Jews
had gone to Palestine (perhaps for a pilgrimage? perhaps to celebrate one of
the festivals?) and having come into contact with the new Jesus-movements
there would have brought some form of Literary Jesus back to Rome and
introduced it into the Roman synagogues. Perhaps a Jesus-movement faction
would have flourished in some synagogues; perhaps entire synagogues were
taken over by a Jesus-movement. The identification of the founder or founders of Roman Christianity, and its initial format, will probably be forever
shrouded in anonymity.

From Jewish Jesus-movement to Roman Christianity

However, some time well before 50 CE, the Roman Jesus-movement seems
to have admitted non-Jews or 'God-fearers' who would not have wanted to
continue contact with the synagogues. In the Roman context, this would

not have been a grave problem; not all Jews there practised in a synagogue, preferring the home for prayer and ritual.

Then, in a dramatic moment, some of the Jewish Jesus-movement people, attached to the synagogues during the reign of Claudius, were expelled for some years in about 49 CE for stirring up trouble among fellow Jews. Around the turn of the century, Suetonius, a Roman historian wrote:

> Since the Jews constantly made disturbances at the instigation of Chrestus, he [the Emperor Claudius] expelled them from Rome. (*Divus Claudius*, 25)

The reference is not absolutely clear. 'Chrestus' could have been a mistaken form of 'Christus'; the first was used as a name, the second would have been unfamiliar to Suetonius. Not all Jews would have been included. It would seem that Jesus-movement Jews were causing trouble and Claudius simply expelled them.

When the Jewish Jesus-movement exiles returned to Rome after the death of Claudius in 54 CE, they would have found that the Roman Jesus-movement they had left behind was mainly Gentile. The Roman Jesus-movement people had cut their moorings with the synagogues and moved into house-churches or *ekklesiae*. For the most part, they were no longer Jewish and the argument was whether they should retain any Jewish heritage.

The Jesus-movement people in Rome, as the Jews before them, struggled to show that they were good citizens and this was all that Rome required. However, as conversions to the Jesus-movement took place, there were problems. Romans belonging to the Jesus-movement were, according to the Roman majority, abandoning the cults of their Roman ancestors and risking the displeasure of gods, a displeasure not only directed against themselves but more importantly directed against the populace and the State.

At some point, when the Jesus-movement people had moved out of the synagogues and into house-churches, when they not only admitted Gentiles but their population was largely Gentile, when they could easily be identified as a separate group, Nero and his administration persecuted them as Jesus-movement people but did not persecute the mainstream Jews. Nero did not act because of their beliefs; he acted because he saw them as civil trouble-makers. The Jesus-movement was cut adrift and became the Christian Church in Rome. Being a Christian was a disadvantage under Nero; it would later become an advantage when the Jews in Jerusalem revolted against the Romans in the 60s CE.

The fact was that Christians in Rome no longer identified with Jews.

There would seem, on the basis of the evidence,[29] to have been a number of separate house-churches. This loose structure of Roman Christianity could have been compared to the loose organization of Judaism itself in Rome, with a number of synagogues but with no overarching authority.

During the 60s, not only the Roman Christians but the Jews of Rome must have lived in great uncertainty. In 66 CE the Jews in Palestine had revolted against Rome, and Roman Jews must have been regarded with suspicion by the Roman authorities. Nero's death in 68 CE brought chaos to the capital with three pretenders to the throne ruling and being disposed of in the one year of 69 CE. Order only came with the accession of the general Vespasian. Jerusalem fell as a result of the siege of his son, Titus, and the Roman army and the spoils of war, including Jewish prisoners, were brought back to Rome in 71 CE.

Between that time and the middle of the third century, the Roman Christians consolidated. They formed a well-constructed society that over the next two centuries would expand greatly. In a letter of Cornelius, the Bishop of Rome 251-253 CE, there is a list of the administrative members of the church in his time: 46 elders or presbyters, seven deacons, seven sub-deacons, 42 acolytes, 52 exorcists and over 1500 widows and indigents. These numbers reflect a total Christian population of something in the tens of thousands; it also reflects a city-wide organization.

Of importance is the link between Peter and this Roman Christianity.

A local elder in Rome, Gaius, wrote in the latter part of the second century CE of a *tropaion* or a memorial erected to Peter in Rome on the Vatican hill. The word *tropaion* can but need not necessarily imply a tomb. But the same Gaius wrote of another *tropaion* to Paul on the Via Ostia. What Gaius wanted to prove was that the Christian teaching in Rome (on topics in which he was furiously involved with opponents outside Rome) had been verified by the stalwarts of Christian tradition, Peter and Paul. Other Christian locations might have their own ideas; the pedigree of Rome's teaching could not be faulted.

> I can show you the trophies (*tropaia*) of the apostles. If, in fact, you go out towards the Vatican or along Via Ostia, you will find the *tropaia* of those who founded this Church. (Cited in Eusebius, *Historia Ecclesiastica*, 2, 25, 6-7)

---

[29] Most attempts to describe the structure of the Jesus-movement at this time rely on the list of greetings in Romans 16:3-16. This list of addressees has its difficulties as we will see. It seems to be addressed to Corinthians, not Romans. We must rely on other sources.

Briefly, the *tropaion* erected in honour of Peter was situated in a second century CE graveyard on the Vatican Hill. It might have been a tomb of Peter; it might more easily have been a monument erected in his honour. Excavations under St Peter's in the twentieth century have recovered the *tropaion*, a rather meagre piece of architecture. The high altar of St Peter's had been centred on this tropaion and no doubt Constantine, the constructor, thought that Peter had been buried beneath. But this was some two centuries after its construction. Bones were found, but it must be remembered that the memorial was erected in a graveyard. Whether the bones of Peter have been recovered from this *tropaion* is a hotly debated matter. There is no convincing evidence that the bones were Peter's or that Peter ever went to Rome.

The two Letters of Peter demonstrate what took place in Rome. 1 Peter begins:

> Peter, apostle of Jesus Christ,
> To the exiles of the Dispersion in Pontus, Galatia, Cappadocia, Asia,
> and Bithynia ...

The term 'apostle' (*apostolos*) is not stated in passing. The letter writer claims to be the Apostle, Peter. Who the writer was or even when exactly the Letter was written is unknown. What we do know is that there was an office of chief *apostolos* in Rome, according to the tradition of the Roman Church. The *apostolos* would have been seen as the successor to Peter. However, whether the *apostolos*-successor ever knew or even had met Peter cannot be determined. What role did the new *apostolos* play? Perhaps something like Clement who headed a home-church in Rome in the 90s CE. He appears as a *primus inter pares* who seems to have been highly regarded in Rome and to be looked up to as a religious foreign minister, having responsibility for other provinces, although no authority over them. He wrote a letter to the Corinthians trying to adjudicate on an issue in their governance. The *apostolos* at some stage morphed into the chief Roman bishop, who was considered to have a special charism because he had inherited the teaching tradition of Peter, surely the most important of all Traditions.

The historical Peter almost certainly had never been in Rome and had no part in its formation. The Jesus-Tradition that had been inherited by Rome and expressed, in its most fulsome statement, was the Gospel of Mark which clearly maintained that the successor of Jesus was Peter. The Roman Christians, seeing themselves at the centre of the Empire, believed that not only the teaching of Peter came to them but Peter did so bodily. The *apostolos* office in Rome looked back to a supposed historical Peter, who had come to Rome towards the end of his life. The holders of that office became 'Peter'. The *tropaion* became more than a memorial; it became a tomb. Hence there began the fiction of Peter in Rome.

ROMAN CHRISTIANITY RETURNS TO THE EAST

At first there would have been the distinction between Roman Christianity, primarily a Gentile structure, and the more Jewish forms of the Jesus-movement still operating in the East. East and West formed a dividing line between versions of the Jesus movement generally. But this distinction was not to last. The Roman Church began to turn back to the East, from where it had first derived its Palestinian version of the new Jesus-movement, and imposed its newly developed version.

From the late 60s CE, the Roman Christians had severed any direct connection with Palestinian Jesus-movements. The Roman Church had its own version of Jesus in the Literary Jesus of the gospels of Mark, Matthew and Luke (which may not have had exactly the texts that have come down to today).

This distinctive form of Roman Christianity was based on the structure of house-churches. Within these some form of the Jesus-Tradition had been received and reworked in a Roman way, with Roman thinking and Roman issues paramount. This reworked Jesus-Tradition was given a formal, written text in the Gospel of Mark. Mark became the principal sacred writing of Rome. Elsewhere in the Empire, with the spread of Roman Christianity, Matthew and Luke's gospels circulated. We have seen that they were based on the gospel of Mark to which they assimilated Sayings of Jesus from the earlier Jesus-Tradition.

Roman Christianity had no problem in identifying Jesus with the Divinity. Their compatriots readily attributed divine power to their outstanding emperors such as Caesar and Octavian. It would have been in Rome, too, with its Games which featured blood-sacrifice that the idea developed that Jesus had died by a sacrifice ordained by The Father and that blood-sacrifice was the means for atoning for the sins of the believers. He became the New Isaac, the Monogenes offered by his Father.

Something has already been said about the symbolism of Isaac in dealing with the title of Monogenes. In short, the Genesis narrative tells of Abraham being asked to sacrifice his Only Son Isaac and although he makes all the preparations, at the last moment, the child was delivered by divine intervention. In Jewish tradition, Abraham thereafter became the Father of Faith, because he carried out the demand of Yahweh, while Isaac became the symbol of the True Israel, who was (almost) sacrificed for his people.

Gradually, as we approach the Christian period, the Jews switched the emphasis on the Abraham and Isaac story from Abraham to Isaac. Isaac was seen as a (near) martyr and the fact that he had not been sacrificed was overlooked. He became the symbol of a suffering people who would overcome their situation. There is evidence that this change affected the Jews of Rome.

It would seem that in Rome there was a confrontation: Jews claimed that Isaac was the symbol of a suffering and persecuted Israel and was almost martyred; Christians claimed that Jesus was the New Isaac, and that Jesus was actually sacrificed.

In short, by the end of the first century CE Roman Christianity was quite different from the various forms of Palestinian Christianity and from Gnosticism.

Then, from the late first century or early second century CE, Roman Christianity travelled in the opposite direction to the Eastern regions of the Empire, first borne by Roman pilgrims visiting the key sacred places mentioned in the Synoptic gospels and later by Christians connected with the Roman administration (merchants, political appointees, military). There, Roman Christianity met the still-existing Palestinian forms of the Jesus-movement.

Two Roman Sites in Palestine

For example, there was a Jesus-movement community in Capernaum, a modest village on the Sea of Galilee, where the Roman Gospel of Mark maintained that Jesus had established his Galilean mission in Peter's house. The village was small, covering some twenty-five acres, and would have supported a population of about 1000. Its buildings were made up of a series of rooms (usually formed by solid ceiling beams supporting a thick bed of reeds and then covered with mud) clustered around a common courtyard.

Archaeologists have found that an octagonal church, dating back to the fifth century CE, was venerated as containing within its walls the presumed house of Peter. Around that time the Jews had also built a synagogue close by. The remains of the so-called House of Peter have been excavated and they reveal a curious series of adaptations. The top stratum is the fifth century church. But, prior to that, there was a fourth century house-church and beneath this was a courtyard home, a focal point of interest since its walls had been covered over many years with graffiti by pilgrims.

How can these excavations be interpreted? In Capernaum, the fourth or fifth century Byzantine church had been built on top of the courtyard home which had been remodelled in the late first century and plastered. In the latter part of the second century its plastered walls had been daubed with graffiti, some undoubtedly written by Roman Christians. Then in the fourth century the room had been enlarged and its ceiling formed into an arch. This is an early shrine doubtless honouring the memory of Peter, whose house was said to be in Capernaum in the Synoptic gospels. Whether this was really the house of Peter is immaterial; Roman Christians coming to the village thought it was.

But the excavated building need not necessarily have ever been a community church for local Jesus-movement people in Capernaum; they would have used the nearby synagogue. They would not have had the Jesus story (including the succession of Peter) as in the gospel of Mark. They did not have the Gospel of Mark. The house shrine honouring Peter would have been a way-chapel catering for Roman pilgrims from the Empire who subscribed to Roman Christianity. It would have become an independent, flourishing Roman Christian centre only after the time of Constantine.

The same is true of other sites such as Nazareth. It may or may not have been the home town of Jesus; the important thing is that readers of the Roman gospels thought it was. In the second century pilgrims arrived from varying parts of the Empire to see the places mentioned in the Synoptic gospels, now appropriated by the Roman Church. By that stage the physical landscape had already changed because of the widespread devastation wrought by the upheavals of the two Jewish revolts against Rome. Many landmarks would have been destroyed. The local Jesus-movements were never particularly interested in these historical details, dear to the Roman Christians.

In the last century, the Crusader church was found to have been built on top of an earlier Greek church. The Greek church had been frequently adorned and there were many new mosaic floors built on top of each other. Beneath this church there lay three caves with plastered walls, a *mikveh* or Jewish ritual bath and a third century synagogue. It would seem that the caves, whose interiors had been plastered, had been venerated by Christian pilgrims, doubtless as the site of the Annunciation by Gabriel to Mary as recorded in Luke. However, once again, there is no evidence that we are dealing with a local Jesus-movement church. This would certainly have been a way-chapel, catering for Roman pilgrims particularly from the Constantinian period, that had been extended over the adjoining area.

The first mention of a Christian shrine in Nazareth comes from Egeria, a pilgrim to the Holy Land, in around 383 CE. She sent a long letter back to a group of women in her native Galicia, perhaps nuns. This has been retained in only a partial copy, later called the *Travels of Egeria*. She mentions seeing a garden 'in which the Lord used to be after his return from Egypt', a 'big and very splendid cave', and an altar placed there. The cave and altar probably refer to the larger of the caves in the grotto of the present basilica.

In other words, there were Jesus-movement people in places like Capernaum and Nazareth who presumably met and acted ritually like Jews and made use of the local synagogue. They would not have been distinguishable from other Jews of the time. However, they would have catered for the spiritual needs of a growing number of Roman Christian visitors as well as for their own economic benefit.

The Cenacle in Jerusalem

Having examined Capernaum and Nazareth, we can now turn to Jerusalem. A long tradition has identified the so-called Cenacle or Supper Room where Jesus was said to have eaten the Last Supper.

It is today found among a conglomerate of buildings to the south of Jerusalem, on Mount Zion[30] just outside the Zion Gate. On the lower floor there is the alleged Tomb of David, while on the first floor there is the alleged Upper Room commemorating the place of both the Last Supper and Pentecost. None of these historical identifications has any verisimilitude. The upper room was built only in 1342 by Franciscans using Cypriot craftspeople and it was one of the rooms in a monastery.

The room containing the cenotaph of David, his tomb, has three floors beneath what can be seen today: Crusader, late Roman or Byzantine and a stone pavement from the second to the third century CE. The least that can be concluded is that a building stood on this site in the second to third century. Is there any documentary evidence to accompany the foundation?

In 394 CE Epiphanius wrote that when Hadrian came to Jerusalem in 130 CE he found the city in ruins, but he did remark on

---

[30] Josephus mistakenly called this area 'Mount Zion'. By his time, it had been forgotten that David was said to have lived on the opposite spur, Ophel. Visitors presumed that David would have lived in the more opulent west side where their own aristocracy lived.

the little church of God on the spot where the disciples went to
the upper room on their return from the Mount of Olives after the
Ascension of the Redeemer. It was built there, namely on Zion,
which escaped destruction, and the houses around Zion and seven
synagogues which remained isolated in Zion like huts, one of which
survived into the time of bishop Maximos and of the emperor
Constantine, like a shanty in a vineyard, as the Scripture says. (*De
mensuris et ponderibus* 14)

This reference to Isaiah 1:8 is repeated by the Bordeaux Pilgrim who
visited Jerusalem in 333 CE (probably later than Epiphanius, who had been
raised in Palestine).

Inside Zion, within the wall, you can see where David had his palace.
Seven synagogues were there, but only one is left – the rest have been
'ploughed and sown' as was said by the prophet Isaiah.

Both writers affirm that in the fourth century there was still a synagogue on Zion. Historically, this is at least unusual since there was no Jewish
presence.

After the destruction of Jerusalem in 70 CE the city was virtually a ruin.
The walls had been largely demolished; the rich houses in the upper part of
the city were destroyed including Herod's palace; the Tyropoeon valley was
filled with masonry and silted up. Roman soldiers of the Tenth Legion had
set up a camp within the city limits near Herod's three great towers.

Jews once more settled back in the Mount Zion region. They could have
worshipped in the seven synagogues mentioned by Epiphanius, since the
Temple Mount was no longer available. Among these Jews would have been
the Jesus-movement people under the leadership now of Simeon.[31] Their
meeting place must have been one of the seven synagogues, since they followed basically a Jewish ritual.

Then in 118 CE Hadrian became emperor. He was an inveterate travel-
ler within the confines of his Empire and he left behind visible signs of his
beneficence in the form of monuments. In 130 CE he came to the ruined
Jerusalem and determined to rebuild it as a gift to the Roman colony of
Judaea. He decided that it would be called Aelia Capitolina, combining his

---

[31] It is debatable whether these Jesus-movement people had been in Pella, as has
been often claimed, since prior to the destruction of Jerusalem. Only Eusebius
posited the flight to Pella and his statement was later taken up by Epiphanius.
Since Pella was a Gentile city, attacked by Jews under Alexander Jannaeus and
again at the beginning of the First Revolt, it would hardly have welcomed the
Jewish Christians. Much more likely, they remained in Jerusalem.

own name (Publius Aelius Hadrianus) and that of the gods of the Roman Capitol to whom the new city would be dedicated. While these plans were executed in good faith, the Jews saw them as the final assault on their religious heritage.

A second revolt was led by Simon Bar Koseba (known by the nickname Bar Kokhba, 'the son of the Star') and his uncle, a priest called Eleazar. With the Tenth Legion absent from Jerusalem quelling guerilla attacks, Koseba took control of Jerusalem and held it for three years. By then the Romans had marshalled their forces and recaptured the city, tracking down Koseba in one of his Judaean strongholds. All Jews were thenceforward banned from entering Jerusalem and Judaea and many moved to Galilee. The decree read:

> It is forbidden for all circumcized persons to enter or stay within the territory of Aelia Capitolina; any person contravening this prohibition shall be put to death. (cited in Avi-Yonah, 1976)

The ban would have applied to all Jews and to Palestinian Jesus-movement people. However, even during the settlement of Aelia Capitolina, some of the Greek and Syrian colonists seemed to have been Roman Christians. Here we can only speculate. It is entirely possible that they took over the synagogue frequented earlier by their distant Jesus-movement confreres. It was outside the boundary of Aelia Capitolina and would not have been included in the general refurbishment of the city wrought by Hadrian. Eusebius remarks on the changed character of the population of Aelia Capitolina, including its Gentile Church:

> And thus, when the city had been emptied of the Jewish nation and had suffered the total destruction of its ancient inhabitants, it was colonized by a different race, and the Roman city which subsequently arose changed its name and was called Aelia, in honor of the emperor Aelius Adrian. And as the church there was now composed of Gentiles, the first one to assume the government of it after the bishops of the circumcision was Marcus. (*Hist Eccl* 4:6)

Over the years Aelia Capitolina rose above the ruins and was dedicated to Jupiter, Juno and Minerva. It was typically a Roman colonial city with a monumental entrance in the north at the Damascus Gate and from the square inside this gate two *cardines* (roads) ran almost its length. In 289 CE the Tenth Legion finally left and it required walls.

The ongoing Roman Christian presence in Aelia Capitolina, despite possible times of discrimination, was illustrated by the appointment of an Alexander as bishop. He came on a pilgrimage in 212 CE and was persuaded to become the auxiliary bishop to the aged Narcissus, whom he then succeeded. He was influential enough to be able to set up a public library within Aelia.

By the beginning of the third century CE, despite the official ban being still operative, Jews began to enter the city once more, but on a small scale. By about 250 CE they were allowed to enter and mourn the destruction of the Temple from the Mount of Olives and the ceremony of commemorating the day of the destruction, *Tisha b'Av*, began some time thereafter.

The 'Little Church of God', conjecturally in the hands of Roman Christians, was reconstructed in the fourth century and became known as the 'Upper Church of the Apostles' and in the fifth century as 'Zion, Mother of all Churches'. There is a remnant of this church – a niche in a six metre broad wall behind the present-day cenotaph of David – which was probably a recess in the exterior wall of the apse of this church. It was only in the fifth century that the church became associated with the tradition of the Last Supper. However, this association would seem to have been based on an earlier fourth century tradition that had already linked the church with the Pentecostal Descent of the Spirit, which also was said to have taken place in an 'upper room'. The 'upper room' motif artificially linked the two traditions.

The Roman Christians would also have laid claim to a throne that was purported to be that of James the Just.

In 326, Constantine's mother, Helena, followed in the steps of early pilgrims to the East. These pilgrims had been satisfied with local traditions and doubtlessly fabricated sites. She bestowed the imperial seal of approval on certain sites and thenceforward their authenticity would not be questioned until more recent times. And so, she identified Golgotha, where Jesus was crucified, and his Empty Tomb nearby. Constantine paid for a large complex to include both sites. He also paid for a Basilica to be built over the supposed site of Jesus' birth in Bethlehem. In Jerusalem, yet another site acknowledged the place from which Jesus ascended into heaven. These were not for the use of locals, but were focal points for Roman pilgrims and other visitors. These were evidence for the historical footprint of Jesus, so necessary to the Roman mentality.

Certainly by the time of Constantine, any juxtaposition between Roman Christianity and the Palestinian Jesus-movements came to an end. Roman Christianity dominated and any remaining Palestinian forms of the Jesus-movement, which might have survived, atrophied. Likewise, from Constantine on, any remaining pockets of Gnosticism were eradicated.

Roman Christianity, for all practical purposes, was all that remained. It was virtually the only Christianity.

Some form of the Jesus-movement had moved from its Palestinian cradle to Rome and it had come back. However, it came back with a changed character. In Palestine the Jesus-movements would have remained within the confines of Judaism or at least on its perimeter. These Jesus-movements generated their own literature and societal structures. On being transported to Rome, because of historical and social influences (for example, being separated from mainstream Judaism, accepting a majority of Gentiles, adapting the Roman culture of the family and hierarchy), the Roman form underwent significant change. This was written back into its origins and transcribed into the Gospel of Mark and later the other Synoptic gospels. This became the religion of the house-churches, quite separate from the synagogues in Rome, ruled at first by elders and in the mid-second century by a bishop with authority over the whole of Rome.

This religion honored (it may even have commissioned) the Literary Jesus of Mark whose main features were:

- Jesus as a figure whose birth, ministry (both of which demonstrated that he was the expected Jewish Messiah), death and physical resurrection and physical ascension had all been affirmed by reliable witnesses;
- the succession of Peter to Jesus, the apostleship of The Twelve (which verified the rule by bishops and elders);
- the betrayal by Judas;
- the blood sacrifice of Jesus (which would eventually require sacrificing priests);
- a specific sacramental system based on a particular interpretation of Baptism and the Eucharist;
- the coming of a Last Day preceded by wondrous events;
- the simultaneous Second Coming of the Messiah;
- the physical resurrection of all believers together with a Final Judgement.

All of this Story had been foretold in the Hebrew Scriptures and was considered to be historical fact.[32] Historicity was endemic to the Roman Jesus-Story and in Mark.

---

[32] The Roman emphasis on historicity can be seen in the Letters of the Roman bishop, Ignatius, written in the second century CE, as he comments on Gnostic teaching to the Christians in Tralles in Asia Minor: [continued ...]

This form of Roman Christianity, because of the historical vicissitudes of the Roman period, was taken back into colonial Palestine. There it diminished drastically any remaining forms of the Palestinian Jesus-movements. The transformation was more or less completed by the end of the Constantinian period.

The period of Constantine saw the triumph of Roman Christianity. He gave it official imperial recognition and considered himself to be its centre. But he wanted to emphasize the Peter element of succession because it would have been involved in the Roman form of the Jesus-Tradition and in the gospel of Mark. This Roman persuasion in non-biblical tradition had already brought Peter to Rome and established his death there. Peter, in Constantine's reading, had possessed supreme religious authority in Rome (and therefore over the now Christian Empire), and Constantine embodied this succession in the very architecture of the first St Peter's Basilica.

Peter became the Founder of all Christianity, the successor to Jesus, and the bishops in Rome who succeeded Peter and The Twelve, in their turn, held the position of leaders. But Peter had never displaced the Emperor. The bishop of Rome was under the authority of Constantine. The first St Peter's was erected by Constantine to Peter, but it was the act of an Emperor towards a past achiever. Constantine saw himself superior to Peter and his successors.

So it was that Constantine, the self-proclaimed vicar of God himself, formally acknowledged that Peter had established the Church in Rome. But he, Constantine, was the representative of God. St Peter's is not a monument to Peter; it is a monument erected by Constantine to himself and his munificence.

They also calumniate his being born of the Virgin; they are ashamed of his cross; they deny his passion; and they do not believe his resurrection. They introduce God as a Being unknown; they suppose Christ to be unbegotten; and as to the Spirit, they do not admit that he exists. Some of them say that the Son is a mere man, and that the Father, Son, and Holy Spirit are but the same person, and that the creation is the work of God, not by Christ, but by some other strange power. (*Epistle to the Trallians*, ch. 6)

And in another place:

Stop your ears, therefore, when any one speaks to you at variance with Jesus Christ, who was descended from David, and was also of Mary; who was truly born, and did eat and drink. He was truly persecuted under Pontius Pilate; he was truly crucified, and truly died, in the sight of beings in heaven, and on earth, and under the earth. He was also truly raised from the dead, his Father restoring him to life, even as after the same manner his Father will so raise up us who believe in him by Christ Jesus, apart from whom we do not possess the true life. (ibid., ch. 9)

Roman Christianity can be constructed in the following way:

YHWH/ now known as Father

↓

The divine Jesus/the Holy Spirit

(Contact achieved)

Peter and 'Peter' (his successors)

↑

Roman Christianity

This was only the skeleton of Roman Christian thinking. When the later theologians of the Roman Church began to deal with deviant beliefs and practices it was often in the context of Greek philosophy. How could the phenomena of Christianity be translated into Greek thought-patterns? There were those who struggled to describe how Jesus could be divine and human at the same time; there were those who struggled to explain how Yahweh (or Father), Jesus as the Divine Son and the mysterious Holy Spirit (also called The Paraclete in John's gospel) could all be God and yet there could be only one God.

The Church Fathers managed to construct the theory of a *trinitas* (the 'threeness'). There was only one God-substance but it consisted of three self-sufficient modes of being (*hypostases* in Greek or *personae* in Latin): the Father, the Son and the Holy Spirit. The Son had proceeded from the Father; the Spirit had proceeded from the Father and the Son (or perhaps, as some maintained, from the Father through the Son). The Son had taken on a human nature but the human and the divine natures were not commingled, the two remained separate, but there was still only one individual. This was called the hypostatic union. All those who thought differently to these orthodox Fathers were denounced.

So it was that Roman Christianity, formulated on Roman soil as a result of what had been received by Jews from the East, had rewritten the traditional text. Then, Roman Christianity had followed the Roman armies and conquered the East for itself.

We now need to look at one of the Christian protagonists whose name has also been appended to the foundation of the Church of Rome – Paul.

NOTES

In an earlier form, this material was published while I was a Visiting Fellow at the Woolf Institute, Cambridge University: Crotty, R. (2001), *Roman Christianity: The Distancing of Jew and Christian*, CJCR Press: Cambridge .

These are references to the archaeological statements made in the above text:

Appolonj-Ghetti B., Ferrua, A., Josi, E., Kirschbaum, E. (1951), 2 vols, *Esplorazioni sotto la Confessione di san Pietro in Vaticano*, Tipografia Poliglotta Vaticana: Rome.

Guidobaldi, F. (1978), *Il complesso archeologico di San Clemente: Risultati degli scavi piu recenti e riesami dei resti architettonici*, 2 vols, Collegio San Clemente: Rome

Richardson, P. (1998), 'Augustan-Era Synagogues in Rome' in K. Donfried & P. Richardson (eds.), *Judaism and Christianity in First-Century Rome*, William B. Eerdmans Publishing Co: Grand Rapids and Cambridge, pp. 17-29.

More general texts on which the material on Roman Christianity has been constructed are:

Barnes, T. D. (1984), *Early Christianity and the Roman Empire*, Variorum: London.

Bowe, B. (1988), *A Church in Crisis: Ecclesiology and Paranesis in Clement of Rome*, ortress Press: Minneapolis

Brown, R. E & Meier, J. P. (1983), *Antioch and Rome: New Testament Cradles of Catholic Christianity*, Paulist Press: New York.

Crotty, R. (1995), 'The Role of Post Mortem Visions in the Jewish Intertestamental Literature', *Pacifica*, 8, pp. 1-8.

Crotty, R. (1996a), *The Jesus Question: the historical search*, Harper-Collins: Melbourne.

Crotty, R. (1996), 'James the Just in the History of Early Christianity', *Australian Biblical Review*, 44, pp.42-52

Crotty, R. (2001), *Roman Christianity: the Distancing of Jew and Christian*, CJCR Press: Cambridge.

Goodman, M. (1994), *Mission and Conversion. Proselytizing in the Religious History of the Roman Empire*, Clarendon Press: Oxford.

Jeffers, J. (1991), *Conflict at Rome: Social Order and Hierarchy in Early Christianity*, Fortress Press: Minneapolis.

Judge, E. & Thomas, G, 'The Origin of the Church at Rome: A New Solution?', *The Reformed Theological Review* 25, pp. 81-94.

Lane, W. (1998), 'Social Perspectives on Roman Christianity during the Formative Years from Nero to Nerva' in K. Donfried & P. Richardson (eds.), *Judaism and Christianity in First-Century Rome*, William B. Eerdmans Publishing Co: Grand Rapids and Cambridge, pp. 196-244.

Leon, H. (1960), *The Jews of Ancient Rome*, Jewish Publication Society of America: Philadelphia.

Limor, O. (1988), 'The Origins of a Tradition: King David's Tomb on Mount Zion', *Traditio*, vol. 44, pp. 453-462.

Murphy-O'Connor, J. (1994), 'The Cenacle and Community: The Background of Acts 2:44-45', in Coogan, M., Exum, J. & Stager L. (eds.), *Scripture and Other Artifacts. Essays on the Bible and Archaeology in honor of Philip J. King*, Westminster John Knox Press: Louisville

Peterson, J. (1969), 'House-churches in Rome', *Vigiliae Christianae* 23, pp. 264-272.

Peterson, J. (1973), 'Some Titular Churches at Rome with traditional New Testament Connections', *Expository Times*, 84, pp. 277-279.

Pinkerfeld, J. (1960), '"David's Tomb": Notes on the History of the Building. Preliminary Report' in *Louis M. Rabinowitz Fund for the Exploration of Ancient Synagogues, Bulletin*, vol. 3, pp. 41-43.

Richardson, P. (1998), 'Augustan-Era Synagogues in Rome', in K. Donfried & P. Richardson (eds.), *Judaism and Christianity in First-Century Rome*, William B. Eerdmans Publishing Co: Grand Rapids and Cambridge, pp. 17-29.

Slingerland, D. (1989), 'Christus-Chrestus?', in A. Avery-Peck (ed.), *The Literature of Early Rabbinic Judaism: Issues in Talmudic Redaction and Interpretation*, University Press of America: Washington, pp. 133-144.

Snyder, G. (1998), 'The Interaction of Jews with Non-Jews in Rome', in K. Donfried & P. Richardson (eds.), *Judaism and Christianity in First-Century Rome*, William B. Eerdmans Publishing Co: Grand Rapids and Cambridge, pp. 69-92.

Strand, K. (1992), 'Peter and Paul in relationship to the episcopal Succession in the Church at Rome', *Andrews University Seminary Studies*, 3, pp. 217-232.

Taylor, J. (1993), *Christians and the Holy Places: the Myth of Jewish-Christian Origins*, Clarendon Press: Oxford.

Walters, J. (1998), 'Romans, Jews and Christians: The Impact of the Romans on Jewish/Christian Relations in First-Century Rome' in K. Donfried & P. Richardson (eds.), *Judaism and Christianity in First-Century Rome*, William B. Eerdmans Publishing Co: Grand Rapids and Cambridge, pp. 175-195.

Wiefel, W. (1977), 'The Jewish Community in Ancient Rome and the Origins of Roman Christianity' in K. Donfried (ed), *The Romans Debate*, Augsburg Press: Minneapolis, pp. 100-119.

Wiefel, W. (1991), 'The Jewish Community in Rome', in K. Donfried (ed.), *The Romans Debate*, 2nd ed., Hendrickson: Peabody, Mass., pp.84-101.

— 6 —
PAUL

UNDOUBTEDLY PAUL WAS ONE OF THE MAIN players in the formation of early Christianity. We know him mainly via his Letters and also via his image in the Acts of the Apostles.

However, Paul has to be treated in the same way as Israel and Jesus. There was certainly an historical Paul. However, we cannot be sure that the 'Paul' proclaimed later within the Christian Church as the Apostle to the Gentiles and the great theologian of Roman Christianity was the same figure as the historical one.

And, as was the case with Israel and Jesus, we must be suspicious of the Biblical Paul, often the subject of modern Christian writings on the man.

THE STUDY OF PAUL

While there is a great deal of information about Paul in the Acts of the Apostles, we need to question its historical value. We do not know the author of Acts; it was not Luke. There are too many differences in style and content. The author of Acts knew the gospel of Luke and repeated the last features of his gospel, but then Acts relied on a variety of sources and constructed, for its own purposes, a coherent narrative from these sources.

Its aim was to establish historical bases for the early Christian Church in Rome from a particular viewpoint. The official transmission of the Christian Church is described as moving from Jesus to the Twelve (accommodating the James group as an aside) and later, and very importantly to Paul; the pathway ends in Rome with Paul's arrival. But the events in Acts need to be balanced against, first of all, the Letters of Paul (with the proviso that some are forgeries and that there could well have been later additions).

We will begin with an analysis of the Acts of the Apostles and then turn to the Letters of Paul.

Paul in the Acts of the Apostles

The Acts of the Apostles has been mentioned in our text several times to this point.

Just as each of the canonical gospels provides a narrative concerning Jesus, so Acts provides a narrative of Paul. Acts contains a theological 'biography' of Paul with certain doctrinal material interspersed along with his missionary activity.

The events narrated from Acts concerning Paul are not necessarily historical facts. Acts relates concerning Paul:

- He was a Jew, born in Tarsus the capital of Cilicia and educated in Jerusalem by the renown Pharisaic teacher, Gamaliel.

- He became a persecutor of members of the newly-established Jesus-movement. In fact, he was present at the execution of Stephen, the leader of the Hellenists.

- He was converted to the Jesus-movement after a Vision of the Risen Jesus on the road to Damascus. In Damascus he was persecuted by Jews and he escaped to 'Arabia'.

- He made a first visit to Jerusalem where his life was threatened by the Hellenists.

- He returned to Tarsus and Antioch.

- On a second visit to Jerusalem he delivered famine relief to believers in Judaea.

- On his first missionary journey he left Antioch and made for Cyprus and Asia Minor, establishing small Jesus communities.

- On a visit to Jerusalem, he met with Peter, James the Brother of Jesus and John. This is sometimes called the 'Jerusalem Council'. It was decided that he would be the Apostle to the Gentiles.

- On a second missionary journey he travelled from Antioch into Cilicia, then Galatia, Troas, Philippi, Thessalonica, Beroea (these last three in Macedonia), Athens, Corinth, Ephesus.

- He made a visit to Jerusalem to 'greet the church'.

- On a third missionary journey he travelled from Antioch to Galatia, Phrygia, Ephesus, Troas, Macedonia, Greece, Miletus, Tyre, Caesarea.

- On a final visit to Jerusalem he was arrested in the Temple and taken before the Jewish authorities and the Roman governor of Caesarea, Felix, and King Agrippa.

- His final journey was to Rome as a prisoner. He arrived in Rome to be welcomed by the members of the Roman Church.

Acts does not begin with Paul. In its first chapters, it demonstrates that the disciples, after having been instructed and prepared by Jesus during his lifetime and then confirmed by his presence after his Resurrection, in turn continue to spread God's new message. The resurrected Jesus is visible to the disciples at first and they are filled with the Spirit of God, God's powerful presence.

After repeating the story of the Ascension from Luke, the Literary Jesus of Luke appears to the disciples in Acts and says:

> It is not for you to know the times or periods that the Father has set by his own authority. But you will receive power when the Holy Spirit has come upon you; and you will be my witnesses in Jerusalem, in all Judaea and Samaria, and to the ends of the earth. (Acts 1:7-8)

Thereafter, Acts begins its Church Story in Jerusalem, where wondrous things occur through the ministry of The Twelve, with Peter at their head. These works are similar to the great things done by Jesus himself earlier: cures, miracles, preaching. Then the disciples move outwards first into Judaea and Samaria and thence, through the ministry of Paul, to Asia Minor and Europe, 'the ends of the earth'. What had begun with Jesus among the Jews had now spread beyond Israel to the whole world.

This is a programmatic statement claiming that what will follow in the tale in Acts will be in accordance with the activity of the Spirit of God. It goes beyond anything envisioned in the gospel of Luke. The text of Acts follows the program with exactitude.

But you will receive power when the Holy Spirit has come upon you;	2:4 All of them were filled with the Holy Spirit and began to speak in other languages, as the Spirit gave them ability.
and you will be my witnesses in Jerusalem,	2:41 So those who welcomed his message were baptized, and that day about three thousand persons were added. 42 They devoted themselves to the apostles' teaching and fellowship, to the breaking of bread and the prayers.

in all Judea and Samaria	[8:1] That day a severe persecution began against the church in Jerusalem, and all except the apostles were scattered throughout the countryside of Judea and Samaria.
	[8:4] Now those who were scattered went from place to place, proclaiming the word. [5] Philip went down to the city of Samaria and proclaimed the Messiah to them. [6] The crowds with one accord listened eagerly to what was said by Philip, hearing and seeing the signs that he did, [7] for unclean spirits, crying with loud shrieks, came out of many who were possessed; and many others who were paralysed or lame were cured. [8] So there was great joy in that city.
and to the ends of the earth	The missionary journeys of Paul accomplish this.
	[28:28] Let it be known to you then that this salvation of God has been sent to the Gentiles; they will listen.'

We are, on the basis of this program, able to provide a structure for Acts:

1. Jerusalem: The Jewish Christian Community: Peter and the Twelve and James the Just and the Brothers (2:1-8:3)
2. Samaria: Philip (8:4-40)
3. Saul/Paul converted (8:40-9:31)
4. Further activity of Peter (9:32-12:24)
5. 'To the ends of the earth': the journeys of Paul (13:1- 28:30)

Acts is the first Church Story, the forerunner of the definitive early Christian history of Eusebius in the time of Constantine. It took its inspiration from Luke and attempted to show how the Spirit theology of Luke had actually worked out in practice. It did so not by history but by Story. Acts is no more historical than Luke.

Acts wove Peter and the Twelve, James the Just and the Brothers, Stephen and the Hellenists and Philip and The Seven into a consistent story displaying the harmony, unity and mutual support of church members after the departure of Jesus. There followed the first stage of Christian outgoing from Jerusalem. For the author of Acts, there was only one Church; it was made up of many proponents but they worked together to spread the word preached by Jesus.

But James, Peter and the Twelve and Stephen and the Hellenists and Philip and his Seven were only the first stage of missionary activity. In a second stage, Acts saw Paul as the true successor of Jesus. It was able to accommodate the other 'successors', but they had been displaced by Paul.

Acts' focus was to show how, from the beginning, the risen Jesus had called Paul to be his missionary and he was elevated above the other leaders.

For sources, Acts used the gospel of Luke, the Letters of Paul (whatever was available at the time), plus oral traditions, and perhaps some written sources, giving brief factual accounts of Paul's missionary endeavours. The end result was a flowing story in which Acts presented Paul as another Jesus (duplicating Jesus' ministry: his arrest in Jerusalem; his trial before the Jewish chief priests and Council; his subsequent trials before Felix the Roman governor and Herod Agrippa the Jewish King; his journey to Rome). Then, full stop. Nothing is said of his death. This was the main point of Acts' second part of the gospel of Luke: Peter had been the initial successor, Paul had established the Roman Church.

However, clearly the gospel of Luke, following Mark, had proposed Peter as the clear successor of Jesus. Acts does not deny it, but presents the succession as the first stage. Peter certainly had been involved in the spread of Christianity and he acted as successor up to the time of Paul. The final narrative about Peter in Acts is an imprisonment from which he is miraculously delivered. The text that follows is important:

> [17] He motioned to them with his hand to be silent, and described for them how the Lord had brought him out of the prison. And he added, 'Tell this to James and to the believers.' Then he left and went to another place.

Peter is not again mentioned; 'he went to another place'. That other place could have been anywhere except Rome – that is the startling statement of Acts. If it had been Rome, Acts would have had to say so. For Acts, Peter did not go to Rome; he did not establish the Church in Rome.

From a literary point of view, Acts follows the genre of the epic history of a past golden era. This was what Homer had done with the Mycenaean Age, what Virgil had done with the beginnings of Rome. Acts needed to explain the qualities of the Church as it existed in a later time and place. So the narrative is set in the Golden Age, the mythic time of the establishment of the Church.

Acts wanted to show that the Apostles agreed with each other and acted in concert. The apostolic foundation in the Golden Age was essential to the Church of the time of Acts; Christianity by the time of Acts was a religion within the Empire centred on Rome. Within this Golden Age, Acts portrayed the Apostolic Council, with Peter, James and John supporting Paul and defending his mission to the Gentiles. This apostolic link was the required guarantee of a direct link to Jesus: from Jesus to Peter and The Twelve and thence to Paul and the Church of Rome.

Acts is a story of struggle to wrest Christianity from Judaism, to wrest Christianity from Jerusalem and to establish it in the Empire at Rome. Hence, in Acts' speeches before Roman dignitaries – Felix, Festus and the Jewish-Roman Herod Agrippa – there is the clear claim that Christianity is a cultural force assisting good Roman citizenship. The Christian Church is presented with its founder, Paul, its earlier apostles, its elders, its rituals of Baptism and Eucharist, its creed of belief.

The Acts of the Apostles is a superb piece of religious writing. It is not historical and it is not based on what we would call historical sources. Endeavouring to write a history of Paul using Acts would be a very difficult exercise.

From the Acts of the Apostles, we turn to the Letters of Paul.

The Letters of Paul

Of the fourteen letters attributed to Paul in the canonical text of the Christian Scriptures, there is scholarly agreement that only seven were his actual output: Romans, 1 and 2 Corinthians, Galatians, Philippians, 1 Thessalonians and Philemon. This opinion is based on the language of the texts, on allusions in the text and evident contradictions. It is very likely that even these seven had later additions inserted, sometimes substantial additions. The other six letters are forgeries (in the sense that they are not written by the one who is claimed to have written them): Ephesians, Colossians, 2 Thessalonians, 1 and 2 Timothy, Titus.[33] Hebrews was never seriously considered to have been written by Paul.

We can isolate three stages in the composition of the Letters of Paul. These stages are based on close attention to every line in their texts.

Stage 1: Letters
Paul began his program of evangelising small communities and he sent Letters to his churches in Asia Minor and Greece in order to maintain control as the founder. This was a ritual letter-writing. He developed his gospel of Jesus in the Letters and the Letters themselves acted with the power of God to affect the hearers. He also trained faithful leaders whom he could use as proxies and who would form the next generation of apostolic workers. The missionaries took his Letters to new locations.

---

[33] 1-2 Timothy plus Titus are known collectively as the Pastoral Letters. The three are forgeries.

Hence, Paul's Letters were transferable and were used in communities he had not sent them to. It was felt that they had a universal value, not tied to any circumstances of time or place. They also continued to be transferred after his death. Slowly, a collection of Letters was forming.

Stage 2: The Letter to the Romans

One of Paul's Letters was sent to the Romans. He himself had never been there. However, it would seem that some of his followers had reached the capital and it was to them that he wrote. They had found a Roman Christianity which assumed that all Christians were Gentiles. Paul had to instruct his own disciples as to how this new direction might be assimilated to what they had been taught. There is no evidence that Paul ever wrote to the whole collection of house-churches in Rome.

Clearly, Paul had his own following in Rome.

Stage 3: The writing of Acts and the Roman image of Paul

Next, came the writing of Acts in which Paul was presented as the true successor of Jesus who went to Rome as its apostle. It was able to accommodate the other 'successors', but they had been displaced by Paul. Acts' focus was to show how, from the beginnings, the risen Jesus had called Paul to be his missionary and he was elevated above the other leaders.

By the time of Acts the Roman Church was taking over the East. In fact, Luke had been written to clarify the situation of those in the East who needed to understand how the Roman Gospel of Mark could be reconciled with the early Jesus Sayings and the Jesus-Tradition. In short, it was the period of the assimilation of Greek, Asia Minor and Palestinian churches, founded by Paul and other Christian missionaries, into Roman Christianity.

Acts gave a new image of Paul and showed how the Letters were being interpreted at a later time after his death.

Stage 4: Roman Christian influence on the Letters of Paul

Roman Christian thinking overlay the teaching of Paul in his Letters. In this period, the Letters were edited or new Letters written as correctives. There were combinations of Letters, there was editing of existing Letters, there were insertions into Letters, there were Pauline forgeries.

On the other hand, other Letters were written in defence of Paul's more original teaching. Colossians and Ephesians were forgeries, written in Paul's name, to repudiate this new assimilation.

In more detail, the Roman influence on Paul's Collection of Letters included:

- Adding 'historical events', mostly in the form of autobiography, into the texts (visible when the seams are clear or when the material is clearly out of place). For example, Paul meeting Peter, James and John in Jerusalem in Galatians.

- Adding Roman theology into the Pauline text. For example, the insertion of the Last Supper text, the Resurrection Visions text and the prohibition of female participation in the liturgy into 1 Corinthians. Also the reference to the 'sacrificed Paschal Lamb' in 1 Corinthians 5:7 is a minor addition.

- Creation of forged Pauline Letters to protect Roman theology against the Gnostic pockets of Pauline Christians. 2 Thessalonians, 1-2 Timothy and Titus were all forged for this purpose.

- (Hebrews was simply added at a much later date to give it an author of repute. It was Roman, from Alexandria, and added to the Roman canon with Paul claimed as author at a much later date. It has no part in this reconstruction)

The end result of this literary activity was that Paul was sanitized for use in Roman Christian communities. Those Christians who had been his explicit followers in Rome must have accepted the inevitable and they too became Roman Christians.

The end result can be seen under Anicetus, Bishop of Rome from 155-166 CE. He compiled a succession list from Jesus for the first time, although our copy is handed on from Irenaeus in about 185. The list is headed, unexpectedly, by the 'Blessed Apostles' – both Peter and Paul!

Later, before the third century CE, this twin leadership would be revoked and the founder would be identified as solely Peter.

With this information on sources, we can now look at the three faces of Literary Paul, Historical Paul and Biblical Paul.

THE THREE PAULS

The study of Paul has examined the sources at the basis of the Pauline image. What we find, as with Israel and Jesus, is that there are a number of 'Pauls'. They must be carefully disentangled and their structure and purpose compared.

The Literary Paul

Literary Paul is the person of Paul presented by the Roman Church up to this day. Literary Paul has been based on the Acts of the Apostles and the thirteen Letters of Paul (Hebrews being usually excluded). The Acts of the Apostles is accepted as the second book written by Luke and it is read in tandem with the four gospels. The Letters of Paul are unquestioned as far as authenticity goes. They all propound the same message and that message expands on the Christian message of the rest of the Christian Scriptures.

Literary Paul is introduced to Christian readers by his dramatic conversion to Jesus on the way to Damascus, described in Galatians as an *apokalypsis* and in Acts in a lurid narrative of being thrown from a horse, light from heaven and a heavenly voice. Paul understood immediately that Jesus was the Son of God who had taken on human form and undergone his death and resurrection. For Paul, Jesus was the glorified Jesus in heaven. The Literary Paul of the Acts of the Apostles then finds his bearings and undertakes a series of missionary journeys, acting as the Apostle to the Gentiles, until his arrest in Jerusalem and his journey to Rome.

Distilling the teaching of Paul from the Letters generally we can find the key points, completing the image of Literary Paul found in Acts:

- All humans are sinful because of the Sin of Adam and personal sinfulness.
- God sent his Son, Jesus Christ, born of a woman, into the world to make satisfaction for this sinfulness.
- Jesus was foretold in detail in the Hebrew Scriptures and he established a New Covenant to replace the Old Covenant with Moses.
- Because of this, Christians do not need to become Jews.
- Christianity is open to all peoples.
- This era will come to an end with the return of Jesus and the final salvation of all believers.
- Jesus the Son is able to communicate saving grace to all who believe in him and are baptized.
- 'Grace' is brought about by the Holy Spirit who then makes a believer an adopted child of God, a member of the body of Christ and an heir to eternal life. The Christian, by baptism, participates in Jesus.

Literary Paul, as presented in the Acts of the Apostles and the Letters of Paul, has been at the cutting edge of subsequent Christian thinking. Augustine, Luther and the German theologians of the twentieth century took their lead from Literary Paul. Literary Paul has been interwoven with the four canonical gospels.

We can now turn to Historical Paul.

The Historical Paul

Historical Paul is the work of historians. They scour the text of the Acts of the Apostles and the texts of the Letters of Paul in order to try to uncover the Paul of History. What they have found has been the evidence of earlier sources, differences between Acts and the Letters and discrepancies that would make it almost impossible to write a history of Paul.

In Literary Paul the conversion, whether according to the description in Acts or in its counterpart in Galatians, is central to his image. But historians have wanted to look further at the account of the conversion.

In the Letter to the Galatians, Paul introduced his apostleship by the fact that he had had a Vision, an apocalypse (*apokalypsis*), an experience of divine interior election:

> But when God, who had set me apart before I was born and called me through his grace, was pleased to reveal [*apokalypsai*] his Son to me, so that I might proclaim him among the Gentiles ... (Gal 1:15-16)

This Vision, to which he also refers in two other Galatians' texts as a revelation, is placed on the same level as those of Peter, James and others. He had been chosen as a leader with equal standing compared to any of the others. Paul is here being compared particularly with James who was a 'Nazirite from his mother's womb' and who was reputed to have received his own Vision of Jesus.

The language in both Acts and Galatians indicates a profound 'conversion', from mainstream Judaism to a Jesus-movement. But its nature must be appreciated. It is not said that Paul ceased to be a Jew. That was never the issue. He simply changed factions within Judaism (although his change was drastic to many Jewish onlookers). He came to some transformative insight about Jesus and his teaching and moved across into the Jesus-movement. But in which Jesus faction did he find a home?

It is clear that he would not be immediately accepted; Paul-the-persecutor had changed overnight to Paul-the-Jesus-follower. There would have been biographical accounts of his missionary activities, including some astounding feats, such as the story of his escape from Damascus thus avoiding 'the Jews' (his former employers). These would have been oral traditions about a great founder.

He undoubtedly became a Christian-movement 'leader', admittedly one among others at that time, with a compulsion to hand on the profound experience he himself had undergone. He was only too clearly never a member of the Peter-group or the Brothers group or the Hellenists.

He seems, therefore, to have created what would have been a novel Christian theology based on Judaism. It is more consistent, but yet more radical, than that attributed to the Hellenists in the Stephen speech. The Stephen speech had maintained that God's revelation was available to 'all', presumably all Jews; Paul went further and specifically included the Gentiles. Their conversion would bring about the final salvation of God's people. The Stephen speech had stated that the Jews had not observed the Law, while Paul extended the boundaries by maintaining that the Law was actually untenable and so adherents were forced to sin. The Stephen speech held that the Temple was superseded; Paul maintained that the Jesus-movement of which he was the spokesperson formed a new, spiritual Temple.

Paul seems to have moved into Asia Minor to pursue his mission. Asia was a Roman term for the area earlier known as Anatolia (a Roman historian of the fourth century CE coined the term Asia Minor or Little Asia). It covered the expanse from the Black Sea to the Mediterranean. Prior to this period, Asia had been under a number of Greek kings and then became hellenized after the time of Alexander the Great in the fourth century BCE. In 133 BCE it came under Roman control although it still kept its Greek ways and institutions.

The Romans organized Asia Minor into a number of provinces. Along the west coast and into the interior there was Asia; along the Black Sea there were Mysia, Bithynia and Pontus; along the southern Mediterranean coast there were Lycia, Pamphylia and Cilicia; east of Asia there were Galatia and Cappadocia.

Roman control meant improvement in communication by well-built roads and safety from bandits.

Acts and Galatians (in a section that clearly shows signs of being a later Roman addition to the original text) relate that fourteen years later Paul went again to Jerusalem, having successfully set up Jesus-movement groups in Asia Minor, and with his new theological justification for accepting Gentiles well in place. He had made a radical break with mainstream Judaism and its hesitation over proselytising non-Jews. We are told in the Letter to the Galatians that, in Jerusalem, Paul confronted the three 'pillars' (*stuloi*): James, Cephas and John.

The meaning of the term *stulos* is not immediately evident. It could be that the term *stuloi* referred originally to 'pillars' as the disciples who established the foundation of a new spiritual temple. However that may be, the term certainly indicates that these *stuloi* in Jerusalem were separate leaders with separate authority and of great importance. Acts' reference would infer that there had been two major Jesus-movement factions from whom Paul required authorization: the group who looked to the leadership of James and that of Cephas and John.

In Galatians, however, the terminology is used very carefully. In reference to both the leadership of the three men and their being 'pillars' Paul points out that the choice of words is not his own. They are only 'considered' or 'acknowledged' (*dokein*) to be leaders and 'pillars'. The term *dokein* is repeated four times in Galatians 2 in relation to them. Its normal usage indicates an appearance without reality, and this seems to be the meaning intended by the text.

What would explain the complexities of this matter is that Acts was relying on an oral or written tradition that Paul had confronted the *stuloi*. In the text he expressed his doubts about their qualification as leaders (he would eventually replace the three of them). Acts reworked the tradition; this narrative was inserted later into Galatians; it was not from Paul's hand.

But the rule of the *stuloi* in Jerusalem could hardly be historical. They were three separate leaders working in three different constituencies. We will see that 'John' was regarded as the leader of Western Asia Christianity, but even in that context the identity of this John is debatable. James the Brother of the Lord was certainly based in Jerusalem, but there is no evidence that Peter had a basis there. The idea of the triumvirate in Jerusalem is a fiction. The Jerusalem Council reflects the conflict between Paul and other established Jesus-movement groups, as would have been reflected in traditions such as that of confronting Peter:

> [11] But when Cephas came to Antioch, I opposed him to his face, because he stood self-condemned; [12] for until certain people came from James, he used to eat with the Gentiles. But after they came, he drew back and kept himself separate for fear of the circumcision faction. [13] And the other Jews joined him in this hypocrisy, so that even Barnabas was led astray by their hypocrisy. [14] But when I saw that they were not acting consistently with the truth of the gospel, I said to Cephas before them all, 'If you, though a Jew, live like a Gentile and not like a Jew, how can you compel the Gentiles to live like Jews?'

Paul had not joined any of the existing Jesus-movement groups. Moreover, it has always been puzzling that Paul was claimed by the later Gnostics as one of their own. Marcion who came to Rome in 140 CE and Valentinus, stalwart Gnostic leaders long after the time of Paul, asserted that he had been a Gnostic leader.

Here, we need to make a surprising claim, an hypothesis based on the analysis of the genuine Letters of Paul. It seems that Paul was a Gnostic. Dissatisfied with the form of Judaism (probably Pharisaic) in which he had been inducted, and probably already dabbling in Greek philosophy, he had turned to the Jesus-movement and saw the possibilities for himself in it. It gave his life purpose and a mission. He had a Gnostic *apokalypsis*.

First, it has long been noted that Paul was never interested in an Historical Jesus. When the Searchers for an Historical Jesus went to their sources they did not begin with Paul. There is nothing there in authentic Paul about Jesus, no events and only a few references to sayings. The Searchers had to begin with Mark or perhaps Thomas. In fact, Paul was interested only in the Divine Jesus.

> [3] For God has done what The Law, weakened by the Flesh, could not do: by sending his own Son in the likeness of sinful Flesh, and to deal with sin, he condemned sin in the Flesh, [4] so that the just requirement of The Law might be fulfilled in us, who walk not according to the Flesh but according to the Spirit. [5] For those who live according to the Flesh set their minds on the things of the Flesh, but those who live according to the Spirit set their minds on the things of the Spirit. [6] To set the mind on the Flesh is death, but to set the mind on the Spirit is life and peace. [7] For this reason the mind that is set on the Flesh is hostile to God; it does not submit to God's Law—indeed it cannot, [8] and those who are in the Flesh cannot please God.
> [9] But you are not in the Flesh; you are in the Spirit, since the Spirit of God dwells in you. Anyone who does not have the Spirit of Christ does not belong to him. [10] But if Christ is in you, though the body is dead because of sin, the Spirit is life because of righteousness. (Romans 8:3-10)

This is a Gnostic statement. Christ in the Flesh could never be the source of Christian salvation. It was the Spirit that gave life. The Jewish Law centred on the Flesh; the sign of belonging in the Flesh was circumcision. To the Philippians he writes about physical circumcision:

> [2] Beware of the dogs, beware of the evil workers, beware of those who mutilate the flesh! [3] For it is we who are the circumcision, who worship in the Spirit of God and boast in Christ Jesus and have no confidence in the flesh – [4] even though I, too, have reason for confidence in the flesh.

Paul claims the exclusivity of a metaphorical 'circumcision' for the spiritual ones, not for those who physically mutilate the human body. Exactly the same contention has been found in the *Gospel of Thomas*:

His disciples said to him: 'Is circumcision beneficial, or not?'
He said to them: 'If it were beneficial, their father would beget them
circumcized from their mother.
But the true circumcision in the spirit has prevailed over everything.'
(logion 53)

What about the historical death of Jesus in Paul?

It is never treated as an historical event. True enough, Paul says that everyone, all sinful humanity, is offered salvation via the death of Jesus on the cross. But how was this achieved? What was the process?

It was not by the Father's sacrifice of Jesus for human sinfulness, as the Synoptics imply and most Christians today continue to uphold. A sacrifice required a physical death, suffering and blood. Paul's approach to the death of Jesus, however, was connected with the notion of participation. The believers participate in Jesus who lived, died and rose again. Jesus came in the Flesh to perform his mission, divested himself of the Flesh through the crucifixion and was resurrected to Eternal Life. But what Paul describes as the death and the resurrection, although real, are nevertheless not physical events. It is from this participation in Jesus' Gnostic Death and Resurrection that Christians attain salvation and experience the Righteousness of the Father.

Nor is there mention of an Empty Tomb or of witnesses to a Jesus-event afterwards. The text in 1 Corinthians, giving a list of those who had Jesus-visions, is a later insertion. Christians are not saved by a blood-sacrifice; they are saved by participation in a divine Being, Christ.

Paul's principal teaching is therefore participation in Jesus.[34] It is based on the Gnostic theme of *gnosis;* it is a profound spiritual experience. Hence, to the Romans he wrote:

How can we who died to sin go on living in it? [3] Do you not know that all of us who have been baptized into Christ Jesus were baptized into his death? [4] Therefore we have been buried with him by baptism into death, so that, just as Christ was raised from the dead by the glory of the Father, so we too might walk in newness of life.

[5] For if we have been united with him in a death like his, we will certainly be united with him in a resurrection like his. [6] We know that our old self was crucified with him so that the body of sin might be destroyed, and we might no longer be enslaved to sin. [7] For whoever has

---

[34] This has curiously become orthodox Christian teaching in more recent times. Paul's texts on participation were the mainstay of the Catholic Church's statement on the Mystical Body of Christ. This Church formulation (summarized in an Encyclical Letter of Pius XII, *Mystici Corporis*, published in 1943), completely misunderstands the Gnostic depths of Paul.

died is freed from sin. [8] But if we have died with Christ, we believe that
we will also live with him. [9] We know that Christ, being raised from
the dead, will never die again; death no longer has dominion over him.
[10] The death he died, he died to sin, once for all; but the life he lives,
he lives to God. [11] So you also must consider yourselves dead to sin and
alive to God in Christ Jesus. (6: 2-11)

This is what Gnostic baptism signifies: that the possessor of *gnosis*
already participates in Jesus and has already been saved.

Participation in the writings of Paul himself also means that there is
no resurrection of the Flesh and certainly no Second Coming at the End of
Times. At this point we should examine the passage in 1 Corinthians 15,
which had Roman correctives inserted.

The text will be interposed with a commentary.

[40]There are both heavenly bodies and earthly bodies, but the glory of
the heavenly is one thing, and that of the earthly is another. [41]There is
one glory of the sun, and another glory of the moon, and another glory
of the stars; indeed, star differs from star in glory.

The first distinction made by Paul is between heavenly bodies and
earthly bodies. Among the heavenly bodies there are distinctions of Glory.
The *pneumatikoi* are 'stars' in this hierarchy of Glory. The term was used
prominently in the Gospel of Judas. Judas was told by Jesus that he is a leading Star:

Lift up your eyes and look at the Cloud and the Light within it and the
Stars surrounding it. The Star that leads the way is your Star. (57)

Paul's text continues, once this distinction has been made.

[42] So it is with the resurrection of the dead. What is sown is perishable,
what is raised is imperishable. [43] It is sown in dishonour, it is raised
in glory. It is sown in weakness, it is raised in power. [44] It is sown a
physical body, it is raised a spiritual body. If there is a physical body,
there is also a spiritual body.

Paul now explains the 'resurrection of the dead' for the Corinthians. For
the *pneumatikoi* there is a new life, no longer controlled by Flesh. What is
the mechanism behind this?

[45] Thus it is written, 'The First Man, Adam, became a living being'; the
Last Adam became a life-giving Spirit. [46] But it is not the spiritual that is
first, but the physical, and then the spiritual. [47] The First Man was from
the earth, a man of dust; the Second Man is from heaven. [48] As was
the Man of Dust, so are those who are of the dust; and as is the Man of

Heaven, so are those who are of heaven. [49] Just as we have borne the image of the Man of Dust, we will also bear the Image of the Man of Heaven.

This is straight Gnostic theology. Adamas, the divine Emanation, had a counterpart in the earthly sphere – Adam and his generation. They were made of dust. But Jesus has come as the Second Man, the Man of Heaven. Those who adhere to Adam remain of the earth. They must adhere to the Second Man, Jesus, to 'bear his Image [*eikon*]'. There is no mention of Roman Christianity's blood sacrifice.

Paul continues:

[50] What I am saying, brothers and sisters, is this: flesh and blood cannot inherit the Kingdom of God, nor does the perishable inherit the imperishable.

Paul makes his case absolutely clear. It is not Flesh, not the Perishable that will achieve the final union.

[51] Listen, I will tell you a mystery! We will not all die, but we will all be changed, [52] in a moment, in the twinkling of an eye [Roman corrective: *at the last trumpet. For the trumpet will sound, and the dead will be raised imperishable, and we will be changed.*] [53] For this perishable body must put on imperishability, and this mortal body must put on immortality. [54] When this perishable body puts on imperishability, and this mortal body puts on immortality, then the saying that is written will be fulfilled:
'Death has been swallowed up in victory.'
[55] 'Where, O Death, is your victory?
Where, O Death, is your sting?'

[Roman corrective: [56] *The sting of Death is sin, and the power of sin is The Law.* [57] *But thanks be to God, who gives us the victory through our Lord Jesus Christ.*]

Paul now makes known the *mysterion*, the divine plan that has existed from the Beginning. When the body of Flesh finds *gnosis*, then there is no real death. The Resurrection has taken place already. But another hand has clearly (and awkwardly) added a comment to Paul's text. This will take place at the End of the World (not now!).

Paul's language, when not muted by modern Christian translations, is only too obviously written in Gnostic language. The NSRV reads in 1 Corinthians 2:

[6] Yet among the mature we do speak wisdom, though it is not a wisdom of this age or of the rulers of this age, who are doomed to perish. [7] But

we speak God's wisdom, secret and hidden, which God decreed before the ages for our glory. [8] None of the rulers of this age understood this; for if they had, they would not have crucified the Lord of glory. [9] But, as it is written,

'What no eye has seen, nor ear heard,
nor the human heart conceived,
what God has prepared for those who love him' ...

This seems acceptable orthodox Roman Christianity. 'The rulers of this age' are the Jews and those linked to them. 'Wisdom' was one of the manifestations of Yahweh in later Jewish thought. The final verse instructs the Corinthians on their future life in Heaven.

But if we translate the same Greek with Gnostic terminology in mind, then we have the following, making sense of the formerly opaque text:

[6] Yet among the *Perfect Ones* we do speak about *Sophia*, though it is not the *Sophia* of *this Aeon* or of the *Archons of this Aeon*, who are doomed to perish. [7] But we speak of *God's Sophia*, secret and hidden, which God decreed before the *Aeons for our Glory*. [8] None of the *Archons of this Aeon* understood this; for if they had, they would not have crucified the *Lord of Glory*. [9] But, as it is written,

'What no eye has seen, nor ear heard,
nor the human heart conceived,
what God has prepared for those who love him' ...

Here is the Gnostic language of Sophia, the Perfect Ones, Aeon, Rulers of this Aeon, Glory, the Lord of Glory. This is not Roman orthodoxy. Paul is speaking, as a Gnostic Leader, to those who were on the way to *gnosis*. Sophia has been returned back to the *Pleroma*; her restitution had been part of the divine plan. The Archons of this Aeon fell into the trap and seemed to crucify Jesus, thus fulfilling the plan for Jesus to divest himself of the appearance of Flesh. The similarity of this ending to the Gospel of Thomas, logion 17, is apparent:

Jesus says: 'I will give you what no eye has seen, and what no ear has heard,
and what no hand has touched, and what has not occurred to the human mind.'

Likewise, in the Gospel of Judas we find this text relative to the revelation of the divinity:

A great invisible Spirit,
which no eye of an angel has ever seen,
no thought of the heart has ever comprehended,
and it was never called by any name.

Thomas and Judas talk of the object of *gnosis*. Are they copying Paul's text? More likely the three are copying a Gnostic source.

In short, Paul was a Gnostic who endeavoured unsuccessfully to make overtures with other Jesus-movement groups. He realized that his preaching on Gnostic matters, with Jesus as the divine Son of God, would not be immediately met with understanding. He adapted himself to the circumstances, as he later explained in 1 Corinthians 9:

> [19] For though I am free with respect to all, I have made myself a slave to all, so that I might win more of them. [20] To the Jews I became as a Jew, in order to win Jews. To those under The Law I became as one under The Law (though I myself am not under The Law) so that I might win those under The Law. [21] To those outside The Law I became as one outside The Law (though I am not free from God's law but am under Christ's law) so that I might win those outside The Law .
> [22] To the weak I became weak, so that I might win the weak. I have become all things to all people, so that I might by any means save some. [23] I do it all for the sake of the gospel, so that I may share in its blessings.

The final events in the life of Paul according to Acts are likewise questionable as an historical narrative. Peter had finally gone to 'another place'. We have already noted that this could be anywhere except Rome according to the author of Acts.

Paul in Acts now becomes the leading character in a Passion play. He is arrested after a scuffle in the Temple. He is brought before the Jewish authorities, the Roman governor and the Jewish king Herod Agrippa (only Luke mentions Jesus being paraded before Herod the Tetrarch). He is subjected to a long journey that ends not on Golgotha but in Rome. The Passion of Paul and his Journey to Rome is too close to the Passion and Journey of Jesus to the Cross to be trusted. His end was described as parallel to that of Jesus. Acts wanted him in Rome at the end to displace the idea that Peter had established Roman Christianity. Paul had been the hero figure.

We have already seen that the Christian elder, Gaius, had written in the second half of the second century that there were two *tropaia* or memorials in Rome: one for Peter and one for Paul. That seems to have been the historical compromise. Roman Christians were split in their allegiance: some looked to Peter, some looked to Paul. Each faction had its own *tropaion*.

Where does archaeology stand on the *tropaion* of Paul? Is it a tomb of Paul? We are in exactly the same position as with the tomb of Peter where there was serious doubt expressed about the historicity of the death and burial of the historical Peter in Rome.

Paul's *tropaion* was on the Via Ostia. It now lies under the Basilica of Saint Paul Outside the Walls. The Basilica was also built by Constantine over the presumed burial place of Paul. From the time of Constantine this Basilica was extended and rebuilt. In the fifth century it was called the *Basilica Trium Dominorum* (the Basilica of the Three Lords) since two other martyrs were said to have been buried with him. Earthquake, pillage and fire have made the present basilica unrecognizable from the Constantinian construction.

There were reports that in the fourth century CE the remains of Paul were placed in a sarcophagus beneath a marble tombstone within the basilica with the inscription: *Paulo Apostolo Mart* (To Paul the apostle and martyr). This is some three centuries after any presumed death of Paul.

The basilica was almost completely destroyed by fire in 1823 and completely rebuilt from its foundations. Although a sarcophagus was recorded as being found in a local Benedictine chronicle, there is no mention of it in the excavators' notes.

Then, in December 2006, the discovery of a white marble sarcophagus under the high altar of St Paul's Outside the Walls by Vatican Museum archaeologist, Giorgio Filippi, was announced. Evidently the archaeological work had been going on since 2002. The inscribed tombstone has three holes – two square and one circular. The circular hole opens into a pipeline into the sarcophagus. The most obvious interpretation would be that the holes would be for pouring libations into the sarcophagus or providing the dead with drink.

By 2009 a hole was drilled into the sarcophagus. Inside was purple cloth, laminated with gold. There were also grains of incense. Tiny fragments of bone were found and dated by Carbon-14 testing to the first or second century.

Benedict XVI announced that the body of Paul had been found in these words: 'This seems to confirm the unanimous and undisputed tradition that these are the mortal remains of the Apostle Paul.' It needs to be said that the evidence behind Benedict XVI's declaration, timed to mark the end of the celebrations of the 2000th anniversary of the birth of Paul, is flimsy.

Constantine had form for 'enhancing' his basilicas both in the East and in Rome. If there were ever a body, it would have been moved many times. The sarcophagus was not inscribed with 'Paul, Apostle and Martyr', as even official statements maintain. It was inscribed with 'To Paul, Apostle and Martyr' which seems to indicate a memorial. The bone shards are dated to the first or second centuries. A second century date would certainly disprove that they came from Paul. There is a long distance between a supposed death of Paul in Rome in the first century and these remains.

In fact, there is no strong evidence that Paul ever went to Rome.

So, we find that there two claimants to being the founder of Christianity in Rome. One was Peter, as in Roman Christian tradition. The other was Paul, as put forward by Acts.

In the contest, Paul lost and Peter was established in the mind of the Roman Christians as leader and his position was absolutely confirmed by Constantine. For Roman Christianity, Peter became the sole founding *apostolos* of Rome.

This has been Historical Paul. Historical Paul is not the object of reverence in the Roman Christian Church of the past or the present. Historical Paul must be seen within the domain of the historian, not in the domain of Christian believers.

Biblical Paul

Most of the faithful in the churches today know only of the Biblical Paul.

Biblical Paul is a mixture of the Historical Paul and the Literary Paul. The image of the Biblical Paul is taken from studies on the Historical Paul (not all astute studies). Based on various sources, a 'life of Paul' is recreated. These sources include of course the Acts of the Apostles and the Letters of Paul. They are supplemented by archaeological finds from the places mentioned in the earlier sources: Jerusalem, Damascus, Tarsus, Galatia, Ephesus, Athens and so on. A historical web, using this archaeology and other data from geography and the social sciences, is then woven around the Biblical Paul.

Biblical Paul, it must be stressed, is not Historical Paul, although it uses Historical Paul. In general, Biblical Paul is a figure who never existed and was never intended to be Literary Paul. Literary Paul carries, by definition, all the discrepancies of events found in Acts and the final edition of the Letters of Paul. This Literary Paul is the image of Paul as another Jesus, but the Jesus as found in the Roman Church.

Biblical Paul offers nothing to either historian or believer.

This study of Paul is vital to the argument in this book. The Historical Paul was a Gnostic. His memory and his writings were over-written by the Roman Church. He became a Roman saint, for some time even regarded as a co-founder of the Roman Church. This was the Literary Paul outcome; it was not history.

What will follow about the Johannine Christianity in Western Asia Minor requires this prior study of Paul as background.

NOTES

There are innumerable studies on Paul, on the Pauline Letters, both in general and in particular, and on Pauline theology.

Some specific studies that have been of help in the construction of this chapter are the following:

Crossan, J. & Reed, J. (2004), *In Search of Paul*, HarperSanFrancisco: New York.

Wills, G. (2006), *What Paul Meant*, Viking: New York.

Westerholm, S. (ed.) (2014), *The Blackwell Companion to Paul*, Wiley Blackwell: Chichester.

Akenson, D. (2000), *Saint Saul: A Skeleton Key to the Historical Jesus*, Oxford University Press: Oxford, New York.

CHRISTIANITY IN
WESTERN ASIA MINOR

WESTERN ASIA MINOR PLAYED a vital part in the story of early Christianity. There were churches established along the Mediterranean coast by Paul and his missionaries. We can tell from the tenor of Paul's genuine Letters that these new establishments were not without their troubles. But Paul also complained about the inroads of other Jesus-movement groups in Asia Minor. He was not the only Christian missionary in those parts.

The same area and some of the same communities were those to whom the Book of Revelation was addressed. It was also in this area that traditionally the writing and first dissemination of John's gospel was said to have circulated.

The general area has been described when dealing with the Historical Paul. The establishments connected with a certain John are on the west coast.

In this section we will concentrate on John of Patmos and the John of the Book of Revelation who flourished in Western Asia Minor. These are antecedents to the John whose name has been appended to the Gospel of John.

JOHN OF PATMOS

The third *stulos* or Christian leader, after Peter and James, was named 'John' in the Acts of the Apostles. Who was this John?

There are, disconcertingly, several Johns (apart from John the Baptist, who is easily recognized) in the early Christian period. There was John who was named by the Synoptics as a member of the Twelve under Peter; he was also one of the inner Synoptic triad of 'Peter, James and John' who accompanied Jesus at key moments in the gospel narrative. Tradition named him as the author of the Gospel of John.

There was also John of Patmos who named himself as the author of the Book of Revelation, addressed to seven Christian communities in Western

Asia Minor. The book was a concoction of Jewish apocalyptic imagery that pointed to the End of Times, but the imagery was set in a Christian context.

There was perhaps one other John who wrote three Letters, contained in the canon of the Christian Scriptures, to certain Christian groups. This John was, from an early date, identified with the author of the gospel.

We will begin with John of Patmos. His name derives from the fact that he identified the location of his calling to be a prophet as being on the island of Patmos, off the coast of modern Turkey.

> [9] I, John, your brother who share with you in Jesus the persecution
> and the kingdom and the patient endurance, was on the island called
> Patmos because of the word of God and the testimony of Jesus. [10] I was
> in the spirit on the Lord's Day, and I heard behind me a loud voice like
> a trumpet [11] saying, 'Write in a book what you see and send it to the
> seven churches, to Ephesus, to Smyrna, to Pergamum, to Thyatira, to
> Sardis, to Philadelphia, and to Laodicea.'

There are some things to note about the seven cities in Western Asia Minor addressed in the Book of Revelation. First, it is notable that six of the seven cities were dominated by Roman imperial temples. These had been built in Asia Minor by local rulers in the aftermath of the assassination of Caesar in 44 BCE. The local rulers had backed Mark Antony and Cleopatra in their quest for power and rued the day they had. In fact, Antony and Cleopatra had set up a centre in Ephesus to try to garner support for their cause against Octavian. When Octavian was victorious in 31 BCE at the decisive Battle of Actium, there was a rush by the same rulers, compromised because of their earlier adhesion to Antony, to build temples in sycophantic honour of the victor, Octavian, and the Roman gods.

Second, some of these cities would at an earlier date have been visited by Paul. Either he or his missionaries would have set up the earliest Gnostic Jesus-movement communities in them. Of the seven cities situated along the western coastline Paul had spent a long period at Ephesus and had certainly established a following there. Explicitly, we also know from Colossians 2 that he had direct contact with Laodicea:

> [1] For I want you to know how much I am struggling for you, and for
> those in Laodicea, and for all who have not seen me face to face.

The reference to 'not seen me face to face' is intriguing. There were obviously other centres in the area, established by his missionaries, who had had no personal contact with Paul. There is no reason to doubt that in the seven churches nominated by John of Patmos, Pauline Christians were long established, even if Paul himself had not visited them.

However, in these seven places, where Roman worship was established and Pauline Gnostic churches flourished, John of Patmos saw the palpable presence of Evil. However, there are some unusual references to such evil; it is found among the existing Christians, not the Gentiles. In Philadelphia, for example, he found some Christians who evidently claimed to be on a par with Jews.

> [9] I will make those of the synagogue of Satan who say that they are Jews and are not, but are lying – I will make them come and bow down before your feet, and they will learn that I have loved you.

This would seem to indicate Pauline Christians to be the culprits, mostly Gentiles, those to whom Paul had addressed this message:

> [27] As many of you as were baptized into Christ have clothed yourselves with Christ. [28] There is no longer Jew or Greek, there is no longer slave or free, there is no longer male and female; for all of you are one in Christ Jesus. [29] And if you belong to Christ, then you are Abraham's offspring, heirs according to the promise. (Galatians 3:28-29)

John of Patmos rejected their claims outright.

John of Patmos also decried the 'prophesying' or ecstatic behaviour which was evidently rife among the Asia Minor Christians. Thus he wrote to the city of Pergamum in chapter 2:15 identifying it with 'Satan's throne' and decrying the fact that they followed the Nicolaitans,

This text made it clear, by its reference to the Nicolaitans (descended, as we have noted earlier, from Nicolaus the Hellenist), that the Enemy in this case was Gnosticism. John of Patmos rejected their claim to be Jews, members of Israel, as well as their claim to divine inspiration for their prophecies.

John of Patmos must have flourished as an apocalyptic preacher on his island home and perhaps he had taken refuge there. This could have been as a result of playing a part in the turmoil after the destruction of Jerusalem in 70 CE and the disturbances connected with subsequent Jewish uprisings. These disturbances would have brought economic strife together with social instability and the whole situation would have been attributed to the Emperor of Rome.

At some time and somewhere John of Patmos had had his Christian experience and became a Jesus-movement follower. He would have come to the Western Asia Minor scene later than other Christian leaders, perhaps towards the end of the first century CE. Christian groups were already firmly established there. He had never been an eyewitness to the Jesus events; he would probably not have been even born then. He was a Christian apocalyptic mystic, schooled in the thinking of Jewish imagery and its Christian counterpart.

Most importantly, he would have been at least indirectly responsible for the Book of Revelation, although he would not have been its major author.

JOHN'S BOOK OF REVELATION

The Book of Revelation is Christian apocalyptic. It belongs to a literary genre that uses symbols to pass judgement on world events and to foretell events that will occur in the future. Essentially the author, narrator or principal personage in this genre is a seer, who has been granted an *apokalypsis* not in its Gnostic sense but in the sense of a penetration into the divine workings and plans lying beneath observable events. The *apokalypsis* has been mediated by a divine being such as an angel, or famous figure from the past, or a heavenly book. The mediation would have taken the form of a vision, an audition or a heavenly journey.

The result is that the seer receives secret knowledge about the unknown working of the cosmos and, perhaps more importantly, the future secret events that will soon take place in the cosmos. Obviously the seers could retain this secret knowledge, but they are constrained to divulge it to a particular audience either by word, action or writing. Apocalyptic writing is simply the written form of the seer's revelation. As such, it acts as a replication of the original *apokalypsis* with a transfer of the secret knowledge to those who can understand.

The texts use mainly mythic imagery from the Hebrew Scriptures such as the Book of Daniel (which in turn at times had made use of wider, Near Eastern imagery).

The text of the canonical Book of Revelation is clearly an amalgam of parts. The seams are quite visible. The Introduction and Conclusion were used to give some earlier apocalyptic items a commonality and to direct them to existing churches in Western Asia Minor. Gathered into the body of the text were three Apocalyptic Discourses. Two of these provided a vision of the future by the use of similar symbols. Some of the symbols overlap in each Discourse (for example, the Sixth Trumpet and the Sixth Bowl). Each Discourse has its own natural conclusion. There is a Third Apocalyptic Discourse describing the Heavenly Jerusalem in mythic terms. Finally, at the end of the Book, there are eight separate apocalyptic statements in no particular order, added as a compendium.

This is not an ordered book. It has gathered together a number of apocalyptic sources and put them into order with a fitting introduction and conclusion. How can John of Patmos and the book of Revelation be situated into a presumed history of Western Asia Minor? First, we need to look at the seven churches named in the book of Revelation: Ephesus, Smyrna, Pergamum, Thyatira, Sardis, Philadelphia and Laodicea. They were Roman strongholds and Roman religion would have prevailed. However, Paul would have had direct or indirect contact with them and his Gnostic churches would have been established from an early date. The mention of the Nicolaitans would indicate that other Gnostic groups had penetrated the area too.

Faced with the evidence we have, the following sequence is suggested:

Stage 1

Jesus-movement communities were set up in Western Asia Minor by unknown early Jesus-movement members. Some of the communities would have been established by Paul. Either personally or through his missionaries his Gnostic influence would have been palpable in the area.

Other communities would have been set up by other Gnostic Christians. The mention of Nicolaus would seem to indicate that The Seven, associated with Stephen, were the leaders of a Christian Gnostic movement.

In this situation, the Letters of Paul must have played a role. In fact, however, we have no genuine Letters of Paul pertaining to Western Asia Minor (Galatia probably refers to the Roman province in the south of Asia Minor). Paul's Letters to the Ephesians and Colossians were written in his name, but after his time. Ephesians upheld Gnostic teaching and attacks on it after Paul's demise; Colossians likewise encouraged its recipients to continue to interpret Jesus from a Gnostic viewpoint. The Pastoral Letters were Pseudo-Paul, whoever their recipients might have been. They uphold a Roman-like system of Christian rule. We are tempted to think that the Collection of Letters (including some or all of the Letters to the Galatians, Corinthians, Thessalonians, Philippians, Philemon and Romans – but without Roman additions) may have circulated in this area too. Certainly, Romans seems to have been later re-directed to addressees among the Ephesians.

Hence, we can conjecture that Paul was one of a number of Christian missionaries in Western Asia Minor, but a very forceful one. He must have founded communities; he may have influenced communities that were already founded. These communities, whether founded by Paul or not, were basically Gnostic.

Stage 2

This situation in Western Asia Minor attracted attention from the Palestinian area. Gnostic Christians saw there a religious haven where they could live in peace. In the Palestinian setting they had not been welcomed, neither by the mainstream Jews nor by the James-Christians nor by groups such as the Peter-Christians. These Gnostics brought with them their own version or versions of the Jesus-Tradition and they joined the existing Gnostic groups. Amongst these traditions there was the collection we have come to know as the Book of Seven Signs, a number of Gnostic Treatises and a number of Gnostic Discourses. These were combined at some time into a Gnostic compendium.

These Palestinian Gnostics looked back to their founder – the Beloved Disciple, a very influential character. The Beloved Disciple's identity will be dealt with later.

Western Asia Minor remained very open to Gnostic thinking. Clement of Alexandria in the third century CE unfavourably includes part of the writings of the Gnostic Theodotos in the previous century in his own work. Theodotos was a Gnostic and came from Asia Minor and can be dated to the second century CE. The Gnostic Montanus, whom we will discuss again, came from the area of Phyrgia. More, the well-known Gnostic, Marcion of Sinope, came from Pontus in Asia Minor where his father was a presbyter. Having fallen into grave trouble with the Christian authorities in Rome he returned to Asia Minor. He claimed, as we mentioned, Paul as a Gnostic leader.

In short, Western Asia Minor was a hive of Gnostic activity during the first century CE.

Stage 3

After the death of Paul and after the presumed arrival of the Palestinian Gnostics, John of Patmos came to Western Asia Minor. He was a charismatic figure. In Asia Minor he was appalled by the Christian thought and practice he found there. He addressed the churches either by preaching or letter. He wanted to instigate Christian apocalyptic thinking with the slaughter of Jesus as an atoning death, the condemnation of Imperial Rome and the glorious *parousia* [the second coming or return] of Jesus to bring the world soon to an end. His apocalyptic was not Roman Christianity, but it was even less Gnostic in tone.

John of Patmos produced apocalyptic sayings and perhaps texts adapted to the Jesus-movement. They were florid accounts of the mysteries of the present and future. These were edited and expanded. A collection of texts, still attributed to John of Patmos although he would probably not have been the author in today's sense of the word, were gathered and directed against seven major churches in Asia Minor by his disciples. The book of Revelation, so formed from three major apocalypses and addressed to the key churches of Asia Minor, was a literary device. It is clear that the choice of seven for the number of addressees is artificial.

Apocalyptic Christianity was confronting Pauline Christianity and Gnosticism in Western Asia Minor.

Stage 4

But there was a new force that came to Western Asia Minor.

Roman Christianity had moved into the East from the first century BCE. The area of Western Asia Minor was already ready for Roman intervention and had been much more open than the rest of the Near East. There was a great deal of political confusion and the last king controlling most of Anatolia had bequeathed his possessions to the Romans in 133 BCE. Roman Christianity, as we have seen, followed the trail of Roman possessions in the Mediterranean area.

Roman Christianity found Christian communities in Western Asia Minor in disarray. There was a Gnostic tendency among the Pauline Christian establishments, there were the Gnostic communities from Palestine and there was an apocalyptic challenge to this Gnosticism from the disciples of John of Patmos. Roman Christianity attempted to impose its own form of the Jesus-movement on the area.

Roman Christianity would have found some form of the Book of Revelation already in circulation. It accepted it because it contained the key ideas of a sacrificed Jesus, a final eschatology and no challenges to its own theology. It read well with its colourful mythic prose alongside Mark, Matthew and Luke. It became a Roman book, eventually a part of its canon.

Of great importance, Roman Christianity also found a final version of a Gnostic gospel with its component parts. It was the loose compendium of Gnostic thinking mentioned earlier. Cleverly, Roman traditions were interposed into the Gnostic collection; Roman editorial additions and corrections were made to its text. The Gospel of John was created from Gnostic antecedent parts and became a Roman gospel.

The gospel was attributed to 'John'. Which 'John'? By this stage the influence of John of Patmos was widespread and he was regarded as a great figure from the past. His apocalyptic teaching had made a huge impression on the area, even if he had not been fully understood. Despite the opposition of John of Patmos to Gnostic thinking, there was a fairly easy compromise between his apocalypticism and Gnosticism. Then, Roman Christians had their point of view inserted. The apocalyptic teaching of the Book of Revelation and the accounts of the Gnostic compendium were adapted to Roman Christian theological thought. The end result was the Gospel of John.

Within Western Asia Minor there was the memory of a great founder, John. This would have been John of Patmos. The Romans made another change: John of Patmos was unknown in the Gospel of Mark. The Roman Christians unseated John of Patmos and instated their own 'John', the son of Zebedee, one of The Twelve in the Gospel of Mark. John of Zebedee became known as the author of the new Gospel of John, the author of the Book of Revelation and the Roman founder of the Christian communities in Western Asia Minor. He was readily identified with the anonymous Beloved Disciple looked upon by the newcomer Gnostics as their leader. John of Zebedee was supreme.

At a later date three letters were issued from a 'John' in Asia Minor but only from about 200-250 CE. The author was 'The Elder' who obviously had control of a group of Christian churches. They show that the seams between the different communities were never quite sealed. The Elder is still battling Gnosticism and still battling those who refuse to accept Roman Christian teaching. But the important fact is that there was still a leader, a Roman Christian and there was still opposition. He was a leader stemming from 'John'.

Together with Cephas and James the Brother of Jesus, John of Zebedee became one of the founders, a *stulos*, of early Christianity. Acts would, first of all, place all three together in Jerusalem in the fictive Jerusalem Council and then dethrone the three of them in favour of Paul.

Stage 5

Eventually, Roman Christianity dominated in Western Asia Minor, even though there were pockets of resistance. The Romanized Gospel of John, the Letters of The Elder, the Book of Revelation became Roman Christian documents. They had to be interpreted within the parameters of the Roman Gospel of Mark.

Having outlined these five stages of development in Western Asian church development and writing, we will attempt to reconcile what has been said about the three *stuloi* with the text of Acts. Acts recognized that after the death of Jesus there was a triumvirate who controlled the Jesus-movements: Peter or Cephas, James the Brother of the Lord and a John. Acts also acknowledged that there was another James who was executed early in the days of the Jesus-movement and this one was the brother of the *stulos*, John. Zebedee, the father of James and John in the Synoptics is, however, never mentioned in Acts. This John of Zebedee was only given a minor part in the text of Acts regarding missionary activity.

What of John's gospel on this matter? He does not even mention a disciple called John, despite the fact that the Beloved Disciple in that gospel is regularly identified with John. The reference in ch. 21 to the 'sons of Zebedee' is in an appended tradition that derived from Roman Christianity.

So we have John of Patmos, John of Zebedee, brother of James, John the author of a Gospel, John the author of three Letters, and the Beloved Disciple (also identified as John, the brother of James of Zebedee). Can we account for these Johns?

Let us suppose that the Markan 'inner triad' of Peter, James of Zebedee and John of Zebedee is a fiction. In fact the case can be proposed that they are a Markan version of 'Peter, James the Brother of the Lord and John of Patmos'. They would never have actually been together in the same time or place. We have also proposed that The Twelve, to which the three Markan apostles (Peter, James and John) belonged, would also have been a later construct. Paul's description in Galatians of his meeting with the three *stuloi* in Jerusalem for a discussion is an addition to the Galatian text, a forged entry. At some time the Roman tradition had made James the Brother of the Lord into James the Brother of John, with a concocted father, Zebedee, and the John lauded as the founder of Christianity in Western Asia Minor as John of Zebedee.

Why? Possibly because there was a fixed memory in the Jesus-Tradition that the three great leaders and founders were Peter, James the Brother of the Lord and 'John'. Peter's identity was clear. James the Brother of the Lord was later adjudged not to have been the actual brother of Jesus and was not accepted into Roman Christianity. By a later time Jesus had been proclaimed as the son of a virgin (clear in the Infancy Stories of Matthew and Luke). How could a virginally conceived Jesus have had a later brother? James was made into the brother of John and both became the sons of a Zebedee. There was a confusion between John of Patmos and John of Zebedee. According to Roman thinking, the churches of Western Asia Minor must have been founded by one of The Twelve. Hence, John of Patmos became identified as John of Zebedee, one of the fictive Twelve.

How long did this identification of 'John' take? Among the Roman churches, a majority of bishops condemned the Book of Revelation and the 'Gospel of John' (which we will see was probably not exactly the canonical Gospel of John). There were reasons for their hesitations. The book had been promoted by the prophetic but heretical Christian, Montanus, in the latter second century CE together with his two female colleagues Priscilla and Maximilla. They were originally situated in Asia Minor, in Phrygia and they were Gnostics. Known as 'The Three' they claimed that their gift of prophecy went back to the daughters of Philip the Evangelist, one of the Hellenist Seven, who had been mentioned in passing in Acts.

> [8]The next day we left and came to Caesarea; and we went into the house of Philip the evangelist, one of the seven, and stayed with him. [9]He had four unmarried daughters who had the gift of prophecy.
> (21:8-9)

'The Three' validated their ecstatic teachings by means of the book of Revelation and the Gospel of John. The latter would have been one of the earlier Gnostic strata of John, very different from what we know as canonical John. The Book of Revelation was also promoted by the followers of Montanus throughout the Empire, together with other esoteric writings.

But even the orthodox would change their minds. Justin Martyr defended the Book. In 160-165 CE he was involved in troubles which would eventually end with his own execution for refusing to offer gifts to the Roman gods. He seems to have recognized contemporary events of his day as similar to those depicted in the Book of Revelation and he identified, and perhaps he was the first to do so, John of Patmos with Mark's John of Zebedee and claimed that the latter also wrote the Gospel of John. By the time of this identification it would have been the mid-second century CE. Some time later, in about 180 CE, the highly orthodox Irenaeus of Lyon wrote of 'John, the disciple of the Lord, who had lain on his breast, himself also published a Gospel, while he was residing at Ephesus of Asia.' For Irenaeus, the one 'John' is John of Patmos, John of Zebedee, John the Beloved Disciple and John the author of the Gospel of John.

At this point, we can turn to the Gospel of John with more confidence. It was not the writing of a mystical poet who had lived with Jesus. It emerged from a complex amalgam of Jesus-movements, Gnostics and Roman Christians which had their influences on a very complex piece of Christian writing.

NOTES

There is a huge output on the Book of Revelation and the Johannine community associated with it. The conclusions drawn by authors are sometime fantastic and discretion must be used. Following are a selection of writings over the past few decades which would give a varied approach to the questions posed in the chapter.

Bauckham R. (2006), *Jesus and the Eyewitnesses*, William B. Eerdmans Publishing: Grand Rapids.

Boxall, I., (2006), *The Revelation of Saint John* (Black's New Testament Commentary), Cambridge University Press: New York.

Brown, R. E. (1997), *Introduction to the New Testament*, Anchor Bible.

Harrington W. J. (1993), *Sacra Pagina: Revelation*, Michael Glazier.

Marvin, P.C. (2010), *Four Views on the Book of Revelation*, Zondervan.

Mounce, Robert H. (1998), *The Book of Revelation*, Eerdmans: Grand Rapids.

Stuckenbruck, L. (2003). 'Revelation', in James, D. G. & William, J., *Eerdemans Commentary on the Bible*, Eerdemans: Grand Rapids.

Sweet, J. P. (1979, updated 1990), *Revelation*, SCM Press: London.

Wall, R. W. (2011), *Revelation*, Baker Books.

Witherington III, Ben (2003), 'Revelation', *The New Cambridge Bible Commentary*, Cambridge University Press; New York.

— 8 —
THE GOSPEL OF JOHN

UP TO THIS POINT WE HAVE CONCENTRATED on methodology, the study of Jesus (in both roles as Literary Jesus and Historical Jesus), the study of his Palestinian successors, Christian Gnosticism, Roman Christianity, Pauline Christianity and the form that Christianity took in Western Asia Minor.

We have seen that there were interconnections, as would be expected, among these. But we have also clearly seen that there was no single line of development that can be easily determined. The social situation of communities throughout the Roman Empire was a determinant.

In particular, we have charted how the Pauline Letters were treated by Roman Christianity in order to make them a Roman Christian property.

All of this background material will be needed to understand the Gospel of John.

What will now follow will be an analysis of the structure and an interpretation, of the Gospel of John. Using the lens of the complex Jesus communities as above, the text will be reconsidered. What fits with the text? What is out of place? How can discrepancies, corrections, expansions be explained against the background that we have been proposing?

We begin with a summary of the study of the Gospel of John. We then apply the methodology outlined above to the texts.

INTRODUCTION TO THE GOSPEL OF JOHN

We have already noted that there are stark differences in language and thought between John[35] and the Synoptics. In the Synoptics, Jesus speaks in homely parables and proverbs, reminiscent of an agricultural society, a simple village life and a suspicion of the colonialists, to get across his mes-

---

[35] Repeating what has been said, in what follows 'John', used in the sense of the author of the Gospel of John, is the handy collective name for the final editor or editors of the canonical gospel. We have no idea who this person was or these persons were and whether a final editor is singular or plural.

sage that the Kingdom of God has arrived and that time is moving towards an end point. The pithy Jesus Sayings from the Jesus-Tradition especially reflect this early stage.

The sayings and proverbs no doubt had an order to them. Apart from the Jesus Sayings and a Greek collection of Thomas sayings, there would have been other collections of proverbs, of sayings, of parables in circulation. These were extended by collections of miracle stories, a Passion narrative, a series of Vision and Empty Tomb stories. As a conglomerate, these traditions make up what we have called the Jesus-Tradition.

Then, at some time, certain Jesus events and sayings were taken from the Jesus-Tradition and transferred to the Roman Church where later they were constructed into a narrative gospel by Mark. In his gospel, by means of a chronological sequence of preaching, bodily cures, nature miracles, exorcisms and debates Jesus demonstrates that he is the Messiah. At the centre of the gospel Peter is nominated as the successor of Jesus. This is culminated by the account of the Passion, Death, Resurrection and Visions of Jesus to followers.

Matthew and Luke used Mark as a template. Matthew added Jesus Sayings and parables from the Jesus-Tradition to Mark, and manipulated the discourse to elaborate on the Markan text. Thus, he spoke not only the language of Rome but also the language of those who adhered to the more earthy Jesus Sayings. Luke followed Matthew and used Mark, the Sayings in Matthew, plus he had access to the earlier Jesus-Tradition.

As against this, John's discourse is largely symbolic. There are no exorcisms; any cures or nature miracles carry with them an overload of subtle spiritual meaning. The reader is not involved in the everyday images of farming, the seasons, local business and colonialism but the terminology of Word and Spirit and Truth and much more that is new. At times the language and the direction of thought is only too clearly Gnostic.

For example, Jesus' extended Discourses in John literally require a Gnostic creed and a glossary (which we have provided above, see pp. 92-104). The Johannine description of Jesus' ministry oscillates from Galilee to Judea, with much of the confrontation with potential believers taking place in the south. There is no gradual opening of the minds of the immediate disciples, as in the Synoptics. They acknowledge from the onset that Jesus is the Messiah, the Son of God, the King of Israel.

The particular quality of John's miracle stories has long been acknowledged. They are called Signs (*semeia*) and reveal the true nature of Jesus' person and mission. Some have argued that the evangelist reworked miracle stories received from the Jesus Tradition for his own purposes. More commonly, there is an assertion that there was an intermediate step. A previous text, The Book of Seven Signs, a Gnostic writing, provided a re-working of some miracle stories in the Jesus-Tradition, and this collection was later incorporated into the gospel.

There are also extensive Discourses, both Dialogues and Monologues, in the gospel. At times they seem to be awkwardly inserted into the text, and it not always possible to vouch for their relevance to it. Again there have been numerous scholars who have claimed that another source, a Revelatory Discourse Source, containing such a collection of Discourses, pre-existed the gospel and was used by it. Others are content that the Discourses simply resulted from the memory of extended teaching and preaching within the Johannine community. However, there has always been an awareness that the Discourses were Gnostic in character.

John's Passion and Death story and his Resurrection story are not compatible with the Synoptics, despite some obvious overlaps in detail. They are clearly separate documents from the Synoptic accounts. There are commonalities, sometimes explained by John's access to the Synoptics. However, the differences from the Synoptics are more significant than the commonalities and the more usual theory is that John had access to the earlier Jesus-tradition to which Mark had also had access and from which he wove his gospel. Events where there is notable similarity between John, as it presently stands, and the Synoptics are the following:

- Ministry and Testimony of John the Baptist.
- Cleansing and Foretelling the Destruction of the Temple.
- Feeding of 5000 people.
- Jesus walking on the Sea of Tiberias.
- Peter's Confession of faith.
- Anointing of Jesus by a woman.
- Triumphal Entry of Jesus into Jerusalem.
- Predictions of Peter's betrayal.
- Appearances to women and disciples.
- Appearance to disciples as they fish (although it is after the resurrection and a Vision in John, and it is before the resurrection and a call-narrative in Luke).

There are other similarities in the description of events or the recording of sayings but they are not strong enough to compel a reader to conclude to anything but access to a previous common body of written and/or oral traditions used by both the Synoptics and John. There is enough evidence to show that, prior to the text of what we call the Gospel of John, there had been sources that were not available or not used by the Synoptics.

Taking into account the overlaps and the distinctiveness of John, there are certain elements that immediately disengage themselves in John. These elements are distinctive because of their common literary forms, their language and their common topics.

In the first place the gospel of John contains detachable discussions of Christian topics but from a Gnostic viewpoint. These have been labelled Gnostic Treatises. They have features common with other Gnostic Treatises in the Nag Hammadi literature.

Second, there are seven sections, clearly defined, dealing with seven significant Jesus events or signs. They can be linked schematically, with interwoven themes and a common Gnostic language.

Third, there is a series of Discourses, always recognized as linguistically expansive, whose Gnostic language is also distinctive. They do not sit comfortably within the narrative texts.

All three categories can be separately detached from their present association in the Gospel of John and they make sense as separate Gnostic documents. Within them, there are incongruous insertion of other material and there are amendments to the texts which are consistent in attempting to neutralize the Gnostic tenor.

As a result of this approach to the literature, these three collections disengage themselves as separate documents, all using Gnostic language and ideas:

- Independent Gnostic Treatises
- The Book of Seven Signs
- Gnostic Discourses

But, disconcertingly, there are other parts of the text of John that clearly propose the thinking of the Synoptics. Too often they cause contradictions and discrepancies. We have labelled them Roman Christian Insertions which take the form of corrections and expansions of texts, both in passing and in large format. Then, there are three Stray Traditions, added after the conclusion to John's Gospel.

On the basis of this preliminary hypothesis, formed on the basis of the study of early Christian literature and history above, we will now examine each of these Johannine collections one by one.

THE SEVEN INDEPENDENT GNOSTIC TREATISES

What follows will be an examination of several texts that have often been seen as unique to the Johannine tradition. They have also caused many problems to commentators. Sometimes in the past, the influence of Gnosticism has been raised as an explanation of their difference, but this is far from generally accepted.

It is clear at times that texts have been tampered with prior to the canonical form of the Gospel of John. There are insertions that are not in keeping with the tone of the text. There are corrections which betray a very different mindset to the original text. There are explanations that likewise show a mentality different to the main thrust of the text. There is the juxtaposition of very different styles of writing that would never have been integrated if the gospel had been written by one hand or from one source.

What the commentary will show is that, once the text is cleared of such corrections and explanations, there emerges a number of Independent Gnostic Treatises as well as the Book of Seven Signs. It will also be demonstrated that the thought world of these items is clearly Gnostic. It will be necessary to explain why the additions to the text have been seen as necessary to later redactors.

Wherever a literary structure is indicated in the text by headings, letters and numbers or lay-out, this is done to allow the reader to see the text in the way in which it is claimed that the original author/editor intended.

It has become very clear that there are a number of rhetorical devices within the Johannine text. All scholars recognize them. One such rhetorical structure is the chiasm where the beginning of the text corresponds to the end, the second part to the second last part, the third to the third last, and so on as follows:

<pre>
        A
          B
            C
              D
            C1
          B1
        A1
</pre>

A chiasm would have been constructed with full deliberation by some scribe and is by no means restricted to Gnostic texts. In fact, many Hebrew Scriptures texts only make sense when this rhetorical device is understood.

Why did ancient writers sometimes go to the trouble of such a precise structure? The chiasm organizes the content of a writing and, in fact, makes it easier for the readers to follow that content. It stresses the pivotal point, the isolated centre, for the sake of the audience and the conclusion explains the line of argument. We can even imagine such a piece of literature being performed in a liturgical assembly.

The isolated centre text, in this case D, is the vital key to understanding what exactly the contents of the chiasm is about.

Another rhetorical device is what has been referred to as a 'framing' effect, in which an important statement is framed between two related statements. For example, in the Gospel of Mark, the following seemingly strange statement about Jesus cursing a fig-tree only becomes comprehensible when the framing surround is made apparent.

> Jesus curses a fig-tree (1:12-14)
>
> Jesus enters the Temple and cleanses it (15-19)
>
> The fig-tree withers (20-25)

The fig-tree story, with a wealth of Hebrew Scriptures allusion, was used as an effective frame for the more important story of Jesus' entrance into the Temple. The fig-tree is the symbol of Israel, as was made clear in some prophetic statements. Jesus curses the fig-tree because, when he arrives at it, it bears no fruit (despite the fact that it was not 'the season for figs'). The surface meaning is nonsense. However, the important statement is that Jesus has come to cleanse the Temple (as once the Hasmoneans had done). This is achieved and the group of disciples return to the fig-tree: it has withered. The time for Israel has passed; the Jesus-movement has replaced it. The message is clear once the framing effect is taken into account.

To ask how the fig-tree actually withered or why Jesus was piqued by the fig-tree is to make nonsense of the religious statement.

As we proceed through the text, following the elements outlined above, these rhetorical structures will be pointed out in the text itself.

As was said above, we can isolate certain sections of the Gospel of John by means of a common topic, a common literary structure and we can make a decision on the dominant theological usage. Treatises follow a common pattern, they are similar in the way they construct their material and their language is obviously Gnostic, as we will demonstrate. We now propose that the following seven separate Independent Gnostic Treatises can be abstracted from the Johannine text:

1. **The Hymn of the Word or *Logos* (1:1-18)**

2. **Foretelling the Destruction of the Temple (2:13-25)**

3. **Anointing by Mary (12:1-11)**

4. **Handing-Over of Jesus (13:1-32 and 18:1-14)**

5. **The Judgement of Jesus (18:28-19:16a)**

6. **The Crucifixion (19:16b-25)**

7. **The Magdalene Vision (20:1-29)**

Each of these, by reason of language and theme, appears to be clearly separate from the surrounding text. It is now impossible to say whether they once belonged to the same Gnostic community, or even what indeed their derivation was. We will take each in turn, sometimes dividing the actual text to indicate its literary structure, and then commenting on the whole section.

1. The Hymn to the Word (*Logos*) (1:1-18)

A In the Beginning was the Word (*Logos*), and the Word was towards God, and the Word was God. [2] He was in the beginning with God.

B [3] All things came into being through him, and without him not one thing came into being. What has come into being [4] in him was Life, and the Life was the Light of all people. [5] The Light shines in the Darkness, and the Darkness did not overcome it.

[6] *There was a man sent from God, whose name was John.* [7] *He came as a witness to testify to the Light, so that all might believe through him.* [8] *He himself was not the Light, but he came to testify to the Light.*

C [9] The true Light, which enlightens everyone, was coming into the World. [10] He was in the World, *and the World came into being through him*; yet the World did not know (*gnosis*) him. [11] He came to his Homeland *(ta idia)*, and his own people (*hoi idioi*) did not accept him.

D [12] But to all who received him, who believed in his name, he gave power to become Children of God, [13] who were born, not of blood or of the will of the Flesh or of the will of man, but of God.

C1 ¹⁴ And the Word became Flesh and lived among us, and we have seen his Glory, the Glory as of a Father's Only Son (*Monogenes*), full of Grace and Truth.

¹⁵ *John testified to him and cried out, 'This was he of whom I said, 'He who comes after me ranks ahead of me because he was before me.''*

B1 ¹⁶ From his fullness we have all received, Grace upon Grace. (¹⁷ *The Law indeed was given through Moses; Grace and Truth came through Jesus Christ.*)

A1 ¹⁸ No one has ever seen God. It is God the Only Son, *Monogenes*, who is in the bosom of Father, who has made him known.

COMMENTARY

A myriad number of commentaries on the Prologue of John have been written; they have sought to find meaning in its symbolic language. Usually the chiastic structure is highlighted. This is only too obviously a Gnostic Hymn or Poem into which the two sections on John the Baptist have been woven to give it some grounding in a life of Jesus; they are quite out of place. Once this premise that the text is Gnostic is accepted the text makes sense.

It was written as a chiasm and the important section highlighted was D. The two Baptist insertions followed the chiastic model, but they were inserted at a later time at C/C1. The editor who made the Baptist insertions understood the chiastic structure.

It may be necessary to refer back, from time to time, to the Gnostic creed and glossary for what follows in the interpretation.

The first protagonists in the Hymn's A section are The Word (the *Logos*) and God. They are both 'in the Beginning', a term used in Genesis 1 to describe the state of being before there was any time or creation. Word and God are together 'in the Beginning'; they accompany each other. The Word is towards (*pros*) God, a general description of Emanation; the Word emanated from God. *Logos* was a Greek philosophical term signifying the invisible principle that permeated all of reality. It was a universal divine Reason, to be found in the World but transcending all the imperfections of the World. It was the unchanging truth beneath the variety of change and oppositions in the World. Here the term *Logos* is being used to cover all of the activity of God, the Great Spirit, with regard to his Emanation towards the World.

In A1 there will be another reflection on The Word, this time as The *Monogenes*, the Only Begotten, existing in the bosom of the Father, who becomes the effective actor in the Word's work in the World. *Monogenes* is more usually named in Gnostic writings as the *Autogenes*, the 'Self-generated'. They are the same.

The God, in section B, produces The Word, and the Word brings Life and that Life became the Light of All Peoples. At this point we are also introduced to the element of Darkness, the antithesis of the Light. However, we are told that The Light shone in the Darkness.

The mention of 'Light' in B has allowed an editor to insert a statement on John the Baptist as the Witness to the Light. As mentioned, the two Baptist insertions cleverly follow the chiastic pattern. Because in the Jesus-Tradition the Baptist was the expected Forerunner, some later editor considered that his role required an insertion into what was essentially an earlier Gnostic hymn, where he had not been originally needed. This section on the Baptist is hopelessly misplaced in the Hymn.

The Hymn continues in C. The Light, which is the Word that has emanated from God, came into the World. An editor has added a phrase to indicate that the Word had created the World: and the World came into being through him. This also interrupts the flow of thought and does not make sense in the context. It does not fit in with the use of 'World' in the rest of John. The Word as The Light comes into the World; the Word does not create the World. But the Word who is Light is not recognized. The Light has come to his Homeland (*ta idia*), but his Own People (*hoi idioi*), who should compose a welcoming group, do not accept him.

The phrases *ta idia* (literarily, 'own places') and *hoi idioi* (literally 'own people') will occur a number of times in John. They are usually ineptly translated in English. There is an interesting parallel to this same idea concerning Wisdom in the Jewish text of 1 Enoch:

[1] Wisdom found no place where she might dwell;
Then a dwelling-place was assigned her in the heavens.
[2] Wisdom went forth to make her dwelling among the children
   of men,
And found no dwelling-place:
Wisdom returned to her place,
And took her seat among the angels.

The Johannine terms refer to a 'dwelling-place' within the hostile World where Jesus is accepted and welcomed. It is a haven for believers, the *pneumatikoi*, until they can find their fulfilment in Heaven.

In D, in dramatic terms, we are told that those living in the World who do accept the Light become Children of God. They are born of God, they have the spark of divinity within themselves and they realize it; they come to *gnosis*. This is the core of the chiasm, the kernel of the Hymn's message.

In C1, The Word takes on the form of Flesh. In Gnostic terminology, Flesh is evil, carnal. It is an obstacle to humans who must divest themselves of it. But Flesh can also indicate the Flesh of The Word, worn as a garment. This is Jesus. The perfect ones experience Jesus with his garment of Flesh as Spirit and Light. The Word displays Glory, the perception of God in a way that enlightened humans can understand. We are now informed that The Word is, in this instance, the Father's *Monogenes*, the Only Child. Within the *Monogenes* is the fullness of the covenant once made with Israel.

'He dwelt among us'. Literally, this vital statement means that 'he pitched his Tent among us' referring to the presence of the Glory of God in the material Tent of Meeting in the book of Exodus 25. A text from Zechariah 2 illustrates this more clearly:

> [10] Sing and rejoice, O daughter Zion! For lo, I will come and dwell in your midst, says Yahweh. [11] Many nations shall join themselves to Yahweh on that day, and shall be my people; and I will dwell in your midst. And you shall know that Yahweh of the Armies has sent me to you.

Just as God had come among the Israelites in the Tent of Meeting (which would eventually morph into the Temple of Jerusalem, a material receptacle for the Glory), so Jesus comes among believers in Flesh. The Word of God lives in a dwelling of Flesh. It is a temporary arrangement, not a substantive one, and cannot last.

Once again, to maintain the symmetry of the Hymn, reference is made to John the Baptist. A phrase is duplicated from John 1:30:

> This is he of whom I said, 'After me comes a man who ranks ahead of me because he was before me'.

The fullness or Pleroma (a Gnostic term for the Divinity) of the Word/Light, as mentioned in B1, has provided 'Grace upon Grace', a new covenant to replace the former one. This is provided for 'us' – the audience to whom the Hymn is addressed. An editorial comment interprets this as Jesus replacing The Law of Judaism.

The final stanza in A1 explains the procedure of *gnosis*. The divine *Monogenes* is within God (in the 'bosom of the Father'; only the *Monogenes* 'sees' God) and has made him known to 'us' as The *Logos*.

At this point we can introduce Gnostic parallels. In the *Second Treatise of the Great Seth*, dating from the third century CE, Jesus brings a conclusion to his revelation by explaining that his audience have lacked *gnosis* because of the 'Fleshly Cloud' that overshadows them. Jesus must be recognized as the divine *Logos* with a garment of Flesh. This is the meaning of the statement: 'I have been in the bosom of the Father from the beginning'.

This imagery is used in other Gnostic writings, including *The Gospel of Truth*, which dates from the second century CE:

> The Father opens his bosom, but his bosom is the Holy Spirit.
> He reveals his hidden self which is his son, so that through the
> compassion of the Father the Aeons may know him, end their
> wearying search for the Father and rest themselves in him, knowing
> that this is rest. After he had filled what was incomplete, he did
> away with form. The form of it is the world that which it served. For
> where there is envy and strife, there is an incompleteness; but where
> there is unity, there is completeness. Since this incompleteness came
> about because they did not know the Father, so when they know the
> Father, incompleteness, from that moment on, will cease to exist. As
> one's ignorance disappears when he gains knowledge [*gnosis*], and as
> darkness disappears when light appears, so also incompleteness is
> eliminated by completeness. Certainly, from that moment on, form is
> no longer manifest, but will be dissolved in fusion with unity. For now
> their works lie scattered. In time unity will make the spaces complete.
> By means of unity each one will understand itself. By means of
> knowledge [*gnosis*] it will purify itself of diversity with a view towards
> unity, devouring matter within itself like fire and darkness by light,
> death by life. (24)

The Hymn of the Word or *Logos*, in a similar vein, has identified that all Divinity has taken its rise by means of Emanations from the Father 'in the Beginning'. Within the Father this Divinity takes the form of The Word who is also The Life and The Light. The Word is the means by which The Divine Spirit can interact with The World. The Word is seen as the *Monogenes*, the Only Child of God, who takes on Flesh. This Word and Flesh is Jesus.

We have been introduced, in the Hymn to the Word or *Logos*, to a Gnostic vocabulary: In the Beginning, Word/*Logos*, God (The Great Spirit), Life, Light, Darkness, The World, Knowledge/*gnosis*, Homeland/*ta idia*, His Own People/*hoi idioi*, Belief, Children of God, Glory, Only Son/*Monogenes*, Fullness/*Pleroma*, Grace, 'In the bosom of The Father'. Only in a Gnostic mindset do these terms make any sense. The Hymn is clearly Gnostic with some attempts at corrections, such as the Baptist insertions and other comments.

The Hymn, minus the Baptist additions and editorial comments, must have circulated among Christian Gnostic circles. There were other texts too. We must not expect complete homogeneity in these Gnostic texts, since there was not complete homogeneity by any means among the Gnostic communities themselves. For example, *Monogenes* is not a favourite Gnostic term and will only be used once more in John. However, the other terms will certainly reappear with regularity and must be interpreted in a Gnostic manner at least in the first instance.

2. Foretelling the Destruction of the Temple (2:13-25)

[13] *The Passover of the Jews was near, and Jesus went up to Jerusalem.*
   [14] In the Temple he found people selling cattle, sheep, and doves, and the money-changers seated at their tables. [15] Making a whip of cords, he drove all of them out of the Temple, both the sheep and the cattle. He also poured out the coins of the money-changers and overturned their tables. [16] He told those who were selling the doves, 'Take these things out of here! Stop making my Father's house a market-place!'
   [17] *His disciples remembered that it was written, 'Zeal for your house will consume me.'*
   [18] The Jews then said to him, 'What Sign [*semeion*] can you show us for doing this?'
   [19] Jesus answered them, 'Destroy this temple, and in three days I will raise it up.'
   [20] The Jews then said, 'This Temple has been under construction for forty-six years, and will you raise it up in three days?'
   [21] *But he was speaking of the temple of his body.* [22] *After he was raised from the dead, his disciples remembered that he had said this; and they believed the scripture and the word that Jesus had spoken.*
   [23] When he was in Jerusalem during the Passover Festival, many believed in his Name because they saw the Signs [*semeia*] that he was doing.
   [24] *But Jesus on his part would not entrust himself to them, because he knew all people* [25]*and needed no one to testify about anyone; for he himself knew what was in everyone.*

COMMENTARY

The next Independent Gnostic Treatise is a short one. This episode of Foretelling the Destruction of the Temple (which historically took place in 70 CE at Roman hands) was seen as generally pivotal in the Jesus-Tradition. It occurs in all canonical gospels, although the Synoptics place it closer to his death and claim it as one of the proximate causes for his arrest. John has much the same storyline but there are no significant verbal parallels (except references to 'money changers' and 'he drove out') between his story and that of the Synoptics.

More likely, this Johannine story has been taken from the Jesus-Tradition and was used as an early 'Sign story' by Gnostics although it did not become part of the Book of Seven Signs. It would have circulated separately as an unattached Gnostic text.

An editor has added it later, after the Sign of Cana (part of the Book of Seven Signs) since it deals also with Signs, and that same editor has moved Jesus from Capernaum to Jerusalem, where the action was situated.

At the mention of 'my Father's house' a later fulfilment text, not in the Synoptics, is taken from Psalm 69:9-10 and a future tense ('will consume me') replaces the original past tense as below:

> [9] It is zeal for your house that has consumed me;
> the insults of those who insult you have fallen on me.
> [10] When I humbled my soul with fasting,
> they insulted me for doing so.

This short account has been expanded, aligning the story with the many Sign stories that involved Jesus (more than those selected in the Book of Seven Signs).

What was the Sign? In the first stage the Sign consisted in the description of the destruction of the Temple (recalling that, by this time of writing, the Temple had been actually destroyed). The Temple was the pivot of mainstream Jewish thinking and practice. Jesus replaced it with another Temple; the New Temple would be the Gnostic religious structure. This Sign differs from those in the Book of Seven Signs insofar as it refers to a future event.

One difficulty has always been that Jesus promised to restore this Temple 'in three days'. What this allusion means is unsure even today. At some stage the detail of the 'three days' was explained by an editorial addition: Jesus was speaking of his body, which was restored in 'three days' by physical resurrection, not of the Temple. This is a much later explanation that would have aligned the story with a Roman outlook.

In short, the original Sign of the Destruction has the meaning that the materiality of Jewish religion, signified by the Temple, has been replaced by the new and spiritual Gnostic Temple that does not need material structure. This straight-forward statement has been blurred by the additions.

3. Anointing by Mary (12:1-11)

[12:1] Six days before the Passover Jesus came to Bethany, the home of Lazarus, whom he had raised from the dead. [2] There they gave a dinner for him. Martha served, and Lazarus was one of those at the table with him. [3] Mary took a pound of costly perfume made of pure nard, anointed Jesus' feet, and wiped them with her hair. The house was filled with the fragrance of the perfume.

[4] But Judas Iscariot, one of his disciples (the one who was about to hand him over), said, [5] 'Why was this perfume not sold for three hundred denarii and the money given to the poor?'

[6] *He said this not because he cared about the poor, but because he was a thief; he kept the common purse and used to steal what was put into it.*

[7] Jesus said, 'Leave her alone. She bought it so that she might keep it for the day of my burial. [8] You always have the poor with you, but you do not always have me.'

[9] When the great crowd of the Jews learned that he was there, they came not only because of Jesus but also to see Lazarus, whom he had raised from the dead. [10] So the chief priests planned to put Lazarus to death as well, [11] since it was on account of him that many of the Jews were deserting and were believing in Jesus.

COMMENTARY

There was a Roman tradition that Jesus was anointed by a woman before his death. It must have been in the Jesus-Tradition, since Mark (followed by Matthew) had access to a Jesus-story about an Anointing while Luke and John had access to a separate but similar account and manipulated it to their own purposes.

John's account names the house of the anointing as that of Lazarus. We will see that he would be the protagonist of Sign 6. His sisters, Martha and Mary, important characters in the earlier Sign, featured here too.

This Gnostic Treatise is of great interest. It is clear that the 'six days before the Passover' has been inserted to situate the story in the chronology of the death of Jesus. John comes closest here to the Synoptics, as would be expected since the two accounts developed in the same milieu. However, the John story has introduced its own chronology and he has his own participants.

This lays open another opportunity to explain the complex interrelationships between the four canonical gospels. The following chart shows the parallels.

	MATTHEW **26:6-13**	**MARK** **14:3-9**	**LUKE** **7:36-50**	**JOHN** **12:1-8**
Location	The house of Simon the Leper in Bethany	The house of Simon the Leper in Bethany	A Pharisee's house	Lazarus' house in Bethany
The Woman	A woman	A woman	A 'woman of the city', a prostitute	Mary of Bethany
Container	Alabaster flask of very costly ointment	Alabaster flask of very costly pure nard	Alabaster flask of ointment	A *litra* of costly ointment of pure nard
Place of anointng	Head	Head	Wets feet with tears from behind, wipes them with hair, kisses them and anoints them	Anoints feet and wipes them with hair
Reaction	Disciples indignant	'Some' indignant	Pharisee wonders why he cannot perceive she is a sinner	Judas Iscariot asks question
Reason for reaction	Large sum of money could have been given to poor	More than 300 denarii could have been given to poor	Prophet would know a sinner	More than 300 denarii could have been given to poor
Jesus' answer to reaction	She has done a beautiful thing; the poor are always there but not Jesus; anointing was for burial.	She has done a beautiful thing; the poor are always there but not Jesus; anointing was for burial.	Parable of Creditor and Two Debtors. Woman is debtor forgiven for a large debt and so she has washed his feet, kissed them, anointed them with ointment.	She should keep the pure nard for the day of his burial; poor are always there but not Jesus.

While John draws no overt conclusion to the Story, the Jesus of Mark and Matthew announce that this story will form part of the gospel to the world for all time. Luke uses it to show that Jesus can forgive sins even of an inveterate prostitute.

There are clear links between John and Mark/Matthew: the situation of the house in Bethany, the costly pure nard, the 300 denarii estimation of a donation for poor, the saying about the 'poor', the statement that the anointing was for his burial. However, there is also the clear link of John with Luke in that the feet are anointed. However, there are no wet tears in John. Mary wipes the feet, as in Luke, but she wipes off the nard, not tears, with her hair.

The parallels are sufficient to show that Mark and Matthew have the same story. Mark had devised this version to show that Jesus simultaneously was anointed by a woman as Messiah (on the head, naturally) and prepared for his burial at the same time, since the Messiah must die to rise again. Matthew has taken his text from Mark and made only some minor changes.

Luke's story is quite different; it centres on divine forgiveness. The woman is named as a sinner; her ritual of weeping and anointing becomes an act of repentance representing as it does the actions of welcome (washing, kissing and anointing) to Jesus. She then receives forgiveness of her sins.

We thus have three versions of an event that clearly must have circulated among early Christians of all types. What would have been the original Jesus-Tradition? Of course there may not have been an original Tradition, perhaps from the beginning there were differing versions. However, we can attempt a broad reconstruction.

- Jesus is at a meal in Bethany at the home of Simon the Leper.
- A woman uses pure nard to anoint him on the feet
- There is outcry centring on the waste of 300 denarii worth of nard, and the predicament of the poor
- Jesus explains the action as being an anointing for his coming burial.

This a clever *tour de force*; it looks as if Jesus is anointed on the feet as a normal welcome; in fact he is being anointed ahead of time for his death. The story of this event had wide circulation and was used in catechetical teaching. As it developed it took on a number of forms, and the details were altered to suit the occasion. Mark changed feet to head to make it announce the Messiahship of Jesus, while secondarily preparing him for death, and so used it immediately prior to the Passion narrative. Matthew followed Mark's text. Luke possibly knew a version that had made use of the story of the anointing of the feet, not the head, and used it in order to instruct the faithful on forgiveness of sins. In this case he followed an alternative to Mark.

The Jesus-Tradition was used and adapted in John's gospel to construct a Gnostic statement. John made use of the three characters who had played roles in the Sign of Lazarus. This had its own purpose: Lazarus had been raised from the tomb after his burial; so would Jesus be.

Judas' role in the story is interesting. He asks a question, a rather naïve one, in which he uses '300 denarii' as in Mark and Matthew. This would indicate that the sum was in the Jesus-Tradition (but not used by Luke). He is identified as 'one of the disciples' and the 'one who was about to hand him over'. Another addition is included – the explanation for his concern being his thieving ways.

We will see that the Gnostic Judas was not a betrayer. He had the noble task of handing-over Jesus so that he might be able to divest himself of The Flesh. This will be seen in the next Gnostic Treatise. Judas simply asks a question, a common rhetorical device in Gnostic stories.

In this Johannine text the importance of the anointing is not as an early embalment (the Gnostic Jesus could not die). Nor is it a moral tale on forgiveness as in Luke. Its meaning can best be understood as the inauguration of one of the Gnostic sacraments mentioned in the *Gospel of Philip*.

> The Lord did everything in a mystery, a baptism and a chrism and a eucharist and a redemption [*apolutrosis*] and a bridal chamber. [...] he said, 'I came to make the things below like the things above, and the things outside like those inside. I came to unite them in the place.' [...] here through types [...] and images. (67)

Baptism, chrism, eucharist and redemption (the word translates the Coptic *apolutrosis*, which means 'redemption' but is otherwise unknown to us as a ritual) seem to be the major sacraments named. *Mysterion* or 'mystery' would be the general term for a Gnostic ritual while entering the Bridal Chamber would depict the final stage of Gnostic salvation. Prior to the final entrance into Gnostic salvation, the inductee would be anointed. Jesus underwent the ritual first; his disciples would hopefully follow.

John's account of anointing is very different from the narrative in Matthew and Mark or the moral tale in Luke. It would have been an account by a Gnostic author to explain why some advanced Gnostics were acknowledged by the sacrament of chrism.

The next Gnostic Treatise is closely related to this one.

4. The Handing-Over of Jesus (13:1-32 and 18:1-14)

Introduction

Now before the festival of the Passover, Jesus knew that his Hour had come to depart from this world and go to the Father. Having loved his own who were in the world, he loved them to the end.

2 The devil had already put it into the heart of Judas son of Simon Iscariot to betray him.

Ritual of Foot-Washing

And during supper 3 Jesus, knowing that the Father had given all things into his hands, and that he had come from God and was going to God, [4] got up from the table, took off his outer robe, and tied a towel around himself. [5] Then he poured water into a basin and began to wash the disciples' feet and to wipe them with the towel that was tied around him.

Misunderstanding of Peter

[6] He came to Simon Peter, who said to him, 'Lord, are you going to wash my feet?'

[7] Jesus answered, 'You do not know now what I am doing, but later you will understand.'

[8] Peter said to him, 'You will never wash my feet.'

Jesus answered, 'Unless I wash you, you have no share with me.'

[9] Simon Peter said to him, 'Lord, not my feet only but also my hands and my head!'

[10] Jesus said to him, 'One who has bathed does not need to wash, except for the feet, but is entirely clean. *And you are clean, though not all of you.'* [11] *For he knew who was to betray him; for this reason he said, 'Not all of you are clean.'*

Meaning of the Foot-Washing Explained

[12] After he had washed their feet, had put on his robe, and had returned to the table, he said to them, 'Do you know what I have done to you? [13] You call me Teacher and Lord– and you are right, for that is what I am. [14] So if I, your Lord and Teacher, have washed your feet, you also ought to wash one another's feet. [15] *For I have set you an example that you also should do as I have done to you.* [16] *Very truly, I tell you, servants are not greater than their master, nor are messengers greater than the one who sent them.* [17] If you know these things, you are blessed if you do them.

[18] *I am not speaking of all of you; I know whom I have chosen. But it is to fulfil the scripture, 'The one who ate my bread has lifted his heel against me.'*

[19] I tell you this now, before it occurs, so that when it does occur, you may believe that I Am. [20] *Very truly, I tell you, whoever receives one whom I send receives me; and whoever receives me receives him who sent me.'*

Ritual of Bread and Wine: Identification of the One who Hands-Over

[21] After saying this Jesus was troubled in spirit, and declared, 'Very truly, I tell you, one of you will hand me over.'

[22] The disciples looked at one another, uncertain of whom he was speaking. [23] One of his disciples—the One whom Jesus Loved – was reclining 'on the bosom of Jesus'; [24] Simon Peter therefore motioned to the disciple to ask Jesus of whom he was speaking.

[25] So while reclining 'on the bosom of Jesus', the disciple asked him, 'Lord, who is it?'

[26] Jesus answered, 'It is the one to whom I give this piece of bread when I have dipped it in the dish.'

So when he had dipped the piece of bread, he gave it to Judas son of Simon Iscariot.

27 After he received the piece of bread, Satan entered into him.

Jesus said to him, 'Do quickly what you are going to do.' *28* Now no one at the table knew why he said this to him.

29 Some thought that, because Judas had the common purse, Jesus was telling him, 'Buy what we need for the festival'; or, that he should give something to the poor.

30 So, after receiving the piece of bread, he immediately went out. And it was night.

31 When he had gone out, Jesus said, 'Now the Son of Man has been glorified, and God has been glorified in him. *32*If God has been glorified in him, God will also glorify him in himself and will glorify him at once'.

The Handing-Over in the Garden

18:1 After Jesus had spoken these words, he went out with his disciples across the Kidron Valley to a place where there was a Garden, which he and his disciples entered.

2 Now Judas, who handed him over, also knew the place, because Jesus often met there with his disciples. *3* So Judas brought a detachment of soldiers together with police from the chief priests and the Pharisees, and they came there with lanterns and torches and weapons.

4 Then Jesus, knowing all that was to happen to him, came forward and asked them, 'For whom are you looking?' *5* They answered, 'Jesus of Nazareth.'

Jesus replied, 'I Am.'

Judas, who handed him over him, was standing with them.

6 When Jesus said to them, 'I Am', they stepped back and fell to the ground.

7 Again he asked them, 'For whom are you looking?'

And they said, 'Jesus of Nazareth.'

8 Jesus answered, 'I told you that I Am. So if you are looking for me, let these men go.'

9 This was to fulfil the word that he had spoken, 'I did not lose a single one of those whom you gave me.'

Misunderstanding of Peter

10 Then Simon Peter, who had a sword, drew it, struck the High Priest's slave, and cut off his right ear. The slave's name was Malchus.

11 Jesus said to Peter, 'Put your sword back into its sheath. Am I not to drink the Cup that the Father has given me?'

The Handing-Over of Jesus to the Jews

So the soldiers, their officer, and the Jewish police arrested Jesus and bound him. First they took him to Annas, who was the father-in-law of Caiaphas, the high priest that year. *Caiaphas was the one who had advised the Jews that it was better to have one person die for the people.*

COMMENTARY

The fourth independent Gnostic text is The Handing-Over of Jesus. Its closest parallel in the Gnostic writings is the *Gospel of Judas*. Either this Treatise is an abbreviation of that text (or something like it) or that text is an expansion of this Treatise. However, in an early time frame, the Handing-Over story as presented here was heavily edited as the italics in the text above indicate. Editors could not comprehend it; they needed to clear up confusions. There were explanatory additions, two fulfilment texts and a general attempt to bring the text into line with the Roman view of Judas the evil Betrayer. These additions are easily identified. They abruptly interrupt the flow of the underlying Gnostic story.

To set the context for this Treatise, John only mentions a Last Supper in passing. There are no details of, or seeming interest in, what happens at it as an actual supper, as regards preparations, menu or the establishment of a bread and wine ritual for the future. Instead, John concentrates on a ritual of Foot-Washing with the meal proceedings as non-essential background. This Foot-Washing is the great finale of the pre-Departure of Jesus. It is also surely the prelude to a sacred ritual in the life of the group.[36] Those present are simply named as 'the disciples'. There is no mention of The Twelve; also present is the Beloved Disciple.

Foot-Washing among the Jews had the everyday implication of welcome to a house. The well-known welcome of Abraham to Yahweh in the guise of Three Men in Genesis 18 is as follows:

> [1] Yahweh appeared to Abraham by the oaks of Mamre, as he sat at the entrance of his tent in the heat of the day. [2] He looked up and saw three men standing near him. When he saw them, he ran from the tent entrance to meet them, and bowed down to the ground. [3] He said, 'My lord, if I find favour with you, do not pass by your servant. [4] Let a little water be brought, and wash your feet, and rest yourselves under the tree.

Jesus in the Foot-Washing is welcoming, on the eve of his Departure, the believing disciples into his Father's Homeland. This Homeland is *ta idia*, and they are His Own, *hoi idioi*. They have seen the Signs, they have responded with faith and now they duly enter into the House of The Father. This is the meaning of the Foot-Washing ritual established by Jesus; they are ready to enter into divinity.

The sequence of the text (with some later Roman Christian additions con-

---

[36] The common but trivial interpretation of the Foot-Washing as an example of Christian humility is much later and inappropriate.

cerning the betrayal by Judas) is a framing structure, with the central narrative based on the identification of the one who will hand-over as its core:

13: 1-5 The Ritual of Foot-Washing

6-11 Misunderstanding of Peter

12-20 The Meaning of the Foot-Washing explained.

21-32 Ritual of Bread and Wine: Identification of the One who Hands-Over

18:1-9 The Handing-Over in the Garden

10-11 Misunderstanding of Peter

12-14 The Handing-Over of Jesus to the Jews

This is a complex piece of literature based on the framing technique. In the first section, the misunderstanding and enlightenment of Peter concerning the Foot-Washing is itself bracketed by Jesus' original action and his instruction to continue the practice of ritual Foot-Washing after his Departure.

The opening structure is matched by another in 18:1-14, which has been at a later date displaced by the insertion of Discourses.[37] This section, 18:1-14, forms the second part of this original Gnostic treatise. Again, a Peter misunderstanding is framed, this time by the Handing-Over in the Garden and then the Handing-Over to the Jews, headed by Annas.

The ritual of the Foot-Washing in the first section announces that the believing disciples, including Judas, are welcomed into The Father's Homeland. This is painstakingly explained to Peter (who often serves the purpose of the obtuse disciple in Gnostic writings) as not being a Head-Washing.[38] Then Jesus, in his interpretation of the ritual, demonstrates that the Foot-Washing is not only for them but for others.

We can state the obvious, that at least for some Gnostics Foot-Washing became a Gnostic sacrament which was performed to welcome a *pneumatikos* into the inner circle. This narrative indicates how they must wash the feet of new *pneumatikoi* when they reach a recognizable stage of *gnosis*. Foot-washing joins chrism as a second Gnostic sacrament.

After the establishment of the Foot-Washing ritual, the Glorification of Jesus begins with the identification of the One who will hand over –

[37] The intrusion of the Discourses into an Independent Gnostic Treatise demonstrates that the Discourses were at least inserted into the complex later than the Treatises.

[38] This reference might be a Gnostic reflection on the immersion ritual and insistence on the head as practised in the Roman Christian Church.

Judas. In Greek, the verb for 'handing-over' (*paradidomi*) means just that, 'to put into someone else's keeping'; it does not necessarily have the pejorative meaning of 'to betray'.

Into this short statement a later editor, certain that Judas was a vile traitor, robber and possessed by Satan, has been dismayed that Jesus applied the Foot-Washing to all the disciples present. He explains that Judas, even though he had had his feet washed, must have been the exception and finds an apposite text from Psalm 41:9:

> [9] Even my bosom friend in whom I trusted,
> who ate of my bread, has lifted the heel against me.

This text would have been current in the Roman Church, as Mark also uses part of it in his Last Supper account. Interestingly, this text uses the same word for 'eating' as that used for the eating of Bread in the Feeding of the 5000. The text is trying to refer to Eucharistic overtones in the passage that are simply not there in John. In fact, the editorial addition distorts the meaning, and it has been successful in distorting it over a long period.

Two more Roman Christian inserts make it clear that the Handing-Over is a betrayal. Jesus is 'betrayed', not just 'handed-over' by Judas; it was an important part of the Roman version of the Christian Story that disdained the Jews and saw Roman Christians as opposed to them. 'Judas', a very common name, meant 'The Jew' and Roman Christians by this time had broken any links with the Jewish synagogues.

The denigration of Judas continued to be invoked throughout other sections of John. Judas' actions would be qualified as evil by additions or insertions in various texts, as editors sought to clarify his evil character. As can be seen, the text above contains three pejorative additions on Judas.

We will advance to the second half of the text in 18:1-14. It has a similar framing structure. In the course of transmission this has been separated from its original context by Gnostic Discourse 12: The Paraclete, Gnostic Discourse 13: The True Vine and Gnostic Discourse 14: The Prayer of Jesus. This is inexpert editing. The second half recounts the actual act of Handing-Over. Judas performs the deed by using both Roman and religious authorities. This was his sacred task. Jesus reveals himself as 'I Am' (*ego eimi*) to the authorities.

'I Am' in Greek is used in John's Gospel to indicate the divinity of Jesus. At some time in the pre-Christian period an epithet had been applied to the general name for God or 'El. This was *Yawi* or Yahweh. The original meaning of the name would have been forgotten by that time, and Yahweh was accepted as a unique, personal name of the God of Israel. In Jewish usage the word would have been long uninterpretable, as the convoluted attempt at a naive etymology in the book of Exodus demonstrates. The text of Exodus, 'ehyeh aser 'ehyeh (literally, 'I am who I am'), has subsequently caused extraordinary exegetical difficulties.[39]

The term was used, for example in texts like Isaiah 43:10-11 and would have been known to Jesus-movement groups:

> [10] You are my witnesses, says Yahweh,
> and my Servant whom I have chosen,
> so that you may know and believe me
> and understand that I Am.
> Before me no god was formed,
> nor shall there be any after me.
> [11] I, I Am Yahweh,
> and besides me there is no Saviour.

While 'I Am' has resonances with Jewish thought about the divinity, the term was also used extensively in Gnosticism. For example, in the Gnostic tract The Thunder: Perfect Mind we read the words of the Divinity revealing the depths of inner being, based on repeated 'I Am' statements:

> For I am the first and the last.
> I am the honoured one and the scorned one.
> I am the whore and the holy one.
> I am the wife and the virgin.
> I am [the mother] and the daughter.
> I am the members of my mother.
> I am the barren one and many are her sons.
> I am she whose wedding is great, and I have not taken a husband.
> I am the midwife and she who does not bear.
> I am the solace of my labor pains.
> I am the bride and the bridegroom, and it is my husband who begot me.
> I am the mother of my father and the sister of my husband and he is my
> offspring.
> I am the slave of him who prepared me.
> I am the ruler of my offspring.
> But he is the one who begot me before the time on a birthday.
> And he is my offspring in [due] time, and my power is from him.
> I am the staff of his power in his youth, and he is the rod of my old age.
> And whatever he wills happens to me.
> I am the silence that is incomprehensible and the idea whose
> remembrance is frequent.

---

[39] Some recent attempts at a translation have been: 'He who creates', 'Preserver', 'I will passionately love whom I love', 'The actuality and existentiality of God', 'I am – that is who I am!'. The simple fact is that the etymology of the sacred name was and is still unknown.

I am the voice whose sound is manifold and the word whose
appearance is multiple.
I am the utterance of my name. (13: 15-30)

The Heavenly Revealer in this text speaks in much the same vein as
Jesus who identifies himself as 'I Am'.[40]

At the centre of these two self-sufficient structures in 13:21-32, there is
the key to the whole passage in a disengaged centre: Judas is finally identified as the one who will be entrusted with the Handing-Over. Jesus delivers
an important statement on this Handing-Over. This independent section is
one of the most important sections of the gospel and one of the most misinterpreted. It concerns the vital role of Judas.

We need to examine what is meant by the Handing-Over. It is said that
this will usher in the Glorification of Jesus. The Beloved Disciple is reclining 'on the breast of Jesus'. It is an unusual pose; it signifies that the Beloved
Disciple and Jesus are as one. Just as *Monogenes* in the Hymn of the Word or
Logos reclines 'on the breast of The Father', so the Beloved Disciple lies 'on
thc breast of Jesus'. It is much more than affection.

This Disciple remains anonymous. The Beloved Disciple receives a message from Peter to enquire who the person so charged with the Handing-
Over actually is. When asked, Jesus answers that he will perform another
ritual: giving the bread dipped in wine to the one so chosen. Although the
details of a Supper have been omitted from this construction, the dipping
of bread morsels into wine, which are then distributed, would have been
considered part of the ceremony.

We have here the inference of a third Gnostic sacrament, the 'eucharist'.
The Gospel of Philip, we have seen, mentions it as one of four: The Lord
did everything in a mystery, a baptism and a chrism and a eucharist and
a redemption [*apolutrosis*] and a bridal chamber. Foot-Washing was meant
for the initiates; chrism for those acknowledged to be on the verge of *gnosis*.
Eucharist was meant for the more advanced Gnostic (like Judas). No-one
else at this Supper received the Gnostic Eucharist.

The Beloved Disciple now knows that Judas is the one who will hand over
Jesus. To the reader this recalls the Gospel of Judas where Jesus says to Judas:

But you will exceed all of them [the other disciples]. For you will
sacrifice The Man that clothes me. (56)

The structure of the framing text contrasts the obtuseness of Peter with
the secret knowledge of the Beloved Disciple.

---

[40] In John's gospel there are other usages similar to these: 'I am the Way, the Truth
and the Life', 'I am the Vine', 'I am the Bread of Life' and so on.

What is central to the story is that Jesus announces that his final Glorification has begun and the Handing-Over is the first, necessary step. The divine Jesus is impeded by his human body, the Flesh. The body is not himself; it is part of the defilement of living in the World. He requires someone who will rid him of that body of Flesh so that he can achieve the final stage of his Glorification. Judas has been chosen by Jesus to put aside his humanity.

In the *Gospel of Judas*, at the time of achieving his life's work of handing over Jesus to those who will destroy his Flesh, Judas enters into 'the Luminous Cloud'. He has become divine. We have seen how Thomas, in the *Gospel of Thomas*, having been entrusted with the deepest and most secret *gnosis* by Jesus, was described as being the 'Twin' of Jesus. In the *Gospel of Philip* those who found the fullness of *gnosis* entered into the 'Bridal Chamber'. In a similar vein in the *Gospel of Judas*, Judas enters the Luminous Cloud, and a Voice comes from the Cloud, although most unfortunately the text that should follow, which would tell us what the Voice announced, is missing.

The Voice is that of *Protennoia*, The First Thought or the First *Ennoia*. (Sometimes the Emanation of Ennoia is called Pronoia; the terms can be used alternatively.) *Protennoia* had taken on three forms. In the first place, *Protennoia* was the Voice of the First Thought who descended as Light into Darkness to minister to those who had fallen. Thereafter she was the Speech of the First Thought and the *Logos* of the First Thought. In a third form she had a human appearance.

The finale of the Gospel of Judas simply recounts Judas' arrangement for the Handing-Over of the human body of Jesus for money. Judas has done what he was divinely commanded to do. He has brought the divine activity of Jesus to its conclusion by arranging the Handing-Over. He has reached a plateau of divinity himself by doing so.

It is the same Judas here in John as in the original text of the Gnostic Treatise. He is charged by Jesus himself with handing himself over for the destruction of his Flesh.

It seems that there was another Roman Christian literary tradition about the betrayal of Jesus. In the canonical literary tradition of the Synoptics, Judas was evil, possessed by Satan, driven by greed for money to betray Jesus with a kiss for thirty coins. Matthew has a tradition about his ignominious death by suicide; he hangs himself. In Acts the same tradition recounts that he projects himself over a precipice.[41] On the contrary, in John he was a noble figure entrusted with the most important moment in the final Glorification of Jesus.

---

[41] In the style of the presentation of a Biblical Jesus, there are scholars who have explained that he hanged himself but the rope broke and he fell over a precipice. For them, there can be no contradiction.

There is no need for us to try to reconstruct the Historical Judas. That is certainly impossible anyway, although it has been often attempted. But we do need to note the Gnostic version. As seen above, in this Gnostic version (not all forms), Judas is the greatest of the disciples, the one entrusted with the sacred task of arranging for Jesus to be freed of the Flesh, his garment during the ministry. He is chosen for the task and this brings into train the Glorification of Jesus.

All four canonical gospels, as they now stand, depict Judas Iscariot as a traitor. In their accounts, he was one of the inner circle of Jesus' followers, but he treacherously laid plans with the Jewish authorities to hand Jesus over to them for payment. This was variously explained as being because of his possession by Satan or his being a thief or both. This betrayal by Judas led directly to the arrest and crucifixion of Jesus. Amongst commentators, there have been attempts to rehabilitate Judas, arguing that his portrayal as a traitor could not have been historical. History is another matter; we are not dealing with history at this moment. In the Synoptic gospels (and the final edited draft of John) he is clearly portrayed as a traitor; however, the traitor designation was originally not in the text of this Gnostic story.

So it is that the formal Handing-Over takes place in a Garden. The un-named Garden immediately evokes memories of The Garden of Eden; there has been a return to the first Eden. At the centre of the new structure is the second misunderstanding of Peter – he is mistaken that Jesus needs to be rescued from this situation. He attacks Malchus. But Jesus rebukes Peter. His rebuke contains the equivalent of the Synoptic story of the Agony in the Garden and the presentation of a Cup to Jesus therein. The Handing-Over must be completed.

The last section of the treatise sees Jesus taken by the soldiers to be delivered to the High Priest, Annas, father-in-law of Caiaphas. The Handing-Over is complete. It was never a humanly-devised plan; it was never one concocted by an evil Judas or the Temple police. It was part of a divine plan and it required the cooperation of Judas as the one who would hand him over.

The final editorial comment is a bitter and ironical statement on Caiaphas.

5. The Judgement of Jesus (18:28-19:16a)

Introduction

[28] Then they took Jesus from Caiaphas to Pilate's Praetorium. It was early in the morning.
They themselves did not enter the headquarters, so as to avoid ritual defilement and to be able to eat the Passover.

A. Initial Condemnation

²⁹ So Pilate went out [*exelthein*] to them and said, 'What accusation do you bring against this man?'

³⁰ They answered, 'If this man were not a criminal, we would not have handed him over to you.'

³¹ Pilate said to them, 'Take him yourselves and judge him according to your law.'

The Jews replied, 'We are not permitted to put anyone to death.'

³² This was to fulfil what Jesus had said when he indicated the kind of death he was to die.

B. Jesus the King

³³ Then Pilate entered [*eiselthein*] the Praetorium again, summoned Jesus, and asked him, 'Are you the King of the Jews?'

³⁴ Jesus answered, 'Do you ask this on your own, or did others tell you about me?'

³⁵ Pilate replied, 'I am not a Jew, am I? Your own nation and the chief priests have handed you over to me. What have you done?'

³⁶ Jesus answered, 'My Kingdom is not from this world. If my Kingdom were from this World, my followers would be fighting to keep me from being handed over to the Jews. But as it is, my Kingdom is not from here.'

³⁷ Pilate asked him, 'So you are a king?'

Jesus answered, 'You say that I am a king. For this I was born, and for this I came into the World, to testify to the Truth. Everyone who belongs to the Truth listens to my voice.'

³⁸ Pilate asked him, 'What is Truth?'

C. The Innocence of Jesus

After he had said this, he went out [*exelthein*] to the Jews again and told them, 'I find no case against him. ³⁹ But you have a custom that I release someone for you at the Passover. Do you want me to release for you the King of the Jews?'

⁴⁰ They shouted in reply, 'Not This Man, but Barabbas!' Now Barabbas was a bandit.

D. Jesus Presented as King

¹⁹:¹ Then Pilate took Jesus and had him flogged. ² And the soldiers wove a crown of thorns and put it on his head, and they dressed him in a purple robe. ³ They kept coming up to him, saying, 'Hail, King of the Jews!' and striking him on the face.

C1 The Innocence of Jesus

⁴ Pilate went out [*exelthein*] again and said to them, 'Look, I am bringing him out to you to let you know that I find no case against him.' ⁵ So Jesus came out, wearing the crown of thorns and the purple robe.

Pilate said to them, 'Here is The Man!'

[6] When the chief priests and the police saw him, they shouted, 'Crucify him! Crucify him!' Pilate said to them, 'Take him yourselves and crucify him; I find no case against him.'

[7] The Jews answered him, 'We have a Law, and according to that Law he ought to die because he has claimed to be the Son of God.'

[8] Now when Pilate heard this, he was more afraid than ever.

B1 Jesus the King

[9] He entered [*eiselthein*] his headquarters again and asked Jesus, 'Where are you from?' But Jesus gave him no answer.

[10] Pilate therefore said to him, 'Do you refuse to speak to me? Do you not know that I have power to release you, and power to crucify you?'

[11] Jesus answered him, 'You would have no power over me unless it had been given you from above; *therefore the one who handed me over to you is guilty of a greater sin.*'

[12] From then on Pilate tried to release him, but the Jews cried out, 'If you release this man, you are no friend of the emperor. Everyone who claims to be a king sets himself against the emperor.'

A1 The Final Condemnation

[13] When Pilate heard these words, he brought Jesus outside [*egagon exo*] and sat on the judge's bench [*bema*] at a place called Lithostrotos, or in Hebrew Gabbatha. [14] Now it was the day of Preparation for the Passover; and it was about noon.

He said to the Jews, 'Here is your King!'

[15] They cried out, 'Away with him! Away with him! Crucify him!' Pilate asked them, 'Shall I crucify your King?'

The chief priests answered, 'We have no king but the emperor.'

[16] Then he handed him over to them to be crucified.

COMMENTARY

This is another independent Gnostic Treatise. Its literary structure is based on Pilate's movements out of (*exelthein*) and into (*eiselthein*) the Praetorium. This device divides the composition into a chiastic form with sections related to each other. The structure, as already inserted in the text above, could not be the result of chance. The final section is marked by a different and stronger verb with the same meaning. It is the dramatic conclusion.

The centre of the chiasm in D comes as a surprise.

When dealing with the Passion of Jesus in the canonical gospels, there are more parallels between John and the Synoptics than in any other sections of the gospel Story. Sometimes the similarities are almost word perfect, at other times there is only a general similarity. It would seem that the Gnostic author, Mark and Luke all had access to the Passion Story in the Jesus-Tradition. They worked on the Tradition in their own way for their own purposes. Matthew edited Mark; Luke edited Mark but also had access to Matthew and the Jesus-Tradition; the Gnostic author also worked on the Jesus-Tradition.

Here are the significant parallels among the four gospels:

'Are you the King of the Jews?' (Mt 27:11; Mk 15:2; Lk 23:3; John 18:33)

'You say so! (with addition that 'I am a King' in John)'. (Mt 27:11; Mk 15:2; Lk 23:3; John 18:37)

'I find no crime in this man (in 'him' in John)'. Lk 23:4; John 18:38

The Barabbas incident is covered in all four gospels, although John's text does not have significant parallels with the other three.

There is a common sequence of the torture of Jesus in Matthew, Mark and John while Luke seems to have his own source:

Mark: scourging, purple cloak, 'plaiting a crown of thorns they put it on him', 'Hail, King of the Jews', struck him with a reed on his head, spat upon him, 'they knelt down in homage to him and mocked him', stripped him of the purple cloak, put his own clothes on him.

Matthew: scourging, scarlet robe, 'plaiting a crown of thorns they put it on his head and put a reed in his right hand', 'they mocked him saying 'Hail, King of the Jews'', he is stripped and they put his own clothes on him.

Luke: Herod treats him with contempt and mocks him; then he puts an elegant robe on him; Pilate proposes scourging but does not carry it out.

John: scourging, 'plaited a crown of thorns and put it on his head', purple robe, 'they came up to him saying, "Hail, King of the Jews"'; 'they give him blows'.

Matthew and Mark are clearly closely related in the description of the torture. Luke has created his own version from the Jesus-Tradition and has alone introduced the Herod character.

John's parallels are not sufficient to demonstrate any direct connection between his text and either Mark/Matthew or Luke. To explain what similarities there are, it is sufficient to invoke access to a Jesus-Tradition, prior to its Synoptic redactions.

One Gnostic document, *The Letter of Peter to Philip*, a Christian Gnostic letter with additional materials on Peter, written perhaps in the late second century CE contains this interesting account of the Passion:

> He [Peter] spoke thus: 'Our Illuminator, Jesus, came down and was crucified. And he bore a crown of thorns. And he put on a purple garment. And he was crucified on a tree and he was buried in a tomb. And he rose from the dead. My brothers, Jesus is a stranger to this suffering. But we are the ones who have suffered through the transgression of the Mother. And because of this, he did everything like us. For the Lord Jesus, the Son of the immeasurable Glory of the Father, he is the author of our life. My brothers, let us therefore not obey these lawless ones, and walk in [...].' (139)

The text of the Letter mentions the crown of thorns, the purple garment and the crucifixion. However, it makes the claim that Jesus was a 'stranger to this suffering'. He took on the appearance of suffering, doing everything that humans do even though he was not human, because his disciples had suffered because of the fall of The Mother, Sophia. For the moment, it is sufficient to remark that in John the regal bearing of Jesus has often been noted. He does not seem to be suffering. We will return to this Gnostic text again to explain the Mother reference.

The real question for the moment is what ideology lies beneath the structure in the Gospel of John.

Within the framework of the Passion Story, John has composed a typical Gnostic scene that distinguishes Inside from Outside (namely, inside and outside the Praetorium). Outside, there is the hostility of the World (represented by the Jews and Pharisees); Pilate is like a stage-manager moving from Inside to Outside. Inside, there is the Gnostic dialogue between himself and Jesus. Pilate struggles with the Gnostic language of Kingship, World, Your Own, Truth, The Man, Son of God. He never does understand. The whole discussion is ironic: it seems that the Jews and The World are condemning Jesus through Pilate, but in fact the Unbelieving World is being itself being condemned by Jesus. Pilate asks naïve questions as is common in Gnostic discourses.

Some of the apparent changes that John made to the original tradition are important. Jesus is clothed with the crown of thorns, the royal purple robe and then enthroned. He is clearly presented as a king. But Jesus is never stripped of his regalia before being led to crucifixion in John. As far as the reader is concerned, he wears the royal regalia to Golgotha. Nor is Jesus 'mocked' in John, as in the Synoptics; instead, he receives blows (*rapismata*);

in fact, he cannot suffer physically. He is rejected as King by those who deliver the blows, but he is not mocked as King. There is an atmosphere of quiet and even regal dignity in John not found in the Synoptics.

The A section of the text sets the scene and gives notice of the charge. Pilate goes Outside to receive it. The charge is not civil, it is religious. It should be judged by the Jews, Pilate decides, but they are already determined on a death sentence.

In B, Pilate, again on the Inside, struggles with the idea of Gnostic kingship. This is the core of the accusation. Jesus responds to him: are you dealing with the notion of Kingship in Jewish parlance or my parlance? He makes it clear that his Kingship is separate from The World. His Kingship is based on his mission to 'testify to the Truth'. The Truth, which Pilate cannot fathom, is the manifestation of The Father that comes about by spiritual adhesion to Jesus. This is Gnostic dialogue with one who has no idea of the idiom.

The two C and C1 sections, which are both on the Outside, insist on the innocence of Jesus: he is not guilty of the charges laid by the Jews. In both of them Pilate asserts this. In C, Barabbas the bandit (lestes) is preferred by the Jews. This lestes is the same term that is found in the Discourse on The Good Shepherd when it refers to the 'bandit'. The lestes causes great problems with the flock, attacks it, disrupts it. However, the Jews prefer Barabbas, the lestes, to Jesus.

In C1 Pilate presents Jesus not as King (despite the fact that he is wearing the crown and the purple robe) but as The Man. In Gnostic language, The True Man, Adamas, comes at the end of time to teach Gnostics the fulness of Truth and to anoint them. *The Hypostasis of the Archons* contains an interpretation of Genesis 1-6, with a discourse between an Angel, Eleleth, and a Gnostic questioner. It dates from the third to fourth century. It would seem that a Gnostic editor has combined the Genesis interpretation with a Gnostic Revelatory Discourse. An enquiry by the questioner about the final freedom from the Archons, the authorities of this World, is answered by Eleleth:

> Then I said, 'Sir, how much longer?'
> He said to me, 'Until the moment when the True Man, within a modelled form, reveals the existence of [the Spirit of] Truth, which The Father has sent.
> Then he will teach them about everything: And he will anoint them with the unction of Life Eternal, given him from the undominated generation.
> Then all the Children of the Light will be truly acquainted with

The Truth and their root, and the father of The All and the Holy Spirit:
They will all say with a single voice, 'The Father's Truth is just, and
The Son presides over The All: and from everyone unto the ages of ages,
'Holy – Holy – Holy! Amen'' (96-97)

Another key text is found in *The Sophia of Jesus Christ*. This is another
Christian Gnostic text but based on an apparently non-Christian Gnostic
source called *Eugnostos the Blessed*, which was also found at Nag Hammadi.
The revised text was directed at Christian Gnostics, some of whom may
have been familiar with Eugnostos the Blessed. In *The Sophia of Jesus Christ*,
a number of disciples ask questions. Here is one of Matthew's questions and
its answer which introduces the topic of The Man:

> Matthew said to him: 'Lord, Saviour, how was The Man revealed?'
> The perfect Saviour said: 'I want you to know that he who appeared
> before the universe in infinity, Self-grown, Self-constructed Father,
> being full of shining light and ineffable, in the Beginning, when he
> decided to have his likeness become a great power, immediately
> the principle [or Beginning] of that Light appeared as Immortal
> Androgynous Man, that through that Immortal Androgynous Man they
> might attain their salvation and awake from forgetfulness through the
> interpreter who was sent, who is with you until the end of the poverty
> of the robbers. (101:4-8)

The irony in John is at its peak. He has Pilate announce to the World and
the Jews that Jesus is The Immortal Androgynous Man. 'Behold, The Man'
seems an innocuous, if unusual, statement. In fact, he is talking Gnostic
language without knowing it. The hearers' response is rejection caused by
profound and culpable ignorance. The reference to 'robbers' is interesting.

Unattached, at the centre of the chiasm (which, to complete the chiasm,
has Pilate 'going in' to The Praetorium twice without any 'coming out') is
the presentation of Jesus as King. He is given a crown of thorns, a royal
purple robe. He is acclaimed in ironic fashion as 'Here is your King', parallel to the earlier 'Here is The Man'. Finally, he is rejected with blows from
the soldiers. This is what the whole Treatise is about: Jesus is the King and
the seeming condemnation is, to those who know, an integral part of the
Glorification.

B1 returns to the theme of Jesus' kingship. Pilate still misunderstands
'power': worldly versus divine. Worldly power is summed up in the constitutional power of the Emperor; it is not comparable to divine power. The
Jews ask if Pilate is a Friend of the Emperor, which was a formal title. Does
he uphold the constitutional power of the Emperor?

The final excerpt in A1 brings the Treatise to a thunderous conclusion. It contains a vital phrase: 'he sat upon the Judge's bench [bema]'. The grammar leaves unanswered who does the sitting. Does Pilate seat himself (as would be expected historically, without doubt, but which would normally require another phrase such as 'himself' after 'sat') or does Pilate seat Jesus on the bema? The latter seems to be intended in the literary creation, unlikely as it would be in historical reality.

Such is the concluding scene. Jesus with his crown and his purple robe is enthroned on the bema. He is dressed as a King and enthroned as a Judge. He faces the Jews. The Hour has come. He is officially proclaimed by Pilate as the King. Yet, he is decisively rejected by the Jews and the World.

For the Gnostic reader this is Jesus – the Word, who is clothed in Flesh. He seems on the Outside to be condemned to death as King, as The Man; yet, on the Inside, he calmly proclaims the true meaning of his Kingship and his status as The Man. He is condemned by The World; in actual fact, The World is condemned by him from the bema seat.

Pilate is next in line to 'hand over' Jesus. Already Judas, his faithful disciple and a Gnostic Good Man, had been instructed to do just that. So, Judas hands him over to the Jewish soldiers; the Jewish soldiers bring him to Annas and Caiaphas; Caiaphas hands him over to Pilate, who hands him back to them.

Following this complex Handing-Over, The Flesh will be destroyed in the crucifixion; the Divine Jesus will then live on, glorified as before.

This is a very theologically dense Gnostic Treatise. There have been several editorial additions that do not assist interpretation. However, it is, in the main, an untouched Gnostic statement that follows on from the earlier Handing-On Treatise.

6. The Crucifixion (19:16b-25)

So they took Jesus; [17]and carrying the cross by himself, he went out to what is called the Place of the Skull, which in Hebrew is called Golgotha. [18]There they crucified him, and with him two others, one on either side, with Jesus between them. [19]Pilate also had an inscription written and put on the cross. It read, 'Jesus of Nazareth, the King of the Jews'. [20]Many of the Jews read this inscription, because the place where Jesus was crucified was near the city; and it was written in Hebrew, in Latin, and in Greek.
[21]Then the chief priests of the Jews said to Pilate, 'Do not write, 'The King of the Jews', but, 'This man said, I am King of the Jews.' '
[22]Pilate answered, 'What I have written I have written.'
[23]When the soldiers had crucified Jesus, they took his clothes and divided them into four parts, one for each soldier. They also took his

tunic; now the tunic was seamless, woven in one piece from the top. [24]So they said to one another, 'Let us not tear it, but cast lots for it to see who will get it.'

This was to fulfil what the scripture says,

'They divided my clothes among themselves,
and for my clothing they cast lots.'

[25]And that is what the soldiers did.

COMMENTARY

The account of the death of Jesus follows the outline found in the Synoptics but again it is not dependent on them. Where there are parallels, there are different emphases in those parallels. The Gnostic Treatise in John takes its rise from the Jesus-Tradition.

Jesus is crucified with two others but there is no comment made on the two malefactors nor is there any conversation with them. The title on the cross is interesting; it has different versions in the four canonical gospels:

Mark: The King of the Jews

Matthew: This is Jesus the King of the Jews

Luke: He is the King of the Jews

John: Jesus the Nazarene, the King of the Jews

Only John has the added detail that the title was written in three languages: Hebrew, Latin and Greek. 'Hebrew' probably refers to the local Aramaic, Latin is the administrative language, and Greek is the international language.

Of more importance is the title inclusion of 'Jesus the Nazarene'. It is not 'Jesus of Nazareth (the town)'. It refers, as we have remarked previously, to 'branch', *nezer,* as used in Isaiah to describe the coming King, the ideal Davidic King, who has come forth, like a Branch, from David. It is only by this link that Nazarene and King can be conjoined.

The Johannine irony is that this is now described on the *titulus* attached to the cross. Jesus is the Branch and the King of Israel, as described by the hand of the Roman governor, Pilate.

For John the crucifixion is the proclamation of the Kingship of Jesus, pure and simple. All detail has been removed. He has been lifted up, exalted. The term 'to lift up' (*hupsoun*) can mean the physical act of lifting, but it can also mean 'exaltation'. Later, in the interpretation of the Gnostic Discourse of Birth and Rebirth, this will be looked at in more detail. The text below from John 8 will be sufficient for our present purposes:

²⁸So Jesus said, 'When you have lifted up the Son of Man, then you will realize that I Am, and that I do nothing on my own, but I speak these things as the Father instructed me.

So, Jesus is lifted up, he is exalted, he becomes openly the King.

John adds to the crucifixion the division of Jesus' clothes. This event occurs in all four gospels. All four describe the soldiers casting lots for the garments, fulfilling the text from Psalm 22:18-19, which John cites, but the others do not.

'They divided my clothes among themselves,
and for my clothing they cast lots.'

The most interesting item among the clothes is the seamless *chiton* or tunic. The *chiton* is described in the text as 'without a seam' and 'woven completely from above [*anothen*]'. There have been innumerable attempts to explain the garment and its relevance. The Gnostic implication is clear: Jesus had worn this garment (his Flesh) from the onset of his time Below when he took on the Flesh, and he had it removed at the Crucifixion. It has been removed, as an indication that his Flesh is removed. The seamless garment is his Flesh. This is one of the more complex of John's metaphors.

In this Gnostic Treatise on the Crucifixion we have Gnostic themes clearly deployed: there is the theme of Jesus being presented as a King, the removal of his Flesh and the exaltation of Jesus as King.

7. The Magdalene Vision (20:1-29)

Final, Canonical Version

Introduction

²¹:¹ Early on the first day of the week, while it was still Dark, Mary Magdalene came to the tomb and saw that the stone had been removed from the tomb.

First Magdalene Report

² So she ran and went towards Simon Peter and towards the other disciple, the One whom Jesus Loved, and said to them, 'They have taken the Lord out of the tomb, and we do not know where they have laid him.'
³ Then Peter and the other disciple set out and went towards the tomb.
⁴ The two were running together, but the other disciple outran Peter and reached the tomb first. ⁵ He bent down to look in and saw the linen wrappings lying there, but he did not go in. ⁶ Then Simon Peter came,

following him, and went into the tomb. He saw the linen wrappings lying there, [7] and the cloth that had been on Jesus' head, not lying with the linen wrappings but rolled up in a place by itself. [8] Then the other disciple, who reached the tomb first, also went in, and he saw and believed.

([9] *For as yet they did not understand the scripture, that he must rise from the dead.*)

[10] Then the disciples returned to their own places.

Mary's Vision

[11] But Mary stood weeping outside the tomb. As she wept, she bent over to look into the tomb; [12] and she saw two angels in white, sitting where the body of Jesus had been lying, one at the head and the other at the feet. [13] They said to her, 'Woman, why are you weeping?'

She said to them, 'They have taken away my Lord, and I do not know where they have laid him.' [14] When she had said this, she turned round and saw Jesus standing there, but she did not know that it was Jesus.

[15] Jesus said to her, 'Woman, why are you weeping? For whom are you looking?'

Supposing him to be The Gardener, she said to him, 'Sir, if you have carried him away, tell me where you have laid him, and I will take him away.'

[16] Jesus said to her, 'Mary!'

She turned and said to him in Hebrew, 'Rabbouni!' (*which means Teacher*).

Conclusion

[17] Jesus said to her, 'Do not keep holding on to me, because I have not yet ascended to the Father. But go to my brothers and say to them, 'I am ascending to my Father and your Father, to my God and your God.' '

Second Magdalene Report

[18] Mary Magdalene went and announced to the disciples, 'I have seen the Lord';

and she told them that he had said these things to her.

The Disciples' Vision

[19] When it was evening on that day, the first day of the week, and the doors of the house where the disciples had met were locked for fear of the Jews, Jesus came and stood among them and said, 'Peace be with you.'

[20] After he said this, he showed them his hands and his side. Then the disciples rejoiced when they saw the Lord.

Conclusion

[21] Jesus said to them again, 'Peace be with you. As the Father has sent me, so I send you.'
[22] When he had said this, he breathed on them and said to them, 'Receive the Holy Spirit. [23] If you forgive the sins of any, they are forgiven them; if you retain the sins of any, they are retained.'

Thomas' Vision

[24] But Thomas (who was called the Twin), *one of The Twelve*, was not with them when Jesus came. [25] So the other disciples told him, 'We have seen the Lord.'
But he said to them, 'Unless I see the mark of the nails in his hands, and put my finger in the mark of the nails and my hand in his side, I will not believe.'
[26] A week later his disciples were again in the house, and Thomas was with them.
Although the doors were shut, Jesus came and stood among them and said, 'Peace be with you.'
[27] Then he said to Thomas, 'Put your finger here and see my hands. Reach out your hand and put it in my side. Do not doubt but believe.'
[28] Thomas answered him, 'My Lord and my God!'

Conclusion

[29] Jesus said to him, 'Have you believed because you have seen me? Blessed are those who have not seen and yet have come to believe.'

COMMENTARY

The seventh Independent Gnostic Treatise is the Magdalene Vision. At some stage and in some Gnostic setting this would have circulated as an independent text, a very important one since it identified the Gnostic successor to Jesus, but in a shorter form than it now appears in the Gospel of John. The original text has undergone considerable redaction and expansion that needs to be explained.

The four gospels include two types of discourse concerning the resurrection of Jesus: Visions and Empty Tomb stories. In each of the canonical gospels as they stand today these types have been fused into one narrative, although the narratives differ.

Taking John's gospel, in order to discriminate between the original material from which the story was fashioned, and the Final Canonical Version, with its insertions into the story by redactors, it will be necessary to look at variations in the text and *aporiai*. These latter are difficulties in the text that cause confusion; they are invariably caused by additions which do not fit into the argument of the original. *Aporiai* require an answer to the question: why was such-and-such put there and who would have done it?

We will look for the *aporiai* that have been commonly recognized in this Final Canonical Version.

Commentators first point out that in v. 2 there is the unexpected use of 'we' in 'we do not know', although Mary Magdalene was presumably the only witness to the Empty Tomb. Verse 2 also includes an awkward extra *kai pros* ('and towards' – although English translations hide this), one referring to Peter and one referring to the 'Other Disciple'.

In the following pericope, in vv. 3-9, there are more jarring *aporiai*. Verse 3 reads in an uneven fashion:

> Then Peter set out (singular) and the other disciple and they went (plural) to the tomb.

In vv. 4-7 there is a double reference to Peter and the Other Disciple seeing the grave clothes; Peter alone sees the cloth that had been on Jesus' head. It is not at all certain, in the present text, what happened in the tomb according to the storyline.

In v. 11 Magdalene has arrived back at the tomb although there had been no mention of her accompanying the two disciples when they ran to it. In v. 12 she sees angels but not the burial clothes, whereas the disciples had seen the reverse.

These *aporiai* can be satisfactorily explained by the fact that there had originally been a Version 1 of the Gnostic text. This underwent two substantial revisions – Version 2 and Version 3 (the Final Canonical Version) – but the revisions caused variations in the storyline and inconsistencies, the *aporiai*, none of which seemed to worry the editors.

The Final Version, as outlined above, is therefore the conglomerate of two major editing processes. We will examine each of the Versions in turn.

VERSION 1

The Text of Version 1

Introduction

21:1 Early on the first day of the week, while it was still Dark, Mary Magdalene came to the tomb and saw that the stone had been removed from the tomb.

First Magdalene Report

2 So she ran and went to [the disciples] and said to them, 'They have

taken the Lord out of the tomb, and we do not know where they have laid him.'

³ Then they set out and went towards the tomb.

(⁹ *For as yet they did not understand the scripture, that he must rise from the dead.*) ¹⁰ Then the disciples returned to their homes.

Mary's Vision

¹¹ But Mary stood weeping outside the tomb. As she wept, she bent over to look into the tomb; ¹² and she saw two angels in white, sitting where the body of Jesus had been lying, one at the head and the other at the feet. ¹³ They said to her, 'Woman, why are you weeping?'

She said to them, 'They have taken away my Lord, and I do not know where they have laid him.'

¹⁴ When she had said this, she turned round and saw Jesus standing there, but she did not know that it was Jesus.

¹⁵ Jesus said to her, 'Woman, why are you weeping? For whom are you looking?'

Supposing him to be The Gardener, she said to him, 'Sir, if you have carried him away, tell me where you have laid him, and I will take him away.'

¹⁶ Jesus said to her, 'Mary!'

She turned and said to him in Hebrew, 'Rabbouni!'

¹⁷ Jesus said to her, 'Do not keep holding on to me, because I have not yet ascended to the Father. But go to my brothers and say to them, 'I am ascending to my Father and your Father, to my God and your God.' '

Second Magdalene Report

¹⁸ Mary Magdalene went and announced to the disciples, 'I have seen the Lord';

and she told them that he had said these things to her.

The Disciples' Vision

¹⁹ When it was evening on that day, the first day of the week, and the doors of the house where the disciples had met were locked for fear of the Jews, Jesus came and stood among them and said, 'Peace be with you.'

²⁰ After he said this, he showed them his hands and his side. Then the disciples rejoiced when they saw the Lord.

²¹ Jesus said to them again, 'Peace be with you. As the Father has sent me, so I send you.'

²² When he had said this, he breathed on them and said to them, 'Receive the Holy Spirit. ²³If you forgive the sins of any, they are forgiven them; if you retain the sins of any, they are retained.'

Thomas' Vision

²⁴ But Thomas (who was called the Twin) was not with them when Jesus came. ²⁵ So the other disciples told him, 'We have seen the Lord.'

But he said to them, 'Unless I see the mark of the nails in his hands, and put my finger in the mark of the nails and my hand in his side, I will not believe.'

[26] A week later his disciples were again in the house, and Thomas was with them.

Although the doors were shut, Jesus came and stood among them and said, 'Peace be with you.'

[27] Then he said to Thomas, 'Put your finger here and see my hands. Reach out your hand and put it in my side. Do not doubt but believe.'

[28] Thomas answered him, 'My Lord and my God!'

[29] Jesus said to him, 'Have you believed because you have seen me? Blessed are those who have not seen and yet have come to believe.'

Version 1 was a Gnostic text, which had been constructed using material from an Empty Tomb/Vision story taken from the Jesus-Tradition, a source also used by the Synoptics. This Version was based on the story, common to the Synoptics in Mark 16:1-8 and parallels in the other Synoptics, of several women going to the tomb on the Sunday morning and finding it open and then returning to the disciples with the news; the Empty Tomb was explained to them by an angel-interpreter. Version 1 has preserved this in vv. 1-2 and 11-13 although it has removed the other women for the specific purpose of highlighting the priority of Magdalene. This removal explains the enigmatic 'we' in 20:2, which presumably was retained since it would have once have referred to the plural 'women' who in some earlier tradition returned with the announcement.

Version 1 only dealt with 'disciples', not specific ones such as Peter or the Beloved Disciple. It also explains why Magdalene is back at the tomb in v. 11 – she returned with the disciples and did not leave again.

The underlying Jesus-Tradition had contained a Vision of Jesus accorded to women, including Mary Magdalene, something similar to Mt 28:9-10.

So they [Mary Magdalene and the Other Mary] left the tomb [after an Angel has explained things to them] quickly with fear and great joy, and ran to tell his disciples. Suddenly Jesus met them and said, 'Greetings!' And they came to him, took hold of his feet, and worshiped him. Then Jesus said to them, 'Do not be afraid; go and tell my brothers to go to Galilee; there they will see me.'

The text is basically similar to the Markan appendix in 16:9-11, which was probably added later to Mark's gospel. However, this appendix records the first Vision as being to Mary Magdalene alone.

This material from the Jesus-Tradition was reworked to provide a Gnostic community with an account of how Mary Magdalene, their leader, had been the first to meet Jesus after his glorification and she attained *gnosis*.

She was the one who handed on Two Reports to the disciples in a very clever literary Treatise.

As mentioned, the 'women' who would have been in the Jesus-Tradition have been replaced here with Mary Magdalene alone. She is the spokesperson of the entire piece and v.2 has been inserted because this is the role of Mary: to speak at the key points in the narrative. Her First Report is: 'They have taken the Lord out of the tomb, and we do not know where they have laid him.'

The statement on 'taking away' has been lifted from the main narrative in v. 13. The fact that the statement has been duplicated and placed at the beginning of the account, where it is illogical (since the tomb at that point had not been examined by her), points to the fact that the Magdalene Reports are not well integrated.

The redactor of Version 1 has gone to considerable trouble to arrange the priority of Mary and to highlight her major statements. We find a Second Magdalene Report in v. 18: 'I have seen the Lord'. An examination of these two statements shows that each statement by Magdalene is followed by a similar structure. First, there is a clarification on the location where the action takes place. Then there is a Vision and finally a conclusion spoken by Jesus.

First Magdalene Report in v. 2: 'They have taken the Lord out of the tomb, and we do not know where they have laid him.'

Location: disciples go to Tomb in v. 3.

Mary's Vision : vv. 11-16

Conclusion: 'Do not keep holding onto me!' v. 17.

This section is held together, in a literary sense, by the stress on the Greek verb for 'to take away (arein)'. Magdalene's original report is that 'they have taken the Lord out [arein] of the tomb'. This statement is then repeated by Mary to the angels in the Vision section and to Jesus himself she states that 'I will take him away [arein]' (v. 15).

Mary's Vision begins with an Angelophany. This is followed by the Christophany, where Mary misidentifies Jesus as The Gardener. In John, the Garden where the Tomb is located is the same as the locus for the Handing-Over of Jesus. It is the New Eden where he was buried awaiting the new creation. Why the error on Mary's part? Who would the Gardener have been? We need to look no further than the Genesis text:

Yahweh Elohim took The Man and put him in the Garden of Eden to till it and keep it. (2:15)

Gnostic Mary thinks that Adam the Gardener is in the Garden and perhaps he had disposed of the body.

Mary Magdalene's misunderstanding has counterparts in the Gnostic literature. For example, in the *First Apocalypse of James*, which lauds James, we read of the latter's misunderstanding:

> James said, 'Rabbi, how, after these things, will you appear to us again? After they seize you, and you complete this destiny, you will go up to Him-Who-Is.' The Lord said, 'James, after these things I shall reveal to you everything, not for your sake alone but for the sake of the unbelief of men, so that faith may exist in them. For a multitude will attain to faith and they will increase in [...].' (29)

In Version 1, there follows an identification. The essential point in the account is Mary's title for Jesus – 'Teacher' – which is the way the text translates *Rabbouni* into Greek. *Rabbouni* is a form of endearment: 'My dear Teacher'.[42] It is a typically Gnostic title; the Revealer is a Teacher. Mary perceives him to be the same Jesus the Teacher who led the group during his earthly ministry. She wants to recapture the experience of the days when Jesus walked the earth, when he was specifically The Teacher. Jesus rejects this attempt with the curt: 'Do not keep on clinging to me'.[43] The reason given by Jesus for this statement is the fact that he has not yet ascended to God.

What is meant is the vital point that Mary and the disciples must give up any notion of a resuscitation of Jesus the Teacher, with the veil of Flesh, of a return to the earthly ministry as it was earlier. The only proper relationship at this point is with the Glorified Jesus who has ascended.

The use of 'brothers' clearly delineates the purpose of the exaltation.

> But go to my brothers and say to them, 'I am ascending to my Father and your Father, to my God and your God.'

'Brothers' sometimes in the additions to John (and in Acts) referred to a particular group of followers. Here, it refers specifically to the believers. Jesus, by means of his Glorification, is to return to The Father and to cement a relationship that can be shared by others who are believers. Mary, in short, had misunderstood the Vision. It did not mean that Jesus would continue his ministry in the World, the active 'teaching' of *gnosis* by Jesus the Teacher, which was a once-and-for-all event. He was about to establish a new rela-

---

[42] John's gospel uses Rabbi eight times in the sense of 'Teacher', a title used by disciples with overtones of familiarity and closeness. Only here does it use *Rabbouni*.

[43] The verb is in the imperfect, denoting continuous action.

tionship with the Father, through his Glorification and Ascension, and that relationship would be shared by believers. He would regain his status of Son and they would become his Brothers.

Version 1 then moves to a second Magdalene Report.

The Second Magdalene Report in v. 18 is: 'I have seen the Lord'. Mary reports her Vision to the disciples and there follows:

Location: The disciples gather in a house v. 19a

The Disciples' vision vv. 19b-21

Conclusion: The final commission v. 22-23

Once again, literary features and content, paralleling those of the first Magdalene Report, suggest that this is an intentional sectional division.

The Second Magdalene Report has also been taken from an already existing tradition, a Vision Story, but it has been reworked to parallel the First Magdalene Report in v. 2. This Second Report is elaborated into a narrative on seeing the Lord in the same way as v. 2 was elaborated into a narrative on the disciples finding the Empty Tomb. The subsequent account in vv. 19-23 is based on a tradition which described the first appearance of the glorified Jesus to the disciples. The account is expanded to include what might have been in the original version (at least implicitly) – the reception of the Spirit. This reception has figured prominently in the Gnostic discourse and was of the greatest importance.

In the first place, the glorified Jesus commissions his disciples. They are to replace him and to continue his ministry. Then he breathes over them.

He breathed on them and said to them, 'Receive the Holy Spirit.' (20:22)

The implication is clear. The only usages of the word used for 'to breathe' (enephysesa, the only usage in the canonical gospels) in the Hebrew Scriptures are the creation account in Genesis 2:7 ('He breathed into his nostrils the breath of life'), its restatement in Wisdom 15:11 ('He breathed a living spirit into them') and the account of the revivification of the dry bones in Ezekiel 37:9 ('Come from the four winds, O Breath, and breathe upon these slain, that they may live').

In short, the ritual action of divine breathing effects a new creation, a group that is vivified by the presence of the Spirit of God. The Spirit of God is the new Paraclete who will substitute for the presence of Jesus in his form of Flesh. Having been glorified, Jesus, in Version 1, has handed on the Spirit. This Version thus sums up the entire momentum of the gospel: Jesus came as The Word clothed in Flesh, Jesus was divested of the Flesh, he was glorified and ascended, he handed on the Spirit and thereby created a new community vivified by that Holy Spirit, the Word finally returned to the Father.

The ritual action of Jesus brings to mind other ritual actions: Jesus being anointed with oil; Jesus washing the feet of his disciples; Jesus giving the eucharist to Judas.

It is conjecture, but the ritual action of breathing could be the fourth sacrament mentioned in the Gospel of Philip after baptism, chrism and eucharist. We have noted that this is simply called *apolutrosis*, something like 'redemption': a baptism and a chrism and a eucharist and a redemption [*apolutrosis*] and a bridal chamber. It would be the fourth and final sacrament acknowledging the acquisition of *gnosis* and the believer's entry into the Bridal Chamber.

The community's newly acquired role that results from the reception of the Holy Spirit is described in the rather awkward logion that follows in v. 23:

> If you forgive the sins of any, they are forgiven them; if you retain the sins of any, they are retained.

It has been reasonably suggested that it is a saying based on something like Isaiah 22:22:

> I will place on his [reference is to Eliakim who has been elevated to the position of Master of the Palace] shoulder the key of the house of David; he shall open, and no one shall shut; he shall shut and no one shall open.

The saying, in some form, could have been handed on, in the Jesus-Tradition, in Aramaic. Matthew's translation of the Aramaic pairing into Greek in 16:19 is 'bind/loose':

> [19] 'I will give you the keys of the kingdom of heaven, and whatever you bind on earth will be bound in heaven, and whatever you loose on earth will be loosed in heaven.'

The Gospel of John's translation into Greek is 'forgive/retain'.[44] The reference is to judging.

The message is that the disciples must continue the discriminatory work of judging that Jesus initiated by his coming in the garment of Flesh, separating the evil from the good, bringing about a judgement in the present.

This statement is expanded by a Vision to Thomas. Thomas was well known in Gnostic circles and his Gospel was regarded highly. He was called

---

[44] Linking this text to authority over the confession of sins is out of place.

the Twin of Jesus in the sense that he too had acquired divinity and became like to Jesus. He is used here as the typical non-participant in the primordial Vision who doubts before he comes to *gnosis*.

There is a parallel account of doubt after the resurrection in Luke 24:36-40. The assembled disciples think that Jesus is a ghost. He reassures them by indicating his hands and feet and by offering to allow them to touch him.

> [36] While they were talking about this, Jesus himself stood among them and said to them, 'Peace be with you.' [37]They were startled and terrified, and thought that they were seeing a ghost. [38]He said to them, 'Why are you frightened, and why do doubts arise in your hearts? [39]Look at my hands and my feet; see that it is I myself. Touch me and see; for a ghost does not have flesh and bones as you see that I have.' [40]And when he had said this, he showed them his hands and his feet.

Version 1 has extended a traditional theme of doubt by introducing the figure of Thomas. In two previous references to him in the gospel he appears dour, even obtuse; he continues to be so in his reply to the disciples' claim to have had a Vision. The disciples repeat the Second Magdalene Report ('I have seen the Lord!'). In fact, the text reads that they 'continued to tell him' the Second Magdalene Report, repeating it over and over. His response is:

> 'Unless I see the mark of the nails on his hands, and put my finger in the mark of the nails and my hand in his side, I will not believe.'

This reflects Jesus' admonition to Magdalene that she must stop clinging to him. The vital point behind Thomas' misunderstanding is that he has refused to accept the word of the other disciples with its insistence that Jesus has been glorified. He wants gross physical evidence that Jesus, identical to the Jesus of the earthly ministry, had been present in the reported Vision. Subsequently, Jesus appears again and offers him his desired 'physical' proof in a distinctly sardonic way. Thomas backs away and does not accept his offer. His response is to bestow the title 'My Lord and my God' on Jesus.

Often this title for Jesus is lauded as the final and greatest of all the faith-expressions in the gospel. This is to gloss over its true significance. The title combines 'Lord' (*kurios* in Greek, referring to Yahweh) and 'God' (*theos* in Greek, referring to *'elohim* in Hebrew). This unusual form of address only occurs in two other readings from the Hebrew Scriptures. They are Genesis 2:7, where Yahweh energizes dust from the earth ('Then Yahweh God [*elohim*] formed man from the dust of the ground and breathed into his nostrils the breath of life') and Ezekiel 37:9, which we saw above when dealing with 'breath', where he energizes the dead bones ("Thus says God [*elohim*] Yahweh "Come from the four winds, O breath, and breathe upon these slain, that they may live""). Both are connected in their contexts with a ritual of breathing and energising the human person.

'My Lord and my God' is intended to be the spontaneous response of any Gnostic with faith to whom a Vision of the exalted Jesus has been made. It is the response of the Gnostic who has attained *gnosis*.

Within the whole of Version 1 we have the message that Jesus has been glorified. He is no longer 'Teacher' (a title appropriate to his mission in this World, clothed in Flesh), but he is 'My Yahweh and my God [*elohim*]' (a title appropriate to the Word, freed of Flesh).

Thomas' Vision closes with a formal blessing in v. 29:

'Blessed are those who have not seen and yet have come to believe.'

The blessing contrasts the two situations of seeing and not-seeing. It does not set out to belittle the experiences of those who 'saw' the evidence of the Empty Tomb and received a physical Vision of Jesus (Mary Magdalene and the disciples). They were unique, once-and-for-all, yet transient events. They were necessary at the beginning because the process had to start somewhere. Those founding experiences of 'seeing' initiated the faith and community. But they were unrepeatable. They are never to be expected again.

Henceforward, the typical Gnostic experience would be a faith-response to the interpreted scriptures (the first sub-section mentions *graphe* or Scripture, the Hebrew Scriptures) and to the preached word (the second sub-section mentions *elegon* or a repetition of the statement of faith). The Christian task, according to this dense gospel story, would be one of interpreting the Scripture and passing on the preached word. Believers would no longer be able to confront an Empty Tomb, but they must interpret Scripture; they would no longer experience a Vision of the glorified Jesus who breathes the Holy Spirit on them, but hear the preached word of other believers and respond by *gnosis*, to be acknowledged by the sacrament of *apolutrosis*. For this Version 1, the Scripture from the past and the Preaching of the present are the bases of Gnostic faith.

But Version 1 was to undergo its own adjustment and correction. In a new socio-religious situation it was considered, as it stood, to be misleading. A second Version was produced.

VERSION 2

The Text of Version 2

Introduction

²¹:¹ Early on the first day of the week, while it was still Dark, Mary Magdalene came to the tomb and saw that the stone had been removed from the tomb.

First Magdalene Report

² So she ran and went to the disciples and Simon Peter and said to them, 'They have taken the Lord out of the tomb, and we do not know where they have laid him.'
³ Then Peter and the disciples set out and went towards the tomb.
⁶ Then Simon Peter went into the tomb. He saw the linen wrappings lying there, ⁷and the cloth that had been on Jesus' head, not lying with the linen wrappings but rolled up in a place by itself.
(⁹ for as yet they did not understand the scripture that he must rise from the dead.)
¹⁰ Then the disciples returned to their homes.

Mary's Vision

¹¹ But Mary stood weeping outside the tomb. As she wept, she bent over to look into the tomb; ¹² and she saw two angels in white, sitting where the body of Jesus had been lying, one at the head and the other at the feet. ¹³ They said to her, 'Woman, why are you weeping?'
She said to them, 'They have taken away my Lord, and I do not know where they have laid him.' ¹⁴ When she had said this, she turned round and saw Jesus standing there, but she did not know that it was Jesus.
¹⁵ Jesus said to her, 'Woman, why are you weeping? For whom are you looking?'
Supposing him to be The Gardener, she said to him, 'Sir, if you have carried him away, tell me where you have laid him, and I will take him away.'
¹⁶ Jesus said to her, 'Mary!'
She turned and said to him in Hebrew, 'Rabbouni!' (which means Teacher).
¹⁷ Jesus said to her, 'Do not keep holding on to me, because I have not yet ascended to the Father. But go to my brothers and say to them, 'I am ascending to my Father and your Father, to my God and your God.' '

Second Magdalene Report

¹⁸ Mary Magdalene went and announced to the disciples, 'I have seen the Lord';
and she told them that he had said these things to her.

The Disciples' Vision

[19] When it was evening on that day, the first day of the week, and the doors of the house where the disciples had met were locked for fear of the Jews, Jesus came and stood among them and said, 'Peace be with you.'

[20] After he said this, he showed them his hands and his side. Then the disciples rejoiced when they saw the Lord.

[21] Jesus said to them again, 'Peace be with you. As the Father has sent me, so I send you.'

[22] When he had said this, he breathed on them and said to them, 'Receive the Holy Spirit. [23] If you forgive the sins of any, they are forgiven them; if you retain the sins of any, they are retained.'

Thomas' Vision

[24] But Thomas (who was called the Twin), one of The Twelve, was not with them when Jesus came. [25] So the other disciples told him, 'We have seen the Lord.'

But he said to them, 'Unless I see the mark of the nails in his hands, and put my finger in the mark of the nails and my hand in his side, I will not believe.'

[26] A week later his disciples were again in the house, and Thomas was with them.

Although the doors were shut, Jesus came and stood among them and said, 'Peace be with you.'

[27] Then he said to Thomas, 'Put your finger here and see my hands. Reach out your hand and put it in my side. Do not doubt but believe.'

[28] Thomas answered him, 'My Lord and my God!'

Conclusion

[29] Jesus said to him, 'Have you believed because you have seen me? Blessed are those who have not seen and yet have come to believe.'

Version 2 is a reworking by a Roman Christian editor of the first Version. We are probably looking at the point at which a Gnostic group or several groups were being assimilated into the Roman Christian context that had subsequently come into Asia Minor. The Gnostics were compelled to assimilate. The substance of the reworking of Version 1 has taken its cue from a separate Roman account of several disciples, headed by Peter, who go to the tomb after hearing the women's report and they are equally amazed to find it empty. This would have been similar to Luke 24:12, which made mention only of Peter.

But Peter got up and ran to the tomb; stooping and looking in, he saw the linen cloths by themselves; then he went home, amazed at what had happened.

This tradition is Roman Christian, acknowledging the priority of Peter over Magdalene and the Beloved Disciple. Peter has been alerted by Mary, true enough, but he is the one who validates the Empty Tomb.

There is something undoubtedly important about the 'linen cloths'; possibly, this report in the text was used in the first instance to validate that this tomb was actually that of Jesus, and not of someone else. Then, there is the introduction of the 'cloth that had been on Jesus' head'. It has been plausibly suggested that the word used for the latter is used to translate the curious reference to Moses' face veil in Exodus 34:33-35.

> [33] When Moses had finished speaking with them, he put a veil on his face; [34] but whenever Moses went in before Yahweh to speak with him, he would take the veil off, until he came out; and when he came out, and told the Israelites what he had been commanded, [35] the Israelites would see the face of Moses, that the skin of his face was shining; and Moses would put the veil on his face again, until he went in to speak with him.

Perhaps the readership of Version 2 may have been expected to pick up the reference and so the meaning of the 'cloth that had been on Jesus' head' in the tomb would be that Jesus as the New Moses had left aside his veil so as to see God, just as Moses had done.[45] In other words, only Peter had understood the full reality of the empty tomb.

Version 2 therefore made it clear that the first one to experience the Empty Tomb was Peter, who understood completely what had transpired.

There are some minor comments added to Version 1.

However, Version 2 would in its turn itself be redacted.

VERSION 3
THE FINAL CANONICAL VERSION

The text of the Final Version is what we have today in the text of John's gospel and it has been reproduced at the beginning of this section above.

At some stage, the already revised Version 2 was corrected by the addition of the Beloved Disciple or Other Disciple and his part in the validation of the Empty Tomb. It was this insertion that caused the difficulties such as the awkwardness of v.3 with its singular and plural verbs and the awkward twofold description of both Peter and the Other Disciple seeing the grave clothes (but Peter still seeing one extra).

---

[45] Lazarus, who had not seen God, came out of the tomb with his head cloth still in place (John 11:44).

The juxtaposition of Peter and the Other Disciple reflects the situation in an assimilated Christian community. The Other Disciple is acknowledged in v.2 to be the Beloved Disciple. The Other Disciple ran the faster, but he defers to Peter and does not enter the tomb. Peter, allowed to enter first, validates that the tomb is empty and that Jesus has put aside 'the cloth that had been on Jesus' head'. Only then did the Other Disciple enter the tomb and believe.

The Other Disciple has a functional importance in this narrative. He stands for the Gnostic believer who shows deference to the authority structure of a hierarchical community. The term 'Beloved Disciple' is not used; it is distinctively Gnostic and the innocuous term 'Other Disciple' is substituted. This Other Disciple might run faster, but he stands back for 'Peter' to make the discovery. The life-situation was the further assimilation of Gnostic groups into the Roman Church, beyond the Asia Minor context. The Gnostic believer is dependent on the structure of Peter's priority and must wait in turn. There is room for both the authoritative leader of the Roman Church and the charismatic leader of the Gnostic community. We will see the same relationship in 21:6-7 where Peter and the Beloved Disciple again contest with each other in a post-Resurrection event.

Who is the Beloved Disciple/the Other Disciple here? It is not Mary Magdalene since she and the Beloved Disciple are mentioned side by side. We will come to a conclusion on this matter when all texts including the Beloved Disciple have been carefully examined.

The literary structure of Version 3 can be confirmed by the orderly message it delivers. We begin with the First Magdalene Report and recognize the importance of this construction: 'They have taken away the Lord and I do not know where thy have laid him'. Mary has been made the spokesperson for the group. Her statement on the Empty Tomb is the statement of a charismatic leader. In vv. 3-10 an editor has taken a traditional Roman narrative and without much literary finesse has inserted the Other Disciple/The Beloved Disciple in order to form an elaboration on this statement. It is obvious that John intended to contrast The Beloved Disciple with Peter, although the disciple does not displace Peter.

What are we to conclude? John 20 began as a Gnostic Vision Story in which Magdalene was accorded the first access to Jesus after the crucifixion. This was because she was regarded by some Gnostics as the leader, the first to come to this *gnosis*. This experience, requiring interpretation, was expanded by weaving in Mary's Angelophany and Christophany. Alerted by Mary, the disciples experienced their own Vision and were commissioned.

Then Thomas, the absent one, came to faith by a personal Vision. At this stage the document was still Gnostic. Jesus was the divine Jesus who had come as the *Rabbouni* to teach his disciples the necessary *gnosis*. He had become 'Lord and God' after divesting himself of Flesh.

At a second stage, material concerning Peter was interpolated. He displaced Mary Magdalene as the leader of the group. He validated the Empty Tomb in the role of an official hierarchical leader.

At a third stage, the whole piece was given a final form by inserting the Beloved Disciple/Other Disciple in order to reconcile the varying interests in a complex Christian context. The Beloved Disciple stood for a charismatic leadership role. In this way what we read today in the canonical text has come into being.

As an appendix, we will now go over the *aporiai* mentioned at the beginning of this commentary:

- Use of 'we' in v. 2. This was because of the original statement in the Jesus-Tradition being delivered by 'women'.

- The extra 'toward' *kai pros* in regard to Peter and the Other Disciple. This was because of the fact that the 'Other Disciple' was interpolated later. Possibly both of them were accorded equal standing; there was no precedence of either one.

- In v. 3 Peter 'sets out (singular) and they went (plural)'. The original form would have had Peter going to the tomb alone. The Other Disciple was a later intrusion in the sentence and required a plural verb.

- In vv. 4-7 the double description of seeing the grave clothes and Peter alone seeing the 'cloth that had been on Jesus' head'. This awkward construction was because of both of them being accorded an equal experience in the tomb. Peter, in Version 2, had seen the grave clothes and the 'cloth that had been on Jesus' head'. The Other Disciple, in Version 3, saw the grave clothes but not the 'cloth that had been on his head'.

- In v. 11 Mary Magdalene is back at the Tomb because she had originally been described as returning with the disciples to the Tomb and not leaving.

- In v. 12 Mary sees angels and not the burial clothes. There are two very different constructions used. Mary has an Angelophany that leads to a Christophany. Peter and the Other Disciple see, at this stage, only the evidence of the grave clothes.

As the text stands in the canonical Gospel of John today, it is a Roman text. It upholds the succession of Peter and the factual resurrection of Jesus. For the Christian, this is the final state of the text. What we have done is simply to show that the text reflects a long transmission that has changed from one religio-social situation to another. In this process, inconsistencies have been acquired. None of the three Versions are put forward as historical. Each speaks correctly to its own constituency.

CONCLUSION TO THE INDEPENDENT GNOSTIC TREATISES

The seven separate Gnostic Treatises would have circulated as individual catechetical pieces intended to instruct believers in the Gnostic Jesus. It is impossible to say anything more about their earlier history. Their language and their mindset are typically Gnostic and they present many difficulties of interpretation if they are read as if they had no transmission history. In fact, apart from the Judgement of Jesus, the other six show that they have been significantly edited once they had entered a Roman Christian setting.

Apart from the Hymn to the Word or *Logos*, they show links with the Jesus-Tradition but not with the Synoptic gospels. This would seem to indicate that the Jesus-Tradition was available to the Gnostics in some substantial form.

All of these Treatises would eventually be integrated into the canonical gospel of John, as we will see. Thereby, they became Roman documents.

We now turn to the next substantial Gnostic text: The Book of Seven Signs.

THE BOOK OF SEVEN SIGNS

This Book of Seven Signs, it is proposed, self-identifies by its clear references to 'signs' (*semeia*). Two events are nominated as *semeia*, but there are other events that fit into the same category. A conclusion refers to 'these [signs] are written so that you may come to believe that Jesus is the Messiah, the Son of God'. This explains the purpose of gathering the Signs together. The number of *semeia* would seem to be seven, a favourite Gnostic number.

The notion of *semeion* is Gnostic; the language in the seven texts is Gnostic; the Jesus of the seven Signs is a Gnostic Jesus. The hypothesis seems warranted that it was a Gnostic book based on the fact that Jesus the Divine Teacher had come and taught not so much by way of words and logical arguments but by Signs. These Signs were Jesus-events which, when correctly interpreted, revealed the true *gnosis* about the mission of Jesus. The Seven Signs are literary objects as they now stand, but they may have been used in oral Gnostic catechesis. They confront the believer with the essential content of *gnosis* and they call for a response of acceptance or non-acceptance. Whether the Jesus-events took place historically would be difficult to prove and irrelevant as far as interpreting the gospel of John is concerned.

So, in the first place, the seven Signs make use of certain elements of the ongoing Jesus-Tradition. The gospel of Mark had put its own order into narrative elements taken from this same Jesus-Tradition and showed how Jesus, by his cures, his exorcisms and his debates, was able to manifest himself as The Messiah. But Mark's Messiah was a real human being some- how related closely to God. John's Messiah is a Divine Being who reveals his Glory to the select few from the beginning. This revelation is prolonged after his departure by the use of the Book of Seven Signs. The Book is something like a Lectionary and something like a Handbook for practical Gnostic instruction.

Once it became incorporated into an orthodox Roman Christian set- ting, as we claim happened in Western Asia Minor, the Book of Seven Signs accumulated expansions, explanations and corrections. It would eventually be divided into its component parts and these were singular- ly distributed throughout the developing canonical text, with significant major interpolations – Independent Gnostic Treatises, Gnostic Discourses and Roman insertions – breaking up the sequence of Seven Signs to such an extent that its primitive outline was lost from view among the broader discourse. Today the Book of Seven Signs can only be reconstructed with difficulty.

The Gnostic link with the idea of Signs was well established. *The Apoca- lypse of Adam* is a revelatory discourse which claims to have been delivered by three Angels from Heaven to Adam. There are no explicitly Christian references in it. Some scholars suggest it should be dated as early as the first century CE and related to the earlier form of Jewish Gnosticism that pre- ceded Christian Gnosticism. In the text Adam describes the Revelation to his son, Seth, who, together with his progeny, become the agents to hand on the *gnosis* to others. Adam explains how he and Eve lost the saving *gnosis* in the first place. However, it has now been transmitted to Seth and then made available to others. In a next phase, however, the evil Creator-God attempted to destroy mankind by the Flood and other means. Then came the Saviour, The Illuminator.

The description of The Illuminator is very interesting as it introduces the topic of Signs:

> And he will perform Signs and Wonders in order to scorn the Powers and their Ruler.
>
> Then the God of the Powers will be disturbed, saying, 'What is the Power of this Man who is higher than we?' Then he will arouse a great wrath against that Man. And the Glory will withdraw and dwell in holy houses which it has chosen for itself. And the powers will not see it with their eyes, nor will they see The Illuminator either. Then they will punish the Flesh of the Man upon whom the Holy Spirit came. (77)

The language of the Gospel of John is already here in this excerpt: Signs, Powers (Archons), the Ruler (Devil), The Man, Glory, the Flesh of the Man, Holy Spirit. The scenario is that of Gnosticism: The Illuminator or The Man will work Signs that will display the Glory of God and will attract the wrath of the Archons and the Creator-God. The Illuminator will be punished in The Flesh. However, the Holy Spirit has come down on The Man. He is not really Flesh. This is a good description of the process that underlies the Book of Seven Signs.

There is no necessity to believe that The Illuminator in this text is Jesus. But similarly there is no doubt that the text could be applied to the memory of Jesus among later Christian Gnostics. Probably that is why it was preserved with the other Christian Gnostic documents at Nag Hammadi; they identified Jesus with The Illuminator, even if originally the text had no Christian context.

Jesus, in a Christian version of this story, would become The Illuminator who came into The World to perform Signs. Some believed in his teaching. However, this display aroused the wrath of the Archons and their allies, the Jews and Pharisees. These conspired to punish The Flesh of The Man by crucifixion. But The Man was only clothed in Flesh; he was the Word and possessed the Holy Spirit and was not himself Flesh. This is the essential Gnostic background to the Book of Seven Signs.

A final editor of this particular book, prior to its placement in the Gnostic form of John, has put together seven of these Signs. There is an admission at the end of the book that there were more than seven. The seven suffice for the purposes of Gnostic instruction. We will see that the seven are arranged in chiastic order. This is yet another substantiation that there was a separate Book of Seven Signs and that the number was seven. The chiasm, tightly constructed as it is, is very important because it explains something of the meaning inherent in the total text. The chiasmic structure is identified by themes and language within the separate Signs:

A Cana and The Mother

   B The cure of the Official's Son

      C The cure of the Crippled Man

         D The Feeding of the 5000

      C1 The cure of the Blind Man

   B1 The raising of Lazarus

A1 The Cross and The Mother

Of the seven Signs, there are three parallel Signs as can be seen in the chiasm: Cana and The Mother/The Cross and The Mother; The cure of the Official's Son/The raising of Lazarus; The cure of the Crippled Man/The cure of the Blind Man. The Feeding of the 5000 is left unattached at the centre; it is the core Sign. It will be demonstrated that there are linguistic and theological cues that illustrate the relationships between the three twin Signs. These will be explained in the Commentary.

What follows in the commentaries on the Seven Signs is, first of all, the retrieval of the text of the Book of Seven Signs from its surroundings within the text of canonical John, where it has been interspersed with Independent Gnostic Treatises, Gnostic Discourses and Roman Christian Insertions, Even when disengaged, each Sign is found to have accrued its own number of editorial expansions and comments. There needs to be a deal of literary dissection. Any later additions in the Signs themselves are marked by italics in the canonical text. In the commentary both the Sign and any additions to their text will be explained.

The Book of Seven Signs comprises the following:

Sign 1. Cana and The Mother (2:1-12)

Sign 2: The Cure of the Official's Son (4:43-54)

Sign 3: The Cure of the Crippled Man (5:1-18)

Sign 4: The Feeding of the 5000 (6:1-34)

Sign 5: The Cure of the Blind Man (9:1-41 and 10:19-21)

Sign 6: Raising of Lazarus (11:1-57)

Sign 7: The Cross and the Mother (19:26-30)

Conclusion to Book of Signs (20: 30-31)

We will now look at each text in turn.

1. Cana and The Mother (2:1-12)

²:¹ On the third day there was a wedding in Cana of Galilee, and the Mother of Jesus was there.

² *Jesus and his disciples had also been invited to the wedding.*

³ When the wine gave out, the Mother of Jesus said to him, 'They have no wine.'

⁴ And Jesus said to her, 'Woman, what concern is that to you and to me? My Hour has not yet come.'

⁵ His Mother said to the servants, 'Do whatever he tells you.'

⁶ Now standing there were six stone water-jars for the Jewish rites of purification, *each holding twenty or thirty gallons [two or three metrata].*

⁷ Jesus said to them, 'Fill the jars with water.' And they filled them up to the brim. ⁸ He said to them, 'Now draw some out, and take it to the chief steward.'

So they took it. ⁹ When the steward tasted the water that had become wine, and did not know where it came from *(though the servants who had drawn the water knew)*, the steward called the Bridegroom ¹⁰ and said to him, 'Everyone serves the good wine first, and then the inferior wine after the guests have become drunk. But you have kept the Good Wine until now.'

¹¹ Jesus did this, the first of his signs, in Cana of Galilee, and revealed his Glory; and his disciples believed in him.

¹² *After this he went down to Capernaum with his Mother, The Brothers, and his Disciples; and they remained there for a few days.*

COMMENTARY

Since the beginnings of Biblical interpretation, scholars have found grave difficulties with this text of the Wedding Feast of Cana. Whose wedding was being celebrated? Who was the Bridegroom addressed by the steward? Why the stern tone in Jesus' address to his mother and his use of the abrasive 'Woman'? Why does the mother go ahead to arrange the Wine event, regardless of his pre-emptory answer? Why was such a large quantity of wine produced – over 200 litres? What is the exact difference between Good Wine and Inferior Wine? Why is this a Sign (a *semeion*, as the conclusion claims)?

This text requires the closest scrutiny if these questions can be answered.

The language of Bridegroom and lack of wine brings to mind a text in the three Synoptics recalling Jesus' self-identification as a Bridegroom.

Now John's disciples and the Pharisees were fasting; and people came and said to him, 'Why do John's disciples and the disciples of the Pharisees fast, but your disciples do not fast?' Jesus said to them, 'The wedding-guests cannot fast while the bridegroom is with them, can they? As long as they have the bridegroom with them, they cannot fast. The days will come when the bridegroom is taken away from them, and then they will fast on that day. (Mark 2: 18-19 and parallels, but note that Matthew uses 'mourn' instead of 'fast')

The Gospel of John's canonical version uses the Bridegroom imagery too, where John the Baptist speaks of Jesus, but it is in a Roman Christian Insertion:

He who has the bride is the bridegroom. The friend of the bridegroom, who stands and hears him, rejoices greatly at the bridegroom's voice. For this reason my joy has been fulfilled. He must increase, but I must decrease.' (3:29-30)

In this short, difficult excerpt, the Bridegroom is obviously Jesus and the 'Friend of the Bridegroom' is John the Baptist. However, we will see that this excerpt was a later addition to the gospel and does not affect the question of the Bridegroom here.

The phrase 'Jesus and his disciples had also been invited to the wedding' is clearly an editorial addition that wants to indicate that the wedding was not that of Jesus, and he was not the Bridegroom. It explains why he and the disciples would have been there in the first case.

In fact, the Wedding was that of Jesus, and he was the Bridegroom.

This entourage of 'disciples' is expanded in the final verse of the Sign: 'his mother, the brothers, and his disciples'. This is another addition to fit the original Sign into the later narrative. The mention of 'brothers' was not in the earlier addition in v. 2 and, in the transmission of the text, there has been an attempt to make it 'his brothers', but this was not widely attested. We have seen that The Brothers refers to an early Jesus-movement group, headed by James the Just, Brother of the Lord, and some well-meaning scribe wanted to include them.

The most important components of the Sign are Jesus, the Bridegroom, the production of the Good Wine, and the Mother of Jesus (significantly, she is never named Mary in John's gospel). The Mother will not appear again in John until the last Sign at the foot of the Cross.

These two Signs, at the beginning and end of the chiastic structure, are clearly related each to the other.

For Christian Gnosticism, Jesus had no human birth and therefore no human mother. In the *Letter of Peter to Philip* he is spoken of as a 'son', but clearly he is the Son of God.

Then, when the apostles had come together, and had thrown themselves upon their knees, they prayed thus saying, 'Father, Father, Father of the light, who possesses the incorruptions, hear us just as thou hast taken pleasure in thy holy child Jesus Christ. For he became for us an Illuminator in the Darkness. Yea, hear us!'

And they prayed again another time, saying, 'Son of life, Son of immortality, who is in the light, Son, Christ of immortality, our Redeemer, give us power, for they seek to kill us!' (133-134)

Since Mary could not have been the physical mother of Jesus in Gnostic thought, the reference to 'Mother' here and in the corresponding Sign at the foot of the cross must have had some other meaning.

In another text taken from the same *Letter of Peter to Philip*, already examined above for a different purpose, Peter explains the predicament of 'The Mother' in Gnostic terminology:

And Peter opened his mouth, he said to his [fellow] disciples, 'Did our Lord Jesus, when he was in the body, show us everything? For he came down. My brothers, listen to my voice.' And he was filled with a Holy Spirit. He spoke thus: 'Our Illuminator, Jesus, came down and was crucified. And he bore a crown of thorns. And he put on a purple garment. And he was crucified on a tree and he was buried in a tomb. And he rose from the dead. My brothers, Jesus is a Stranger to this suffering. But we are the ones who have suffered through the transgression of The Mother. And because of this, he did everything like us. For the Lord Jesus, the Son of the immeasurable glory of the Father, he is the author of our life. (139)

The Mother in this context is Barbelo or Sophia. She was within The Pleroma but brought about an Emanation of the Demiurge without due permission from her consort, The Divine Spirit. She fell from grace and, with the Demiurge-Creator, Yaldabaoth, she had a part in the creation of the world. The Demiurge breathed the spiritual soul from Sophia into Adam. Sophia wanted to protect this spiritual soul. We repeat the text of the *Apocryphon of John*:

'And the Sophia of the *Epinoia*, being an Aeon, conceived a thought from herself and the conception of the Invisible Spirit and foreknowledge. She wanted to bring forth a likeness out of herself without the consent of the Spirit, – he had not approved – and without her consort, and without his consideration. And though the person of her maleness had not approved, and she had not found her agreement, and she had thought without the consent of the Spirit and the knowledge of her agreement, (yet) she brought forth. And because of the invincible power which is in her, her thought did not remain idle, and something came out of her which was imperfect and different from her appearance, because she had created it without her consort. And it was dissimilar to the likeness of its mother, for it has another form.

And when she saw [the consequences of] her desire, it changed into a form of a lion-faced serpent. And its eyes were like lightning fires which flash. She cast it away from her, outside that place, that no one of the immortal ones might see it, for she had created it in ignorance. And she surrounded it with a luminous cloud, and she placed a throne in the middle of the cloud that no one might see it except the Holy Spirit who is called the mother of the living. And she called his name Yaltabaoth. (9-10)

Yaldabaoth (or Yaltabaoth) now continues independently. He is arrogant and ignorant. The Mother, Sophia, repents of her untimely action. Then there is the Emanation of another who will become the Perfect Man in order to right the error caused by Sophia, his Mother.

This is the first Archon who took a great power from his mother. And he removed himself from her and moved away from the places in which he was born. He became strong and created for himself other aeons with a flame of luminous fire which [still] exists now. (9-10)

And the Arrogant One took a power from his mother. For he was ignorant, thinking that there existed no other except his mother alone. And when he saw the multitude of the angels which he had created, then he exalted himself above them. (13)

And when the mother recognized that the garment of darkness was imperfect, then she knew that her consort had not agreed with her. She repented with much weeping. And the whole Pleroma heard the prayer of her repentance, and they praised on her behalf the invisible, virginal Spirit. And he consented; and when the invisible Spirit had consented, the Holy Spirit poured over her from their whole Pleroma. For it was not her consort who came to her, but he came to her through the Pleroma in order that he might correct her deficiency. And she was taken up not to her own aeon but above her son, that she might be in the Ninth[46] until she has corrected her deficiency.

And a voice came forth from the exalted aeon-heaven: 'The Man exists and the son of Man.' And the chief archon, Yaltabaoth, heard [it] and thought that the voice had come from his Mother. And he did not know from where it came. And he taught them, the holy and perfect Mother-Father, the complete foreknowledge, the image of the Invisible One who is the Father of the all [and] through whom everything came into being, the first Man. For he revealed his likeness in a human form. (13-14)

Her plight is further elaborated in the *Valentinian Exposition*. Sophia fell from the Pleroma because she acted without permission. This fall could only be corrected by her Son, who had the fullness of divinity as The Perfect Man, and by no other.

---

[46] In Gnostic thought, the 'Ninth' was the highest stage of spiritual enlightenment.

Since it is a perfect form that should ascend into the Pleroma, he did not at all want to consent to the suffering, but he was detained [...] him by Limit, that is, by the syzygy, since her correction will not occur through anyone except her own Son, whose alone is the fullness of divinity. He willed within himself bodily to leave the powers and he descended.

And these things [passions] Sophia suffered after her son ascended from her, for she knew that she dwelt in a [...] in unity and restoration. They were stopped [...] the brethren [...] these. A [...] did not [...]. I became [...]. Who indeed are they? The [...], on the one hand, stopped her [...], on the other hand, [...]. with the [...] her. These moreover are those who were looking at me, these who, [...] these who considered [...] the death. They were stopped [...] her and she repented and she besought the Father of the truth, saying, 'Granted that I have renounced my consort. Therefore I am beyond confirmation as well. I deserve the things [passions] I suffer. I used to dwell in the Pleroma putting forth the Aeons and bearing fruit with my consort' And she knew what she was and what had become of her. (33-34)

The *Apocryphon of John* now explains that Adam is the creation of the great powers and Yaldabaoth is tricked into giving the Man a breath of divinity.

'And when the mother wanted to retrieve the power which she had given to the chief archon, she petitioned the Mother-Father of the All, who is most merciful. He sent, by means of the holy decree, the five lights down upon the place of the angels of the chief archon. They advised him that they should bring forth the power of the Mother. And they said to Yaltabaoth, 'Blow into his face something of your spirit and his body will arise.' And he blew into his face the spirit which is the power of his mother; he did not know [this], for he exists in ignorance. And the power of the mother went out of Yaltabaoth into the natural body, which they had fashioned after the image of the one who exists from the beginning. The body moved and gained strength, and it was luminous. (19)

This was Adam, the likeness of the divine First Man, Adamas. The final stage in the mythology is the role of Eve, the Epinoia. She is hidden in Adam.

'But the blessed One, the Mother-Father, the beneficent and merciful One, had mercy on the power of the Mother which had been brought forth out of the chief archon, for they [the archons] might gain power over the natural and perceptible body. And he sent, through his beneficent Spirit and his great mercy, a helper to Adam, luminous Epinoia which comes out of him, who is called Life. And she assists the whole creature, by toiling with him and by restoring him to his fullness and by teaching him about the descent of his seed [and] by teaching him about the way of ascent, [which is] the way he came down. And the luminous Epinoia was hidden in Adam, in order that the archons might not know her, but that the Epinoia might be a correction of the deficiency of the mother. (20)

Eve is the human equivalent of Sophia. Adam is awakened by Sophia or Epinoia. Both Adam and Eve are enlightened by her. It is Sophia who has come to make up for the deficiency caused by her error.

'And he [Adam] saw the woman beside him. And in that moment the luminous Epinoia appeared, and she lifted the veil which lay over his mind. And he became sober from the drunkenness of Darkness. And he recognized his counter-image, and he said, 'This is indeed bone of my bones and flesh of my flesh.' Therefore the man will leave his father and his mother, and he will cleave to his wife, and they will both be one flesh. For they will send him his consort, and he will leave his father and his mother ... [3 lines unreadable] (23)

'And our sister Sophia [is] she who came down in innocence in order to rectify her deficiency. Therefore she was called Life, which is the mother of the living, by the foreknowledge of the sovereignty of heaven. And through her they have tasted the perfect Knowledge. I appeared in the form of an eagle on the tree of knowledge, which is the Epinoia from the foreknowledge of the pure light, that I might teach them and awaken them out of the depth of sleep. For they were both in a fallen state, and they recognized their nakedness. The Epinoia appeared to them as a light; she awakened their thinking. (23)

Only at this point does the unusual dialogue and the context of the first Sign begin to make sense.

There is a wedding feast. No Gnostic would fail to recognize the context: it is the implementation of the Bridal Chamber, the locus where the final consummation of divinity takes place with those who have attained the fullness of *gnosis*. We can cite the *Gospel of Philip* yet again:

The Lord did everything in a mystery, a baptism and a chrism and a eucharist and a redemption and a bridal chamber. (6)

The Bridal Chamber is the final destination of those who have fully achieved *gnosis*. Jesus is The Bridegroom of this Cana narrative. The Mother of Jesus, Sophia, is present. She requires rehabilitation and is endeavouring to right her wrong. 'They have no Wine', she says. She is describing the human condition, the condition of all humans at that moment, without the Wine of spiritual enlightenment, of *gnosis*.[47] And who is the Bride? Anomalous as it seems, it is Sophia (even if she is named as the 'Mother of Jesus' – the Gnostic Jesus did not have a real humanity, could not have had a human mother and could not have had a sexual partner). She has her counterpart, Eve or Sister, with her. Later Mary Magdelene will take on the role of the

---

[47] In the *Gospel of Philip* we read: Spiritual love is wine and fragrance. (77)

counterpart to Sophia/Eve. Sophia is the first partner of Jesus; there will be more *pneumatikoi* to follow.

Then occurs one of the most troublesome texts for those who try to follow the literal meaning of a text where Jesus is said to have casually gone to a normal wedding feast where the wine has run out. It makes sense only as a Gnostic text.

> And Jesus said to her, 'Woman, what concern is that to you and to me? My Hour has not yet come.'

'Woman' has nothing to do with gender or disrespect. It is an alternative for Sophia and Eve. Then follows a Hebrew-like clause: 'What concern is that to you and to me?". The phrase was used in the book of Judges:

> Then Jephthah sent messengers to the king of the Ammonites and said, 'What is there between you and me that you have come to me to fight against my land?' (11:12)

Jephthah did not want to be involved with the king. He saw no reason for any participation in conflict. Likewise, using the same Hebrew idiom, Jesus does not want to bring about the conclusion of his mission prematurely. His Hour has not yet come; he is unwilling to proceed to the completion of his mission, which would entail offering salvation to all.

He does however, at the behest of the Woman, provide a Sign of the future reconciliation: Water is changed to Wine. It is a Sign that points to *gnosis*, but not the fulfilment of *gnosis*. Water was the revelation of the Father brought into the World by Jesus; it is to be followed by the Wine of the Gnostic insight, the profound experience of *gnosis*. The changing of the Water of revelation into The Wine of *gnosis* describes Jesus' mission in the World. Just as he changes six stone water-jars of Water into Wine (*oinos*) here in the first Sign, in the seventh Sign, he himself will drink from a *skeuos*, a seventh container, which is a much more common receptacle than the stone water-jars at Cana.

There were six of those stone water-jars. They were unusual objects, although instances have been found in conjunction with first century CE Palestinian houses of the upper classes. Six is the number of incompletion. Seven is needed for completion. The seventh jar will be described in the seventh Sign, the death of Jesus, and the seventh container will be the common *skeuos*.

But the text, not surprisingly, has always caused difficulties. In Hebrew thought, Wine was one of the harbingers of the fullness of time when all would be restored. When the final time came, there would be much Wine.

The following is one of several abundance-of-wine texts:

The time is surely coming, says Yahweh,
when the one who ploughs shall overtake the one who reaps,
and the treader of grapes the one who sows the seed;
the mountains shall drip sweet wine,
and all the hills shall flow with it. (Amos 9:13)

Building on this key concept from mainline Judaism, the reference that the water-jars were meant 'for the Jewish rites of purification' was added. They are Jewish water jars. An editor has added 'each holding two or three *metrata*' – over two hundred litres. It hints at the meaning, quite out of context here, that Christianity, the abundant Good Wine, has supplanted Judaism, the Water. It is a later interpretation and a quite different interpretation of the changing of Water to Wine.

The Mother, Sophia, now recedes from the Gnostic gospel of John until the scene at the foot of the Cross, the seventh Sign, when she re-appears. She must wait until The Hour.

Cana and The Mother began as a Gnostic statement of great profundity. There is a wedding feast. This is the formal establishment of the Bridal Chamber, as discussed in the *Gospel of Philip*. The Bridegroom is Jesus. Sophia, The Mother, is present as the Bride. She has brought about the dire situation of humans, now entrapped in The World. She asks, on behalf of humanity, for Jesus – the Word who has taken on Flesh – to right the deficiency caused by Yaldabaoth here and now.

Jesus refuses and rebukes her as The Corruptible Woman, as she was named in some Gnostic texts. The Hour for rehabilitating humanity has not yet come. But he does give the first Sign. He changes water into wine and those who are *pneumatikoi* can understand. Wine is *gnosis*; the abundance of wine is the Sign that *gnosis* is now about to be made available to the believer. The Sign, like the other six, are preparatory. The Hour has not yet come.

The narrative ends with a typical Gnostic statement: Sign, Glory and Belief. The disciples penetrate the Sign and see the Glory, the manifestation of divinity. They believe. This is the reaction expected of all who read the text of the first Sign correctly.

This first Sign will link with the seventh Sign, The Cross and the Mother. There, The Mother, The Woman, The Hour, the Wine will all occur again. The two Signs should be read in close tandem.

2. The Cure of the Official's Son (4:43-54)

[43] *When two days were over, he went from that place to Galilee*

[44] *For Jesus himself had testified that a prophet has no honour in the prophet's own country.*

[45] *When he came to Galilee, the Galileans welcomed him, since they had seen all that he had done in Jerusalem at the Festival; for they too had gone to the Festival.*

[46] Then he came again to Cana in Galilee where he had changed the water into wine.

Now there was a royal official whose son lay ill in Capernaum. [47]When he heard that Jesus had come from Judea to Galilee, he went and begged him to come down and heal his son, for he was at the point of death.

[48]Then Jesus said to him, 'Unless you see signs and wonders you will not believe.'

[49]The official said to him, 'Sir, come down before my little boy dies.'

[50]Jesus said to him, 'Go; your son will live.'

The man believed the Word that Jesus spoke to him and started on his way. [51]As he was going down, his slaves met him and told him that his child was alive. [52]So he asked them the hour when he began to recover, and they said to him, 'Yesterday at one in the afternoon the fever left him.' [53]The father realized that this was the hour when Jesus had said to him, 'Your son will live.'

So he himself believed, along with his whole household.

[54]Now this was the Second Sign that Jesus did after coming from Judea to Galilee.

COMMENTARY

The second Sign concerns the cure of a Royal Official's son. The Official is presumably a Gentile and this would have given a reason for the interpolation of the two parallel Discourses about a Jew and a Samaritan in the preceding section: Jew (Nicodemus), Samaritan (the Samaritan Woman), Gentile (Royal Official). It should be mentioned that the idea of Jesus ministering to Gentiles and Samaritans is surely a Johannine creation. It reflects the later Christian attitude of supersessionism, that Christianity superseded Judaism and opened itself to all who might believe, not just Jews. This is why Jesus pits himself, at various points in the Gospel of John, against the great ones of Jewish lore: Abraham, Jacob, David and so on.

The transition phrase in vv. 43-45 has been inserted by an editor and based on a popular saying: 'A prophet has no honour in his own country'. In the Synoptics the phrase applied to Galilee; here it seems to apply to Jerusalem and Judaea. The Galileans, who are said to have seen the Cleansing of the Temple in Jerusalem, are praised. This reflection has no connection with the second Sign which takes place, like the first, in Cana, apart from the need to return Jesus from Jerusalem to Cana. At an earlier stage the Second Sign simply followed the First.

There is a similar text to this Sign in Matthew 8:5-13 and Luke 7:1-10 although those texts deal with a centurion rather than a royal official and there are no noticeable verbal parallels between John and the two Synoptics. As the text was not derived from Mark and there are parallels in Matthew and Luke, it is possible that a text, dealing with the Temple, has been adapted from the Jesus-Tradition. John must have depended on this earlier form of the story in the Jesus-Tradition. Clearly, a common tradition has been used by both the Synoptics and John and redacted in quite different ways.

In the Synoptics it is unclear whether the centurion is referring to his son or his servant (both are possible translations of the Greek *pais*). In John the term for 'son' (*huios*) is clearly used and later 'little boy' (*paidion*, a term which is also used for 'disciple'). The son is close to death and he is cured from a distance by the words of Jesus ('Your son will live!'). The meaning of the Gnostic Sign is clear enough – Jesus brings life, in this case to someone on the brink of death.

There is an obvious connection with the raising of Lazarus, its chiastic pair. In this case of the centurion's son there is less certainty about the closeness of death. Lazarus has been entombed and already putrefaction has set in. The Jesus statement to the official ('Your son will live!') is paralleled by his statement to Martha ('Your brother will rise again!'). Lazarus is the ideal believer in Jesus who does not see death; *paidion*, as noted above with regard to the boy, is also used for a Jesus disciple. The restoration of life and the notion of resurrection were closely aligned in Gnostic thought.

It is clearly noted at the end of the passage that this is the Second Sign.

3. The Cure of the Crippled Man (5:1-18)

5:1 *After this there was a Festival of the Jews, and Jesus went up to Jerusalem.*
2 Now in Jerusalem by the Sheep Gate there is a pool, called in Hebrew Beth-zatha, which has five porticoes. 3 In these lay many invalids – blind, lame, and paralysed. 5 One man was there who had been ill for thirty-eight years.
6 When Jesus saw him lying there and knew that he had been there a long time, he said to him, 'Do you want to be made well?'
7 The sick man answered him, 'Sir, I have no one to put me into the pool when the water is stirred up; and while I am making my way, someone else steps down ahead of me.'

[8] Jesus said to him, 'Stand up, take your mat and walk.'

[9] At once the man was made well, and he took up his mat and began to walk.

Expansion

Now that day was a Sabbath. [10] *So the Jews said to the man who had been cured, 'It is the Sabbath; it is not lawful for you to carry your mat.'*

[11] *But he answered them, 'The man who made me well said to me, 'Take up your mat and walk.' '*

[12] *They asked him, 'Who is the man who said to you, 'Take it up and walk'?'*

[13] *Now the man who had been healed did not know who it was, for Jesus had disappeared in the crowd that was there.*

[14] *Later Jesus found him in the temple and said to him, 'See, you have been made well! Do not sin anymore, so that nothing worse happens to you.'*

[15] *The man went away and told the Jews that it was Jesus who had made him well.* [16] *Therefore the Jews started persecuting Jesus, because he was doing such things on the sabbath.*

[17] *But Jesus answered them, 'My Father is still working, and I also am working.'*

[18] *For this reason the Jews were seeking all the more to kill him, because he was not only breaking the Sabbath, but was also calling God his own Father, thereby making himself equal to God.*

COMMENTARY

The Third Sign has no Synoptic parallel, apart from the general similarity with the Synoptic story of the cure of a paralytic in Mark 2: 1-12 and its parallels in Matthew and Luke, but the respective details are quite different.

It takes place on a 'Festival of the Jews', later identified as the Sabbath in an extension to the text.

The tradition would seem to have given specific details about a site in Jerusalem called the Sheep Gate, Beth-zatha (the manuscripts disagree over its name, and perhaps it should be 'Bethesda', as a Bethesda Pool is described in one of the Dead Sea Scrolls from cave 3). More recent archaeological evidence in Jerusalem shows that, at one site in the grounds of St Anne's Church, two pools with five porticos did exist in the first century. However, this identification is merely a setting for the Sign and would have given an earlier story its context. The exact geographical identification is of passing historical interest.

The crippled man is waiting to be immersed in water. He is seeking renewal. He is not able to achieve this. He is waiting by the pool with five porticoes along with many others – blind, lame and paralysed. The reference to the five-book Torah and the expectations of Jews is only too obvious.

He has been waiting thirty-eight years. Why such exactitude in a Sign story? What would the readers or hearers of the Sign have understood (or have had pointed out to them)?

The Exodus story concerning the wandering of the first generation of the People of Israel in the wilderness, as found in Deuteronomy 2, states:

> [14]And the length of time we had travelled from Kadesh-barnea until we crossed the Wadi Zered was thirty-eight years, until the entire generation of warriors had perished from the camp, as Yahweh had sworn concerning them.

The cripple is the Jew of a new generation, when those who has lost their way in the wilderness for thirty-eight years had passed on. He is asked whether he wants to be 'cured'. The allusion is too obvious. Are the Jewish people, following the practices of the Law, satisfied with their results at this point? Do they want another way?

The crippled man is cured of his ailment and walks. His cure is paired with that of a Blind Man in the fifth Sign. In both these cases the seeming impossibility of the ailment being cured is stressed.

The message of the Sign is simply that Jesus the Teacher brings new life and ability to those who are crippled and blind within the Jewish people. These are not physical ailments; they are the ailments of those who do not have *gnosis*.

At some stage there has been an extension added to the Sign, in which the contentious issue is not the meaning of the cure of the cripple but the fact that the cure was done on the Sabbath. This was much more topical. This addition must have been set in place at a time when the issue of Jewish observance was still paramount between Jew and Christian. Should Jesus-movement people still observe the Torah regulations? Had they been exempted from them because of Jesus?

This extension also brings the first mention of the charge of blasphemy, which would be later laid against Jesus. Here it is out of place.

The Sabbath issue is raised also in the corresponding Fifth Sign of the Blind Man in the chiastic structure. The two additions in each place would seem to have come from the same editorial hand. By this stage the Sign element has not been understood.

4. The Feeding of the 5000 (6:1-34)

> [6:1] After this Jesus went to the other side of the Sea of Galilee, *also called the Sea of Tiberias*.

[2] A large crowd kept following him, because they saw the signs that he was doing for the sick. [3] Jesus went up The Mountain and sat down there with his disciples. [4] Now the Passover, the festival of the Jews, was near. [5] When he looked up and saw a large crowd coming towards him, Jesus said to Philip, 'Where are we to buy bread for these people to eat?'

[6] *He said this to test him, for he himself knew what he was going to do.*

[7] Philip answered him, 'Six months' wages would not buy enough bread for each of them to get a little.'

[8] One of his disciples, Andrew, Simon Peter's brother, said to him, [9] 'There is a boy here who has five barley loaves and two fish. But what are they among so many people?'

[10] Jesus said, 'Make the people sit down.'

Now there was a great deal of grass in the place; so they sat down, about five thousand in all. [11] Then Jesus took the loaves, and when he had given thanks, he distributed them to those who were seated; so also the fish, as much as they wanted. [12] When they were satisfied, he told his disciples, 'Gather up the fragments left over, so that nothing may be lost.'

[13] So they gathered them up, and from the fragments of the five barley loaves, left by those who had eaten, they filled twelve baskets [*kophinoi*].

[14] When the people saw the Sign that he had done, they began to say, 'This is indeed The Prophet who is to come into the world.'

[15] When Jesus realized that they were about to come and take him by force to make him king, he withdrew again to The Mountain by himself.

Expansion

[16] *When evening came, his disciples went down to the Sea,* [17] *got into a boat, and started across the Sea to Capernaum. It was now Dark, and Jesus had not yet come to them.* [18] *The lake became rough because a strong wind was blowing.* [19] *When they had rowed about twenty-five or thirty stadia [about six kilometres], they saw Jesus walking on the Sea and coming near the boat, and they were terrified.*

[20] *But he said to them, 'I Am; do not be afraid.'*

[21] *Then they wanted to take him into the boat, and immediately the boat reached the land towards which they were going.*

[22] *The next day the crowd that had stayed on the other side of the Sea saw that there had been only one boat there. They also saw that Jesus had not got into the boat with his disciples, but that his disciples had gone away alone.* [23] *Then some boats from Tiberias came near the place where they had eaten the bread (after the Lord had given thanks).* [24] *So when the crowd saw that neither Jesus nor his disciples were there, they themselves got into the boats and went to Capernaum looking for Jesus.*

[25] *When they found him on the other side of the lake, they said to him, 'Rabbi, when did you come here?'*

[26] *Jesus answered them, 'You are looking for me. Very truly, I tell you not*

because you saw Signs, but because you ate your fill of the loaves. [27] *Do not work for the food that perishes, but for the food that endures for eternal life, which the Son of Man will give you. For it is on him that God the Father has set his seal.'*

[28] *Then they said to him, 'What must we do to perform the works of God?'*

[29] *Jesus answered them, 'This is the work of God, that you believe in him whom he has sent.'*

[30] *So they said to him, 'What Sign are you going to give us then, so that we may see it and believe you? What work are you performing?* [31] *Our ancestors ate the manna in the wilderness; as it is written, 'He gave them bread from heaven to eat.' '*

[32] *Then Jesus said to them, 'Very truly, I tell you, it was not Moses who gave you the Bread from Heaven, but it is my Father who gives you the True Bread from Heaven.* [33] *For the Bread of God is that which comes down from Heaven and gives life to the World.'*

[34] *They said to him, 'Sir, give us this bread always.'*

COMMENTARY

The Feeding of the 5000 in John has its clear counterpart in the Synoptics. Comparing John to Mark we find the following parallels in their stories:

John 6:1-15 Feeding of 5000

(Both Mark and Matthew have a second Feeding of 4000)

John 6:16-21 Walking on Sea

John 6: 22-34 Jesus ministers to the crowd

The text of John will later be expanded with the insertion of a Discourse on the Bread of Life in 6:36-59 and an insertion of a Roman Christian tradition on Peter's Confession in 6:60-69, which has clear parallels to the Synoptic tradition. These are not parts of the Sign text.

The fact that John does not have a Second Feeding of 4000 is interesting. It tends to show that the Second Feeding of 4000 (with its seven baskets of fragments of bread) was a Markan construction, followed by Matthew but rejected by or unknown to Luke. In Mark the Second Feeding is of vital importance to his Jesus Story.

Mark has distinguished a Feeding of 5000 with five loaves and a Feeding of 4000 with seven loaves. From the first there are twelve baskets of fragments and from the second seven baskets of fragments. In the later discussion on the Feedings in Mark 8:19-21, Mark's Jesus asks:

[19] When I broke the five loaves for the five thousand, how many baskets (*kophinoi*) full of broken pieces did you collect?' They said to him,

'Twelve.' [20] 'And the seven for the four thousand, how many baskets (*spyrides*) full of broken pieces did you collect?' And they said to him, 'Seven.' [21] Then he said to them, 'Do you not yet understand?'

The obvious answer is that the numbers are of paramount importance. Five and twelve are typical Jewish numbers reflecting the five books of the Torah and the Twelve Tribes of Israel. Four and seven are universal numbers, the four ends of the earth and the number of completion, seven. The curious change in the word for basket is also important: a *kophinos* was a specifically Jewish type of fish basket; a *spyris* was the common word for basket used by all. The Markan message of the numbers is that Jesus is Messiah, as Peter soon acknowledges on behalf of the group, of both the Jews, who used the *kophinos*, and the Gentiles who used the *spyris*.

As in other instances, there is evidence that Matthew had some form of Mark in front of him, Luke had some form of Mark but also access to the Jesus-Tradition from which Mark had mined his gospel and subtly adapted it. Luke must have known there was only one Feeding, that of 5000, in the Jesus-Tradition. John did not have access to the Synoptics but to the Jesus-Tradition.

The Jesus-Tradition must have included a miracle-story about Jesus feeding a multitude. This is not surprising and it would have belonged to that early form of miracle-stories comparing Jesus with Elisha as in 2 Kings 4:

[42] A man came from Baal-shalishah, bringing food from the first fruits to the man of God: twenty loaves of barley and fresh ears of grain in his sack. Elisha said, 'Give it to the people and let them eat.' [43] But his servant said, 'How can I set this before a hundred people?' So he repeated, 'Give it to the people and let them eat, for thus says Yahweh, 'They shall eat and have some left.' ' [44] He set it before them, they ate, and had some left, according to the word of Yahweh.

This was the template in the Jesus-Tradition which adapted the Elisha miracle story to the Jesus context and must have added the fish (since they are in all four canonical gospels) together with the numbers five and twelve. Mark (followed by Matthew), Luke and John adapted the Jesus-Tradition story to their own purposes.

The 'fish' are interesting. In the Feeding of the 5000, Mark, Matthew and Luke refer to 'two fish (*ichthus*)'; John refers to 'two fish', but in the form of dried fish (*opsarion*) which were eaten with bread. In the Feeding of the 4000, found only in Mark and Matthew, both refer to a 'few small fish (*ichthus*)'. What is the meaning of 'fish' in an event that is highly symbolic in meaning? The only possible solution would be that the Jesus-Tradition had been written partly in Aramaic and this included the story of the Feeding taken from 2 Kings. The Aramaic word for 'fish', *nun*, might have been translated into Greek as both *ichthus* and *opsarion*. The Synoptics used *ichthus* (although Luke uses an alternative plural to Mark and Matthew) and John used *opsarion*. The only other usage that makes similar use of *ichthus/ opsarion* is the call-story in Luke and the post-resurrection story in John where Jesus provides an abundance of fish. We will refer to the usage in dealing with the Stray Tradition of the Catch of 153 Fish.

It would seem that 'fish' in the mainstream Jesus-movements was a symbol for disciples gathered by the original group. Just as fish might be attracted by bait, so followers are attracted by the teaching and insight of the first disciples. Bread and Fish are therefore clarified in general: the bread is God's revelation (as it was used in Jewish tradition earlier) and the fish are the result of spreading that revelation to others. However, this does not mean that the two symbols necessarily retain the same message when they enter two different social contexts of John's Gnostic circle and Roman Christianity.

Originally, the Fourth Sign was the story of Jesus feeding 5000 people with five loaves and two fish together with the collection of twelve baskets (*kophinos*) of fragments. Here, only the numbers five and twelve and the use of *kophinos* are seen as significant. As we saw above, they are Jewish numbers and a Jewish basket and they must have been in the Jesus-Tradition story. Jesus is seen feeding his people with Bread and Fish. The Feeding with Bread recalls the Exodus event in which Yahweh fed his people in the wilderness. Later there will be parallels drawn between the Manna of the Exodus. But the Bread from Heaven for the Gnostic Sign is specifically *gnosis*. Fish is the symbol for a group of believers attracted by the preaching of the eye-witnesses.

This event takes place on The Mountain in John. This is not a geographical notice and any search for a geographical mountain in the area would be fruitless. The Mountain is the equivalent of Sinai or Horeb. Jesus is the fulfilment, in this instance, of all that Moses and the people of Israel offered. Jesus from the Mountain dispenses *gnosis,* the Bread, to the Fish.

In short, it seems that a Jesus-Tradition about the Feeding has been used by Mark, Luke and John. Each has adapted the Tradition.

John's central Sign, the hub of the other six Signs, is that Jesus has come to provide this Bread, *gnosis* or the new Manna, for his people, the Fish. They are the new People of Five and Twelve, the true People of The Father. However, the populace still do not understand since they wish to make him into a worldly King. He is a King, but not of the World. He retreats to The Mountain, to the new Sinai.

To this Sign there has been added, first of all, the Walking on the Water and then the Ministry of Jesus' Ministry to the Crowd. These are Roman insertions that do nothing for the Sign, even though the terminology of 'sign' occurs.

The context against which the story of Walking on Water in John, Mark and Matthew need to be read is the Exodus and the Crossing of the Jordan. The People have received their Bread in the wilderness and now Jesus, the fulfilment of Joshua, leads the people dry-shod across the Jordan into the Promised Land

This Christophany (probably, in the Jesus-Tradition, a post-Resurrection Revelation) has Jesus proclaim, in all three gospels, his identification as I Am (*ego eimi*). Mark and Matthew will not use it again. We have seen already that John's gospel makes strategic use of the title as an expression of divinity referring to Yahweh whose name is interpreted in Exodus 3:14 as 'I Am who I Am'.

The next small section is confused. At some stage an editor has tried to put in clarifying details about other boats coming to the desert place. The sole purpose is to bring the audience who had shared in the Feeding back to Jesus, as in the Synoptic version.

The discussion in vv. 25-34 gives an interpretation of the Feeding, appended to the original Sign at some point. Its usage of 'sign' is in accord with the Synoptic idea of a work of power that convinces the audience. The Roman Christian text distinguishes between the Manna of the Exodus and the Bread of God. They are very different. The crowd is still looking for a 'sign' and do not realize that it is not the Manna of the Exodus. It has a new reality as the Bread of God.

But this line of argument is not part of the Gnostic text.

5. The Cure of the Blind Man (9:1-41 and 10:19-21)

[9:1] As he walked along, he saw a man blind from birth. [2] His disciples asked him, 'Rabbi, who sinned, this man or his parents, that he was born blind?'

[3] Jesus answered, 'Neither this man nor his parents sinned; he was born blind so that God's works might be revealed in him. [4] We must work the works of him who sent me while it is day; Night is coming when no one can work. [5] As long as I am in the World, I am the Light of the World.'

[6] When he had said this, he spat on the ground and made mud with

the saliva and spread the mud on the man's eyes, [7]saying to him, 'Go, wash in the pool of Siloam' (*which means Sent*).

Then he went and washed and came back able to see.

Expansion

[8] *The neighbours and those who had seen him before as a beggar began to ask, 'Is this not the man who used to sit and beg?'*

[9] *Some were saying, 'It is he.' Others were saying, 'No, but it is someone like him.' He kept saying, 'I am the man.'* [10] *But they kept asking him, 'Then how were your eyes opened?'*

[11] *He answered, 'The man called Jesus made mud, spread it on my eyes, and said to me, 'Go to Siloam and wash.' Then I went and washed and received my sight.'*

[12] *They said to him, 'Where is he?' He said, 'I do not know.'*

[13] *They brought to the Pharisees the man who had formerly been blind.* [14] *Now it was a Sabbath day when Jesus made the mud and opened his eyes.* [15] *Then the Pharisees also began to ask him how he had received his sight.*

He said to them, 'He put mud on my eyes. Then I washed, and now I see.'

[16] *Some of the Pharisees said, 'This man is not from God, for he does not observe the Sabbath.' But others said, 'How can a man who is a sinner perform such Signs?' And they were divided.*

[17] *So they said again to the blind man, 'What do you say about him? It was your eyes he opened.'*

He said, 'He is a prophet.'

[18] *The Jews did not believe that he had been blind and had received his sight until they called the parents of the man who had received his sight* [19] *and asked them, 'Is this your son, who you say was born blind? How then does he now see?'*

[20] *His parents answered, 'We know that this is our son, and that he was born blind;* [21] *but we do not know how it is that now he sees, nor do we know who opened his eyes. Ask him; he is of age. He will speak for himself.'* [22] *His parents said this because they were afraid of the Jews; for the Jews had already agreed that anyone who confessed Jesus to be the Messiah would be put out of the synagogue.* [23] *Therefore his parents said, 'He is of age; ask him.'*

[24] *So for the second time they called the man who had been blind, and they said to him, 'Give glory to God! We know that this man is a sinner.'*

[25] *He answered, 'I do not know whether he is a sinner. One thing I do know, that though I was blind, now I see.'*

[26] *They said to him, 'What did he do to you? How did he open your eyes?'*

[27] *He answered them, 'I have told you already, and you would not listen. Why do you want to hear it again? Do you also want to become his disciples?'*

[28] *Then they reviled him, saying, 'You are his disciple, but we are disciples of Moses.* [29] *We know that God has spoken to Moses, but as for this man, we do not know where he comes from.'*

³⁰ *The man answered, 'Here is an astonishing thing! You do not know where he comes from, and yet he opened my eyes.* ³¹ *We know that God does not listen to sinners, but he does listen to one who worships him and obeys his will.* ³² *Never since the world began has it been heard that anyone opened the eyes of a person born blind.* ³³ *If this man were not from God, he could do nothing.'*

³⁴ *They answered him, 'You were born entirely in sins, and are you trying to teach us?' And they drove him out.*

³⁵ *Jesus heard that they had driven him out, and when he found him, he said, 'Do you believe in the Son of Man?'*

³⁶ *He answered, 'And who is he, Sir? Tell me, so that I may believe in him.'*

³⁷ *Jesus said to him, 'You have seen him, and the one speaking with you is he.'*

³⁸ *He said, 'Lord, I believe.' And he worshipped him.*

³⁹ *Jesus said, 'I came into this world for Judgement so that those who do not see may see, and those who do see may become blind.'*

⁴⁰ *Some of the Pharisees near him heard this and said to him, 'Surely we are not blind, are we?'*

⁴¹ *Jesus said to them, 'If you were blind, you would not have sin. But now that you say, 'We see', your sin remains.*

Conclusion

¹⁰:¹⁹ Again the Jews were divided because of these words. ²⁰ Many of them were saying, 'He has a demon and is out of his mind. Why listen to him?' ²¹ Others were saying, 'These are not the words of one who has a demon. Can a demon open the eyes of the blind?'

COMMENTARY

The Fifth Sign has no direct parallels with the Synoptics apart from the fact that some blind people were also restored their sight in their stories. The only parallel is with the Third Sign, the cure of the paralytic. However, the unusual use of saliva as part of the healing ritual for curing a Blind Man occurs in both John and Mark. This certainly shows, once again, that an earlier story in the Jesus-Tradition has been manipulated by these two evangelists. The Jesus-Tradition story must have included a saliva-ritual.

Mark tellingly uses a two-stage cure of the man (first, the man sees vaguely, then he sees clearly) for his own effect: the blind man's cure parallels the two-fold realization that Jesus is a wonder-worker and then that he is the Messiah. At two key points in his narrative Mark has the cure of a Blind Man. After the first, as outlined above, Peter makes his Confession of Jesus the Messiah. After the second, the disciples resolutely set their face towards Jerusalem and the final events of Jesus' mission.

John uses his Sign for a different purpose and Jesus himself gives the interpretation of this Sign: 'I am the Light of the World' – a key Gnostic statement. An original cure story from the Jesus-Tradition, which included the saliva-ritual, has been fashioned into a typical Sign with the message that Jesus is the Light of the World. This is Gnosticism.

There is a long expansion, similar to that in the Third Sign, in which the Pharisees discuss the cure. Once again the point is not the cure itself but the fact that it broke the Sabbath observance. The text seems to be completely disconnected from the Sign of the Blind Man, apart from the fact that the Sign-story is used as a provocation and the issue would seem to be the same as the extension of the Third Sign: are Jesus-movement people subject to the Torah?

The extension contains these elements, which are only loosely connected:

Neighbours: The cured Blind Man recognized as a conundrum
Pharisees: Explanation – Jesus broke the Sabbath
Jews: Debate with Blind Man on his blindness
Jesus: Identifies himself as Son of Man and explains real Blindness
Pharisees: Debate with Jesus on real Blindness

The Expansion has made use of this loose content, and outlined a typical Jesus-community versus Pharisees and Jews confrontation. The material has come from that context and may even record a commentary on the Sign after the time it was abstracted from its original setting in the Book of Seven Signs. What the Jews contend against the Blind Man who has been cured is typically what later mainstream Jews (identified as followers of Moses, not Jews) contended against Jesus-movement people. For non-observance of the Torah and the dubious recognition of Jesus as Messiah, the Jesus-movement people were threatened with exclusion from the synagogues, and accused of an alleged sinful state and even demon-possession.

The natural conclusion to the fifth Sign in 10:19 has been separated from the original Sign story by the insertion of the Discourse on the Good Shepherd.

6. The Raising of Lazarus (11:1-57)

[1] Now a certain man was ill, Lazarus of Bethany, *the village of Mary and her sister Martha.* [2] *Miriam was the one who anointed the Lord with perfume and wiped his feet with her hair; her brother Lazarus was ill.*

³ So the sisters sent a message to Jesus, 'Lord, he whom you love is ill.'

⁴ But when Jesus heard it, he said, 'This illness does not lead to death; rather it is for God's glory, so that the Son of God may be glorified through it.'

⁵ Accordingly, though Jesus loved Martha and her sister and Lazarus, ⁶ after having heard that Lazarus was ill, he stayed two days longer in the place where he was.

⁷ Then after this he said to the disciples, 'Let us go to Judea again.'

⁸ The disciples said to him, 'Rabbi, the Jews were just now trying to stone you, and are you going there again?'

⁹ Jesus answered, 'Are there not twelve hours of daylight? Those who walk during the day do not stumble, because they see the Light of this World. ¹⁰ But those who walk at Night stumble, because the Light is not in them.'

¹¹ After saying this, he told them, 'Our friend Lazarus has fallen asleep, but I am going there to awaken him.'

¹² The disciples said to him, 'Lord, if he has fallen asleep, he will be all right.'

¹³ *Jesus, however, had been speaking about his death, but they thought that he was referring merely to sleep.*

¹⁴ Then Jesus told them plainly, 'Lazarus is dead. ¹⁵ For your sake I am glad I was not there, so that you may believe. But let us go to him.'

¹⁶ Thomas, who was called the Twin, said to his fellow-disciples, 'Let us also go, that we may die with him.'

¹⁷ When Jesus arrived, he found that Lazarus had already been in the tomb for four days. ¹⁸ *Now Bethany was near Jerusalem, some two miles away,* ¹⁹ and many of the Jews had come to Martha and Miriam to console them about their brother. ²⁰ When Martha heard that Jesus was coming, she went and met him, while Miriam stayed at home.

²¹ Martha said to Jesus, 'Lord, if you had been here, my brother would not have died. ²² But even now I know that God will give you whatever you ask of him.'

²³ Jesus said to her, 'Your brother will rise again.'

²⁴ Martha said to him, 'I know that he will rise again in the resurrection on the last day.'

²⁵ Jesus said to her, 'I am the Resurrection and the Life. Those who believe in me, even though they die, will live, ²⁶ and everyone who lives and believes in me will never die. Do you believe this?'

²⁷ She said to him, 'Yes, Lord, I believe that you are the Messiah, the Son of God, the One Coming into the World.'

²⁸ When she had said this, she went back and called her sister Miriam, and told her privately, 'The Teacher is here and is calling for you.' ²⁹ And when she heard it, she got up quickly and went to him.

(³⁰ *Now Jesus had not yet come to the village, but was still at the place where Martha had met him.* ³¹ *The Jews who were with her in the house, consoling her, saw Miriam get up quickly and go out. They followed her because they thought that she was going to the tomb to weep there.*)

³² When Miriam came where Jesus was and saw him, she knelt at his

feet and said to him, 'Lord, if you had been here, my brother would not have died.' ³³ When Jesus saw her weeping, and the Jews who came with her also weeping, he was greatly disturbed in spirit and deeply moved.

³⁴ He said, 'Where have you laid him?'

They said to him, 'Lord, come and see.' ³⁵ *Jesus began to weep.*
³⁶ *So the Jews said, 'See how he loved him!' ³⁷ But some of them said, 'Could not he who opened the eyes of the blind man have kept this man from dying?'*

³⁸ Then Jesus, again greatly disturbed, came to the tomb. It was a cave, and a stone was lying against it. ³⁹ Jesus said, 'Take away the stone.' Martha, the sister of the dead man, said to him, 'Lord, already there is a stench because he has been dead for four days.'

⁴⁰ Jesus said to her, 'Did I not tell you that if you believed, you would see the glory of God?'

⁴¹ So they took away the stone.

And Jesus looked upwards and said, 'Father, I thank you for having heard me. ⁴² I knew that you always hear me, but I have said this for the sake of the crowd standing here, so that they may believe that you sent me.'

⁴³ When he had said this, he cried with a loud voice, 'Lazarus, come out!' ⁴⁴ The dead man came out, his hands and feet bound with strips of cloth, and his face wrapped in a cloth. Jesus said to them, 'Unbind him, and let him go.'

⁴⁵ Many of the Jews therefore, who had come with Miriam and had seen what Jesus did, believed in him.

Expansion

⁴⁶ *But some of them went to the Pharisees and told them what he had done. ⁴⁷ So the chief priests and the Pharisees called a meeting of the council, and said, 'What are we to do? This man is performing many signs. ⁴⁸ If we let him go on like this, everyone will believe in him, and the Romans will come and destroy both our holy place and our nation.'*

⁴⁹ *But one of them, Caiaphas, who was High Priest that year, said to them, 'You know nothing at all! ⁵⁰ You do not understand that it is better for you to have one man die for the people than to have the whole nation destroyed.' ⁵¹ He did not say this on his own, but being High Priest that year he prophesied that Jesus was about to die for the nation, ⁵² and not for the nation only, but to gather into one the dispersed children of God.*

⁵³ *So from that day on they planned to put him to death.*

⁵⁴ *Jesus therefore no longer walked about openly among the Jews, but went from there to a town called Ephraim in the region near the wilderness; and he remained there with the disciples.*

⁵⁵ *Now the Passover of the Jews was near, and many went up from the country to Jerusalem before the Passover to purify themselves. ⁵⁶ They were looking for Jesus and were asking one another as they stood in the Temple, 'What do you think? Surely he will not come to the Festival, will he?'*

⁵⁷ *Now the chief priests and the Pharisees had given orders that anyone who knew where Jesus was should let them know, so that they might arrest him.*

COMMENTARY

The raising of Lazarus[48] is the chiastic analogue of the Cure of the Official's Son. In one case the request comes from a father on behalf of his son; in the other it is the sisters on behalf of their brother. In the first, the father is assured that 'Your son lives!' and in the second Martha is told 'Your brother will rise!'. This latter word for resurrection is *anastasis,* which only occurs here and in John 5.29, where it is used in a corrective expansion of the text.

The first sentence is a title. 'Mary' is written in Greek – *Maria.* In the rest of the Sign she is given the Hebrew name of *Miriam.* This would seem to indicate that the first phrase of an explanatory addition in v.1 came from a different hand to the comment in v.2.

There are various comments, which stand out as additions, made by an editor-reader who is anxious to tidy up possible items of misunderstanding by readers. They are indicated above in italics. They intend to make Jesus more human than the Gnostic text warranted.

We return to the text. Resurrection in the Jewish tradition had a compli- cated history. In Mesopotamian belief generally, life after death was restrict- ed to an attenuated life in some great cavern under the earth. In the Jewish tradition, which shared the Mesopotamian thought-world in this respect, this cavern became known as *she'ol.*[49] Normally, *she'ol* was a dead-end, a half-life of sleepiness; there was no exit point. Both just and unjust ended in *she'ol.*

But there were obvious inequities in this outcome. In order for equity to be achieved, the just had to receive any reward (such as long life, wealth, honour and respect) for their righteousness in this life not the next – and it did not always seem that such was the case. In the books of Daniel (written some time in the second century BCE) and 2 Maccabees (written around the same time) there was a proposed solution: the world would come to an End, and this would be brought about by divine intervention. A final battle of the forces of good and the forces of evil would precede the End. At that point, those just ones who survived the battle would enter the Kingdom of God where there would be everlasting peace and happiness. Those who had died in battle on the just side and the just ones from the past would be resurrected, raised up, from *she'ol* and join the victors in the final Kingdom of God. The unjust would be left in *she'ol* (although some later Jewish and

---

[48] His name is the Greek form of Eleazar, 'God helps', a very common Hebrew name.

[49] Despite many attempts the meaning of *she'ol* has not been deciphered.

Christian statements made it clear that they would undergo punishment there as well).

Other Jewish books from a somewhat later period such as Wisdom (written sometime between 30 BCE and 50 CE) and 4 Maccabees (written around the middle of the first century CE) told a different story, but with the same final outcome. Just people died and they went immediately, in a spiritual state, into the presence of God. The unjust simply disappeared at death. This second option was much more in the Platonic vein of thinking and was that taken up by the Gnostic tendencies within Judaism.

Jesus identifies himself in this narrative as the Resurrection and the Life. The term 'Life' or 'Eternal Life' has been frequently used in a number of Johannine contexts. In John, the term refers to a return to the Aeon in the sense of a return to the Divinity. It has a close connection with other Gnostic terminology. Life was the hub of the cure of the Official's son, with which the Lazarus Sign is paired. Here, the more traditional term *anastasis* is added to life. In the context of John's gospel it is not the same as the resurrection of Jesus or the resurrection of the dead as understood in the Synoptics (and earlier in Daniel and 2 Maccabees). In the case of Lazarus there is clearly a body in question and it should be in a state of putrefaction.

What is being depicted in the Lazarus story is not the mainstream Jewish idea of rescue of the physical being from *she'ol*. The story presumes the Proto-Gnostic Jewish idea, reflected in Wisdom and 4 Maccabees seen above, that, instead of waiting for a future physical resurrection, the action took place immediately. Those who had been martyred in the fight against the Greeks had gone immediately into the divine realm. Likewise the Gnostic went into the divine realm upon death. Jesus as Resurrection means that the Gnostics who had attained the fullness of *gnosis* were already resurrected; they had already achieved the fullness of life. Lazarus had never died in any real sense. Hence, Jesus' delaying tactics, there is no hurry, and his assurance that Lazarus was 'asleep'.

The *anastasis* of Lazarus is acknowledged by Jesus four days after internment. In Jewish law, three days were required before putrefaction was beyond doubt and legal death could be declared. Jesus' resurrection was declared after three days; Lazarus is left another day beyond the legal limit. There can be no doubt about his physical death and his putrefied body. What emerges cannot be the fleshly body of his life in the World.

At Jesus' proclamation that he is Resurrection and Life, Martha bestows three titles on Jesus: Messiah, Son of God and The One Coming into the World.

It is only too clear that the raising of Lazarus is in parallel with the Independent Gnostic Treatise on Mary's Vision, which was covered earlier. The points of intersection dealing with Lazarus and Jesus are as follows:

- **Lazarus**: In v. 34 Jesus asks: 'Where have you laid him?' (*pou tetheikate auton*).
  Jesus: This is the same expression that is used by Mary to the Gardener in 20:15: *pou ethekas auton.*

- **Lazarus**: It was a cave, and a stone was lying against it. ([39] Jesus said, 'Take away the stone.')
  Jesus: [20:1] Early on the first day of the week, while it was still dark, Mary Magdalene came to the tomb and saw that the stone had been removed from the tomb.

- **Lazarus**: Jesus said to her, 'Did I not tell you that if you believed, you would see the glory of God?'
  Jesus: Mary Magdalene went and announced to the disciples, 'I have seen the Lord'; and she told them that he had said these things to her.

It would seem that the Sixth Sign and the Independent Gnostic Treatise on the Vision of Mary circulated together at some stage. One drew on the other for meaning. The *anastasis* of Jesus and the *anastasis* of Lazarus are deliberately paralleled. Later, in John, any further references to Lazarus are in Roman Christian Insertions. For the Book of Signs, Lazarus has been resurrected and plays no further part in the earthly arena.

There is at this vital point an editorial expansion dealing with the Pharisees. It is a distraction, relative to the Sign of Lazarus. It is similar to the expansions in the Third and Fifth Signs with their account of an approach to the Jewish authorities. Caiaphas is introduced and irony is used in his speech. He foretells that Jesus will die for his people (which will be proved correct for Roman Christians) and that his death will gather together the dispersed (also correct in Roman Christianity). The threat to arrest and kill him is repeated. This is a later, Roman Christian expansion.

While the sixth Sign corresponds to the second Sign and there are significant parallels, it also is the prelude to the seventh and final Sign. Lazarus' death was not real. Jesus' death is not real. Lazarus' 'death' prepares the reader for the 'death' of Jesus.

7. The Cross and the Mother (19:26-30)

Meanwhile, standing near the cross of Jesus were his Mother, and his Mother's Sister, Mary *of Clopas,* and Mary Magdalene.

[26] When Jesus saw his Mother and the Disciple Whom he Loved standing beside her, he said to his mother, 'Woman, here is your Son.'

[27] Then he said to the Disciple, 'Here is your Mother.'

And from that Hour the Disciple took her into The Homeland [*ta idia*].

[28] After this, when Jesus knew that all was now finished, he said *(in order to fulfil the scripture),* 'I am thirsty.'

[29] A jar full of sour Wine was standing there. So they put a sponge full of the Wine on a branch of hyssop and held it to his mouth.

[30] When Jesus had received the Wine, he said, 'It is finished.'

Then he bowed his head and handed over The Spirit.

COMMENTARY

The final Sign, the seventh, is the culmination of the Book of Signs. It is short, but packed with meaning and, in many ways, the most difficult to interpret. It has also been grossly misinterpreted since the time of its insertion in the canonical book of John with its Roman Christian perspective. Like the first Sign, it was deliberately confused; the redactors did not want the original meaning (which they could hardly have comprehended) to be easily transmitted.

The reader of the Book of Seven Signs had been expected, in the Book's original Gnostic version, without the expansions and other additions, to have moved from one Sign to the next. That is the purpose of a chiasm. The reader has been expected to draw the faith conclusions from each Sign, with mounting requirement of faith as described in the commentaries. Believers should proclaim that Jesus is The Bridegroom who supplies The Wine and atones for The Mother, that Jesus is the One who bestows Life, that Jesus cures the Jew who is maimed, that Jesus is the New Moses who feeds his People in the desert, that Jesus is the Light who gives sight to the Jew who cannot see, that Jesus is the Resurrection and the Life for the believers who face death.

Finally, there is this seventh Sign.

The Seven Signs, as we have seen from their analysis, are organized thus:

A Cana and The Mother – Jesus, The Son, answers the request of
The Mother, his Bride.

   B The cure of the Official's Son – Jesus brings Life

      C The cure of the Crippled Man – Jesus the Healer of
a crippled Jew

         D The Feeding of the 5000 – Jesus the New Moses
who feeds his people with Bread

      C1 The cure of the Blind Man – Jesus the Light of a
blind Jew

   B1 The raising of Lazarus – Jesus the Resurrection and the Life

A1 The Cross and The Mother – The Mother and her Sister and Mary
Magdalene. The Hour has come.

It is clear that there is correspondence between B/B1, C/C1. There must
be a correspondence between A/A1.

The culmination of the Book of Seven Signs is this scene at the foot
of the Cross. On first appearances, there seem to be three people present
with Jesus in the final text: his Mother, Mary of Clopas (in Greek this is
simply 'of Clopas' and could therefore be daughter, sister or wife of the said
Clopas), and Mary Magdalene. But these women have caused great toil for
the interpreters from the beginning. Some scholars have endeavoured to
find at the foot of the Cross only two women (his Mother, who was Mary the
daughter/sister of Clopas, and Mary Magdalene), or three women (as above
– his Mother, her sister who was Mary the daughter/sister/wife of Clopas
and Mary Magdalene) or even four women (his Mother, her unnamed sister,
Mary the daughter/sister/wife of Clopas and Mary Magdalene).

The reason for these desperate measures is that, first, no other gospel
records the Mother of Jesus being at the foot of the Cross. Second, where did
Mary of Clopas come from? Clopas is only mentioned here in the Christian
Scriptures.

The other gospels relate the following:

Mark: From afar there are many women, among whom are Mary
Magdalene, Mary the mother of James and Joseph and the mother of
the Zebedees.

Matthew: From afar there are many women and among them Mary
Magdalene, Mary, the mother of James the Younger and Joses, and
Salome

Luke: From afar there are all his acquaintances and women.

Only John's Gospel has the Mother of Jesus and Mary, the daughter/sister/wife of Clopas, and Mary Magdalene present and, unlike the Synoptic accounts, the three of them are close enough for a conversation with Jesus.

The rather obvious solution raises further issues. The unexpected mention of 'Mary of Clopas' was inexpert and intended to respond to a deeper problem. The original text would have run:

> Meanwhile, standing near the cross of Jesus were his Mother, her Sister Mary and Mary Magdalene.

An early, well-meaning scribe has seen the problem: no-one knew of Mary the Mother of Jesus having a sister (also called Mary). A much later Christian tradition handed on the writing of Hegesippus had identified one of the blood relatives of Jesus, elected as a successor in Jerusalem, as Clopas.

> And, profound peace being established in every church, they remained until the reign of the Emperor Trajan, and until the above-mentioned Simeon, son of Clopas, an uncle of the Lord, was informed against by the the heretics, and was himself in like manner accused for the same cause before the governor Atticus. And after being tortured for many days he suffered martyrdom and all, including even the proconsul, marvelled that, at the age of one hundred and twenty years, he could endure so much. And orders were given that he should be crucified.

Clopas was named as 'the uncle of Jesus'. If so, then presumably he was considered to be the brother of the Virgin Mary. No other sibling is mentioned. Hence, the 'Mary' who is the 'Sister' must be Mary the wife (not sister and not daughter) of Clopas who would thereby be both sister (in-law) of the Virgin Mary and called Mary. So, a later editor inserted 'Mary of Clopas' into the text. Sister-in-law is not quite 'sister', then or now. Did the scribe have any evidence that 'Mary, wife of Clopas' actually had a sister-in-law also called Mary? We will probably never know, and the issue is inconsequential.

But we need to turn to the Gospel of Philip to see where this text is going.

> There were three who always walked with the Lord: Mary, his mother, and her sister, and Magdalene, the one who was called his companion. His sister and his mother and his companion were each a Mary. (58)

This solves many problems. 'Mary' is not one; 'Mary' is the name given to Sophia. Sophia has a human counterpart, *Havvah* (which means nothing in Hebrew but is close to *hayyah*, 'the living') or Eve in English. She is 'Mother of all the Living' in the text of Genesis. Jesus and Eve are a syzygy, brother and sister if you like. During the time of Jesus' mission in the Flesh, Mary Magdalene became, because of her acquisition of *gnosis*, the *koinonos* of Jesus, his spiritual companion. She reached the spiritual heights of Sophia and Eve. She was the Sophia and Eve of the final times. The three of these 'Marys' are to be found at the foot of the Cross. At this point we need to re-examine the Gnostic text of the Apocryphon of John cited above in the commentary on the first Sign:

> And when the mother [Sophia] recognized that the garment of darkness was imperfect, then she knew that her consort had not agreed with her. She repented with much weeping. And the whole Pleroma heard the prayer of her repentance, and they praised on her behalf the invisible, virginal Spirit. And he consented; and when the invisible Spirit had consented, the Holy Spirit poured over her from their whole Pleroma. For it was not her consort who came to her, but he came to her through the Pleroma in order that he might correct her deficiency. And she was taken up not to her own Aeon but above her Son that she might be in the Ninth until she has corrected her deficiency (13-14)

Sophia or The Woman or The Mother caused Yaldabaoth to come into being, a deformed divinity. Her 'deficiency' in producing the monster could only be 'corrected' by The Son. Sophia was linked to Adamas, the Archetypal Man, and they became part of the Garden in the World created by Yaldabaoth – in the forms of Adam and Eve.

Adam responded to the divine Form of Adamas; Eve responded to the divine Form of Sophia. Sophia had been more vaguely recognized in Wisdom (*hochmah*) of Proto-Gnostic Judaism. The Gnostic Jesus acknowledges her as His Mother. Jesus was the 'Son of Man', son of Adamas (who was also the Great Seth). Sophia and Jesus were in spiritual consummation in the Bridal Chamber at Cana. There the final exoneration of Sophia could not take place; the Hour had not yet come. Jesus was still engaged in the emancipation of the *pneumatikoi*.

What of Mary Magdalene? We need to go beyond any historical reconstructions of this Mary.[50] She was seen by some Gnostics as a representation

---

[50] I do not think that the historian can say much more about Mary Magdalene than that she was probably from Magdala (where recent excavations have taken place); she must have been a woman of means and freedom since she seems to have become a travelling disciple of Jesus. And there history must give up the search ... there is new data discovered beyond what we have at the present. The Histori-...gdalene is a different being to the Gnostic Magdalene.

of Sophia, the Wisdom. She and Eve were accordingly comingled in their stories. She became the Gnostic consort of Jesus, just as Sophia was.

The Sign of Cana and The Mother show Jesus being led into the Bridal Chamber by The Mother. Sophia wants her 'correction of deficiency' to take place forthwith. She is told rather peremptorily that it is too early. The Hour has not come.

Now, in the Sign of The Cross and the Mother, the Hour has come.

First, Jesus indicates the Disciple Whom He Loved who is at the foot of the Cross. This Disciple can only be one of the three women; no other presence has been recorded; no mention of a male such as John has been made. The Beloved Disciple must be Mary Magdalene.[51] Just as Adamas corresponds with Adam and Sophia with Eve, the generation of Seth with Jesus, so Sophia corresponds with Mary Magdalene. Mary Magdalene is a human form of Sophia. She will care for Sophia.

At the foot of the cross there is the Mother of Jesus, her Sister Eve and Mary Magdalene.

Speaking to his Mother, Sophia, Jesus says:

'Woman, here is your Son'.

This designation of 'Son' has always seemed to indicate a male Beloved Disciple (who is nowhere named as being at the foot of the cross) but 'The Son' in this instance has no gender. The Son is the Emanation from the divine Spirit. Jesus was the Son of God, the Divine Son. He had taken on Flesh and was about finally to divest it. Now Jesus indicates that Mary Magdalene, the counterpart of Sophia, will continue the role of The Son. The Beloved Disciple, Mary Magdalene, will be the successor to Jesus the Son of God.

Next Jesus speaks to The Disciple whom He Loved, Mary Magdalene: 'Here is your Mother.'

She is to assume responsibility for the Mother of Jesus, and the Magdalene takes her, Corruptible Sophia now rehabilitated, into the Homeland of the saved, His Own Ones.

Jesus, having fulfilled the task of rehabilitating Sophia, wants to bring his mission to its completion and calls for a drink: 'I am thirsty (dipso).' They give him common wine (oxos) on a branch of hyssop; this is the equivalent of Jesus accepting the Cup at Gethsemane in the Synoptics (there is a similar story in the Synoptics about the dying Jesus being tormented by thirst, but

---

[51] We will see, in a study below, that this does not mean that Mary Magdalene was the only claimant to the title of Beloved Disciple.

that is not the import of the Johannine text). The Wine in the *skeuos* is the symbol of the fullness of *gnosis* which Jesus has brought, just as it was at Cana. Cana and the Cross once more dovetail. There, in the Cana story, the abundance of wine was proleptic; on the Cross the Wine is the final *gnosis* offered to believers. At Cana there were six stone water-jars, the number of incompletion. This is the seventh jar (*skeuos*) of Wine which Jesus now solemnly drinks. The container is not that of the once-privileged Jews; it is a container for everyday use, available to all.

This wine is called *oxos* not *oinos*. *Oinos* (the term for wine used in the Cana story) was a refined, sweet wine drunk by the upper classes. *Oxos* was a sour wine, an everyday cheap drink used by Roman soldiers and Roman lower classes. Why the change in terminology? First, because the Jesus Tradition, repeated in the four evangelists, had identified this *oxos* as that foretold in Psalm 69:21:

> They gave me poison for food,
>   and for my thirst (*dipsan*) they gave me vinegar (*oxos*) to drink.

Second, *oxos* was the wine of the people, open to all, like its container (*skeuos*), neither of them restricted to a particular class of people.

Having drunk the Wine, he brings his earthly mission to a conclusion: 'It is finished'.

'It is finished [*tetelestai*]' cannot be glossed over. It does not mean 'it is all over'. At the beginning of the Gnostic Treatise of the Handing-Over of Jesus, the text opens thus:

> Now before the festival of the Passover, Jesus knew that his hour had come to depart from this world and go to the Father. Having loved his own who were in the world, he loved them to the end [*telos*]. (13:1)

The Hour has come and this will be The End (*telos*). In Greek, the word implies 'purpose', 'consummation'.

Other references to The End are masked in translation. Thus in the Final Prayer of Jesus, to be discussed below, we read:

> [23] I in them and you in me, that they may become completely one [be brought to the *telos* as one], so that the world may know that you have sent me and have loved them even as you have loved me.

'It is finished' means that he has done completely what he was sent to do in the World, clothed in Flesh. He has brought The Mother back into the Pleroma and he has brought *gnosis* to the believers. Everything that he purposed to do, he has done.

He then bows his head and hands over The Spirit;[52] it is handed over to Mary Magdalene. The work for which he took on Flesh, worked in the World and acquired a group of believers has been completed. The Leader is now Mary Magdalene, The Son and the protector of Sophia, the bearer of The Spirit.

The parallels with the First Sign, Cana and the Mother, are unmistakeable. The two pericopes are the only ones to feature his Mother. In both she is specifically identified as The Woman. In both there is talk of The Hour: at Cana it has not come, and on the Cross it has arrived. In both there is The Wine of *gnosis*.

The Corruptible Sophia has been rehabilitated, the evil in the World has been conquered, the Archons no longer have power, the *pneumatikoi* have access to *gnosis*.

No more fitting final Sign could be envisaged to conclude the Book of Seven Signs. Those who have persevered in the reading or hearing of the text to this point would be regarded as initiated Gnostics.

The final action of Jesus handing-over The Spirit corresponds with the sacrament of *apolutrosis* in the Magdalene Treatise. The sacrament signifies what has been achieved.

Conclusion to the Book of Seven Signs (20:30-31)

[30] Now Jesus did many other Signs in the presence of his disciples, which are not written in this book. [31] But these are written so that you may come to believe that Jesus is the Messiah, the Son of God, and that through believing you may have Life in his Name.

COMMENTARY

The Book of Seven Signs is a separate Gnostic 'gospel'. It begins, in the first Sign, with the cosmic problem of The Mother, Sophia, who had brought disorder into the world and now requires rehabilitation. Then Jesus in the following five Signs reveals himself as the centre of Gnostic expectation. Finally, in the seventh Sign Jesus announces that his work has been completed, that The Mother's cosmic mistake has been corrected and she is returned to *ta idia*, that *gnosis* is available to believers through the ministry of Mary Magdalene, the Beloved Disciple and the recipient of The Spirit.

---

[52] The term to 'give up the ghost' became, in English, a common enough term for death. However, prior to its usage in John and its translation in the King James' Version, the term was never known in this sense. The translation of *pneuma* by 'ghost' rather than 'spirit' added to this misconception.

The Book is a Handbook of Gnostic induction. Gnostic initiates would have been expected to read, or to hear, the successive Signs and express a response of faith. By the seventh Sign they would be inducted into the search for *gnosis*. This would have been no intellectual endeavour; it was experiential.

The conclusion to the Book of Seven Signs starkly announces this in formal language.

It comes to its conclusion with a terse statement, replete with Gnostic theological meaning. If we interpose the theological statements with explanations it would read like this:

> Now Jesus did many other Signs [*'signs' are human actions of Jesus that reveal a divine message and his identity to an audience*] in the presence of his disciples, which are not written in this book [*disciples only need the ones in this Book of Seven Signs*]. But these are written so that you may come to believe that Jesus is the Messiah [*'Messiah' is the one sent by God to those in the World*], the Son of God [*an alternative title stressing the divine origin of the Messiah from the Eternal Spirit*], and that through believing you may have Life [*this 'life' is the fullness of life, not human life, but the life of the Aeons in the Pleroma*] in his name [*'name' implies the special God-given power of this Jesus who has undertaken the mission*].

This is a fitting conclusion to the exhaustive procedure of reading and interacting with the Book of Seven Signs, reacting to the many life-changing challenges of faith it requires from its readers.

The Book of Seven Signs reads well as a Gnostic catechetical tool when detached from the total text of the gospel of John and released from its extensions and correctives.

From the Book of Seven Signs, we turn to the Gnostic Discourses. They are strategically placed at various places in the Gospel of John. Usually there is a logical reason for the placement; at other times the reason is not so apparent. Always, they disrupt the flow of the Seven Signs and can be easily recognized. We will take them in the order they occur in the Gospel of John.

THE FOURTEEN GNOSTIC DISCOURSES

This series of fourteen Jesus-statements or Discourses is very much in the Gnostic tradition. We often find similar Discourses in the Nag Hammadi literature. Their language here in John is clearly Gnostic at times (with some non-Gnostic expansions and corrections). In some cases we find Discourses which are Monologues, where Jesus discusses protracted matters of Gnostic theology. Other Discourses are Dialogues where, in a genre common in the Gnostic writings, Jesus is confronted by questioners who, sometimes with great naivety, put forward doctrinal queries on Gnostic teaching.

The end result is a veritable catechism of Gnostic teaching. Put together, the fourteen statements can be considered another early Gnostic source that has subsequently been expanded and occasionally corrected. The expansions endeavour to explain some of the more difficult points, not always successfully, while the corrections show that some Gnostic teachings were felt to deviate too far from later orthodox requirements. The result is that the collection itself is not necessarily coherent and balanced. There is no necessary connection between any one Discourse and the other thirteen, although there are undoubtedly overlaps. Nor do the Discourses always fit precisely into the context in which they have been placed in the narrative of the gospel. As they now stand they have been interspersed at a later date among the Seven Signs.

Whereas the Book of Seven Signs was certainly once a coherent book, the Discourses might never have been one collection. They overlap, they are repetitious. They could have been culled from a number of Gnostic writings in order to be inserted into the Book of Seven Signs. They are consistent with a very general statement of the Gnostic Myth.

The fourteen Discourses are listed below. The titles are sometimes my own, taken from the major content of each one:

1. **Birth and Rebirth (3:1-21 and 31-36)**

2. **The Water of Life (4:4-42)**

3. **The Father and Son (5:19-47)**

4. **The Bread of Life (6:35-65)**

5. **Excerpts within a Tradition (7:1-52)**

6. **The Light of the World and Testimony (8:12-20)**

7. **Above and Below (8:21-30)**

8. **The Father and Abraham (8:31-59)**

9. **The Good Shepherd (10:1-21)**

10. **The Works of the Father (10:22-42)**

11. **The Hour and Glory (12:19-50)**

12, **The Paraclete (13:33-14:31)**

13. **The True Vine (15:1-16:33)**

14. **The Prayer of Jesus (17:1-26)**

We will now examine and analyse these one by one.

1. Birth and Rebirth (3:1-21 and 31-36)

^{3.1} Now there was a Pharisee named Nicodemus, a leader [*archon*] of the Jews. ² He came to Jesus by Night and said to him, 'Rabbi, we know that you are a teacher who has come from God; for no one can do these Signs that you do apart from the presence of God.'

³ Jesus answered him, 'Very truly, I tell you, no one can see the kingdom of God without being 'born from above'.'

⁴ Nicodemus said to him, 'How can anyone be born after having grown old? Can one enter a second time into the mother's womb and be born?'

⁵ Jesus answered, 'Very truly, I tell you, no-one can enter the Kingdom of God without being born of water and Spirit. ⁶ What is born of the Flesh is Flesh, and what is born of the Spirit is Spirit. ⁷ Do not be astonished that I said to you, 'You must be 'born from above'.' ⁸ The wind blows where it chooses, and you hear the sound of it, but you do not know where it comes from or where it goes. So it is with everyone who is born of the Spirit.'

⁹ Nicodemus said to him, 'How can these things be?'

¹⁰ Jesus answered him, 'Are you a teacher of Israel, and yet you do not understand these things? ¹¹ 'Very truly, I tell you, we speak of what we know and testify to what we have seen; yet you do not receive our testimony. ¹² If I have told you about earthly things and you do not believe, how can you believe if I tell you about heavenly things? ¹³ No one has ascended into Heaven except the One who Descended from Heaven, the Son of Man. ¹⁴ And just as Moses lifted up the serpent in the wilderness, so must the Son of Man be lifted up, ¹⁵ that whoever believes in him may have Eternal Life.

Correction

¹⁶ *'For God so loved the World that he gave his only Son, so that everyone who believes in him may not perish but may have Eternal Life.* ¹⁷ *'Indeed, God did not send the Son into the world to condemn the world, but in order that the world might be saved through him.*

¹⁸ 'Those who believe in him are not condemned; but those who do not believe are condemned already, because they have not believed in the Name of the only Son of God. ¹⁹ And this is the Judgement, that the Light has come into the World, and people loved Darkness rather than Light because their deeds were evil. ²⁰ For all who do evil hate the Light and do not come to the Light, so that their deeds may not be exposed. ²¹ But those who do what is true come to the Light, so that it may be clearly seen that their deeds have been done in God.'

³¹ 'The one who comes 'From Above' is above all; the one who is 'Of the Earth' belongs to the earth and speaks about earthly things. 'The One who Comes from Heaven' is above all. ³² He testifies to what he has seen and heard, yet no one accepts his testimony. ³³ Whoever has accepted his testimony has certified this, that God is True. ³⁴ He whom God has sent speaks the words of God, for he gives the Spirit without measure. ³⁵ The Father loves the Son and has placed all things

in his hands. [36] Whoever believes in the Son has Eternal Life; whoever disobeys the Son will not see Life, but must endure God's wrath.'

COMMENTARY

This first Discourse is a dialogue with a Jew, Nicodemus. He is one of the Archons or leaders in Jerusalem. The term *archon* is specifically Gnostic, referring to a leader of this World, usually pitted against Jesus. However, Nicodemus is open to the new teaching, even if he is rather obtuse about understanding it. He has come out of the night or Darkness. He is used as a handy questioner in the Dialogue.

Jesus discusses the salvation of Gnostic disciples with him. They are reborn 'from Above'. The Greek term *anothen* actually has two meanings: being born 'from Above' or being born 'again' or for a second time. Nicodemus' reply shows he has misunderstood the term as referring to a second birth, and the Dialogue progresses on the basis of the misunderstanding.

Jesus explains that, having been reborn, the believers enter the Kingdom of God (the only two usages in John). However, this is not the Kingdom of the Synoptics which is expected to come at the end of time. There is immediate entry for the Gnostic believer into the Kingdom of God.

The Gospel of Philip shows us that this statement about being born 'from above' or re-born was not unfamiliar to the Gnostics:

> A bridal chamber is not for the animals, nor is it for the slaves, nor for defiled women; but it is for free men and virgins.
> Through the Holy Spirit we are indeed begotten again, but we are begotten through Christ in the two. We are anointed through the Spirit. When we were begotten, we were united. None can see himself either in water or in a mirror without light. Nor again can you see in light without mirror or water. For this reason, it is fitting to baptism in the two, in the light and the water. Now the light is the chrism. (69)

Jesus now analyses 'born from Above' further. It means 'born of the Water and the Spirit' playing on the fact that, both in Hebrew and Greek, the term for Spirit (*pneuma*) can also mean 'wind'. In this case the practice of baptizing among the Gnostics (a foot-washing), recognising the link with the Spirit, is contrasted with the water baptism of John. Nicodemus is uncomprehending.

Jesus replies with a terse statement that the only one who has been in Heaven (in the presence of The Father) is The One Who Descended from Heaven, the Son of Man. Presumably this statement negates any of the earlier Jewish statements about those who were supposed to have gone up to Heaven such as Enoch or Moses. This Son of Man was prefigured by the Bronze Serpent raised up by Moses to bring healing to the Israelites; the Son of Man will also be raised up to bring salvation and Eternal Life to believers.

We have already seen that the term 'raise up' (*hupsoun*) has the symbolic meaning of 'exalt'. The Son of Man will be 'exalted' on the Cross.

There is an interesting parallel to the mention of Moses and the Bronze Serpent (related in the book of Numbers) in the Gnostic *Testimony of Truth*:

> Again it is written [Nm 21:9], 'He made a serpent of bronze [and] hung it upon a pole ...
> ... [*1 line unrecoverable*]
> ... which [...] for the one who will gaze upon this bronze serpent, none will destroy him, and the one who will believe in this bronze serpent will be saved.' For this is Christ; those who believed in him have received life. Those who did not believe will die. (48-49)

In this instance the action of Moses is seen as having been fulfilled in Jesus. He has replaced Moses. Being born from Above, in short, means that the believer finds Eternal Life in the realm of Heaven by the action of The Spirit.

The theme of Exaltation or 'lifting up' (*hupsoun*) is distinctive to John. In the Synoptics, Jesus foretells the sequence of his Passion, Death and Resurrection. In John, Jesus announces his Exaltation. The term may have originated from its usage in the description of the Suffering Servant in Isaiah 52:13:

> [13] See, my servant shall prosper;
> he shall be exalted and lifted up,
> and shall be very high.

The meaning here is that the crucifixion of Jesus is primarily a declaration that he is a King; he is performing an exercise of regality.[53] He divests himself of The Flesh. He manifests himself as the divine being. From this vantage point Jesus attracts those who finally see The Truth in what he has done.

There then follows a correction. It had been written by a commentator in an effort to give a reliable summary of what has been dealt with in the Dialogue. However, the attempt tries to tone down the Gnostic teaching. It tries to form a bridge between what Gnostics might have been saying in the Discourse and what was more orthodox Roman doctrine. The Son of Man is now identified as the Monogenes (the term for 'Only Begotten' used only

---

[53] This point is made in some late Jewish writings (such as 1 Maccabees and Daniel) where the appointment of a king is described as an 'exaltation'

here and the first chapter of John). But here it has the sense it bears in the Synoptics: Jesus is the New Isaac whose father sacrificed him. More, the World is actually good; no Gnostic would have written that 'God loves the World'.

Then the Discourse proper takes up again and concludes.

At some stage the first two Discourses (Birth and Rebirth, The Water of Life) operated as a pair. Nicodemus, the Jew who has come out of the Dark, and the Samaritan Woman in the next Discourse were exemplars of the universalist thrust of Christian Gnosticism. The two Discourses have been placed as the foreword to the Sign of the Cure of the Gentile official's Son to give the sequence of Jew, Samaritan and Gentile. Jesus as the source of Rebirth and the source of Living Water reveals the very substance of Gnostic belief, open to all believers.

2. The Water of Life (4: 4-42)

⁴ But he had to go through Samaria. ⁵ So he came to a Samaritan city called Sychar, near the plot of ground that Jacob had given to his son Joseph. ⁶ Jacob's well was there, and Jesus, tired out by his journey, was sitting by the well.

The hour was about noon.

⁷ A Samaritan woman came to draw water, and Jesus said to her, 'Give me a drink'.

⁸ *(His disciples had gone to the city to buy food.)*

⁹ The Samaritan woman said to him, 'How is it that you, a Jew, ask a drink of me, a woman of Samaria?'

(Jews do not share things in common with Samaritans.)

¹⁰ Jesus answered her, 'If you knew the gift of God, and who it is that is saying to you, 'Give me a drink', you would have asked him, and he would have given you Living Water.'

¹¹ The woman said to him, 'Sir, you have no bucket, and the well is deep. Where do you get that Living Water? ¹² Are you greater than our ancestor Jacob, who gave us the well, and with his sons and his flocks drank from it?'

¹³ Jesus said to her, 'Everyone who drinks of this water will be thirsty again, ¹⁴ but those who drink of the Water that I will give them will never be thirsty. The Water that I will give will become in them a Well of Water gushing up to Eternal Life.'

¹⁵ The woman said to him, 'Sir, give me this Water, so that I may never be thirsty or have to keep coming here to draw water.'

¹⁶ Jesus said to her, 'Go, call your husband, and come back.'

¹⁷ The woman answered him, 'I have no husband.'

Jesus said to her, 'You are right in saying, 'I have no husband'; ¹⁸ for you have had five husbands, and the one you have now is not your husband. What you have said is true!'

¹⁹ The woman said to him, 'Sir, I see that you are a Prophet. ²⁰ Our ancestors worshipped on this mountain, but you say that the place where people must worship is in Jerusalem.'

²¹ Jesus said to her, 'Woman, believe me, the Hour is coming when you will worship the Father neither on This Mountain nor in Jerusalem.

²² *You worship what you do not know; we worship what we know, for salvation is from the Jews.*

²³ But the Hour is coming, and is now here, when the true worshippers will worship the Father in Spirit and Truth, for the Father seeks such as these to worship him. ²⁴ God is Spirit, and those who worship him must worship in Spirit and Truth.'

²⁵ The woman said to him, 'I know that Messiah is coming' (*who is called Christ*). 'When he comes, he will proclaim all things to us.'

²⁶ Jesus said to her, 'I Am, the one who is speaking to you.'

²⁷ Just then his disciples came. They were astonished that he was speaking with a woman, but no one said, 'What do you want?' or, 'Why are you speaking with her?'

²⁸ Then the woman left her water-jar and went back to the city. She said to the people, ²⁹ 'Come and see a man who told me everything I have ever done! He cannot be the Messiah, can he?'

³⁰ They left the city and were on their way to him.

Expansion 1

³¹ *Meanwhile the disciples were urging him, 'Rabbi, eat something.' ³² But he said to them, 'I have food to eat that you do not know about.' ³³ So the disciples said to one another, 'Surely no one has brought him something to eat?' ³⁴ Jesus said to them, 'My food is to do the will of him who sent me and to complete his work. ³⁵ Do you not say, 'Four months more, then comes the harvest'? But I tell you, look around you, and see how the fields are ripe for harvesting. ³⁶ The reaper is already receiving wages and is gathering fruit for eternal life, so that sower and reaper may rejoice together. ³⁷ For here the saying holds true, 'One sows and another reaps.' ³⁸ I sent you to reap that for which you did not labour. Others have laboured, and you have entered into their labour.'*

Expansion 2

³⁹ *Many Samaritans from that city believed in him because of the woman's testimony, 'He told me everything I have ever done.' ⁴⁰ So when the Samaritans came to him, they asked him to stay with them; and he stayed there for two days. ⁴¹ And many more believed because of his Word.*
⁴² *They said to the woman, 'It is no longer because of what you said that we believe, for we have heard for ourselves, and we know that this is truly the Saviour of the World.'*

COMMENTARY

The next Dialogue, as was pointed out, is parallel to the previous one with Nicodemus. It engages Jesus with a Samaritan woman and it is situated at Sychar near Jacob's Well.[54] The well provides the scenario for a Discourse dealing with water. Just as in the Nicodemus Dialogue, in which Jesus placed himself in contrast to Moses, so in this section he places himself in contrast to Jacob (later he will also place himself above Abraham). These comparisons with the principal Jewish figures of the past must reflect some early debates between Jesus-movement people and the mainstream Jews.

The Samaritans were Jews. They accepted only the five books of Moses as their Torah. They expected a Prophet-like-Moses (or more simply, The Prophet) to come and restore true Jewish worship, not in the Jerusalem Temple but in their own sanctuary on Mount Gerizim. The idea of this Prophet comes from the book of Deuteronomy, according to their interpretation.

> Yahweh your God will raise up for you a Prophet-like-me from among your own people; you shall heed such a prophet. (18:15)

Again there are minor interruptions by a friendly scribe who tries to explain any inconsistencies. However, one indignant comment explains that no one should understand that Jesus accepted Gerizim as a legitimate place of worship, because true worship was limited to the Jewish practice in Jerusalem.

Some other explanatory additions are made to the text to explain how Jesus came to be alone at the well (his disciples had gone off to buy food), why the woman would be taken back at his request for water (Jews kept apart from Samaritans) and how the woman came to return to Sychar.

Whereas Nicodemus misunderstood 'born from Above' because of its double meaning, so the Woman misunderstands 'living water' (*hudor zon*) because it too has a double meaning. The term can mean 'water that gives Life' or 'fresh water'. She wrongly chooses the latter, just as Nicodemus misunderstood 'born from Above'.

Jesus now patiently explains, as he did with Nicodemus, that he means 'Water gushing up to Eternal Life'.

The Dialogue turns to Jesus' insight into her troubled marital status. It allows the woman to question him as to whether he is The Prophet and the legitimacy of the Samaritan claim to have their centre of worship on

---

[54] Sychar is probably modern Aska, a short distance from the purported well.

The Mountain or Gerizim. Mountain is pitted against Mountain: Can Sinai/ Horeb be found in Jerusalem or Gerizim? Jesus side-steps this argument. Gnostic worshippers will worship 'in Spirit and Truth'; they will not need a Mountain.

Finally, Jesus reveals himself as 'I Am' to her. This brings about belief not only on the part of the woman but of the other Samaritan citizens.

An expansion deals with the return of the disciples, whose absence an earlier editorial comment had attributed to the need to get food. It deals with the topic of food and bread in vv.31-38. Stray sayings on food and bread, some of them similar to those in the broader Jesus-Tradition, have been linked, not always successfully or clearly.

A final but much later editorial comment in vv. 39-42 makes it clear that the Samaritan Woman was acting as an evangelist, which all converted believers should do.

These two expansions are not Gnostic and they do nothing to further the Discourse on Living Water.

These two Discourses with Nicodemus and the Samaritan Woman have centred on Water and Washing. The Gnostic was intended to understand the reference to Baptism in the Gnostic ritual, the Foot-Washing.

3. The Father and Son (5:19-47)

5:19 Jesus said to them, 'Very truly, I tell you, the Son can do nothing on his own, but only what he sees the Father doing; for whatever the Father does, the Son does likewise. 20 The Father loves the Son and shows him all that he himself is doing; and he will show him greater works than these, so that you will be astonished. 21 Indeed, just as the Father raises the dead and gives them Life, so also the Son gives Life to whomsoever he wishes.

22 The Father judges no one but has given all Judgement to the Son, 23 so that all may honour the Son just as they honour the Father. Anyone who does not honour the Son does not honour the Father who sent him. 24 Very truly, I tell you, anyone who hears my Word and believes him who sent me has Eternal Life, and does not come under Judgement, but has passed from death to life.

Expansion 1

25 'Very truly, I tell you, The Hour is coming, and is now here, when the dead will hear the voice of the Son of God, and those who hear will live. 26 For just as the Father has Life in himself, so he has granted the Son also to have Life in himself; 27 and he has given him authority to execute Judgement, because he is the Son of Man. 28 Do not be astonished at this; for The Hour is coming when all who are in their graves will hear his voice 29 and will come out –

those who have done good, to the resurrection of Life, and those who have done evil, to the resurrection of condemnation.

[30] 'I can do nothing on my own. As I hear, I judge; and my Judgement is just, because I seek to do not my own will but the will of Him who Sent Me.

[31] 'If I testify about myself, my testimony is not true. [32] There is another who testifies on my behalf, and I know that his testimony to me is true.

Expansion 2

[33] *You sent messengers to John, and he testified to the Truth. [34] Not that I accept such human testimony, but I say these things so that you may be saved. [35] He was a burning and shining lamp, and you were willing to rejoice for a while in his light. [36] But I have a testimony greater than John's.*

The works that the Father has given me to complete, the very works that I am doing, testify on my behalf that the Father has sent me. [37] And the Father who sent me has himself testified on my behalf. You have never heard his voice or seen his form, [38] and you do not have his Word abiding in you, because you do not believe Him Whom He Has Sent.

[39] 'You search the scriptures because you think that in them you have Eternal Life; and it is they that testify on my behalf. [40] Yet you refuse to come to me to have Life. [41] I do not accept Glory from human beings. [42] But I know that you do not have the love of God in you. [43] I have come in my Father's Name, and you do not accept me; if another comes in his own name, you will accept him. [44] How can you believe when you accept glory from one another and do not seek the Glory that comes from the one who alone is God? [45] Do not think that I will accuse you before the Father; your accuser is Moses, on whom you have set your hope. [46] If you believed Moses, you would believe me, for he wrote about me. [47] But if you do not believe what he wrote, how will you believe what I say?'

COMMENTARY

The third Discourse is a Monologue on the Father and Son and it has been inserted at this point because it refers to an important item in the preceding Third Sign:

> [5:17] But Jesus answered them, 'My Father is still working, and I also am working.'

Jesus has raised an Official's Son and has cured the Crippled Man. The Discourse explains how it is that Jesus is able to achieve these works, with the main thesis being:

> [21] Indeed, just as the Father raises the dead and gives them Life, so also the Son gives Life to whomsoever he wishes.

This Discourse is, therefore, a Gnostic explanation of the two roles of Father and Son. It shows how the Father is understood by The Son, who follows the Father's initiative as he prepares the Son for his mission into The World. Those who believe, by accepting the Son who has been sent into The World, will acquire Eternal Life. This is a theology of Emanation.

At this point, a very important notion is introduced: death yielding to life. For the Gnostics death has a particular meaning as can be seen from this extract from *The Apocryphon of John*. Written in the earlier second century CE, this document is a commentary on Genesis 1-6. It is based on ten questions. One aspect of The Apocryphon of John needs explanation before the text below makes sense – *Pronoia* ('Forethought') is a Saviour figure.

Early in the text Jesus is said to have come forth from *Pronoia*. It is in the form of Jesus that *Pronoia* descends three times into the lower realms and there she, in the form of Jesus, preaches the true *gnosis* and awakens those who believe from their sleep of death. Jesus speaks:

> 'Still for a third time I went – I am the light which exists in the light, I am the remembrance of the Pronoia – that I might enter into the midst of darkness and the inside of Hades. And I filled my face with the light of the completion of their aeon. And I entered into the midst of their prison, which is the prison of the body. And I said, 'He who hears, let him get up from the deep sleep.' And he wept and shed tears. Bitter tears he wiped from himself and he said, 'Who is it that calls my name, and from where has this hope come to me, while I am in the chains of the prison?' And I said, 'I am the Pronoia of the pure light; I am the thinking of the virginal Spirit, who raised you up to the honoured place. Arise and remember that it is you who hearkened, and follow your root, which is I, the merciful one, and guard yourself against the angels of poverty and the demons of chaos and all those who ensnare you, and beware of the deep sleep and the enclosure of the inside of Hades.
>
> 'And I raised him up, and sealed him in the light of the water with five seals, in order that death might not have power over him from this time on.' (30-31)

In dealing with Salvation, the *Apocryphon of John* explains that Jesus came to remind humans of their heavenly origins; this knowledge is *gnosis*. Those who possess this saving *gnosis* are enabled to return to The Light (in this case, the non-believers will be endlessly reincarnated until they do achieve *gnosis*). Thus, Death is the state of those who have not achieved *gnosis*; they are the unawakened ones who live in the imprisonment of their flesh. The Gnostic believers hear the preaching of Jesus and respond, and in this way they are delivered from Death. This is the meaning of 'passing from Death to Life'.

However, a Roman editor has seen the need for a correction of this realized eschatology whereby the saved pass immediately from Death to Life. It did not seem compatible with the developing orthodox Roman teaching on death, the resurrection of the dead, future judgement, reward and punishment. Accordingly, the correction outlines a future eschatology. The Hour, a Gnostic idea, is redefined as a point of time in the future when the general resurrection of the dead would take place, after which there would be a rewarding of the just and punishment of the unjust.

The main text continues with the original Discourse but the mention of 'testimony' (*martyrein*) attracts another correction about John the Baptist. It is said that actually he did give testimony as a temporary measure in the divine plan. Therefore, his 'testimony' to the Father was human, even if admirable for the purpose. Likewise he was not the Light, but comparable only to a lamp, in contradistinction to The Light itself.

Rejoining the main Discourse text again, we are confronted with Jesus' dismissal of the Hebrew Scriptures as sources for Eternal Life. The Scriptures (equivalent to 'Moses') are not the full testimony. Moses foretold the coming of Jesus but this was only a preliminary function. Now the time has come to lay him and his Scriptures aside. Jesus has arrived and the full *gnosis* with him.

This Gnostic Discourse with its delineation of the roles of The Father and The Son is an important statement of the basic mechanism of Gnosticism. All else in Gnostic thought takes its rise from this relationship of Father and the Son who has emanated from him.

4. The Bread of Life (6:35-65)

35 Jesus said to them, 'I am the Bread of Life. Whoever comes to me will never be hungry, and whoever believes in me will never be thirsty. ³⁶But I said to you that you have seen me and yet do not believe. ³⁷Everything that the Father gives me will come to me, and anyone who comes to me I will never drive away; ³⁸for I have come down from Heaven, not to do my own will, but the will of Him Who Sent Me.

Expansion 1

³⁹*And this is the will of Him Who Sent Me that I should lose nothing of all that he has given me, but raise it up on the last day.* ⁴⁰*This is indeed the will of my Father that all who see the Son and believe in him may have Eternal Life; and I will raise them up on the last day.'*

41 Then the Jews began to complain about him because he said, 'I am the Bread that came down from Heaven.' ⁴²They were saying, 'Is not

this Jesus, the son of Joseph, whose father and mother we know? How can he now say, 'I have come down from heaven'?'

⁴³Jesus answered them, 'Do not complain among yourselves. ⁴⁴No one can come to me unless drawn by the Father who sent me; *and I will raise that person up on the last day. ⁴⁵It is written in the prophets, 'And they shall all be taught by God.'* Everyone who has heard and learned from the Father comes to me. ⁴⁶Not that anyone has seen the Father except the one who is from God; he has seen the Father. ⁴⁷Very truly, I tell you, whoever believes has Eternal Life. ⁴⁸I am the Bread of Life. ⁴⁹Your ancestors ate the manna in the wilderness, and they died. ⁵⁰This is the Bread that comes down from Heaven, so that one may eat of it and not die. ⁵¹I am the Living Bread that came down from Heaven. Whoever eats of this Bread will live for ever; *and the Bread that I will give for the Life of the World is my Flesh.'*

Expansion 2

52 The Jews then disputed among themselves, saying, 'How can this man give us his flesh to eat?'

⁵³So Jesus said to them, 'Very truly, I tell you, unless you eat the Flesh of the Son of Man and drink his Blood, you have no Life in you. ⁵⁴Those who eat my Flesh and drink my Blood have Eternal Life, and I will raise them up on the last day; ⁵⁵for my Flesh is true food and my Blood is true drink. ⁵⁶Those who eat my Flesh and drink my Blood abide in me, and I in them. ⁵⁷Just as the living Father sent me, and I live because of the Father, so whoever eats me will live because of me. ⁵⁸This is the Bread that came down from Heaven, not like that which your ancestors ate, and they died. But the one who eats this Bread will live for ever.'

⁵⁹He said these things while he was teaching in the synagogue at Capernaum.⁶⁰ When many of his disciples heard it, they said, 'This teaching is difficult; who can accept it?'

⁶¹But Jesus, being aware that his disciples were complaining about it, said to them, 'Does this offend you? ⁶²Then what if you were to see the Son of Man ascending to where he was before? ⁶³It is the Spirit that gives Life; the Flesh is useless. The words that I have spoken to you are Spirit and Life. ⁶⁴But among you there are some who do not believe.'

For Jesus knew from the first who were the ones that did not believe, and who was the one that would betray him.

⁶⁵And he said, 'For this reason I have told you that no one can come to me unless it is granted by the Father.'

COMMENTARY

The editors of John have added this Gnostic Discourse on the Bread of Life at the end of Fourth Sign concerning the Feeding of the 5000. It was a logical position for it. Jesus has revealed himself as the Bread of Life, has come to renew and fulfil the expectations of Israel, and this requires Gnostic explanation.

Accordingly a collection of five of the fourteen Discourses, containing much of Gnostic teaching, have been inserted at this point:

The Bread of Life (6:35-65)

Excerpts within a Tradition (7:1-52)

The Light of the World and Testimony (8:12-20)

Above and Below (8:21-30)

The Father and Abraham (8:31-59)

Beginning with the Bread of Life, these constitute a considerable outline of Gnostic teaching, following the pivotal Fourth Sign.

It should be noted that apart from 'Bread of Life', there is the terminology of 'Bread of God' and 'Bread of Heaven'. These terms are synonyms.

We have already noted above that 'Bread' had had a long history in Jewish religious thought. In the first place, in developing Jewish thinking, bread was a synonym for the guiding revelation of God: he fed his people with bread in the wilderness; he continues to feed them thereafter. This became the interpretation of the manna stories in the book of Exodus.

However, with the coming of Jesus, there is a new emphasis on Jesus as The Bread of Life or God or Heaven in Gnostic circles. Jesus is said to have brought the Bread of Heaven in the *Gospel of Philip*:

> Before Christ came, there was no bread in the world, just as Paradise, the place were Adam was, had many trees to nourish the animals but no wheat to sustain man. Man used to feed like the animals, but when Christ came, the perfect man, he brought bread from heaven in order that man might be nourished with the food of man. The rulers thought that it was by their own power and will that they were doing what they did, but the Holy Spirit in secret was accomplishing everything through them as it wished. Truth, which existed since the beginning, is sown everywhere. (55)

This Discourse is a brief Dialogue, dealing with Jesus' self-identification as the Bread of Life. The opening statement in the Discourse contains a rather illogical remark 'and whoever believes in me will never be thirsty'. This possibly refers to the Gnostic Eucharist, which consisted of both bread and wine (but with different connotations to the Roman practice).

A correction uses the point concerning 'the will of him who sent me' to add a remark on Roman Christian ideas on the resurrection of the dead on a Last Day. This is final eschatology in contrast to the tenor of the Dialogue. The text then resumes from where it left off.

The reference to the 'Jews' is interesting. They 'complain'. This is a reminder of the complaints of the Jews in the wilderness over the manna, as recorded in Exodus.

> [11] Yahweh spoke to Moses and said, [12] 'I have heard the complaining of the Israelites; say to them, "At twilight you shall eat meat, and in the morning you shall have your fill of bread; then you shall know that I am Yahweh your God."' (16:11-12)

The Jews misunderstand the term 'came down from Heaven' that Jesus appended to the title of Bread. It is not the manna of the wilderness. That was in the past; in the present there is Jesus, the new Bread of Heaven.

Jesus explains more on the Bread of Life. There are two corrections that may be from different hands. One tries again to include a final eschatology. The other makes use of a vague text, *'And they shall all be taught by God'* (conflated from Isaiah 54:13 and Jeremiah 31:34), to answer the problem set by the Jews.

The text is yet again interrupted by a later correction that links the eating of the Bread of Life with the practice of the Roman Eucharist. The Jews ask the question about actually eating the flesh of Jesus (an idea certainly abhorrent and foreign to Gnostics, not so to Romans accustomed to the idea of sacrifice) and receive an affirmation that indeed that is what the saying means. This is one of the many divergences between Gnostics and Roman Christians on the sacraments.

It is clear that some of the Gnostic statements about realized eschatology and about eating Bread have been corrected and re-directed. Realized eschatology is corrected to final eschatology; the metaphorical 'eating' is changed to a literal reception of the Eucharist (in the form of eating and drinking the body and blood of Jesus), with an overtone that the bread is physically Jesus.

Unfortunately, as it stands, the text cannot be read as an integral and flowing piece. It does not make sense as such. It is more like a poem with a quizzical editor adding comments and making suggestions on the margin, not all of them appropriate. The readers of the present text have a Romanized Christian version of the Discourse in front of them; it has many anomalies but it has been skewed to apply to the Roman Eucharist. The original version of the Discourse had no such intention.

5. Excerpts Within a Tradition (7:1-52)

Expansion 1

> *After this Jesus went about in Galilee. He did not wish to go about in Judea because the Jews were looking for an opportunity to kill him.*

[2] *Now the Jewish Festival of Booths was near.*

[3] *So his brothers said to him, 'Leave here and go to Judea so that your disciples also may see the works you are doing;* [4] *for no one who wants to be widely known acts in secret. If you do these things, show yourself to the world.'* [5] *(For not even his brothers believed in him.)*

[6] *Jesus said to them, 'My time has not yet come, but your time is always here.* [7] *The World cannot hate you, but it hates me because I testify against it that its works are evil.* [8] *Go to the Festival yourselves. I am not going to this Festival, for my time has not yet fully come.'*

[9] *After saying this, he remained in Galilee.*

[10] *But after his brothers had gone to the Festival, then he also went, not publicly but as it were in secret.*

[11] *The Jews were looking for him at the Festival and saying, 'Where is he?'*

[12] *And there was considerable complaining about him among the crowds. While some were saying, 'He is a Good Man', others were saying, 'No, he is deceiving the crowd.'* [13] *Yet no one would speak openly about him for fear of the Jews.*

[14] *About the middle of the Festival, Jesus went up into the Temple and began to teach.*

[15] *The Jews were astonished at it, saying, 'How does this man have such learning, when he has never been taught?'*

[16] Then Jesus answered them, 'My teaching is not mine but his who sent me. [17] Anyone who resolves to do the will of God will know whether the teaching is from God or whether I am speaking on my own. [18] Those who speak on their own seek their own glory; but the one who seeks the Glory of him who sent him is true, and there is nothing false in him. [19] 'Did not Moses give you the Law? Yet none of you keeps the Law. Why are you looking for an opportunity to kill me?'

[20] The crowd answered, 'You have a demon! Who is trying to kill you?'

[21] Jesus answered them, 'I performed one work, and all of you are astonished. [22] Moses gave you circumcision *(it is, of course, not from Moses, but from the patriarchs)*, and you circumcize a man on the Sabbath. [23] If a man receives circumcision on the Sabbath in order that the Law of Moses may not be broken, are you angry with me because I healed a man's whole body on the Sabbath? [24] Do not judge by appearances, but judge with right judgement.'

Expansion 2

[25] *Now some of the people of Jerusalem were saying, 'Is not this the man whom they are trying to kill?* [26] *And here he is, speaking openly, but they say nothing to him! Can it be that the authorities really know that this is the Messiah?* [27] *Yet we know where this man is from; but when the Messiah comes, no one will know where he is from.'*

[28] Then Jesus cried out as he was teaching in the Temple, 'You know me, and you know where I am from. I have not come on my own. But

the One who Sent Me is true, and you do not know him. ²⁹ I know him, because I am from him, and he sent me.'

Expansion 3

³⁰ *Then they tried to arrest him, but no one laid hands on him, because his Hour had not yet come.*

³¹ *Yet many in the crowd believed in him and were saying, 'When the Messiah comes, will he do more Signs than this man has done?'*

³² *The Pharisees heard the crowd muttering such things about him, and the chief priests and Pharisees sent temple police to arrest him.*

³³ Jesus then said, 'I will be with you a little while longer, and then I am going to Him Who Sent Me. ³⁴ You will search for me, but you will not find me; and where I am, you cannot come.'

³⁵ The Jews said to one another, 'Where does this man intend to go that we will not find him? Does he intend to go to the Dispersion among the Greeks and teach the Greeks? ³⁶ What does he mean by saying, 'You will search for me and you will not find me' and, 'Where I am, you cannot come'?'

³⁷ *On the last day of the festival, the great day, while Jesus was standing there, he cried out:*

> 'Let anyone who is thirsty come to me,
> ³⁸ *and let the one who believes in me drink.*

As the scripture has said, 'Out of his heart shall flow rivers of living water.' '

³⁹ *Now he said this about the Spirit, which believers in him were to receive; for as yet there was no Spirit, because Jesus was not yet glorified.*

⁴⁰ *When they heard these words, some in the crowd said, 'This is really The Prophet.'*

⁴¹ *Others said, 'This is the Messiah.'*

But some asked, 'Surely the Messiah does not come from Galilee, does he? ⁴² Has not the Scripture said that the Messiah has descended from David and comes from Bethlehem, the village where David lived?'

⁴³ So there was a division in the crowd because of him. ⁴⁴ Some of them wanted to arrest him, but no one laid hands on him.

Expansion 4

⁴⁵ *Then the temple police went back to the chief priests and Pharisees, who asked them, 'Why did you not arrest him?'*

⁴⁶ *The police answered, 'Never has anyone spoken like this!'*

⁴⁷ *Then the Pharisees replied, 'Surely you have not been deceived too, have you? ⁴⁸ Has any one of the authorities or of the Pharisees believed in him? ⁴⁹ But this crowd, which does not know the Law—they are accursed.'*

⁵⁰ *Nicodemus, who had gone to Jesus before, and who was one of them, asked, ⁵¹ 'Our Law does not judge people without first giving them a hearing to find out what they are doing, does it?'*

⁵² They replied, 'Surely you are not also from Galilee, are you? Search and you will see that no prophet is to arise from Galilee.'

COMMENTARY

An analysis of the fifth Discourse demonstrates extreme difficulties in interpretation. The Discourse is very different to any of the others. In fact, the whole piece is more a narrative than a Discourse. Reading the narrative sections only (in italics above) there is good sense in the text. The narrative takes precedence and excerpts of a Jesus Discourse have then been inserted at appropriate places. The end result is an awkward text in the extreme, combining Narrative and Discourse. It is more like a Dialogue, where the questions are not raised by the interrogators but by events.

More likely, the narrative existed first. The Discourse was then inserted into it.

The narrative centres on the fact that Jesus came from Galilee and ministered there. This was used later on by Jewish opponents of the Jesus-movements to deny claims to his Messiahship. No prophet was foretold as coming from Galilee. Judea (and specifically Bethlehem therein) was considered the locus for the origin of The Prophet or The Messiah. The text of John as it stands is made up of the following elements, with an indication of the weaving of narrative and Discourse:

Theme 1: Galilee or Judea – where should Jesus minister?

Narrative (7:1-9)

Jesus' ministry is in Galilee not Judea; this is for fear of the Jews in Judea.

The Brothers announce they are going to Judea for the Festival of Booths; they invite Jesus to come. (A secondary comment denounces The Brothers as non-believers.)

Jesus refuses: the Jews of Jerusalem hate him but not the Brothers. He will come to Jerusalem to fulfil The Hour.

Jesus remains in Galilee

Theme 2: Jesus in Jerusalem for the Festival of Booths (10-13)

(Transition: Jesus goes secretly from Galilee to Jerusalem.)

His presence in Jerusalem causes 'complaining' among the Jewish Crowd.

Discourse (14-31)

He teaches in the Temple on the middle day of the Festival.

Admiration of Crowd, but we find problem 1: The Messiah was supposed to come from an unknown place.

Narrative (7:32-36)

The Jews make attempts to arrest him (but his Hour has not come).

The Crowd believes on the basis of Signs, which highlights problem 2: The Messiah was expected to perform Signs openly.

Temple police are sent by the chief priests and Pharisees to arrest him.

Discourse (7:37-39)

Jesus preaches on the Water of Life on the final day of the Festival.[55]

There are additions to this Discourse. First, there is a reference to a fulfilment text, of uncertain origin, that foretells living water coming out of Jerusalem, and then a correction that identifies the Water with the Spirit, although it is made clear that the Spirit will be a post-Resurrection phenomenon.

Narrative (7:40-52)

The crowd responds with acclamation of The Prophet, The Messiah. But there is problem 3: the Messiah was supposed to come from Bethlehem.

The Temple police return, impressed by his teaching.

Nicodemus, one of the Jews, defends Jesus' teaching using his interpretation of The Law.

Jews exasperated: No prophet has ever come from Galilee.

The life-situation of this narrative must have been a period after the formation of a particular Gnostic community. They had two opponents. The first opponent was the Jews (also depicted as the Pharisees and the chief priests, backed up by the Temple police). The second opponent was Palestinian Christianity, depicted as The Brothers of the Lord. We have already dealt with this group of Jesus-movement people. They had been situated in Jerusalem under James, the Brother of the Lord. Neither opponent accepted the fact that a Messiah could arise and minister in Galilee.

---

[55] The ritual of the Feast of Booths required priests to take water drawn from Siloam and to circle the Temple altar seven times. The crowds would gather, bearing harvest offerings while the priests then poured the water onto the ground through a funnel. This is the contrived situation for Jesus' claim to be the source of Living Water, written in typical Hebrew verse.

The narrative takes their arguments in turn: Jesus did go to Jerusalem; the claims against his Messiahship (his origins should be unknown;[56] he does not perform Signs openly; he should have been born in Bethlehem[57]) are because of misinterpretations of The Law or ignorance. The Crowd and Nicodemus argue against the Jews on the matter.

Into this narrative – which reflects the debate between Jews, Palestinian Christians and Gnostics – excerpts from Jesus Discourses have been interpolated. Together, they do not make up a whole Discourse. They are excerpts from Discourses, otherwise unattested, that respond to particular issues raised in the narrative.

Issue: Where does Jesus' 'learning' come from? (*'How does this man have such learning, when he has never been taught?'* v. 15)

Response: His teaching originated from the realm of the divine, from the divine Father. (*'My teaching is not mine but his who sent me.'* v. 16)

Issue: Why do the Jews want to kill him? (*'Who is trying to kill you?'* v. 20)

Response: Because he cured a 'man's whole body' (this could have been an earlier story of the cripple, the blind man or another) on the Sabbath. The argument about circumcision on the Sabbath is used as a response (with an aside that the Patriarchs introduced circumcision, not Moses, mistaking 'Moses' for the character not The Torah). (*'Are you angry with me because I healed a man's whole body on the Sabbath?'* v. 23)

Issue: The origins of Jesus are known, which should not be the case if he was The Messiah (*'Yet we know where this man is from.'* v. 27)

Response: He has come from the unknown realms of The Father. (*'I have not come on my own. But the One who Sent Me is true, and you do not know him.'* v. 28)

---

[56] Justin Martyr (in Dialogue 8:4) related that the Jewish belief was that the Messiah would be hidden until he was revealed by Elijah (and hence the Synoptic effort to align John the Baptist with Elijah).

[57] Matthew and Luke of course solve this problem in a more forthright way. Their Infancy Gospels claim that Jesus actually was born in Bethlehem. For Matthew, Mary lived with Joseph in Bethlehem where Jesus was born and later went to Nazareth. For Luke, Mary and Joseph lived in Nazareth, but they went to Bethlehem for a census and the child was born there. In both instances they returned to Nazareth. Neither account has any historical foundation.

Issue: Where is the elusive Jesus going? (*'Where does this man intend to go that we will not find him?* v. 35)

Response: This present time is the 'Little While'. It will only be when the Little While is completed that Jesus, according to the divine plan, could be arrested. (*'I will be with you a little while longer, and then I am going to Him Who Sent Me.'* v. 33)[58]

This manipulated Discourse stands alone. In many ways it is not a Discourse. It is a commentary, in Discourse terms, on a narrative. In other instances expansions work in the opposite direction: they are set in Discourses in order to explain them further. Here the parts of Discourses are used as expansions to elaborate on the narrative.

6. The Light of the World and Testimony (8:12-20)

[12] Again Jesus spoke to them [the Pharisees], saying, 'I am the Light of the World. Whoever follows me will never walk in Darkness but will have the Light of Life.'

[13] Then the Pharisees said to him, 'You are testifying on your own behalf; your testimony is not valid.'

[14] Jesus answered, 'Even if I testify on my own behalf, my testimony is valid because I know where I have come from and where I am going, but you do not know where I come from or where I am going. [15] You judge by human standards; I judge no one. [16] Yet even if I do judge, my judgement is valid; for it is not I alone who judge, but I and the Father who sent me. [17] In your Law it is written that the testimony of two witnesses is valid. [18] I testify on my own behalf, and the Father who sent me testifies on my behalf.'

[19] Then they said to him, 'Where is your Father?'

Jesus answered, 'You know neither me nor my Father. If you knew me, you would know my Father also.'

[20] He spoke these words while he was teaching in the treasury of the Temple, but no one arrested him, because his Hour had not yet come.

COMMENTARY

This is a short excerpt from some larger Discourse.

It begins with a statement on the Light of the World and then progresses to Testimony (*marturein*). 'Testimony' has been defined in the glossary. As well as a term that was used in Jewish religious thought, 'Light' is also a con-

---

[58] In the final Issue and Response, the Response is actually given before the Issue has been raised.

sistently-used Gnostic term and its usage here is much closer to the Gnostic usage. The Father is Eternal Light. This image was intended to convey the idea of infinite power. Jesus is the Word who comes from the Highest God, as was described in the Gnostic Hymn of John 1. As an Emanation from the fullness of divinity, there is a moving description of him as 'Light from Light' in the fourth century CE *Teachings of Silvanus*. This was not a Gnostic book but was written in the Wisdom strain and, in fact, looked upon Gnosticism pejoratively. However, it was found bound into a codex at Nag Hammadi and presumably served the purposes of a Gnostic audience.

> O Lord Almighty, how much glory shall I give Thee? No one has been able to glorify God adequately. It is Thou who hast given glory to Thy Word in order to save everyone, O Merciful God. [It is] he who has come from Thy mouth and has risen from Thy heart, the First-born, the Wisdom, the Prototype, the First Light.
>
> For he is Light from the power of God, and he is an Emanation of the pure glory of the Almighty. He is the spotless mirror of the working of God, and he is the image of his goodness. For he is also the Light of the Eternal Light. (112-113)

The Discourse would have been seen as an adequate Gnostic description of Jesus the Light.

After the statement on Light in the Discourse there is a return to what, for a Jewish mind, was important – Testimony. The Law in Deuteronomy 17:6 had stated that two or three witnesses were required for testimony in any capital case.

> On the evidence of two or three witnesses the death sentence shall be executed; a person must not be put to death on the evidence of only one witness.

Jesus now counts the witnesses in the present judgement: himself and The Father; there are two.

The Pharisees then misunderstand the meaning of 'Father' and Jesus dismisses them.

7. Above and Below (8:21-30)

> [21] Again he said to them [the Jews], 'I am going away, and you will search for me, but you will die in your sin. Where I am going, you cannot come.'
> [22] Then the Jews said, 'Is he going to kill himself? Is that what he means by saying, 'Where I am going, you cannot come'?'
> [23] He said to them, 'You are from Below, I am from Above; you are

of this World, I am not of this World. [24] I told you that you would die in your sins, for you will die in your sins unless you believe that I Am.'

[25] They said to him, 'Who are you?'

Jesus said to them, 'Why do I speak to you at all? [26] I have much to say about you and much to condemn; but the one who sent me is true, and I declare to the world what I have heard from him.'

[27] They did not understand that he was speaking to them about the Father.

[28] So Jesus said, 'When you have lifted up the Son of Man, then you will realize that I Am, and that I do nothing on my own, but I speak these things as the Father instructed me. [29] And the one who sent me is with me; he has not left me alone, for I always do what is pleasing to him.'

[30] As he was saying these things, many believed in him.

COMMENTARY

This section is another short Dialogue dealing with the departure of Jesus to The Father. The Jews misunderstand his saying about 'going away' to mean suicide, a rather far-fetched interpretation.

Jesus then distinguishes once again The Above of heavenly fullness from The Below, where sin and death abounds in The World. The Idea of 'Above' has already been seen in the glossary and the Nicodemus Discourse. The Jews do not understand and ask for his self-identification. Jesus identifies himself as 'I Am', the divine designation.

There is a further comment showing that the Jews do not understand about The Father, who sent Jesus on his mission to the World and to whom Jesus will now return. Their question indicates their ignorance. Jesus, in response to their quandary, explains the mechanism of his Return.

To enable his Return, he will be 'lifted up' in the sense of 'exalted' (as seen also in the Nicodemus Discourse), although it also refers to the lifting-up by his crucifixion. This term is now linked with 'I Am'. It is in the lifting-up or glorification, effected by the crucifixion, that he will be manifested as 'I Am' and it will be clear what relationship he has with his Father.

This is a concise and astute statement of Gnostic theology. Jesus has come as God from Above to Below, but he will 'go away'. His going-away will be brought about by his Glorification, which is synonymous with the crucifixion, the mechanism for his 'going away' from Below to Above. In short, his exaltation by crucifixion will divest him of The Flesh, his Glory will be revealed and he will be seen as I Am and then he will return to the Father.

8. The Father and Abraham (8:31-59)

[31] Then Jesus said to the Jews who had believed in him, 'If you continue in my Word, you are truly my disciples; [32] and you will know the Truth, and the Truth will make you free.'

[33] They answered him, 'We are descendants of Abraham and have never been slaves to anyone. What do you mean by saying, 'You will be made free'?'

[34] Jesus answered them, 'Very truly, I tell you, everyone who commits sin is a slave to Sin. [35] The slave does not have a permanent place in the household; the son has a place there for ever. [36] So if the Son makes you free, you will be free indeed. [37] I know that you are descendants of Abraham; yet you look for an opportunity to kill me, because there is no place in you for my Word. [38] I declare what I have seen in the Father's presence; as for you, you should do what you have heard from the Father.'

[39] They answered him, 'Abraham is our father.'

Jesus said to them, 'If you were Abraham's children, you would be doing what Abraham did, [40] but now you are trying to kill me, a Man who has told you the Truth that I heard from God. This is not what Abraham did. [41] You are indeed doing what your father does.'

They said to him, 'We are not illegitimate children; we have one father, God himself.'

[42] Jesus said to them, 'If God were your Father, you would love me, for I came from God and now I am here. I did not come on my own, but he sent me. [43] Why do you not understand what I say? It is because you cannot accept my Word. [44] You are from your Father the Devil, and you choose to do your father's desires. He was a murderer from the beginning and does not stand in the truth, because there is no truth in him. When he lies, he speaks according to his own nature, for he is a liar and the Father of Lies. [45] But because I tell the Truth, you do not believe me. [46] Which of you convicts me of sin? If I tell the Truth, why do you not believe me? [47] Whoever is from God hears the words of God. The reason you do not hear them is that you are not from God.'

[48] The Jews answered him, 'Are we not right in saying that you *are a Samaritan and* have a demon?'

[49] Jesus answered, 'I do not have a demon; but I honour my Father, and you dishonour me. [50] Yet I do not seek my own Glory; there is one who seeks it and he is the judge. [51] Very truly, I tell you, whoever keeps my word will never see Death.'

[52] The Jews said to him, 'Now we know that you have a demon. Abraham died, and so did the prophets; yet you say, 'Whoever keeps my word will never taste death.' [53] Are you greater than our f ather Abraham, who died? The prophets also died. Who do you claim to be?'

[54] Jesus answered, 'If I glorify myself, my glory is nothing. It is my Father who glorifies me, he of whom you say, 'He is our God', [55] though you do not know him. But I know him; if I were to say that I do not know him, I would be a liar like you. But I do know him and I keep his

word. [56] Your ancestor Abraham rejoiced that he would see my day; he saw it and was glad.'

[57] Then the Jews said to him, 'You are not yet fifty years old, and have you seen Abraham?'

[58] Jesus said to them, 'Very truly, I tell you, before Abraham was, I Am.'

[59] So they picked up stones to throw at him, but Jesus hid himself and went out of the temple.

COMMENTARY

This Discourse is a contrived Dialogue between Jesus and the Jews about their relationship to their past. The term 'Jews' in this instance simply indicates inhabitants of Judea, not necessarily people inherently evil in their intent. They are faced with a dilemma of choosing between Jesus and their own Jewishness, represented in this instance by Abraham. They have chosen to believe in Jesus, and Jesus now dialogues about their 'continuance' in belief in their Jewish past.

No doubt the Dialogue was used in the situation where Jews, wanting to follow the Gnostic Jesus, were uncertain about their links to their past in Judaism. The stylistic Discourse follows the pattern of questions, mistaken in their import, and answers that are not understood.

The Dialogue begins with Jesus introducing the Gnostic idea of Truth. The Truth, the reader knows, is achieved by *gnosis;* it is divine knowledge made available in a form that humans can comprehend. When a person reads or perceives a Sign and interprets the Sign, not as a human event but as a point where divine knowledge breaks through into the human sphere, then that person receives the Truth and it will bring freedom from the shackles of being human in the World. The purpose of Jesus' mission has thus been to bring Truth into the World; he is in fact himself The Truth that brings freedom. These ideas are identical to those elaborated in the *Gospel of Philip*:

> He who has knowledge of the Truth is a free man, but the free man does not sin, for 'He who sins is the slave of sin'. Truth is the mother, knowledge [*gnosis*] the father. Those who think that sinning does not apply to them are called 'free' by the world. Knowledge of the Truth merely makes such people arrogant, which is what the words, 'it makes them free' mean. It even gives them a sense of superiority over the whole world. But 'Love builds up'. In fact, he who is really free, through knowledge, is a slave, because of love for those who have not yet been able to attain to the freedom of knowledge. Knowledge makes them capable of becoming free. Love never calls something its own, [...] it [...] possess [...]. It never says, 'This is yours' or 'This is mine,' but 'All these are yours'. Spiritual love is wine and fragrance. (77)

The Jews respond by misunderstanding and taking up the peripheral issue of their freedom on the basis of their descent from Abraham. The fact that their sacred story recounted, from the time of Abraham onwards, instances of foreign bondage and slavery seems to be overlooked.

Jesus' answer is based on the notion that the World is a place of sin, and accepting sinfulness renders the individual a slave. The status of a slave means that the person is outside the household of The Father, His Own Ones. Jesus ends with the exhortation that his listeners should attend to The Father.

Their answer is as naive as the previous one: they only have one father, Abraham.

Jesus' answer is brutal. He distinguishes between Father Abraham and Father the Devil (*diabolos*) who rules The Below. The Jews react by claiming their legitimacy: they are the children of The Father, not the children of the Devil, and they are proud of their sexual uprightness and deny any sexual impropriety (*porneia*) which could refer to illegitimacy.

This claim is now demolished by Jesus. If they were the children of The Father, they would listen to the Truth about The Father. Instead, they are the children of Father the Devil. He was a murderer 'from the beginning' (probably referring to Cain whom some Jewish Targumim understood to be son of the Devil after he refused to master his 'evil inclination') and a Liar, who has no Truth in him. In short, they are illegitimate, children of the Devil.

The reply of the Jews is to counter-charge: they claim Jesus is possessed by a demon (*daimonos*). At some point an editor has added 'a Samaritan' to the charge of demon-possession. Presumably this charge of being a Samaritan made sense in the context of the editor's time; possibly one of the charges brought by Jews against John's version of Jesus was that he accepted the Samaritans, looked upon as Jewish heretics. The Samaritan issue is not taken up in the response and Jesus refutes the claim of demon-possession and progresses the Gnostic argument claiming that he reflects the Father and those who follow him will escape from Death.

This side statement becomes the new focus for the Jews. Is he claiming to be greater than Abraham and the Prophets? Jesus restates his relationship to The Father using the terminology of Glory, Knowledge and Word. Abraham is said to have rejoiced over the coming of Jesus. Beneath this is probably a tortured exegesis that accepted that the name Isaac, through whom the promise was to be transmitted, is close to 'laughter' or 'rejoicing' in the Hebrew story.

Once again the Jews take up a peripheral issue: has Jesus had contact with the ancient Abraham? This gives Jesus the opportunity to end the Dialogue with a declaration that he is 'I Am'. He is outside time.

The Jews cut off their association with Jesus by attempting to kill him with stones, the approved execution for a blasphemer.

As was always possible for The Word, he hides himself.

9. The Good Shepherd (10:1-21)

10:1 'Very truly, I tell you, anyone who does not enter the sheepfold by the gate but climbs in by another way is a thief (*kleptes*)and a bandit [*lestes*]. [2] The one who enters by the gate is the shepherd of the sheep. [3] The gatekeeper opens the gate for him, and the sheep hear his voice. He calls his own sheep by name and leads them out. [4] When he has brought out all his own [*ta idia*], he goes ahead of them, and the sheep follow him because they know his voice. [5] They will not follow a stranger, but they will run from him because they do not know the voice of strangers.'

[6] *Jesus used this figure of speech [paroimia] with them,*
But they did not understand what he was saying to them.

[7] So again Jesus said to them, 'Very truly, I tell you, I Am the Gate for the Sheep. [8] All who came before me are thieves [*kleptai*] and bandits [*lestai*]; but the sheep did not listen to them. [9] I Am the Gate. Whoever enters by me will be saved, and will come in and go out and find pasture. [10] The thief comes only to steal and kill and destroy. I came that they may have life, and have it abundantly.

[11] 'I Am the Good Shepherd. The Good Shepherd lays down his Life for the Sheep. [12] The hired hand, who is not the shepherd and does not own the sheep, sees the wolf coming and leaves the sheep and runs away—and the wolf snatches them and scatters them. [13] The hired hand runs away because a hired hand does not care for the sheep. [14] I Am the Good Shepherd. I know my own and my own know me, [15] just as the Father knows me and I know the Father. And I lay down my life for the Sheep.

[16] *I have other Sheep that do not belong to this fold. I must bring them also, and they will listen to my voice. So there will be one Flock, one Shepherd.*

[17] For this reason the Father loves me, because I lay down my Life in order to take it up again. [18] No one takes it from me, but I lay it down of my own accord. I have power to lay it down, and I have power to take it up again. I have received this command from my Father.'

[19] Again the Jews were divided [*schisma*] because of these words.

[20] *Many of them were saying, 'He has a demon and is out of his mind. Why listen to him?'*

[21] *Others were saying, 'These are not the words of one who has a demon. Can a demon open the eyes of the blind?'*

COMMENTARY

The next two Discourses are linked by the theme of Shepherd. In the first one, the Good Shepherd Discourse, we read:

> [17]For this reason the Father loves me, because I lay down my Life in order to take it up again. [18]No one takes it from me, but I lay it down of my own accord. I have power to lay it down, and I have power to take it up again. I have received this command from my Father.'

Jesus here refers to the fact that he has complete control over his Flesh. He decides when he will remove it.

In the next Discourse 10, the Works of the Father, we read:

> [28]I give them Eternal Life, and they will never perish. No one will snatch them out of my hand. [29]What my Father has given me is greater than all else, and no one can snatch it out of the Father's hand. [30]The Father and I are one.'

This continues the theme of Jesus' Life and his power over its conferral to believers. The content of both Discourses was seen to be complementary, related to the notion of Jesus the Good Shepherd, and placed in the text consecutively.

The analogy of shepherd and caring for sheep in reference to Yahweh was common enough in Jewish thinking. Psalm 23 begins thus:

> Yahweh is my shepherd, I shall not want.
> He makes me lie down in green pastures;
> he leads me beside still waters;
> [3] he restores my soul.
> He leads me in right paths
> for his name's sake.
>
> [4] Even though I walk through the darkest valley,
> I fear no evil;
> for you are with me;
> your rod and your staff—
> they comfort me. (vv. 1-4)

The prophecy of Ezekiel makes use of the same analogy. After decrying the practices of the so-called 'shepherds of Israel', the appointed leaders, the prophecy depicts Yahweh as taking over the role of Shepherd himself:

> [11]For thus says the Lord Yahweh: I myself will search for my sheep, and will seek them out. [12]As shepherds seek out their flocks when they are among their scattered sheep, so I will seek out my sheep. I will rescue them from all the places to which they have been scattered on

a day of clouds and thick darkness. ¹³I will bring them out from the peoples and gather them from the countries, and will bring them into their own land; and I will feed them on the mountains of Israel, by the watercourses, and in all the inhabited parts of the land. ¹⁴I will feed them with good pasture, and the mountain heights of Israel shall be their pasture; there they shall lie down in good grazing land, and they shall feed on rich pasture on the mountains of Israel. ¹⁵I myself will be the shepherd of my sheep, and I will make them lie down, says the Lord Yahweh. ¹⁶I will seek the lost, and I will bring back the strayed, and I will bind up the injured, and I will strengthen the weak, but the fat and the strong I will destroy. I will feed them with justice. (34:11-16)

The image of Jesus as the Good or Authentic Shepherd makes sense from this point of view. No doubt there were some pastoral images regarding sheep in the Jesus-Tradition. This is how Luke develops the theme:

3 So he told them this parable: ⁴'Which one of you, having a hundred sheep and losing one of them, does not leave the ninety-nine in the wilderness and go after the one that is lost until he finds it? ⁵When he has found it, he lays it on his shoulders and rejoices. ⁶And when he comes home, he calls together his friends and neighbours, saying to them, 'Rejoice with me, for I have found my sheep that was lost.' ⁷Just so, I tell you, there will be more joy in heaven over one sinner who repents than over ninety-nine righteous people who need no repentance. (15:3-7)

The Gnostics used the same Jesus-Tradition, although with a somewhat different application from the Synoptic gospels. For example, there is a clear usage in the *Gospel of Truth*, a Christian Gnostic text, which has often been attributed to the heresiarch Valentinus, dating the text to the second century. In general, the teaching takes items from the Jesus-Tradition and, with great skill, puts them into Gnostic settings. Almost certainly, the aim was to present Gnostic teachings to an audience of the orthodox Roman Church. One application from the *Gospel of Truth* is as follows:

He is the shepherd who left behind the ninety-nine sheep which had not strayed and went in search of that one which was lost. He rejoiced when he had found it. For ninety-nine is a number of the left hand, which holds it. The moment he finds the one, however, the whole number is transferred to the right hand. Thus it is with him who lacks the one, that is, the entire right hand which attracts that in which it is deficient, seizes it from the left side and transfers it to the right. In this way, then, the number becomes one hundred. This number signifies the Father.
He laboured even on the Sabbath for the sheep which he found fallen into the pit. He saved the life of that sheep, bringing it up from the pit in order that you may understand fully what that Sabbath is, you who possess full understanding. It is a day in which it is not fitting

that salvation be idle, so that you may speak of that heavenly day which has no night and of the sun which does not set because it is perfect. Say then in your heart that you are this perfect day and that in you the light which does not fail dwells. (31-32)

John's extended Monologue on Jesus the True or Authentic Shepherd follows the Gnostic line of thinking, and not the Synoptic. The Shepherd is first distinguished from 'the thief' (kleptes) and 'the bandit' (lestes)'.[59] Those who belong to the Shepherd belong to the Heavenly Homeland (ta idia). A helpful editor explains that this Shepherd metaphor is a *paroimia*, a proverb or parable which makes sense to insiders but not to outsiders, as an explanation for the hearers' failure to understand.

The Ezekiel dissertation on God the Shepherd had come to a fulsome conclusion:

> [30] They shall know that I, Yahweh their God, am with them, and that they, the house of Israel, are my people, says the Lord Yahweh. [31] You are my sheep, the sheep of my pasture, and I am your God, says the Lord Yahweh. (34:30-31)

Likewise, the revelation that Jesus is the Shepherd ends with a declaration that 'I Am the Gate' and 'I Am the Good Shepherd'. Jesus as the Gate probably refers to himself as the opening to Heaven, the Way. He had told Nathanael that angels would ascend and descend on the Son of Man. It is not inconsistent with this image of the Gate and the Shepherd.

A statement on the death of the Shepherd is interrupted by an addition that points out that there are Jesus-movement followers who do not belong to the Gnostic community. Jesus looks to the time when there will be only one Flock and one Shepherd. The text continues with its discussion of his death: he will die only so that he can resume living; he has the power to do this in himself and The Father has commanded it.

Typically his teaching divided the audience by causing a division or *schisma*. This gives us a clue as to what happened in the elaboration of the Book of Seven Signs. The term was used by John in the previous Sign of the Cure of the Blind Man in chapter 9.

> [16] Some of the Pharisees said, 'This man is not from God, for he does not observe the sabbath.' But others said, 'How can a man who is a sinner perform such signs?' And they were divided [schisma].

Schisma also appears in the conclusion to one of the narrative sections of the Discourse, Excerpts Within a Tradition.

---

[59] It is interesting that Barabbas was named as a *lestes*.

[43] So there was a division [*schisma*] in the crowd because of him. [44]Some of them wanted to arrest him, but no one laid hands on him.

This *schisma* was a formal way for the Gnostics to define the split between believers and unbelievers.

10. The Works of the Father (10:22-42)

[22] At that time the Festival of the Dedication took place in Jerusalem. It was winter, [23] and Jesus was walking in the temple, in the portico of Solomon.

[24] So the Jews gathered around him and said to him, 'How long will you keep us in suspense? If you are the Messiah, tell us plainly.'

[25] Jesus answered, 'I have told you, and you do not believe. The works that I do in my Father's Name testify to me; [26] but you do not believe, because you do not belong to my Sheep. [27] My sheep hear my voice. I know them, and they follow me. [28] I give them Eternal Life, and they will never perish. No one will snatch them out of my hand. [29] What my Father has given me is greater than all else, and no one can snatch it out of the Father's hand. [30] The Father and I are one.'

[31] The Jews took up stones again to stone him.

[32] Jesus replied, 'I have shown you many good works from the Father. For which of these are you going to stone me?'

[33] The Jews answered, 'It is not for a good work that we are going to stone you, but for blasphemy, because you, though only a human being, are making yourself God.'

[34] Jesus answered, 'Is it not written in your Law, 'I said, you are gods'? [35] If those to whom the word of God came were called 'gods'—*and the scripture cannot be annulled*— [36] can you say that the One whom the Father has sanctified and sent into the world is blaspheming because I said, 'I am God's Son'? [37] If I am not doing the Works of my Father, then do not believe me. [38] But if I do them, even though you do not believe me, believe the works, so that you may know and understand that the Father is in me and I am in the Father.'

[39] Then they tried to arrest him again, but he escaped from their hands.

Expansion

[40] *He went away again across the Jordan to the place where John had been baptizing earlier, and he remained there.* [41] *Many came to him, and they were saying, 'John performed no sign, but everything that John said about this man was true.'* [42] *And many believed in him there.*

COMMENTARY

Once again there is the insertion of a Gnostic Dialogue and it concerns the Jews in the sense of inhabitants of Judaea. They ask him if he is the Messiah.

Jesus' response shows that this Dialogue is connected with the previous Monologue on the Good Shepherd. His answer is a typical Gnostic explanation of The Messiah put into the context of the Good Shepherd who is engaged in calling together his sheep.

The Jews' attempt to stone him is forestalled by a question from Jesus: which good work is the cause of death by stoning? They reply that this is not the issue, the issue is that he has claimed to be God. Stoning was the usual penalty for blasphemy. Here, the irony of the text becomes apparent: Jesus, himself a divine Emanation, is threatened by stoning for blasphemy.

Jesus uses a very Jewish argument against them. First, he takes a text of The Law,

> [6] I say, 'You are gods,
> children of the Most High, all of you;
> [7] nevertheless, you shall die like mortals,
> and fall like any prince.' (Psalm 82:6)

Next he argues that if the Scriptures (whose divine authority an editor has emphasized in case of any misunderstanding) can identify humans as 'gods', then *a fortiori* the One who has been consecrated by The Father can claim the title without being charged with blasphemy.

The Jews react by trying to arrest him but once again he has the facility to escape them.

The expansion in vv. 40-42 has nothing to do with the Discourse. It was intended as a general conclusion to his public ministry, as chronicled in the Roman Christian format of the gospel. The ministry had begun with his interaction with John the Baptist. He returns to John the Baptist territory and is acclaimed by believers who acknowledge that John had only a preparatory role. At some stage in the redaction of the gospel, this text functioned as a conclusion to what was seen as the public ministry of Jesus. It has been secondarily attached to the Discourse.

11. The Hour and Glory (12: 19-50)

> [19] The Pharisees then said to one another, 'You see, you can do nothing. Look, the World has gone after him!'
> [20] Now among those who went up to worship at the Festival were some Greeks. [21] They came to Philip, who was from Bethsaida in Galilee, and said to him, 'Sir, we wish to see Jesus.'
> [22] Philip went and told Andrew; then Andrew and Philip went and told Jesus.

²³ Jesus answered them, 'The Hour has come for the Son of Man to be glorified. ²⁴ Very truly, I tell you, unless a grain of wheat falls into the earth and dies, it remains just a single grain; but if it dies, it bears much fruit. ²⁵ Those who love their Life lose it, and those who hate their Life in this World will keep it for Eternal Life. ²⁶ Whoever serves me must follow me, and where I am, there will my servant be also. Whoever serves me, the Father will honour.

²⁷ 'Now my soul is troubled. And what should I say – 'Father, save me from this Hour'? No, it is for this reason that I have come to this Hour. ²⁸ Father, glorify your Name.'

Then a Voice came from Heaven, 'I have glorified it, and I will glorify it again.'

²⁹ The crowd standing there heard it and said that it was thunder. Others said, 'An angel has spoken to him.'

³⁰ Jesus answered, 'This Voice has come for your sake, not for mine. ³¹ Now is the Judgement of this World; now the Ruler of this World will be driven out. ³² And I, when I am lifted up from the earth, will draw all people to myself.'

³³ *He said this to indicate the kind of death he was to die.*

³⁴ The crowd answered him, 'We have heard from the Law that the Messiah remains for ever. How can you say that the Son of Man must be lifted up? Who is this Son of Man?'

³⁵ Jesus said to them, 'The Light is with you for a little longer. Walk while you have the Light, so that the Darkness may not overtake you. If you walk in the Darkness, you do not know where you are going. ³⁶ While you have the Light, believe in the Light, so that you may become Children of Light.'

After Jesus had said this, he departed and hid from them.

Expansion 1

³⁷ *Although he had performed so many Signs in their presence, they did not believe in him.* ³⁸ *This was to fulfil the word spoken by the prophet Isaiah:*

'Lord, who has believed our message,
and to whom has the arm of the Lord been revealed?'

³⁹ *And so they could not believe, because Isaiah also said:*

⁴⁰ *'He has blinded their eyes*
and hardened their heart,
so that they might not look with their eyes,
and understand with their heart and turn—
and I would heal them.'

⁴¹ *Isaiah said this because he saw his Glory and spoke about him.*
⁴² *Nevertheless many, even of the authorities, believed in him. But because of the Pharisees they did not confess it, for fear that they would be put out of the synagogue;* ⁴³ *for they loved human glory more than the Glory that comes from God.*

⁴⁴ Then Jesus cried aloud: 'Whoever believes in me believes not in me but in Him Who Sent Me. ⁴⁵ And whoever sees me sees Him Who Sent Me. ⁴⁶ I have come as Light into the World, so that everyone who believes in me should not remain in the Darkness. *⁴⁷ I do not judge anyone who hears my Words and does not keep them, for I came not to judge the World, but to save the World. ⁴⁸ The one who rejects me and does not receive my Word has a judge; on the last day the Word that I have spoken will serve as judge, ⁴⁹ for I have not spoken on my own, but the Father who sent me has himself given me a commandment about what to say and what to speak. ⁵⁰ And I know that his commandment is Eternal Life. What I speak, therefore, I speak just as the Father has told me.'*

COMMENTARY

Discourses 11-14 are loosely connected by the theme of 'Little While'. The Little While is the period between Jesus assuming Flesh and the Time of his Exaltation and Glorification. Hence, during his mission in The World there is the Time-Before-The Hour or the 'Little While'. The theme has originally been sounded in Discourse 5: Excerpts Within a Tradition in John 7. The text clearly outlines the program:

> ³³ Jesus then said, 'I will be with you a Little While [*eti chronon micron*], and then I am going to him who sent me. ³⁴ You will search for me, but you will not find me; and where I am, you cannot come.'

The theme of Little While then continues in the Discourses from 11 to 13:

Discourse 11: The Hour and Glory, the present Discourse (12:19-50)

> ³⁵ Jesus said to them, 'The Light is with you for a Little While [*eti micron chronon*]. Walk while you have the Light, so that the Darkness may not overtake you.

Discourse 12: The Paraclete (13:33-14:31)

> ¹³:³³ Little children, I am with you only a Little While [*eti micron*]. You will look for me; and as I said to the Jews so now I say to you, 'Where I am going, you cannot come.'

and

> ¹⁴:¹⁹ In a Little While [*eti micron*] the world will no longer see me, but you will see me; because I live, you also will live.

Discourse 13: The True Vine (15:1-16:33)

> ¹⁶ 'A Little While [*micron kai*] and you will no longer see me, and again a Little While [*kai palin micron*], and you will see me.'

The final Discourse 14: The Prayer of Jesus (17:1-26) opens with a thunderous proclamation. The Little While is over. The Hour has come.

> 17:1 'Father, The Hour has come [*eleluthen he hora*]; glorify your Son so that the Son may glorify you, 2since you have given him authority over all people, to give Eternal Life to all whom you have given him.

Reading the Discourses as a sequence, the tension builds inexorably. Who is Jesus? Where has he come from? Where is he going? When will he go? By Discourse 14 these questions have been answered.

We return now to the present Discourse 11: The Hour and Glory.

This Discourse is another Monologue that has been placed into a special context. The issue is the participation of non-Jews or Greeks in the whole venture of acquiring *gnosis*. The context is intensified by Greeks (presumably God-fearing Gentiles) who ask to see Jesus. They approach Philip and Andrew. These are the only two of Jesus' named disciples who have Greek names and they came from Bethsaida, which at least in Greek thinking was part of the Gentile hinterland. Jesus reacts by seeing in this event the coming of The Hour and the time of Glorification. He links this to his coming death, using a common proverb about a seed dying to produce life. The form of the seed must disappear, if the new life is to emerge. So Jesus must dispose of his earthly appearance of Flesh, if he is to fully regain his Divine stature.

In the face of death, the removal of the Flesh, Jesus undergoes an agony. In the three Synoptics the Agony is a public and physical affair enacted in the Garden of Gethsemane with three disciples who are not really witnesses since they sleep through it. In John it is a private anguish, drawing on a similar source (there is a clear parallel with Mark 14:34: And he said to them, 'I am deeply grieved, even to death; remain here, and keep awake'). The Jesus-Tradition seems to have contained a cry of anguish to the Father and a request to be delivered (from the Cup in the Synoptics and from The Hour in John, although the 'cup' imagery is used in the Treatise on Handing-Over).

His cry of pain is answered by a Voice. We have already referred to the *Trimorphic Protennoia* where Protennoia is the heavenly First Thought who, as already seen, communicates as a Voice. Protennoia is also Barbelo.

> I [am] the Thought of the Father, Protennoia, that is, Barbelo, the perfect Glory, and the immeasurable Invisible One who is hidden. I am the Image of the Invisible Spirit, and it is through me that the All took shape, and [I am] the Mother [as well as] the Light which she appointed as Virgin, she who is called 'Meirothea', the incomprehensible Womb, the unrestrainable and immeasurable Voice. (9)

As mentioned earlier, Protennoia takes on three forms. In the first place, Protennoia is the Voice of the First Thought who descends as Light into Darkness to minister to those who have fallen. Thereafter she is the Speech of the First Thought and the *Logos* of the First Thought. The third form entails the assumption of a human appearance.

What occurs in John is that Protennoia, the Voice of the First Thought, assures the company that Jesus will be glorified through his exaltation on the Cross. Jesus explains that the Voice has spoken to enlighten the audience, not himself. He does not need enlightenment. The fact that some of the audience only hear thunder or imagine an angel stresses their inability to comprehend what is occurring, their ignorance.

The Jews now take up a peripheral issue: if Jesus is the Messiah then he cannot be exalted and removed from the World. They claim confirmation from The Torah. What the reference might have been (or whether it perhaps came from a now unknown Jewish commentary) is immaterial.

Jesus' response is that the Light, which is himself, is about to leave. There will only be Darkness once again thereafter. They have only a limited time to decide. Once again Jesus hides, as he was always capable of doing. This is the end of the original Monologue.

An expansion has been added to this text. It takes up the fact that the Signs are regularly met with disbelief. No doubt this was a matter that required explanation, particularly as the Jewish community took stringent measures against some of the Jesus-movement groups, including in particular the Christian Gnostics. The editor explains that this disbelief was foretold by Isaiah in 53:1 and cites the verse. The editor then uses another Isaiah text from 6:10 to elaborate. This literary device attempts to explain the procedure whereby some people, notably the Jews, do not believe. They hear what Jesus had to say but, out of fear of their position in society, they will not react with faith to that word as they should.

A summary has been appended. It is Gnostic. It takes up the issue mentioned in the previous expansion on belief. This could easily have been an excerpt from another Discourse. This section deals, in Gnostic terms, with the topic of Judgement and its relationship to belief: Jesus is the Messenger sent by The Father. He is The Light. He comes as Judge, and there is immediate judgement based on the reaction of hearers to his coming: belief or unbelief. A Roman editor has made another insert, attempting to delay this judgement to the Last Day, but the text has already insisted that the judgement is immediate. Jesus has come as Judge only in as much as non-believers judge themselves by their failure to believe.

12. The Paraclete (13:33-14:31)

[33] Little children, I am with you only a little longer. You will look for me; and as I said to the Jews so now I say to you, 'Where I am going, you cannot come.' [34] I give you a New Commandment, that you love one another. Just as I have loved you, you also should love one another. [35] By this everyone will know that you are my disciples, if you have love for one another.'

[36] Simon Peter said to him, 'Lord, where are you going?'

Jesus answered, 'Where I am going, you cannot follow me now; but you will follow afterwards.'

[37]*Peter said to him, 'Lord, why can I not follow you now? I will lay down my Life for you.'*

[38]*Jesus answered, 'Will you lay down your Life for me? Very truly, I tell you, before the cock crows, you will have denied me three times.*

[14:1] 'Do not let your hearts be troubled. Believe in God, believe also in me. [2] In my Father's house there are many dwelling-places. If it were not so, would I have told you that I go to prepare a place for you? [3] And if I go and prepare a place for you, I will come again and will take you to myself, so that where I am, there you may be also. [4] And you know the Way to the place where I am going.'

[5] Thomas said to him, 'Lord, we do not know where you are going. How can we know the Way?'

[6] Jesus said to him, 'I am the Way, and the Truth, and the Life. No one comes to the Father except through me. [7] If you know me, you will know my Father also. From now on you do know him and have seen him.'

[8] Philip said to him, 'Lord, show us the Father, and we will be satisfied.'

[9] Jesus said to him, 'Have I been with you all this time, Philip, and you still do not know me? Whoever has seen me has seen the Father. How can you say, 'Show us the Father'? [10] Do you not believe that I am in the Father and the Father is in me? The words that I say to you I do not speak on my own; but the Father who dwells in me does his works. [11] Believe me that I am in the Father and the Father is in me; but if you do not, then believe me because of the works themselves. [12] Very truly, I tell you, the one who believes in me will also do the Works that I do and, in fact, will do greater Works than these, because I am going to the Father. [13] I will do whatever you ask in my name, so that the Father may be glorified in the Son. [14] If in my Name you ask me for anything, I will do it.

[15] 'If you love me, you will keep my commandments. [16] And I will ask the Father, and he will give you another Paraclete, to be with you for ever. [17] This is the Spirit of Truth, whom the World cannot receive, because it neither sees him nor knows him. You know him, because he abides with you, and he will be in you.

[18] 'I will not leave you orphaned; I am coming to you. [19] In a Little While the World will no longer see me, but you will see me; because I live, you also will live. [20] On that day you will know that I

am in my Father, and you in me, and I in you. [21] They who have my commandments and keep them are those who love me; and those who love me will be loved by my Father, and I will love them and reveal myself to them.'

[22] Judas *(not Iscariot)* said to him, 'Lord, how is it that you will reveal yourself to us, and not to the World?'

[23] Jesus answered him, 'Those who love me will keep my Word, and my Father will love them, and we will come to them and make our home with them. [24] Whoever does not love me does not keep my Words; and the Word that you hear is not mine, but is from the Father who sent me.

[25] 'I have said these things to you while I am still with you. [26] But the Paraclete, the Holy Spirit, whom the Father will send in my Name, will teach you everything, and remind you of all that I have said to you. [27] Peace I leave with you; my peace I give to you. I do not give to you as the World gives. Do not let your hearts be troubled, and do not let them be afraid. [28] You heard me say to you, 'I am going away, and I am coming to you.' If you loved me, you would rejoice that I am going to the Father, because the Father is greater than I. [29] And now I have told you this before it occurs, so that when it does occur, you may believe. [30] I will no longer talk much with you, for the Ruler of this World is coming. He has no power over me; [31] but I do as the Father has commanded me, so that the world may know that I love the Father. *Rise, let us be on our way.*

COMMENTARY

This Twelfth Discourse is a Dialogue between Jesus and four of his disciples: Simon Peter, Philip, Thomas and Judas (whom a Roman editor has assured readers was not the vile Iscariot; however, in the original text, Judas Iscariot would certainly have been the questioner). Four questions from the four disciples, fairly basic questions, allow Jesus to discourse on the new arrangements after he returns to the Father as the divine Word, and the Paraclete takes over his role.

After an opening statement by Jesus, which refers once more to 'Little While', Peter begins the Dialogue by showing misunderstanding about where Jesus is going. Jesus answers him and then a Roman Christian addition has been made: Peter offers to follow him now and give his life. The addition explains the fact that later, in a Roman insertion to the text, Peter will deny Jesus three times and the cock will crow. This was seen as an appropriate time to place the prophecy of the denials into the text.

In response to the original question from Peter, Jesus discourses on The Above under the analogy of a house with subsidiary dwellings. In Jewish apocalyptic 'the house' was a common image for Heaven. Jesus uses 'I Am' as a descriptor of his own future state. Then he raises the question of The Way. Thomas does not comprehend the meaning of The Way and allows Jesus to advance the Dialogue.

Jesus explains, in Gnostic terminology, the meaning of The Way. The Way is the pathway that humans can take in order to find ultimate meaning, the divinity within themselves. That Way is very simply summed up as being provided by Jesus himself. He is the Way, first of all because he is Truth. He by his very revelation of Truth has revealed the meaning of The Father, Ultimate Divinity. Someone reading the Jesus-events, his Signs (into which these Discourses have been inserted), understands this Truth. He is also as a consequence the one who has brought The Life. The Way to the Father is by means of that *gnosis* brought into the World by Jesus. The *gnosis* is The Truth and brings to believers Eternal Life, the life of the Aeon to come.

Next, Philip's question provides the opportunity for Jesus to take this Gnostic thinking further. No human is capable of coming to The Father directly. They require Jesus who is the reflection of the Father, the Emanation from The Father and therefore The Way.

Jesus announces the arrangements following his return to The Father. He will be replaced by the Paraclete. The term comes from the Greek *parakalein*, 'to call to the side of', or 'to encourage, give comfort'. It refers to someone called to another's side, such as a Court Assistant, or someone who bestows encouragement and guidance. Who will be the replacement of Jesus? It will be the Spirit of Truth. The Spirit is still Jesus but not now in the human form of Flesh. This Spirit will still bring divine knowledge to believers. He will remain with believers from this point onwards. For subsequent believers, after the departure of Jesus, the Paraclete or Spirit is the paramount factor in direct mediation.

Judas asks a question that distinguishes once again between believers and The World. It is only the believers among whom The Father and The Word will dwell. They will make a home amongst themselves prior to their possession of a Heavenly dwelling place. This is *ta idia* and they are *hoi idioi*. The Spirit will continue the role of teaching and explaining which Jesus, in the Flesh, had done in a limited timeframe.

This question ('Lord, how is it that you will reveal yourself to us, and not to the World?') is not so different to the one asked by Judas in the *Gospel of Judas*:

> 'When will you tell me these things, and [when] will the great day of light dawn for the generation?' (25-26)

This points to the fact that it was Judas Iscariot who asked the question in the Discourse.

There is a final statement by Jesus that sums up all that the Dialogue has produced about Jesus departing and the coming of the Paraclete. Jesus calls for calm even as the Archon of The World, the Evil force, is on his way. Although he has no power over Jesus, Jesus will submit because that is the plan of The Father for the salvation of believers.

With its Introduction, four questions and Final Statement this Dialogue is a neat outline of the Gnostic mission of Jesus into the World and the preparations for his Departure.

13. The True Vine (15:1-16:33)

[1] 'I am the True Vine, and my Father is the Vine-grower. [2] He removes every branch in me that bears no fruit. Every branch that bears fruit he prunes to make it bear more fruit.

[3] *You have already been cleansed by the Word that I have spoken to you.*

[4] Abide in me as I abide in you. Just as the branch cannot bear fruit by itself unless it abides in the vine, neither can you unless you abide in me. [5] I am the Vine, you are the branches. Those who abide in me and I in them bear much fruit, because apart from me you can do nothing. [6] Whoever does not abide in me is thrown away like a branch and withers; such branches are gathered, thrown into the fire, and burned. [7] If you abide in me, and my Words abide in you, ask for whatever you wish, and it will be done for you. [8] My Father is glorified by this, that you bear much fruit and become my disciples. [9] As the Father has loved me, so I have loved you; abide in my love. [10] If you keep my commandments, you will abide in my love, just as I have kept my Father's commandments and abide in his love. [11] I have said these things to you so that my joy may be in you, and that your joy may be complete.

[12] 'This is my Commandment, that you love one another as I have loved you. [13] No one has greater love than this, to lay down one's Life for one's friends. [14] You are my friends if you do what I command you. [15] I do not call you servants any longer, because the servant does not know what the master is doing; but I have called you Friends, because I have made known to you everything that I have heard from my Father. [16] You did not choose me but I chose you. And I appointed you to go and bear fruit, fruit that will last, so that the Father will give you whatever you ask him in my Name. [17] I am giving you these commands so that you may love one another.

[18] 'If the World hates you, be aware that it hated me before it hated you. [19] If you belonged to the World, the World would love you as its own. Because you do not belong to the World, but I have chosen you out of the World—therefore the World hates you. [20] Remember the Word that I said to you, 'Servants are not greater than their master.' If they persecuted me, they will persecute you; if they kept my Word, they will

keep yours also. [21] But they will do all these things to you on account of my Name, because they do not know Him Who Sent Me. [22] If I had not come and spoken to them, they would not have sin; but now they have no excuse for their sin. [23] Whoever hates me hates my Father also. [24] If I had not done among them the works that no one else did, they would not have sin. But now they have seen and hated both me and my Father.

[25] *It was to fulfil the word that is written in their Law, 'They hated me without a cause.'*

[26] 'When the Paraclete comes, whom I will send to you from the Father, the Spirit of Truth who comes from the Father, he will testify on my behalf. [27] You also are to testify because you have been with me from the beginning.

[16:1] **'I have said these things to you** to keep you from stumbling. [2] They will put you out of the synagogues. Indeed, an Hour is coming when those who kill you will think that by doing so they are offering worship to God. [3] And they will do this because they have not known the Father or me.

[4] **But I have said these things to you** so that when their hour comes you may remember that I told you about them. 'I did not say these things to you from the beginning, because I was with you. [5] But now I am going to Him Who Sent Me; yet none of you asks me, 'Where are you going?'

[6] **But because I have said these things to you,** sorrow has filled your hearts. [7] Nevertheless, I tell you the Truth: it is to your advantage that I go away, for if I do not go away, the Paraclete will not come to you; but if I go, I will send him to you. [8] And when he comes, he will prove the World wrong about Sin and Righteousness and Judgement: [9] about Sin, because they do not believe in me; [10] about Righteousness, because I am going to the Father and you will see me no longer; [11] about Judgement, because the Ruler of this World has been condemned.

[12] **'I still have many things to say to you**, but you cannot bear them now. [13] When the Spirit of Truth comes, he will guide you into all the Truth; for he will not speak on his own, but will speak whatever he hears, and he will declare to you the things that are to come. [14] He will glorify me, because he will take what is mine and declare it to you. [15] All that the Father has is mine. For this reason I said that he will take what is mine and declare it to you. [16] 'A little while, and you will no longer see me, and again a little while, and you will see me.'

Expansion

[17] *Then some of his disciples said to one another, 'What does he mean by saying to us, 'A little while, and you will no longer see me, and again a little while, and you will see me'; and 'Because I am going to the Father'?' [18] They said, 'What does he mean by this 'a little while'? We do not know what he is talking about.'*

[19] *Jesus knew that they wanted to ask him, so he said to them, 'Are you discussing among yourselves what I meant when I said, 'A little while, and*

you will no longer see me, and again a little while, and you will see me'? [20] *Very truly, I tell you, you will weep and mourn, but the World will rejoice; you will have pain, but your pain will turn into joy.* [21] *When a woman is in labour, she has pain, because her hour has come. But when her child is born, she no longer remembers the anguish because of the joy of having brought a human being into the world.* [22] *So you have pain now; but I will see you again, and your hearts will rejoice, and no one will take your joy from you.* [23] *On that day you will ask nothing of me. Very truly, I tell you, if you ask anything of the Father in my Name, he will give it to you.* [24] *Until now you have not asked for anything in my name. Ask and you will receive, so that your joy may be complete.*

[25] *'I have said these things to you in figures of speech* [paroimiai]*.* The Hour is coming when I will no longer speak to you in figures, but will tell you plainly of the Father. [26] On that day you will ask in my Name. I do not say to you that I will ask the Father on your behalf; [27] for the Father himself loves you, because you have loved me and have believed that I came from God. [28] I came from the Father and have come into the World; again, I am leaving the World and am going to the Father.'

[29] His disciples said, 'Yes, now you are speaking plainly, not in any figure of speech [paroimia]! [30] Now we know that you know all things, and do not need to have anyone question you; by this we believe that you came from God.'

[31] Jesus answered them, 'Do you now believe? [32] The Hour is coming, indeed it has come, when you will be scattered, each one to his home, and you will leave me alone. Yet I am not alone because the Father is with me. [33] I have said this to you, so that in me you may have peace.

In the World you face persecution. But take courage; I have conquered the World!'

COMMENTARY

This is a long and complex Discourse. It is situated after an editorial conclusion to the previous Discourse in 14:31 ('Rise, let us be on our way'). It is linked to the Final Discourse, The Prayer of Jesus in chapter 17, and linked to the preceding Discourses as it raises the question of the Little While again. This section seems to be an insertion, but a Gnostic one.

For the most part it is a Monologue. It stands by itself and takes up many of the Gnostic themes dealt with in other places.

Thematically, it is based on the Vine analogy which introduces both the notion of the disciples' incorporation in Jesus and the spectre of persecution. This is followed by a five-part statement on the teaching of the Gnostic Jesus with a Conclusion. Into this an expansion has been inserted, a Gnostic reflection on 'Little While'.

The five-part statement is very similar in content to the earlier Discourse on The Paraclete in 13:33-14:31. Both speak of Jesus' departure, the coming of the Paraclete and the work of The Father. Possibly an earlier form of the Discourse on the Paraclete had contained the five statements; it has been revised, and inserted here.

The Discourse begins with the analogy of the Vine. This was not a novelty. In the Hebrew Scriptures, in Isaiah 5 for example, this was a well-used description of the people of Israel with God as the Vine-grower.

> 5:1 Let me sing for my beloved
> my love-song concerning his vineyard:
> 2 My beloved had a vineyard
> on a very fertile hill.
> He dug it and cleared it of stones,
> and planted it with choice vines;
> he built a watch-tower in the midst of it,
> and hewed out a wine vat in it;
> he expected it to yield grapes,
> but it yielded wild grapes.
>
> 3 And now, inhabitants of Jerusalem
> and people of Judah,
> judge between me
> and my vineyard.
> 4 What more was there to do for my vineyard
> that I have not done in it?
> When I expected it to yield grapes,
> why did it yield wild grapes?
>
> And now I will tell you
> What I will do to my vineyard
> I will remove its hedge,
> and it shall be devoured;
> I will break down its wall,
> and it shall be trampled down.
> 6 I will make it a waste;
> it shall not be pruned or hoed,
> and it shall be overgrown with briers and thorns;
> I will also command the clouds
> that they rain no rain upon it.
>
> 7 For the vineyard of Yahweh of the Armies
> is the house of Israel,
> and the people of Judah
> are his pleasant planting;
> he expected justice,
> but saw bloodshed;
> righteousness,
> but heard a cry!

Isaiah's poem described the People of Israel as a Vineyard that needed to be tended and indeed pruned with vigour. John's Jesus now identifies himself as the True or Authentic Vine. This self-identification as The Authentic Vine is a claim that he has replaced Israel. Jesus extends the metaphor by identifying his disciples as branches, who have no life unless they are attached to him as The Vine.

Again he takes up the description of the New Commandment of mutual love. He makes use of the term Friends (philoi) to describe the family of those who love him. The Friends, perhaps better translated as 'Loved Ones', have gnosis and they bear the fruit of gnosis. Returning to The Vine image, he states that it is the branches that will bear fruit. .

Again, he counterposes the Vine-Branches to The World. The disciples cannot be expected to receive from the World anything less than Jesus himself received, since the branches are linked to the Vine. This reaction of the World will be persecution. An editor has found a handy fulfilment text.

The next section, taking up the Gnostic theme of Departure and Return, is artificially divided by the use five times of the phrase: 'I have said these things to you' or similar. The Vine analogy had stressed the bond between Branches and Vine; this section is intended to prepare the listeners for a time when Jesus the Vine will no longer be with them in the Flesh. The section, as stated earlier, is a parallel to Discourse 12 and has a very forceful and dramatic conclusion. The five-fold division is as follows:

1. 16: 1-3 Jesus announces coming persecution
2. 4-5 Jesus announces that he will be leaving them before the time of their persecution
3. 6-11 Jesus will depart, but the Paraclete will judge the World
4. 12-16 The Paraclete or Spirit of Truth will continue Jesus' mission (17-24 Gnostic expansion: Meaning of 'Little While') 25-28 The role of The Father
5. Conclusion 29-33: A final statement of faith by the disciples, and Jesus' prediction of their suffering.

The general theme is sounded in section 1 with the statement that persecution is coming. The text continues in 2 with the complementary announcement that Jesus will be departing.

Curiously, section 2 maintains that no disciple up to that point has asked him where he is going. This has already been done amply in 13:36-14:6. This is not a contradiction. The two Discourses of The Paraclete and the second part of The True Vine were originally quite separate, but the two have used overlapping themes. The theme of Jesus' departure was treated as an answer to a question in The Paraclete Discourse, and as a question posed by Jesus here.

A further indication of the difference in the two Discourses 12 and 13 is found in section 3, which shows that Jesus attributes a subsidiary forensic role to the Paraclete. The Paraclete will judge The World. This is paralleled in section 4 by a similar statement that the Spirit of Truth will continue the mission of Jesus.

There follows an insertion of a later collection of sayings, a response by Jesus following the private question among the disciples, about the 'Little While'. Jesus will go but the Paraclete will come. Joy after pain and more specifically motherhood after birth pain are used to give the group some hope in a persecuted future.

The final section, 5, returns to the role of The Father and the whole purpose of Jesus' coming into the World.

In the conclusion there is a statement on the disciples coming to faith. Up to this point Jesus has been speaking in metaphorical language (*paroimiai*); now they understand him and he speaks openly, plainly. The disciples finally understand the plain language. But Jesus' final response once more emphasizes the reality of persecution in the future.

The Discourse of The Vine has covered almost the entire Christian Gnostic teaching. It has explained the relationship of Jesus to The Father, of Jesus to the believing disciples. It has told of the future: persecution of the believers (no doubt a reality to an original readership); the departure of Jesus and the coming of The Paraclete or Holy Spirit. The community has advanced from uncomprehending disciples to full believers who now have full *gnosis*, not relying on the *paroimiai* of earlier times.

14. The Prayer of Jesus (17:1-26)

[1] After Jesus had spoken these words, he looked up to Heaven and said, 'Father, The Hour has come; glorify your Son so that the Son may glorify you, [2] since you have given him authority over all people, to give Eternal Life to all whom you have given him. [3] And this is Eternal Life that they may know you, the only true God, and Jesus Christ whom you have sent. [4] I glorified you on earth by finishing the work that you gave me to do. [5] So now, Father, glorify me in your own presence with the Glory that I had in your presence before the world existed.

[6] 'I have made your Name known to those whom you gave me from the World. They were yours, and you gave them to me, and they have

kept your Word. ⁷Now they know that everything you have given me is from you; ⁸for the Words that you gave to me I have given to them, and they have received them and know in Truth that I came from you; and they have believed that you sent me. ⁹I am asking on their behalf; I am not asking on behalf of the World, but on behalf of those whom you gave me, because they are yours. ¹⁰All mine are yours, and yours are mine; and I have been glorified in them. ¹¹And now I am no longer in the World, but they are in the World, and I am coming to you. Holy Father, protect them in your Name that you have given me, so that they may be one, as we are one. ¹²While I was with them, I protected them in your Name that you have given me.

I guarded them, and not one of them was lost except the one destined to be lost, so that the scripture might be fulfilled.

¹³But now I am coming to you, and I speak these things in the World so that they may have my joy made complete in themselves. ¹⁴I have given them your Word, and the World has hated them because they do not belong to the World, just as I do not belong to the World. ¹⁵I am not asking you to take them out of the World, but I ask you to protect them from the Evil One. ¹⁶They do not belong to the World, just as I do not belong to the World. ¹⁷Sanctify them in the Truth; your Word is Truth. ¹⁸As you have sent me into the World, so I have sent them into the World. ¹⁹And for their sakes I sanctify myself, so that they also may be sanctified in Truth.

²⁰'I ask not only on behalf of these, but also on behalf of those who will believe in me through their Word, ²¹that they may all be one. As you, Father, are in me and I am in you, may they also be in us, so that the world may believe that you have sent me. ²²The Glory that you have given me I have given them, so that they may be one, as we are one, ²³I in them and you in me, that they may become completely one, so that the world may know that you have sent me and have loved them even as you have loved me.

²⁴Father, I desire that those also, whom you have given me, may be with me where I am, to see my Glory, which you have given me because you loved me before the foundation of the world.

²⁵'Righteous Father, the World does not know you, but I know you; and these know that you have sent me. ²⁶I made your Name known to them, and I will make it known, so that the love with which you have loved me may be in them, and I in them.'

COMMENTARY

The Final Discourse is written in the genre of a Prayer. It may have been based on a prayer form from the Jesus-Tradition, similar to what would become the Lord's Prayer in Matthew and Luke. The Prayer is addressed to The Father and would not have been intended for public usage by a community, as the Synoptic version was. There are elements of 'Hallowed be Your Name', 'Your Kingdom Come', 'Your will be done on Earth as in Heaven',

'Deliver Us from the Evil One'. The Matthew Lord's Prayer was written in a different context and for a different audience but its outline is visible in this Gnostic Prayer.

The stress again is on the departure of Jesus. The Hour will bring the final glorification of Jesus and the assurance to his believers that they have received The Father's Words and understand The Truth.

A Roman editorial aside again ensures that the evil Judas Iscariot is not included.

The community of believers are being left in the World and they will be succeeded by others who will believe not because they saw the Signs of Jesus but because they were presented with his Word by earlier Gnostic believers.

The prayer now turns to the required unity of believers. We will not go into the ongoing controversy as regards the authors or provenance of *The Community Rule* at Qumran but a text therein refers to its group as a *yahad* ('unity') or community (1 QS 5:7). It states that the members enter the Covenant with God and are thereby 'gathered into unity'. This is the same sort of description as we have in this Prayer.

The finale, a dramatic statement of Gnosticism, stresses *gnosis* as the explanation of the entire scenario of Jesus coming into the World, sent by The Father, to form a unity/community of Love.

> 'Righteous **Father**, the **World** does not **know** you, but I **know** you; and these **know** that you have sent me. I made your name **known** to them, and I will make it **known**, so that the **love** with which you have **loved** me may be in them, and I in them.'

This text must have been a treasured statement for the Gnostic communities. It would have been a prayer (giving profound access to the mind of the Gnostic Jesus), a last testament, a final expression of hope.

CONCLUSION TO THE GNOSTIC DISCOURSES

The fourteen Discourses have been divided between Monologues and Dialogues. In Gnostic literature, as was said, both genres are well attested. Most are free standing and we can presume that they were used in various ways by more than one Gnostic community. Some, especially Excerpts within a Tradition, are fragmentary. They all present a fairly standard Gnostic approach although there are different Gnostic emphases between some.

No doubt they have been edited to ensure some general coherence. They have then been inserted into the context of John's gospel. They occur between the elements of the Book of Seven Signs, where they must have seemed relevant to an editor, and then form an almost complete and separate section leading up to the Passion story.

At various points in the Discourses there are later additions. Some of these are insignificant: some editor has interpreted a difficult point; some editor has found a fitting fulfilment text; some editor has made an insertion that must have previously lived its own life and now needed to find a place in a suitable context; some editor has made a correction, usually in the direction of Roman Christianity. These are fairly easy to distinguish. They break the flow of the statement: they are sometimes a distraction to the argument, they are sometimes trying to introduce a fulfilment of the Scriptures relative to an event or saying or even to make a correction in regard to a difficult text. All of these additions have been incorporated into the final text of John, as we have it today.

As a whole, the Discourses, detached from their expansions and corrections, give an overall account of Christian Gnosticism. Christian Gnosticism was not the Christianity of the Palestinian sects (represented by the Jesus-Tradition in its early stages) and was not the Christianity of Roman Christianity (represented by Mark and then Matthew and Luke). It was part of what the Gnostic Paul attempted to construct in his foundations.

We will now turn to the specific Roman Christian insertions into the Gospel of John.

THE FIVE ROMAN CHRISTIAN INSERTIONS

As Roman Christianity moved around the Mediterranean, within Roman dominated areas such as Western Asia Minor, it found persistent Gnosticism. Roman Christianity insisted that a hierarchy of bishops and elders had been established to continue after the time of Peter and The Twelve. It had its own theology, outlined in the gospel of Mark. The Gnostics capitulated and assimilated. They retained their own world view but they eventually accepted the broad outline of the Roman Jesus teaching. It was inevitable. Other Gnostics continued as before in other parts of the Roman world. These were also faced eventually with assimilation or destruction.

This assimilation of Gnostics to Roman Christianity was not without pain. The three so-called Letters of John reflect the turmoil of accepting the Gnostic visionaries into the structures of an existing Roman Christianity. Already Ignatius of Antioch in 110 CE, as Roman Christian as one could have been, had reprimanded Christians in Asia Minor who did not believe that Jesus was a true human.

> There is one Physician who is possessed both of flesh and spirit; both made and not made; God existing in flesh; true life in death; both of Mary and of God; first passible and then impassible, even Jesus Christ our Lord. (*Letter to the Ephesians,* ch. 7)

Ignatius also acknowledged that there were a variety of Christians among his flock.

> Take note of those who hold heterodox opinions on the grace of Jesus Christ which has come to us, and see how contrary their opinions are to the mind of God ... They abstain from the Eucharist and from prayer because they do not confess that the Eucharist is the flesh of our Saviour Jesus Christ, flesh which suffered for our sins and which that Father, in his goodness, raised up again. They who deny the gift of God are perishing in their disputes. (*Letter to the Smyrnaeans,* 6:2–7:1)

Somewhere in the second century CE the First Letter of John was written to local communities probably in Asia Minor. We have already seen that in it the author called himself the *apostolos.* The author exhorted them but also warned against some of the excesses of dissidents. These excesses included not maintaining the commandment of love, deceiving the believers and acting as Anti-Christs, not acknowledging that Jesus came as real Flesh. This Letter seems, after a Prologue, to have reviewed an already existing Gospel of John with its discussion of the Book of Seven Signs (in 1 John 1:5-3:10) and the other collected material, sometimes known as the Book of Glory (in 1 John 3:11-5:12). If the text is to be understood in this way, then 1 John was trying to explain how the Gospel of John should be interpreted in its new form and in a new setting.

The text of 1 John has much of the terminology of John's gospel, but that terminology is placed in a new context and therefore takes on a new meaning. We can recognize familiar Johannine words: Darkness, Blood of Jesus, new commandment, World, Flesh, Hour, Truth, Eternal Life, Children of the Devil, Spirit, Son and Saviour, Judgement. However, these are now placed in a Roman context and it is clear that the Letter intends that the Gospel of John should be read in this new context. The Letter is claiming that there has been evil and sinfulness in the World from the time of Cain the murderer. Humans have generally been caught up with this sinfulness and are threatened with eternal death because of mortal sin. Jesus has come in human form, the Flesh, to save humans from this impasse.

There will be accordingly a final Day of Judgement at the End of the world; the Hour of John's gospel is changed to the Last Hour of human existence which is proximate; the Archon of this World is changed to a future Antichrist.

> 2:18 Children, it is the Last Hour! As you have heard that Antichrist is coming, so now many antichrists have come. From this we know that it is the Last Hour.
> 4: 17 Love has been perfected among us in this: that we may have boldness on the Day of Judgement, because as he is, so are we in this world.

It is now made quite clear that Jesus achieved salvation for humanity not by his teaching on *gnosis* but by a blood sacrifice:

> 1:7 But if we walk in the light as he himself is in the light, we have fellowship with one another, and the blood of Jesus his Son cleanses us from all sin.
> 2:2 And he is the atoning sacrifice for our sins, and not for ours only but also for the sins of the whole world.

The Spirit of Truth is given a new role, pitted against the Spirit of Error. The Paraclete is described as the Risen Jesus under a new title.

> 4:6 We are from God. Whoever knows God listens to us, and whoever is not from God does not listen to us. From this we know the Spirit of Truth and the Spirit of Error.
> 2:1 Little children, I am writing these things to you so that you may not sin. But if anyone does sin, we have a Paraclete with the Father, Jesus Christ the righteous [*zaddik*].

This shows that at some time in the second century the Gospel of John was explained in a Roman Christian manner. The meaning of the Gnostic terminology in that Gospel was tamed. Roman additions and explanations would have been made in the text itself.

The Second Letter of John, written around the same time as the first Letter, claims 'The Elder (*presbyteros*)' as its author. In tradition he has also been given the name of 'John' to add to the confusion over names and writers. This Letter was sent to the same addressees as the First Letter of John. The term 'The Elder' possibly refers to an office, like Bishop, in an Asia Minor community. It warns the same audience of local Christians against any association with separatist groups.

The Third Letter of John was written probably some fifty years later, but still claims to be written by The Elder, and by that time the office would certainly have had a new occupant. It describes contact among house-churches in the area being maintained by travelling missionaries who required support. These were sent by The Elder himself; he had also made pastoral visits. The third Letter is a plea for hospitality to be given to these missionaries. A certain Diotrephes had evidently refused this welcome and he is reprimanded. The travelling missionaries could well have been Roman Christian inspectors, charged with maintaining Roman Christian teaching. The dissension among the Christian groups is palpable.

What we learn from this literature is that there was unrest and there was a period of dissension in which some Jesus movement people held to a divine Jesus-Revealer and some to a human Jesus-Saviour who had died in a sacrificial rite for the sins of humanity. Compromise was being sought and the Gospel of John, in its final canonical form, was that compromise.

The re-reading of religious texts was an entrenched Jewish and Christian practice. Re-reading is precisely what happened in this instance. The magnificent Gnostic texts – already shaped and combined into the form of the Gnostic Book of Seven Signs/Gnostic Treatises/Discourses – were first expanded, explained and corrected with Roman Christian editorial additions where clearly the changes were considered necessary. Then the entire corpus of writings was placed into a Roman Christian narrative framework.

The Roman Christian texts stressed certain narrative aspects of the Jesus story never found in a Gnostic Jesus or texts related to him. This was a solidly historical framework, with every step seemingly logical in its progression:

Jesus was truly a human being as well as a divine being, born of Mary and the Holy Spirit.

Jesus was initially acknowledged by John the Baptist, the Forerunner of the Messiah.

Key events in the life and ministry of Jesus had been foretold with exactitude by the earlier Jewish Prophets.

Jesus' life had followed a strict chronological and historically verifiable sequence.

Jesus had selected twelve disciples to be his travelling companions. They were known as The Twelve. (He also had an inner council of Peter, James and John of Zebedee).

Jesus nominated Peter as the leader of The Twelve.

Jesus was betrayed by the evil Judas Iscariot, one of The Twelve.

Jesus died by crucifixion for the sins of humanity and his very real death was a blood-sacrifice.

Jesus was placed in a tomb as a dead man, and the dead body and
burial were witnessed.

The empty tomb was discovered three days after the death, with due
witnesses, and the resurrected Jesus was clearly seen by witnesses in
Visions.

Jesus ascended into Heaven, an event also witnessed reliably.

The Christian Church established itself in Jerusalem but then moved
outwards into Palestine and to 'the ends of the world', by which Rome
should be understood.

The Gnostic texts were allowed to stand but they had to be loosely inserted into this new historical framework, whether it was suitable or not for
this purpose. Additions and corrections were made to ensure broad agreement with the Roman Christian thought-world; texts were dismantled and
placed in a sequence. The Gnostic form of John survived but only within a
new format that the Roman Church could live with.

Because of the poetic and mystical bent of the Gnostic sections of the
Gospel of John, even in this revised and muted format, it became popular
and it was accepted in Rome. It eventually became part of the official canon
of the Roman Church and was read as a Roman Christian text.

What follows are a set of significant Roman Christian additions to the
Johannine text, relating to the new framework. Naturally, there are other
parallels in John to the Synoptic writings but this is because of the fact that
both the Synoptics and John had access to the same Jesus-Tradition. We
have found no evidence that John's gospel had direct access to any of the
three Synoptics. The passages below were Roman texts, self-standing not
just added comments inserted into the Johannine story. They do not reveal
any contact with Gnostic thought or practice.

1. **John the Baptist (1:19-51 and 3:22-30 and 4:1-3)**

2. **Confession of Peter (6:66-71)**

3. **Entry into Jerusalem (12:12-19)**

4. **Peter's Denials and the Trial before the Sanhedrin (18: 15-
   27)**

5. **The Burial (19:31-42)**

We will now examine these in turn.

1. John the Baptist (1:19-51 and 3:22-30 and 4:1-3)

Introduction: First Day

[19] This is the testimony given by John when the Jews sent priests and Levites from Jerusalem to ask him, 'Who are you?'

[20] He confessed and did not deny it, but confessed, 'I am not the Messiah.'

[21] And they asked him, 'What then? Are you Elijah?'

He said, 'I am not.'

'Are you the Prophet?'

He answered, 'No.'

[22] Then they said to him, 'Who are you? Let us have an answer for those who sent us. What do you say about yourself?'

[23] He said,

'I am the voice of one crying out in the wilderness,
'Make straight the way of the Lord' ',
as the prophet Isaiah said.

[24] Now they had been sent from the Pharisees.

[25] They asked him, 'Why then are you baptizing if you are neither the Messiah, nor Elijah, nor the Prophet?'

[26] John answered them, 'I baptize with water. Among you stands One whom you do not know, [27] the One who is coming after me; I am not worthy to untie the thong of his sandal.'

[28] This took place in Bethany-Across-The-Jordan where John was baptizing.

Second Day

[29] **The next day** he saw Jesus coming towards him and declared, 'Here is the Lamb of God who takes away the sin of the world! [30] This is he of whom I said, 'After me comes a man who ranks ahead of me because he was before me.' [31] I myself did not know him; but I came baptizing with water for this reason, that he might be revealed to Israel.'

[32] And John testified, 'I saw the Spirit descending from Heaven like a dove, and it remained on him. [33] I myself did not know him, but the One who sent me to baptize with water said to me, 'He on whom you see the Spirit descend and remain is the One who baptizes with the Holy Spirit.' [34] And I myself have seen and have testified that this is the Son of God.'

Third Day

[35] **The next day** John again was standing with two of his disciples, [36] and as he watched Jesus walk by, he exclaimed, 'Look, here is the Lamb of God!'

[37] The two disciples heard him say this, and they followed Jesus.

[38] When Jesus turned and saw them following, he said to them,

'What are you looking for?'

They said to him, 'Rabbi' (*which translated means Teacher*), 'where are you staying?'

[39] He said to them, 'Come and see.'

They came and saw where he was staying, and they remained with him that day. It was about the tenth hour. [40] One of the two who heard John speak and followed him was Andrew, Simon Peter's brother. [41] He first found his brother Simon and said to him, 'We have found the Messiah' (*which is translated Anointed*). [42] He brought Simon to Jesus, who looked at him and said, 'You are Simon son of John. You are to be called Cephas' (*which is translated Peter*).

Fourth Day

[43] **The next day** Jesus decided to go to Galilee. He found Philip and said to him, 'Follow me.'

[44] Now Philip was from Bethsaida, the city of Andrew and Peter. [45] Philip found Nathanael and said to him, 'We have found him about whom Moses in The Law and also the prophets wrote, Jesus son of Joseph from Nazareth.'

[46] Nathanael said to him, 'Can anything good come out of Nazareth?'

Philip said to him, 'Come and see.'

[47] When Jesus saw Nathanael coming towards him, he said of him, 'Here is truly an 'Israelite in whom there is no deceit'!'

[48] Nathanael asked him, 'Where did you come to know me?'

Jesus answered, 'I saw you under the fig tree before Philip called you.'

[49] Nathanael replied, 'Rabbi, you are the Son of God! You are the King of Israel!'

[50] Jesus answered, 'Do you believe because I told you that I saw you under the fig tree? You will see greater things than these.' [51] And he said to him, 'Very truly, I tell you, you will see heaven opened and the angels of God ascending and descending upon the Son of Man.'

Conclusion

[3:22] **After this** Jesus and his disciples went into the Judean countryside, and he spent some time there with them and baptized. [23] John also was baptizing at Aenon near Salim because water was abundant there; and people kept coming and were being baptized.

[24] *John, of course, had not yet been thrown into prison.*

[25] Now a discussion about purification arose between John's disciples and a Jew. [26] They came to John and said to him, 'Rabbi, the one who was with you across the Jordan, to whom you testified, here he is baptizing, and all are going to him.'

[27] John answered, 'No one can receive anything except what has been given from Heaven. [28] You yourselves are my witnesses that I said, 'I am not the Messiah, but I have been sent ahead of him.' [29] He who

has the bride is the Bridegroom. The friend of the Bridegroom, who stands and hears him, rejoices greatly at the Bridegroom's voice. For this reason my joy has been fulfilled. [30] *He must increase, but I must decrease.'*

4:1 Now when the Lord learned that the Pharisees had heard, 'Jesus is making and baptizing more disciples than John'— [2] although it was not Jesus himself but his disciples who baptized— [3]he left Judea and started back to Galilee.

COMMENTARY

The connection of Jesus with John the Baptist in Roman Christianity was considered a solid fact and an essential proof that Jesus was the Messiah. It was therefore felt necessary to introduce John as the Forerunner into John's text.

There is difficulty in reconstructing the historical John the Baptist, and this would only be of passing interest for the non-historian. It is not so much a matter of deciding who he was, but of deciding how the early Jesus-movement groups regarded him. However, this latter search may be clarified by indulging in some historical reconstruction.

Clearly John the Baptist needs to be put into the context of Herod Antipas (about 20 BCE-39 CE), who was responsible for John's execution according to Josephus. The generation around the time of Jesus in Lower Galilee would have been brought up with the memory of being once incorporated into a Temple-state system by the Hasmoneans, being invaded by the Roman general Pompey, of being subjected to the Idumean Herod and then of being ruled by Herod Antipas who wished to rejuvenate the area by means of a Romano-Hellenistic building program. It would not have been a time for savouring liberation or nationalism.

Into this context came the historical John the Baptist. We can put together some of the material in the canonical gospels and Josephus to conjecture about his activity. It seems that his reported offer of a baptism in the Jordan was of a piece with other messianic movements also described by Josephus. John's purpose, it seems, was to gather together a group who would be ready to form a New Israel that could then stand up to the Romans and associated authorities, a New Israel that would re-present the great events of the Jewish past. Thus, the Exodus motif is evident in the descriptions of his baptismal activity. Just as the people under Moses had crossed the Sea of Reeds and Joshua had led the remnant of the Exodus group across the Jordan River, so John devised a ritual immersion in the Jordan to initiate his community as the New Israel.

From this point we can try to put together the historical connection between Jesus and John. There is no certainty here. It could have been that in Galilee, around the same time, the family of Jesus – Jesus and his physical brothers – was involved in a spiritual revival movement within local Judaism. It would have been acknowledged as a messianic family, descended from David, with hopes of reviving Galilean Judaism. However, Jesus had sided with John the Baptist as the way to go, something not done by the other members of the family. When those other family members moved to Jerusalem, Jesus remained in Galilee with the Baptist faction but gradually extricated himself from it. He had gathered a Jewish group of families around himself and the ascetic John was something of an embarrassment.

At some later point the Jesus group, now grown numerically strong, also went down to Jerusalem, where Jesus was executed by the Romans on the grounds of disturbing the peace (no trivial charge in the heated context of Jerusalem at Passover time) and later acknowledged as a Messiah who would return some day. James, the brother of Jesus, whether reconciled to him prior to his death or not, claimed succession. But, as we have seen earlier, so did others. At some stage Jesus was acknowledged as the Davidic Messiah; James was acclaimed as the Priestly Messiah.

So much for an attempt at historical reconstruction. We return to the question: how did the early Jesus-movement groups, and for our purposes the Roman Christian Church in particular, regard John?

Roman Christianity saw John the Baptist as vitally important for the identification of Jesus as the Messiah. Only his approbation could give authority to the recognition that Jesus was the Davidic Messiah. There was widespread expectation among the Jews that the Messiah would be preceded by a Forerunner. The Forerunner was expected to be a prophet and there was a belief that he would be Elijah-*redivivus*. Elijah had been taken up to heaven in a fiery chariot, still alive according to the text of 2 Kings, and was expected to return prior to the end of the world. There were biblical texts too which seemed to describe explicitly the role of such an Elijah-like Forerunner. One was Malachi:

> See, I am sending my Messenger to prepare the way before me, and the
> Lord whom you seek will suddenly come to his temple. The Messenger
> of the Covenant in whom you delight – indeed, he is coming, says
> Yahweh of the Armies. But who can endure the day of his coming, and
> who can stand when he appears? (3:1-2)

There was another text in Isaiah 40:3:

A voice cries out:
'In the wilderness prepare the way of Yahweh,
make straight in the desert a highway for your God.'

Mark's text had ineptly combined the two texts and then applied them to John the Baptist. He is clearly identified with the Forerunner. He is active 'in the wilderness' (since the text of Isaiah was mistakenly read: A voice cries out in the wilderness: 'Prepare the way ...'); he was 'clothed with camel's hair' which was the typical clothing of the Prophet according to Zechariah and wearing a leather belt, which had been sufficient for king Ahaziah to identify Elijah in 2 Kings.

> 1:7 He [Azariah] said to them, 'What sort of man was he who came to meet you and told you these things?' 8 They answered him, 'A hairy man, with a leather belt around his waist.' He said, 'It is Elijah the Tishbite.'

John 'proclaims' a baptism. Why? Because the Forerunner was expected to announce a message, according to the texts of Isaiah and Malachi, not baptize. The baptism of John was a ritual that identified those people within Israel who were prepared for the Messiah's coming and that was sufficient for it to be ranked as a 'message'. He gave identity to the group by this baptism with water. It was a 'baptism of repentance for the forgiveness of sins'. Once a person had acknowledged the coming of the Messiah, joined the welcoming committee as it were, then a drastic change of lifestyle would be required. Nothing in life could be the same. Everything must be reassessed. That is the meaning of 'repentance', it is a dramatic change of direction, in which the believer's life would be renewed.

John's baptism was later described by some Jesus-movements, including Roman Christianity, as only preparatory. Once the Messiah had arrived a new ritual would be required. This would be another baptism, but one 'with the Holy Spirit'. It is worth repeating something on The Holy Spirit. There was frequent mention among the Jewish people of the Holy Spirit, or the Spirit of Holiness, that is the Spirit of God. In Judaism, 'Spirit' was the dynamic action of God, the agitation that he aroused in nature, among peoples, in human events. Prophets were overwhelmed by the Spirit of God; military commanders were animated by his Spirit. This Spirit is what Jesus offers in the Synoptic tradition by Christian baptism. As we have seen 'Holy Spirit' has another quite different meaning in Gnostic texts. In this text Holy Spirit has its Synoptic meaning. This version of John the Baptist was taken into the Synoptic gospels as part of the Roman tradition.

This Roman Christian tradition, not specifically in the format of the Synoptic tradition, was used as an essential part of the Roman outline for the Gnostic collections. As we now have it as an insertion into the Johannine collection, the activity is divided between an introductory section in which John identifies himself as The Voice in the Wilderness, as in the mistranslation of Isaiah, but points to the coming of Jesus with a superior baptism.

Then there is the calling of Jesus' disciples, the first ones of whom are taken from those of John's following. This is the First Day

The traditional material is artificially divided into three other successive days, after an Introduction

1. Second Day: The Testimony of John to Jesus in person. (Titles given to Jesus: 'Lamb of God', possibly from the Suffering Servant Song in Isaiah 53:7 and 'Son of God'.)

2. Third Day: The first disciples are called: Andrew and an unnamed disciple. Jesus says, 'Come and see.' Andrew calls Simon. (Titles given to Jesus: 'Rabbi' and 'Messiah'; Simon is given the title of 'Peter'.) The 'tenth hour' indicates that this day is coming to an end.

3. Fourth Day: More disciples are called: Philip is told: 'Follow me'. He calls Nathanael and says, 'Come and see.' Nathanael hesitates: the one issuing the call is 'Jesus son of Joseph from Nazareth'.

On the third day the pattern of gathering disciples is outlined. Importantly, John in this storyline encourages two of his disciples, Andrew and an unnamed disciple, to approach Jesus. They are called and they respond, staying with Jesus. They bestow the title of 'Rabbi' on him. Then, Andrew calls his brother, Simon, giving the title of 'Messiah' to Jesus. In turn, Jesus gives the new name of 'Cephas/Peter' to Simon.

The fourth day repeats this pattern. Jesus calls Philip. As was the case in Andrew's calling of Simon, Philip calls another – Nathanael. Philip now uses the same language as Jesus: 'Come and see'. Nathanael sums up the concatenation of titles: Rabbi, Son of God (both previously used), King of Israel.

The text dealing with Nathanael has caused a number of problems. Having heard from Philip that Jesus is 'Jesus, son of Joseph from Nazareth', Nathanael questions the value of the hamlet of Nazareth. However, we have seen that Nazareth and 'Nazarene' are related to the Hebrew for 'Branch' (nezer) and in Isaiah this tree metaphor was applied to the ideal Davidic king of the future. From the original kingship an entirely new dynasty, a nezer, will emerge. Thus, Nathanael is presented with the fact that Jesus is claiming to be the Branch, not one from the hamlet of Nazareth, and he responds with the new and appropriate title of 'King of Israel'.

Nathanael himself is given the title of an 'Israelite in whom there is no deceit'. The reference is to the book of Genesis' Jacob (who was given the new name of 'Israel'). His father Isaac spoke about him after Jacob had deceived his brother in Genesis 27:

> [35] But he [Isaac] said [to Esau], 'Your brother came deceitfully, and he has taken away your blessing.' [36] Esau said, 'Is he not rightly named Jacob [*'the heel-grabber'*]? For he has supplanted me these two times. He took away my birthright; and look, now he has taken away my blessing.'

Jacob's name was etymologically imagined to be 'heel-grabber' or 'supplanter (by guile)'. Nathanael is now acknowledged as Jacob/Israel but without the guile. We can go further with the allusions.

The unusual remark of Jesus, 'I saw you under the fig tree before Philip called you', is probably an allusion to Micah 4:2-4 and its description of the End of Times:

> [2] And many nations shall come and say:
> 'Come, let us go up to the mountain of Yahweh,
> to the house of the God of Jacob;
> that he may teach us his ways
> and that we may walk in his paths.'
> For out of Zion shall go forth instruction,
> and the word of Yahweh from Jerusalem.
> [3] He shall judge between many peoples,
> and shall arbitrate between strong nations far away;
> they shall beat their swords into ploughshares,
> and their spears into pruning-hooks;
> nation shall not lift up sword against nation,
> neither shall they learn war anymore;
> [4] but they shall all sit under their own vines and under their
> own fig trees,
> and no one shall make them afraid;
> for the mouth of Yahweh of the Armies has spoken.

Jesus' reply ('Very truly, I tell you, you will see heaven opened and the angels of God ascending and descending upon the Son of Man') becomes clearer. It refers to the 'Ladder of Jacob' in Genesis 28:12:

> [12] And he [Jacob] dreamed that there was a ladder set up on the earth, the top of it reaching to heaven; and the angels of God were ascending and descending on it.

Nathanael is the True Jacob and he sees the Way to the opened heaven.

What must be recognized in this Call section is the importance of names. For the Semitic mind the name and the person were identical. To act 'in someone's name' meant that the person's interior reality had been penetrated and understood. In these cases, not only Jesus but Simon Peter and Nathanael have their interior reality made clear for all.

The final paragraph covers the joint baptismal activity of John and Jesus. An editorial addition explains that this took place before the execution of John (which has not even been recorded in the Johannine text) and that Jesus did not actually baptize (even though the text clearly says that he did). The use of 'Lord' (kyrios) is not Johannine. It is only used in editorial additions (6:23 and 11:2).

This introductory material was considered necessary for the Roman Christians. It is headed:

> [19] This is the testimony given by John when the Jews sent priests and Levites from Jerusalem to ask him, 'Who are you?'

The 'testimony' was then written back into the opening Hymn. Whoever was responsible for this Roman Insertion was also certainly responsible for the editing of the Hymn of the Word with the two Baptist additions.

The Roman Insertion set the stage for the Roman Christian understanding of the mission of Jesus, which had been prepared and foretold by The Forerunner, but it has no place in a Gnostic document.

2. Confession of Peter (6:66-71)

> [6:66] Because of this many of his disciples turned back and no longer went about with him.
> [67] So Jesus asked The Twelve, 'Do you also wish to go away?'
> [68] Simon Peter answered him, 'Lord, to whom can we go? You have the words of Eternal Life. [69] We have come to believe and know that you are the Holy One of God.'
> [70] Jesus answered them, 'Did I not choose you, The Twelve? Yet one of you is a devil.'
> [71] He was speaking of Judas son of Simon Iscariot, for he, though one of The Twelve, was going to betray him.

COMMENTARY

This is a short but important Roman insertion. Peter, for the Roman Christians, as we have seen, was the vicar of Jesus, the Leader who had been designated by Jesus himself to have authority over the entire Jesus-movement.

We have also seen that there was a Peter-group, established in Antioch.

Peter's leadership would have been highly contested, but the tradition that had come to Rome had that leadership woven into its fabric.

In the Gnostic sections of John, Peter is one of the disciples. He is not designated as a leader. This Insertion of Peter's Confession has been placed artificially at the end of the Bread of Life Discourse by Roman Christians.

The contrast between this story in John and its equivalent in Mark is interesting. To some extent that contrast leads us into the very matrix of the gospel construction that is taking place here.

In Mark's gospel the Confession of Peter is the central point of an elaborate argument concerning the Jesus-event. We have already examined the peculiar structure of Mark's gospel on pp. 36-37. We need to repeat some of it, but now in more detail.

Following a Prologue concerning John the Baptist as the Forerunner who baptizes Jesus, who is then subjected to The Testing by Satan, Mark shows, in three cycles of material derived from the Jesus-Tradition and artificially contrived, that Jesus had revealed himself as the Messiah.

Each of the three cycles has a similar outline containing four phases:

- An opening summary of Jesus' messianic activity
- Jesus makes ready his group of disciples
- Jesus manifests himself as the Messiah by word and by work
- Jesus is rejected

The first cycle is found in Mark 1:14 to 3:6, and catalogues the typical works of a Messiah – curing, exorcising demons, debating with obtuse minds. The second cycle in 3:7-6:6a repeats the outline with different material. The third cycle in 6:6b-8:26 concludes with the curing of a blind man, strange because the cure requires two stages. No other miracle story told of Jesus required two attempts. In the first stage the blind man, having been involved in a saliva-ritual involving his eyes, sees something vaguely:

'I can see people, but they look like trees, walking.'

His vision is indistinct and mistaken; he cannot perceive the Messiahship of Jesus, although he knows that there is something remarkable about him. Then Jesus lays his hands on him and he sees everything with clarity. The two stages of healing have a vital purpose in Mark's narrative.

The blind man epitomizes the first group of disciples for Mark. At first they only understand Jesus vaguely, imperfectly. Then they understand clearly.

Mark's gospel reached its climax at this point. Jesus had exorcized evil spirits, healed the sick, debated with those in the throes of ignorance and explained the parables. People were trying to understand him. He asks for their response. Their response is the equivalent of the imperfect vision of the blind man who saw people as trees. He is told that some interpret him as John the Baptist raised from the dead or as Elijah who was expected to return to earth or as the Prophet who would precede the Messiah (8:27-28). They are rejected as vague, imperfect, mistaken responses to what had been perceived.

Jesus now turns to The Twelve and asks the most telling question in Mark's gospel: 'But who do you say that I am?' Peter gives the group's solemn response when he says: 'You are the Messiah.' (8:29) He expresses simply but adequately the faith-response of the group. Like the blind man, cured in the second stage, the group see things clearly.

This is highly symbolic literature. Mark has taken material from the Jesus-Tradition and woven it into a clever theological statement. Matthew and Luke will utilize Mark and, indeed, Matthew will elaborate on Jesus' response to Peter, making it abundantly clear that Peter is not only the spokesperson for the group but the leader-designate who will succeed him.

In order to construct this narrative, Mark has used the Jesus-Tradition in the form that it was received in Rome. Matthew and Luke have used Mark, although Luke also used some version of Matthew's sayings and seems to have had access to the more original Jesus-Tradition.

But Gnostic John does not exalt Peter. Hence, there was need for a Roman Christian insertion. This passage relates the role of Peter as spokesperson, it contains the first mention of The Twelve[60] and the designation of Judas as the Betrayer. John's title for Jesus in this account is 'Holy One of God'. Mark used 'Messiah', which is followed by Matthew (who expands it with 'Son of the Living God') and then Luke introduces 'Holy One of God', the same as John. It is more likely that the more original title in the Jesus-Tradition was 'Holy One of God', changed by Mark to suit the tenor of his gospel but not followed by Luke.

Hence, the Confession of Peter was inserted at this point in the sequence.

3. Entry into Jerusalem (12:12-19)

12:12 The next day the great crowd that had come to The Festival heard that Jesus was coming to Jerusalem. 13 So they took branches of palm trees and went out to meet him, shouting,

---

[60] The Twelve are only mentioned in John's gospel in this section and in Version 2 of the Magdalene Vision in 20:24.

'Hosanna!
Blessed is the one who comes in the Name of the Lord—
the King of Israel!'

[14]Jesus found a young donkey and sat on it; as it is written:

[15] 'Do not be afraid, daughter of Zion.
Look, your king is coming,
sitting on a donkey's colt!'

Expansion

[16] *His disciples did not understand these things at first; but when Jesus was glorified, then they remembered that these things had been written of him and had been done to him.*

[17] So the crowd that had been with him when he called Lazarus out of the tomb and raised him from the dead continued to testify.
[18] It was also because they heard that he had performed this Sign that the crowd went to meet him.
[19] The Pharisees then said to one another, 'You see, you can do nothing. Look, the world has gone after him!'

COMMENTARY

This acclamation of Jesus entering Jerusalem is common to the four canonical gospels. It is a Roman Christian insertion. The four canonical gospels can, with some interest, be compared.

	MATTHEW 21:1-9	MARK 11:1-10	LUKE 19:28-40	JOHN 12:12-19
Location	Jerusalem, Bethphage at the Mount of Olives	Jerusalem, Bethphage and Bethany at the Mount of Olives	Jerusalem, near to Bethphage and Bethany, at the Mount of Olives	Jerusalem
Jesus' order	Bring back an ass and colt	Bring back a colt	Bring back a colt	No order. Jesus 'finds an ass'.
Fulfil-ment text	[5] 'Tell the daughter of Zion, Look, your king is coming to you, humble, and mounted on an ass, and on a colt, the foal of an ass.'	No text	No text	[15] 'Do not be afraid, daughter of Zion. Look, your king is coming, sitting on a ass's colt!'

Prepar-ation for Entry	Put garments on ass and colt and Jesus sits on both	Threw garments on colt and Jesus sits on it	Threw garments on colt and they place Jesus on it.	Jesus sits on the ass
Actions of Crowd	Most spread garments and branches on road	Many spread garments and others spread leafy branches on road	As Jesus rides crowd spread garments on road	Crowd carry branches of palm trees to meet him
Crowd's acclam-ation	'Hosanna to the Son of David! Blessed is the One who comes in the name of the Lord! Hosanna in the highest heaven!'	'Hosanna! Blessed is the One who comes in the name of the Lord! Blessed is the coming kingdom of our ancestor David! Hosanna in the highest heaven!'	'Blessed is the king who comes in the name of the Lord! Peace in heaven, and glory in the highest heaven!'	'Hosanna! Blessed is the One who comes in the name of the Lord— the King of Israel!'
Pharisees	No text	No text	They ask Jesus to rebuke crowd	They conclude the World has turned to him

From this grid, it is clear that Mark was the original Synoptic account. Matthew has corrected Mark (e.g. his geography) and expanded the text. The principal expansion is the inclusion of the actual text of Zechariah 9:9:

Rejoice greatly, O daughter Zion!
Shout aloud, O daughter Jerusalem!
Lo, your king comes to you;
triumphant and victorious is he,
humble and riding on an ass,
on a colt, the foal of an ass.

However, Matthew misunderstands the poetic doublet, a common feature of Hebrew poetry, in the final two lines. He counts two animals and then ensures that the prophecy is fulfilled by Jesus instructing the disciples to gather two animals and then riding astride on both.

John is not dependent on the Synoptics but shares a common source in the Jesus-Tradition. He leaves the one animal in the original and then abbreviates this search with Jesus simply 'finding' an ass, either by himself or with the disciples' help.

The actions of the crowd are similar to those in the Synoptics but John has a different scenario. The crowds come out with branches to greet him with a shout taken from Psalm 118:25-26.

[25] Save us [Hosanna is shortened form of this], we beseech you,

O Yahweh!
O Yahweh, we beseech you, give us success!
[26] Blessed is the One who Comes in the name of Yahweh.
We bless you from the house of Yahweh.

In common with the other three, John uses the title 'The One Who Comes' but, in common with Luke only, he uses King as a second title, since it is mentioned in the Zechariah text. Mark had expanded this acclamation to include a welcome to the coming of David's Kingdom (which the other Synoptics do not repeat). Matthew adds a new but related title 'Son of David'.

John's version follows the basic storyline but there are few verbal intersections. He would seem to have had access to the Jesus-Tradition before it was adapted by the Synoptics.

There are three largely disconnected editorial statements in the Expansion. One deals with the fact that the disciples did not yet understand what the Entry really meant (otherwise, how would they have been so dense when Jesus was arrested) and the second two tried to explain the reaction of the crowd (they recalled the sign of Lazarus' raising from the dead). The two explanations were probably quite separate statements.

The Roman Christian tradition has endeavoured to connect the Sign of Lazarus, from the Book of Seven Signs, to the growing belief among the Crowd in favour of Jesus and the growing hostility against him among The Pharisees. This is more in keeping with the Roman view of the effect of Jesus on the Jewish people. For Roman Christians the Entry into Jerusalem was the formal beginning of the Passion and Death story. It would later be presented as such in the Roman liturgy.

4. Peter's Denials and the Trial before the Sanhedrin (18:15-27)

[15] Simon Peter and an Other Disciple followed Jesus. Since that disciple was known to the High Priest, he went with Jesus into the courtyard of the High Priest, [16] but Peter was standing outside at the gate. So the Other Disciple, who was known to the High Priest, went out, spoke to the woman who guarded the gate, and brought Peter in. [17] The woman said to Peter, 'You are not also one of this man's disciples, are you?' He said, 'I am not.'

A [18] Now the slaves and the police had made a charcoal fire because it was cold, and they were standing round it and warming themselves. Peter also was standing with them and warming himself.

B [19] Then the High Priest questioned Jesus about his disciples and about his teaching. [20] Jesus answered, 'I have spoken openly to the World; I have always taught in synagogues and in the Temple, where all the Jews come together. I have said nothing in secret. [21] Why do you ask me? Ask those who heard what I said to them; they know what I said.'

C [22] When he had said this, one of the police standing nearby struck Jesus on the face, saying, 'Is that how you answer the High Priest?' [23] Jesus answered, 'If I have spoken wrongly, testify to the wrong. But if I have spoken rightly, why do you strike me?'

B1 [24] Then Annas sent him bound to Caiaphas the High Priest.

A1 [25] Now Simon Peter was standing and warming himself.

They asked him, 'You are not also one of his disciples, are you?'

He denied it and said, 'I am not.'

[26] One of the slaves of the High Priest, a relative of the man whose ear Peter had cut off, asked, 'Did I not see you in the garden with him?'
[27] Again Peter denied it, and at that moment the cock crowed.

COMMENTARY

As has been said earlier, Peter was at the centre of Roman Christianity. He was seen as the Vicar of Jesus who had ended his ministry in Rome. But he was also seen as a flawed character. In fact, he and Judas provided an opposition. Peter betrayed Jesus; but Peter also repented. Judas betrayed Jesus; but Judas did not repent and met an untimely death.

This Roman Christian insertion dealing with Peter's betrayal and Jesus' affirmation is in the form of a chiasm. Historically, Annas was the High Priest from 7-14 CE. He set up a dynasty under Roman protection, as was previously noted, and was succeeded by his son Eleazar who held the position for a year before being himself succeeded by Annas' son-in-law Caiaphas, who remained in that position until 35/36 CE.

In John's account, Peter is accompanied by an 'Other Disciple'. Commonly, this Other Disciple is identified by commentators with the Beloved Disciple and in one editorial addition to the text in the Magdalene Visions the two are actually named as one and the same; we have seen that this identification is secondary and therefore this identification is most unlikely. Why would a writer use two terms for such an important figure? Here the reference to the 'Other Disciple' is of no consequence, simply supplying an addition to the text to explain how Peter might have made an unlikely entry to the interior of the High Priest's palace and how the event might have been recorded later.

The events in the High Priest's courtyard are in all four canonical gospels. The comparison is interesting.

	MATTHEW 26:57-68	MARK 14:53-65	LUKE 22:54-71	JOHN 18:13-24
Setting	Peter enters courtyard by himself and sits with guards	Peter enters courtyard by himself and sits with guards, warming himself	Peter sits with 'them' who have kindled a fire	The Other Disciple bring Peter in to the court because he knows the maid. After a first Denial he warms himself at a charcoal fire lit by servants and officers. (action of warming repeated soon after in v. 25)
First Denial	To maid	To maid	To maid	To maid
Second Denial	To another maid	To same maid	To someone else	To 'them'
Third Denial	To bystanders when challenged by his accent	To bystanders because of 'being a Galilean'	To 'another' because of 'being a Galilean'	To kinsman of Malchus
Cock crow	Cock crows once	Cock crows a second time	Cock crows once and Jesus looks at Peter	Cock crows once
Reference to Jesus fore-telling	Three denials before cock crows	Three denials before cock crows twice	Three denials before cock crows	No reference
Finale	Peter repents	Peter repents	Peter repents	No reference

There is no advantage in trying to divine what really happened and how the denials could be reconciled. That Peter could gain access to the High Priest's palace and become involved in discussion with the attendants is historically implausible. Matthew and Luke had some form of the Markan story before them. Matthew has edited the text. He has first named Caiaphas as the High Priest and removed the 'chief priests' because this term seems to reflect Roman religion and not Jewish religion. He has inverted the order of 'elders and scribes' because he knew the latter come first in the social hierarchy. The reference to 'guards' is removed, possibly because that seems to make the scenario even more unlikely. He also removes the homely act of Peter 'warming' himself. He adds 'another' to 'maid' because it seems unlikely that the same maid would have twice accused him. He explains to a non-Jewish audience how being a Galilean would have been obvious; it was because of the accent. He removes the reference to the cock crowing twice, since any earlier crowing had not been noted in Mark's text. It seems clear that Matthew has followed Mark, but with his own editorial changes.

Luke makes other but not drastic changes to a Markan original. He refers only to the High Priest's house and does not detail the members who are present. Nor is there mention of guards. 'They', whoever they are, light the fire but there is no reference to Peter warming himself. Luke makes it appear that the questioning of Jesus takes place in the same courtyard as the denials of Peter, with Peter observing. Luke solves Mark's problem of the same maid posing the second question by making it 'someone else'. Likewise he changes the third questioner to 'another' although he keeps the basis of the charge as 'being a Galilean'. Like Matthew he removes the enigmatic second cock crow, which had not happened.

In neither case does there seem to be sufficient evidence that Matthew and Luke used any other source for this event than Mark which they have each edited.

John clearly does not follow the Synoptics. His version is based on the earlier Jesus-Tradition although this text is still a Roman Insertion. He names the High Priest as Annas, although his son-in-law Caiaphas was actually High Priest. At that time, High Priests were regularly appointed and deposed by the Romans. Possibly, there was some circumstance that allowed both to be acknowledged as High Priests.

The one curious link with the Synoptics is the reference to 'warming'. Mark, followed by Luke, refer to a fire and Mark, but not Luke, states that Jesus warms himself. John has Peter and the Other Disciple warming themselves and uses the 'warming' as part of a chiasm. There must have been such a reference in the Jesus-Tradition shared by Mark and John. Matthew and Luke put aside the homely image. John makes an interesting addition: it is a charcoal fire (anthrakia). There are only two places in the Christian Scriptures where this word occurs: here and the post-Resurrection meal of bread and fish in John.

The text can be divided as follows.

Introduction: Jesus is brought to Annas, and Peter is brought into the court-yard of the High Priest by another disciple. (18:12-16). An editor has made a clarifying note in v. 12.

(This Introduction leads into a tightly knit chiasmus in vv. 17-27).

A First Denial to the Woman Guarding the Gate (17)

   B Peter warms himself (18)

      C Annas the High Priest questions Jesus (19-21)

         D Temple policeman gives Jesus a blow,
            rapisma(22-23)

      C1 Annas sends Jesus to Caiaphas, also High Priest (24)

   B1 Peter warms himself (25a)

A1 Second Denial to a general 'they' and to a relative of Malchus (25b-27)

There are three denials in John – to the woman guarding the gate, to 'them' and to the relative of Malchus. This fulfils the prediction of Jesus inserted into the Handing-Over Treatise by an editor, although it is likely that the 'prediction' was added after this section had been inserted. Malchus' relative was chosen because presumably he was considered as identifiable and could be a witness to the final denial.

Jesus makes a clear statement on why he should not reveal his teaching. He has preached openly and not in secret. His followers know his teaching.

However, the focus of the chiasm is on the rejection of Jesus by a blow, a *rapisma*. The term was already used in the Judgement of Pilate Treatise. It signifies rejection. The scene is meant to highlight the rejection by the 'Jews' of the clear proclamation of Jesus. It seems that the denials of Peter were firmly set in the Roman Christian version in the lead-up to the crucifixion. The Synoptics all make mention of the immediate repentance of Peter. Despite being a flawed man he became the chosen Leader. This account of the denials was an important link in the Roman Christian story. Hence, this Roman Christian insertion, with some later editing, was made.

5. The Burial (19:31-42)

[19:31] Since it was the Day of Preparation, the Jews did not want the bodies left on the cross during the Sabbath, especially because that Sabbath was a day of great solemnity.

So they asked Pilate to have the legs of the crucified men broken and the bodies removed.

[32] Then the soldiers came and broke the legs of the first and of the other who had been crucified with him. [33] But when they came to Jesus and saw that he was already dead, they did not break his legs.

[34] Instead, one of the soldiers pierced his side with a spear, and at once Blood and Water came out.

³⁵ *He who saw this has testified so that you also may believe. His testimony is true, and he knows that he tells the Truth.*

³⁶ These things occurred so that the Scripture might be fulfilled, 'None of his bones shall be broken.'

³⁷ And again another passage of scripture says,

'They will look on the one whom they have pierced.'

³⁸ After these things, Joseph of Arimathea, who was a disciple of Jesus, though a secret one because of his fear of the Jews, asked Pilate to let him take away the body of Jesus. Pilate gave him permission; so he came and removed his body.

³⁹ *Nicodemus, who had at first come to Jesus by Night, also came, bringing a mixture of myrrh and aloes, weighing about a hundred litras.*

⁴⁰ They took the body of Jesus and wrapped it with the spices in linen cloths, according to the burial custom of the Jews.

⁴¹ Now there was a Garden in the place where he was crucified, and in the Garden there was a new tomb in which no one had ever been laid. ⁴² And so, because it was the Jewish Day of Preparation, and the tomb was nearby, they laid Jesus there.

COMMENTARY

The dimensions of this small excerpt on the dead body of Jesus and its burial are easily identified because there is an *inclusio* in its two references to the Jewish Day of Preparation at the beginning and the end. The recognition of the death of Jesus and his subsequent burial, physical facts that had been witnessed by reliable people, was important to Roman Christianity.

John's narrative is introduced by the breaking of the legs of the two others crucified and the piercing of Jesus' side. Blood and Water emerge. There have been other references to the Blood of Jesus in John but they are not in Gnostic contexts. This reference does not seem to be Gnostic either. The Blood in this instance signifies sacrifice and this is specifically Roman Christian.

The text on the piercing of Jesus' side and the decision not to break his legs occurs only in John, not the Synoptics.

An editor has added a reassurance that this piercing actually happened and was seen by a trustworthy witness. This is followed by two fulfilment passages. The first deals with the unbroken bones and is close enough to the text concerning the Paschal Lamb in Exodus 12:46:

⁴⁶ It [the Lamb] shall be eaten in one house; you shall not take any of the animal outside the house, and you shall not break any of its bones.

Jesus is, in this imagery, depicted as a sacrifice to God. This is quite contrary to the mainstream Gnostic thought.

The second fulfilment text is from Zechariah 12:10 where the Hebrew text reads:

> [10] And I will pour out a spirit of compassion and supplication on the house of David and the inhabitants of Jerusalem, so that, when they look on the one whom they have pierced, they shall mourn for him, as one mourns for an only child, and weep bitterly over him, as one weeps over a firstborn.

The original Hebrew text was probably quite different.[61] However, the sense of the quotation as recorded in John above is: 'They will look on the one whom they have pierced.' This has been literally applied to Jesus' piercing with a lance (which *'daqar'* in Hebrew could mean). That the text with this meaning was in circulation is shown by the fact that there is a similar allusion in Revelation 1:7:

> [7] Look! He is coming with the clouds;
> every eye will see him,
> even those who pierced him;
> and on his account all the tribes of the earth will wail.
> So it is to be. Amen.

Both of these fulfilment texts are in line with the Roman Christian view of Jesus' death as a blood sacrifice for all humanity.

So what is the significance of Blood and Water coming from the side of Jesus. The idea that it is a medical reference is an obvious nonsense. A relevant related reference to this event is 1 John 5: 6-7

> [6] This is the One who came by water and blood, Jesus Christ, not with the water only but with the water and the blood. And the Spirit is the one that testifies, for the Spirit is the truth. [7] There are three that testify: [8] the Spirit and the water and the blood, and these three agree.

We have already seen that 1 John was a letter written by Roman Christians to assimilated Christians in Asia Minor. The context is an argument against dissidents who deny 'blood' coming with 'water'. While the author will accept that faith is the source of Eternal Life, what is not accepted is

---

[61] The Hebrew text is tortured both textually and in its interpretation. In Zechariah, Yahweh is speaking of the renewal of the people by a new Spirit. The original text probably continued thus:

> 'They shall look to me [Yahweh] and they shall mourn for him whom they have pierced [or 'offended']'.

It is possible that the word here translated as 'pierced' (*daqar*) should be translated as 'offended'. The reference could be to a victim of the Jerusalemites, who has been slain.

that the coming of the Spirit is associated only with the water of baptism. It is also associated with Blood, the blood of Jesus' crucifixion. This thinking has been behind the Roman insertion. It insisted that the death of Jesus was a sacrifice and this brought about the water of salvation in the sacrament of Roman baptism.

In the next part of the text, the actual burial seems to follow the Synoptic story although it is abbreviated.

	MATTHEW 27:57-61	MARK 15: 42-47	LUKE 232: 50-56	JOHN 19:38-42
Insti-gator	A rich man from Arimathea, named Joseph	Joseph of Arimathea, a respected member of the Council	Joseph from the Jewish town of Arimathea. He was a member of the Council and a good and righteous man who had not consented to the evil deed.	Joseph of Arimathea
Religious standing	Disciple of Jesus	Looking for the Kingdom of God	Looking for the Kingdom of God	Disciple of Jesus but secretly, for fear of the Jews
Other partici-pant	Nil	Nil	Nil	Nicodemus with hundred *litrai* of myrrh and aloes
Burial wrappings	Clean linen *sindon* or shroud (takes away body, presumably removed from cross)	Linen *sindon* or shroud (takes down body)	Linen *sindon* or shroud (takes down body)	Linen *othonioi* or cloths, with the spices (takes away body, presumably removed from cross)
Tomb	Joseph's tomb hewn in rock; stone rolled to door	Tomb hewn out of the rock; stone rolled against the door	Rock-hewn tomb, unused.	Unused tomb in a Garden
Time of burial	No indication	No indication	Day of Preparation	Jewish Day of Preparation
Witnesses	Mary Magdalene and other Mary	Mary Magdalene and Mary mother of Joses	Women from Galilee. (Later they prepare spices and ointments)	No witnesses apart from Joseph and Nicodemus

The Jesus-Tradition would have recounted a story that Joseph of Arimathea, a disciple of Jesus but previously unmentioned, brought a linen cloth or cloths to wrap Jesus after he had been taken down from the cross.

He then laid Jesus in an unused rock tomb with a large rolling stone blocking the entrance. The witnesses were Galilean women who brought spices to anoint Jesus. This took place on the Day of Preparation.

Mark used this tradition. He identified the burial cloth as a *sindon*, a shroud, and the tomb as a cave with its rolling stone. There is no mention of the cave belonging to Joseph and no mention of it being previously unused. The witnesses are named specifically as Mary Magdalene and Mary of Joses, neither of whom anointed the corpse, since Jesus has already been anointed by 'a woman' in Mark.

Matthew and Luke follow Mark with minor alterations. However, as in John, Luke mentions that the tomb was unused,

As with the Synoptics, Joseph of Arimathea is a quite new character in John. John, like Matthew, claims him to have been a disciple of Jesus, although a secret one, probably to cover the fact that he has never been previously named in the gospel.

An editor has also introduced Nicodemus, the Jew mentioned in the Discourse on Water, into the burial task. He brings a hundred *litrai* of myrrh and aloes, a hundred times more than Mary used for the Anointing of Jesus in Bethany, an enormous amount. It must be symbolic. One guess is that 100 is the equivalent of Love, *agape* in Greek.

In some ancient languages (for example, Akkadian, Hebrew and Greek) the letters of the alphabet could serve as numerals. Hence, a sequence of numbers could also be read as a word, and a word or sequence of words could be read as a number. In Greek this was called *Isopsepha,* or *Gematria* in Hebrew (although this simply transliterates the Greek word for 'geometry'). Hence, a number can have a textual meaning if the numbers are translated into a linguistic message.[62] We can apply this to the numbers inserted (certainly later) into the text. With a = 1, g = 3, p = 80, e = 8, we get 101 which is 'about a hundred'. But why the message? If the conjecture is

---

[62] See more in B. Blake (2010), *Secret Language: Codes, Tricks, Spies, Thieves and Symbols*, OUP: New York, pp. 122-126. Blake gives an interesting Hebrew example in Genesis 49:10:

> The sceptre shall not depart from Judah, nor a lawgiver from beneath his feet, until Shiloh shall come; and unto him shall the gathering of the people be.

'Shilo shall come' is in Hebrew *Sylh yh'*. The total, using the Hebrew alphabet, comes to 358. The word for Messiah, *msy*, also comes to 358. The writer is saying, to those prepared to delve beneath the surface of the text, that the Messiah is coming. A more explicit Greek inscription involving numbers from a text in Pompeii is the following: 'I love her whose number is 545'. Unfortunately, we may never know the woman who was 545!

correct, then some editor has identified Nicodemus as bringing his Love. Possibly, this would identify him with the Beloved Disciple. Later in dealing with the Johannine additions in chapter 21, this methodology will be used again, but with a different result.[63]

John, together with Luke, notes that the tomb has been unused (they do not acknowledge it as Joseph's own intended tomb like Matthew). Both John and Luke note that it is the Day of Preparation and that the body was anointed. It would seem that John and Luke both had independent access to the Jesus-Tradition, which Luke was able to compare to Mark and make changes to the text. John's version had been fashioned from the Jesus-Tradition alone with a Gnostic editor introducing the added character of Nicodemus.

In short, this whole section is a construction inserted into the Passion and Death story, based on a digression on the Pierced One, as understood from Zechariah, and on the Burial as in the Jesus-Tradition, also used by Mark. It is a Roman Insertion apart from the addition of Nicodemus; it maintains that Jesus was sacrificed in blood on the cross and then buried with very specific witnesses who would have testified to his very real death.

CONCLUSION TO THE ROMAN CHRISTIAN INSERTIONS

These Insertions were the last major redactional change to what we know as the Gospel of John. They indicate that when the Gnostic form of the Gospel of John was considered for use in church groups that had been founded by the Roman Christians, probably in Western Asia Minor, then the Gnostic material required adaptation. A minimum number of pivotal Roman stories had to be inserted.

It was necessary to import material on John the Baptist into John. In the Roman Church, John the Baptist was esteemed as the Jew who heralded Christianity, whose testimony acknowledged Jesus as the true Leader and who sent his own disciples to become disciples of Jesus. John was essential to the verification of Jesus as the Messiah.

Equally, it was necessary to situate Peter as the established Leader. There was already a tradition that 'Peter' was the vicar of Jesus; Rome claimed him as its own Apostle.

The Gnostics had Treatises on Foretelling the Destruction of the Temple, the Anointing by Mary, the Handing-Over of Jesus, the Judgement of Jesus and the Magdalene Vision. They also had a Sign dealing with the Cross

---

[63] See K. Linforth (2014), *The Beloved Disciple: Jacob the Brother of the Lord*, Vivid Publishing, Fremantle, pp. 198-199.

and the Mother. But these composed a meagre outline for the narrative of Jesus. The Romans introduced John the Baptist, the Confession of Peter, the Entry into Jerusalem, the Denials of Peter and the Burial of Jesus. These insertions provided a more fulsome schema, in the eyes of the Romans, for the presentation of a gospel of Jesus.

And from where did the Roman Christians, adapting the existing John text, obtain their materials? It was primarily from the Jesus-Tradition. This would also be mined by Mark, who was copied by Matthew (with the addition of the Jesus Sayings and some other sources) and by Luke (also with the addition of Matthew's Jesus Sayings and some other sources). But Luke had ready access to the Jesus-Tradition, prior to Mark's adaptations. Sometimes he reverted to the Jesus-Tradition and, in doing so, came closer at times to John.

The Gospel of John was not constrained in the least to contradict the Synoptics and it was reworked to that effect. What the Roman editors considered pivotal moments in the Roman Jesus-story were inserted into the Gnostic text. For convenience, we now repeat the content of the Roman Jesus-Story as stated earlier:

This Jesus-Story honored the Literary Jesus of the Synoptics as a figure whose birth, ministry (both of which demonstrated that he was the expected Jewish Messiah), death and physical resurrection and physical ascension (all affirmed by reliable witnesses), the succession of Peter to Jesus, the apostleship of The Twelve (which verified the rule by bishops and elders), the betrayal by the evil Judas, the blood sacrifice of Jesus (which would eventually require sacrificing priests), a specific sacramental system based on a particular interpretation of Baptism and the Eucharist, the coming of a Last Day preceded by wondrous events, the simultaneous Second Coming of the Messiah, and the physical resurrection of all believers. All of this Story had been foretold in the Hebrew Scriptures and was an historical fact.

Historicity and evidence was endemic to the Roman Jesus-Story.

Of further importance are some Stray Traditions in the Gospel of John. We will turn to them.

THREE STRAY TRADITIONS

The sections that follow have long been recognized as stray traditions. They never had a part in the mainstream text of the Gospel of John. While other additions have been inserted into the text at various times and in various places and have formed part of the final format of the Gospel of John, Stray Traditions 2 and 3 were Johannine traditions that circulated in the communities in Western Asia Minor but were never made part of the gospel at any stage of its construction. Stray Tradition 1 does not even belong to the text of the Gospel of John and had its own textual life. (It has even been called the 'Fifth Gospel'). Because of their obvious authority and relevance however, the latter two at some point in time were collected as an Appendix.

It is a small list:

1. **The Adulterous Woman (7:53-8:11)**

2. **The Catch of 153 Fish (21:1-23)**

3. **Two conclusions (21:24-25)**

We will deal with each Stray Tradition in turn.

1. The Adulterous Woman (7:53-8:11)

[53] Then each of them went home, [8:1] while Jesus went to the Mount of Olives. [2] Early in the morning he came again to the temple. All the people came to him and he sat down and began to teach them. [3] The scribes and the Pharisees brought a woman who had been caught in adultery; and making her stand before all of them, [4] they said to him, 'Teacher, this woman was caught in the very act of committing adultery. [5] Now in The Law, Moses commanded us to stone such women. Now what do you say?' [6] They said this to test him, so that they might have some charge to bring against him. Jesus bent down and wrote with his finger on the ground.

[7] When they kept on questioning him, he straightened up and said to them, 'Let anyone among you who is without sin be the first to throw a stone at her.' [8] And once again he bent down and wrote on the ground.

[9] When they heard it, they went away, one by one, beginning with the elders; and Jesus was left alone with the woman standing before him.

[10] Jesus straightened up and said to her, 'Woman, where are they? Has no one condemned you?'

[11] She said, 'No one, sir.'

And Jesus said, 'Neither do I condemn you. Go your way, and from now on do not sin again.'

COMMENTARY

This was a stray gospel passage. It does not find a ready home in any of the four canonical gospels. Only after the third century CE are manuscripts found with it inserted into John. It should not be included in any reconstruction of John.

It is a typically Jewish text, describing how the scribes and Pharisees set a snare to catch Jesus out. Instead, Jesus shows that he is a Wise Man (in the tradition of the wise Solomon) by turning the tables on them. There are similar stories in the Synoptics (for example, the tribute coin story in Mark 12:13-17 and parallels).

The Stray Tradition was probably placed here much later as an introduction to the Discourse on the Light of the World, breaking the nexus with the previous Discourse. Also, it is a handy illustration of John 8:15:

> [15]You judge by human standards; I judge no one.

The passage has no bearing on our analysis of John's gospel.

2. The Catch of 153 Fish (21:1-23)

Part A

[21:1] After these things Jesus showed himself again to the disciples by the Sea of Tiberias; and he showed himself in this way. [2]Gathered there together were Simon Peter, Thomas called the Twin, Nathanael of Cana in Galilee, the sons of Zebedee, and two others of his disciples.

[3]Simon Peter said to them, 'I am going fishing.'

They said to him, 'We will go with you.'

They went out and got into the boat, but that night they caught nothing.

[4]Just after daybreak, Jesus stood on the beach; but the disciples did not know that it was Jesus. [5]Jesus said to them, 'Children, you have no fish [*prosphagion*], have you?'

They answered him, 'No.'

[6]He said to them, 'Cast the net to the right side of the boat, and you will find some.'

So they cast it, and now they were not able to haul it in because there were so many fish [*ichthus*].

[7]That Disciple whom Jesus Loved said to Peter, 'It is the Lord!'

When Simon Peter heard that it was the Lord, he put on some clothes, for he was naked, and jumped into the lake. [8]But the other disciples came in the boat, dragging the net full of fish [*ichthus*], for they were not far from the land, *only about 200 stadia off.*

[9]When they had gone ashore, they saw a charcoal fire [*anthrakia*] there, with fish [*opsarion*] on it, and bread.

[10]Jesus said to them, 'Bring some of the fish [*opsarion*] that you have just caught.'

[11]So Simon Peter went aboard and hauled the net ashore, *full of large fish* [*ichthus*], *a hundred and fifty-three of them*; and though there were so many, the net was not torn.

[12]Jesus said to them, 'Come and have breakfast.'

Now none of the disciples dared to ask him, 'Who are you?' because they knew it was the Lord.

Part B

¹³ Jesus came and took the bread and gave it to them, and did the same with the fish [*opsarion*].

¹⁴ *This was now the third time that Jesus appeared to the disciples after he was raised from the dead.*

¹⁵ When they had finished breakfast, Jesus said to Simon Peter, 'Simon son of John, do you love me more than these?'

He said to him, 'Yes, Lord; you know that I love you.'

Jesus said to him, 'Feed my lambs' [*boske ta arnia mou*].

¹⁶ A second time he said to him, 'Simon son of John, do you love me?'

He said to him, 'Yes, Lord; you know that I love you.'

Jesus said to him, 'Tend my sheep' [*poimaine ta probate mou*].

¹⁷ He said to him the third time, 'Simon son of John, do you love me?'

Peter felt hurt because he said to him the third time, 'Do you love me?' And he said to him, 'Lord, you know everything; you know that I love you.'

Jesus said to him, 'Feed my sheep' [*boske ta probate mou*].

¹⁸ *Very truly, I tell you, when you were younger, you used to fasten your own belt and to go wherever you wished. But when you grow old, you will stretch out your hands, and someone else will fasten a belt around you and take you where you do not wish to go.'*

¹⁹ (He said this to indicate the kind of death by which he would glorify God.)

After this he said to him, 'Follow me.'

Part C

²⁰ Peter turned and saw the Disciple whom Jesus Loved following them; he was the one who had reclined on the breast of Jesus at the supper and had said, 'Lord, who is it that is going to betray you?'

²¹ When Peter saw him, he said to Jesus, 'Lord, what about him?'

²² Jesus said to him, 'If it is my will that he remain until I come, what is that to you? Follow me!'

²³ *So the rumour spread in the community that this Disciple would not die. Yet Jesus did not say to him that he would not die, but, 'If it is my will that he remain until I come, what is that to you?'*

COMMENTARY

This Stray Tradition has been constructed from some pre-existing texts that have been joined together, not always without seam. Its innate difficulties are caused by persistent editorial additions. The link between the Vision Story and what preceded is made by a very general 'after these things' and 'again'. We can distinguish three sections whose topics overlap:

PART A: A Vision Story (catch of fish/breakfast)
PART B: A Call Story (breakfast/ Peter)
PART C: Peter and the Beloved Disciple (Peter/ Beloved Disciple)

There is no necessary connection between the three parts apart from the deliberate linking of Fish/Breakfast, Breakfast/Peter, Peter/Beloved Disciple and the fact that in Parts A and C, Peter and the Beloved Disciple are pitted one against the other.

The first section is a Vision Story. It is not linked with the previous Vision stories since in this instance the group of disciples have resumed their occupation, seemingly not aware of the Visions or commissioning in John 20. The group numbers seven, a typical number: Simon Peter, Thomas, Nathanael, two Sons of Zebedee and two other disciples. One of these seven is presumably the Beloved Disciple to be mentioned later.

The story line is shared only with Luke, who uses it as a call-story whereby Simon (Peter) and the two Sons of Zebedee are converted to Jesus' following. The parallels are too obvious to be accidental.

	LUKE 5:1-11	JOHN 21:1-11
Location	On the shore of Gennesaret presumably during day	On the Sea of Tiberias during night and early morning.
Participants	Simon, two sons of Zebedee	Simon Peter, Thomas, Nathanael, Sons of Zebedee, two others.
Activity	Jesus boards boat and orders them to use nets	From shore (a note that the boat is about 200 stadia off), Jesus orders them to use a net (singular)
Result	Great shoal of fish, nets were breaking, ship about to sink	A quantity of fish (153 in number). The single net did not break.
Reaction	Peter acknowledges himself as sinful before Lord	Beloved Disciple recognizes Jesus as Lord
Outcome	The three men follow Jesus	The Seven are invited to share breakfast

In the first place the overlap in detail (and the considerable differences) can only be explained by the common use of an item from the Jesus-Tradition that gave details of Jesus supplying a catch of a huge quantity of fish to his disciples. What implication the story in the earlier Jesus-Tradition might have had is beyond our knowledge, but Luke has subsequently used this as a call-story while John has used it for another purpose. It would seem to be more readily recognizable as a call-story.

The *aporiai* or contradictions in John's text are only too evident. Jesus asks the disciples to bring the fish just caught, but he already has fish cooking. Peter brings the fish ashore alone, even though the disciples had struggled to contain the load. The disciples hesitate over the identity of Jesus, although the Beloved Disciple has already revealed it to them. It seems that two stories have been combined, with some difficulty, in John. The first was the call-story (as used by Luke) and the second was a post-resurrection meal-story. The fish are meant to play a part in both.

Another *aporia* is the variant use of the word used for 'fish'. The first usage (*prosphagion*) does not necessarily mean 'fish'. It means 'something that can be eaten with bread' and was quite often, but not always, a fish-relish. The disciples then have a haul of fish (*ichthus*), the more common word for fish. However, once they come ashore they find Jesus cooking *opsarion*, a dried fish usually eaten with bread. This was the same term used in the Feeding of the 5000 Sign in John 6 (although the Synoptics did use *ichthus* in the parallels). There is a reversion to *ichthus* for the reference to 153 fish, which also raises the question of the exactitude of the number of fish and also the need to inform the reader that the catch took place 'only about 200 stadia' from shore.

There is an obvious identification of the two stories – the call-story and the meal-story – by the naming of the fish. The call-story uses *prosphagion* as a general enquiry about something that will go with bread; then it uses the normal word for fish, *ichthus*. These are compatible. The meal-story uses *opsarion* (as used in John's Sign of the Feeding of the 5000) except for the phrase about the 153 fish (*ichthus*) which, we will see, is an addition.

This *aporiai* can therefore be explained.

The passage began as a call-story in the Jesus-Tradition where the name for fish was *prosphagion* and *ichthus* (as in Luke). This was then combined with a post-Resurrection meal-story of fish being cooked on a charcoal fire where *opsarion* was used as in the Feeding of the 5000 in John 6. Into this combined unit there was the message inserted about the number 153, using *ichthus,* and the message about the 200 stadia.

It seems that the two remarkable notes about the exact numeration of fish and distance are additions: they were about 200 *stadia* from land; they had caught 153 fish. Why the precision? Earlier, when dealing with the 100 *litrai* of spices brought by Nicodemus, we became aware of the possibility that the use of numbers could also be read as a word. This, we pointed out, was called *Isopsepha*. If we use the Greek letters for the numbers as words, then one possibility for 153 is the Greek *(h)e Magdalene* (where the initial aspirate 'h' does not occur in the Greek script). If the letters are computed as we have seen already by *Isopsepha* (e = 8, m = 40, g = 3, d = 4, l = 30, n = 50), then the total is 153.[64] The answer to '153 fish' is The Magdalene.

Looking at Mary's Hebrew name, *Mariam*, which Jesus specifically uses at key times in John, then its letters add up to 192 (m = 40, a = 1, r = 100; i = 10) which is 'around 200', and the distance of the boat from shore ('only about 200 *stadia*'). The fish are not normal-sized fish. They are 'large', in Greek *ichthuon megalon*. Why the stress on 'large', *megalon*? It just could be because Mary came from the town of Magdala, whose name derived from *gdl* or 'large, great'. Related to it is a noun, *mgdl*, a 'tower' and the town of Magdala would seem to have been named with reference to some such architectural feature.[65] It is a reasonable conclusion that an editor is trying to identify the Beloved Disciple in the storyline as Mary Magdalene, one of the two unnamed disciples, and has added the Isopsepha of 200 and 153 to indicate this clearly.

What might have been the purpose, as a whole, of this stray narrative dealing with the Beloved Disciple and Peter? The complete text, as it now stands, is a Vision story that has made use of a previous call-story. It circulated in the same context as the Gospel of John. However, it was never part of the Gospel of John. The fact that the disciples are addressed in v. 5 by the appellative 'Little Children' and nowhere else in the gospel is indicative of the fact that this is a later construction. In 1 John 2:14, a much later writing, the term is used again.

> [14] I write to you, Little Children,
> because you know the Father.
> I write to you, fathers,
> because you know him who is from the Beginning.
> I write to you, young people,
> because you are strong
> and the word of God abides in you,
> and you have overcome the Evil One.

In short, the narrative in the Gospel of John first presents, in Part A, a Vision of Jesus, unconnected with any other. If we accept the identification

---

[64] On this see M. Starbird (2005), *Mary Magdalene: Bride in Exile*, Bear and Co. Vermont, p. 83; K. Linforth (2014); *The Beloved Disciple: Jacob the Brother of the Lord*, Vivid Publishing, Fremantle, pp. 205-9.

[65] See again Linforth (2014), pp. 206-7.

of Mary Magdalene with the Beloved Disciple then the Vision Story is a parallel to the more extensive Gnostic Magdalene Treatise in John 20.

There is another intriguing element: Jesus has a charcoal (*anthrakia*) fire for cooking the fish that make up, with bread, the meal. We saw that the only other time this word is used in the Christian Scriptures was the scene where Peter was warming himself in the High Priest's courtyard just before his three denials. This was a Roman Christian Insertion. Here Peter and the others eat fish from a charcoal fire. Peter has been rehabilitated. He warmed himself as he denied Jesus over a charcoal fire (*anthrakia*); in repentance, he shares a meal with Jesus over a charcoal fire (*anthrakia*). Part B pretends to continue on from the Vision Story and be an extension of it. Basically it is a meal-story and the fish for the meal has already been provided by Jesus. It recounts the special call of Peter and his response when he follows Jesus. This is the inauguration of the rehabilitated Peter as the successor of Jesus. The dialogue of Jesus with Peter produces three Jesus statements:

Boske ta arnia mou Feed my lambs

Poimaine ta probata mou Pasture my sheep

Boske ta probata mou Feed my sheep

There is no obvious progression here and the three-fold questioning, despite Peter's typical misunderstanding, has a purpose. The three affirmations relate to the three denials in the Roman insertion on the Denials of Peter. The inquisition ends with a typical call to follow Jesus.

There are enough connections with the Roman Insertion on the Denials of Peter to see here the hand of a Roman Christian redactor.

In Part C there is an added and originally unconnected tradition concerning Peter and the Beloved Disciple. Peter asks the divine Jesus about the Beloved Disciple. The main purpose of this complex stray tradition is to counterpose the Beloved Disciple with Peter. In some community context, where reverence for both Peter and the Beloved Disciple was operative, this was a necessary task. A number of traditions are combined. Peter is seen as the headstrong leader who has been rehabilitated and given the role of Shepherd of the Flock. The Beloved Disciple is the mystic who is able to perceive the presence of Jesus from the distant boat and whose presumed death at some stage needed explanation.

In an assimilated community these traditional snippets have been combined. The central figures are 'Peter' and 'Beloved Disciple'. In this instance neither are intended to be an historical character. 'Peter' represents the community leader, the *apostolos,* in charge of the pastoral care and direction of that community. 'The Beloved Disciple' is the Gnostic leader, who directs the Christian thinking of that community. The three-part narrative indicates that both functions are required in a community.

The 'Beloved Disciple' recognizes the Lord. 'Peter' leads the way to the breakfast with the Lord. 'Peter' is officially inducted as the Pastor. What of the 'Beloved Disciple'? 'Leave him be', says the Lord. The two can co-exist in this community. Eventually, with the spread of Roman Christianity and the suppression of even this mitigated form of Gnosticism, the 'Beloved Disciple' role would be neglected. 'Peter' will reign alone as the Roman Christian Church becomes more bureaucratic.

At some stage a later hand has inserted the '153 fish' and the '200 stadia' to show that, at least for their group, the founding Beloved Disciple was Mary Magdalene. We will later spend more time on this provocative issue.

Another supplementary question was inserted: would the Beloved Disciple last through to the final consummation, whereas Peter would die? Waiting for the consummation and The End would not have been a Gnostic preoccupation. Gnostics would have said that The Beloved Disciple had already found salvation in the divine Jesus and would not die, could not die. An editorial explanation has been added, pointing out that Jesus was not speaking of avoiding physical death and there is an admission that a past interpretation was mistaken. The founding Beloved Disciple would pass through physical death and perhaps had already done so.

This narrative would have had a separate history to the other Independent Gnostic Treatises, later adapted to the Roman Christian mentality. It would have circulated among assimilated Gnostics. At some stage it was thought proper to append it to the finished gospel. In its final form it is Roman Christian.

3. Two conclusions (21:24-25)

Conclusion 1

[24] This is the disciple who is testifying to these things and has written them, and we know that the testimony of this disciple is true.

Conclusion 2

[25] But there are also many other things that Jesus did; if every one of them were written down, I suppose that the world itself could not contain the books that would be written.

COMMENTARY

There are two editorial conclusions (even though the Book of Seven Signs had provided its own conclusion at the end of chapter 20, and there was a conclusion to the public ministry of Jesus in 10:40-42).

The first of these conclusions could belong to the foregoing tradition of a Beloved Disciple (who is only identified as 'a disciple', perhaps male or perhaps female). This Beloved Disciple is the one who testifies to the events in the gospel. The use of Gnostic terminology such as disciple (*mathetes*), testimony (*marturein*) and truth (*aletheia*) point to the Beloved Disciple rather than a later scribe as the witness and author. It is likely that this was a stray colophon appended to the Book of Signs, attributing their veracity to the Beloved Disciple.

The second conclusion seems to be the sort of colophon that a scribe might append to a great work of art, such as the Gospel of John in its final form, commenting that the 'author' has done the best possible under the circumstances. It may have originally come earlier prior to the Stray Traditions. It refers more to an editorial hand that has put together the Gnostic material, the Roman material, the additions and the corrections into some semblance of order.

IDENTIFYING THE BELOVED DISCIPLE

At this point, as an important aside, we need to face the question of the Beloved Disciple which has been largely allowed to lay in abeyance, although some suggestions have been made. We have hinted that the usual equation of The Beloved Disciple with John of Zebedee,[66] one of The Twelve, is not satisfactory, at least as a universal solution. There are reasons in the text of John for identifying Mary Magdalene as the Beloved Disciple or, less likely, Nicodemus.

We have already noted that, in the *Gospel of Philip*, Mary Magdalene had been identified as the one whom Divine Jesus particularly loved.

> There were three who always walked with the Lord: Mary, his mother, and her sister, and Magdalene, the one who was called his companion. His sister and his mother and his companion were each a Mary. (58)

---

[66] We have seen that Irenaeus had suggested the identification. Polycrates of Ephesus (c. 130-196) is quoted in Eusebius' *Historia Ecclesiastica* as also opting for John, as both author of the fourth gospel and the Beloved Disciple.

> John, who was both a witness and a teacher, who reclined upon the bosom of the Lord, and, being a priest, wore the sacerdotal plate. He fell asleep at Ephesus.

But there have been many other possibilities identified by scholars, more than the three above: Lazarus, James the Brother of Jesus, Jude the Brother of Jesus, John Mark, Matthias (the replacement of Judas), Thomas, Nathanael, Judas, a symbolic figure representing True Christian Faith or Gentile Christianity or an Itinerant Prophetic Community.

But we are not looking for an historical character. We are looking for the identification of a figure in the Gospel of John which is not historical. We need to look at the evidence for these claims. The 'Beloved Disciple' appears at various points in the Gospel of John. Thomas' claim to the title is only based on his title of Didymos or Twin. This does not seem sufficient for identification; he achieved *gnosis*, but he was never said to be loved in a particular way by Jesus. Nor is there any strong argument for Nathanael. Nicodemus only has the weak claim based on his 'one hundred *litrai*', used at Jesus' funeral arrangement, meaning *agape* or love. Judas appears at the final meal as the one who hands over, and the Beloved Disciple is the one who indicates this; it cannot be Judas at least in this instance. Lazarus, James and Jude likewise have little to encourage their claims. The two more probable identifications would seem to be Mary Magdalene and John of Zebedee.

The references to the Beloved Disciple in the Gospel of John should now be compared, with some comments on their respective qualifications of either Mary Magdalene or John of Zebedee for the role:

Independent Gnostic Treatise 4: Handing-Over of Jesus (13:1-32 and 18:1-14)

John 13: 23 -25. The Beloved Disciple reclines beside Jesus at the Last Supper and this one (*ekeinos,* referring to the masculine form of *mathetes* and therefore not necessarily male) asks Jesus, at Peter's request, who it is that will betray him. This narrative would be open to Mary Magdalene being the Beloved Disciple, but also John of Zebedee.

Sign 7: The Cross and the Mother (19:26-30)

John 19: 26-27. On Golgotha John relates: When Jesus saw his Mother and the Disciple whom he Loved standing beside her, he said to his mother, 'Woman, here is your Son.' This saying would seem at once to exclude both John (since he is not verified as being there!) and also Mary Magdalene (she is not a 'Son'). However, we have surmised that the Woman at Golgotha is not the Virgin Mary of Matthew or Luke's gospels. She is the Gnostic Mother, Sophia. 'Son' would not be a biological term, but refer to the

Emanation from the Father without gender. There is no reference to male gender but to 'The Disciple' (*ho mathetes*). Mary Magdalene emerges as a distinct possibility. In fact, of the three people at the foot of the Cross, Mary is the only possibility for the title.

Independent Gnostic Treatise 7: The Magdalene Vision (20:1-29)

John 20:1-10. Mary Magdalene (only previously mentioned at the foot of the Cross) runs to tell Peter and the Beloved Disciple about the Empty Tomb. The Beloved Disciple, called the Other Disciple in the text, reaches the tomb first, but allows Peter to enter ahead of him. This narrative would exclude Mary Magdalene, but we have seen that the reference to the Other/ Beloved Disciple is in a later addition to the text from a Roman Christian hand. That addition would probably intend the Beloved Disciple to be John of Zebedee.

In John 18:15-16, the account of Peter's denials, a Roman Christian Insertion, there had been an earlier mention of The Other Disciple. This person gains entrance for Peter to High Priest's courtyard. In this case there is no need to think of anyone than an unnamed disciple. The Other Disciple in that passage is not the Beloved Disciple. The literary device of introducing an 'Other Disciple' demonstrates how knowledge of the event in the courtyard could have been obtained. The use of 'Other Disciple' is not significant. In the case of John 20 it explicitly refers to the Beloved Disciple who accompanied Peter.

Stray Tradition 2: The Catch of 153 Fish (21:1-23)

John 21: 4-14. John 21 is a collection of later, stray and unconnected texts. The Beloved Disciple (*ho ekeinos mathetes*, without gender) is one of seven fishers. The dead Jesus appears and they gather 153 fish when they are around 200 *stadia* from the shore. We have already seen that the numbers would seem best to suit 'The Magdalene' and 'Mariam'. This narrative would be open to Mary Magdalene being the Beloved Disciple, even apart from the insertion making the numerical claim. John of Zebedee is acknowledged as present, but why not identify him as the Beloved Disciple, if he was intended?

John 21: 20-23. In the same collection of stray traditions, Peter is reprimanded by Jesus for questioning the Beloved Disciple's (*ho mathetes ekeinos*, no gender) continued presence. This saying would be open to Mary Magdalene being the Beloved Disciple as well as John.

Stray Tradition 3: Two conclusions (21:24-25)

John 21:24. Also in the final chapter, there is a statement that possibly the Gospel of John is based on the testimony of the Beloved Disciple (*ho mathetes*). While this is usually taken as proof that the Beloved Disciple, John of Zebedee, is behind the writing of the fourth Gospel, this reference would be open to Mary Magdalene as well.

The first salient point to be faced is: why has the Gospel of John not identified the Beloved Disciple? Answers have suggested the Beloved Disciple's modesty, or a need to hide from Jewish persecutors; these presume the Beloved Disciple is also the author of the gospel. There does not seem to be any validation for these solutions in the sources.

A second important point is that the Beloved Disciple is in competition with Peter. We can examine the following four passages:

> [13:23] One of his disciples – the One whom Jesus Loved—was reclining next to him; [24] Simon Peter therefore motioned to him to ask Jesus of whom he was speaking.

> [2] So she [Mary Magdalene] ran and went to Simon Peter and to the other disciple, the One whom Jesus Loved, and said to them, 'They have taken the Lord out of the tomb, and we do not know where they have laid him.'
> [3] Then Peter and the other disciple set out and went towards the tomb.

> [21:7] That Disciple whom Jesus Loved said to Peter, 'It is the Lord!' When Simon Peter heard that it was the Lord, he put on some clothes, for he was naked, and jumped into the lake.

> [21:20] Peter turned and saw The Disciple whom Jesus Loved following them; he was the one who had reclined next to Jesus at the supper and had said, 'Lord, who is it that is going to betray you?' [21] When Peter saw this one, he said to Jesus, 'Lord, what about this one?' [22] Jesus said to him, 'If it is my will that this one remain until I come, what is that to you? Follow me!'

In each instance it is the Beloved Disciple who confidently knows what is to be done, has the insight, and is in control of the situation. Peter is the journeyman, the Pastor who cares for the flock but does not have extensive spiritual insight. The Beloved Disciple is the one who has *gnosis*, who can recognize Jesus in a new situation. Peter is the operator who takes care of the daily running of the community.

Who then is the Beloved Disciple? From the evidence it would seem that a likely answer is that The Beloved Disciple was not a particular person at all, but a textual paradigm. 'The Beloved Disciple' was a title and the occupant of the time would have been well known to the group using it. It could have been similar to titles like The Teacher of Righteousness at Qumran or The Messiah in Jewish expectation, or in more modern times The Pope or the Archbishop of Canterbury. It can be legitimately asked: who had been first in line for the title? Perhaps that person was an unknown or contested. This had happened with the Teacher of Righteousness. The ongoing case of The Roman Pope raises the very same question. Each Bishop of Rome has claimed to be 'Peter'. 'Peter' had also become a textual paradigm, doubtless built on the memory of a real person, but used to convey the notion of apostolic authority. There was not a single 'Peter'; there have been many 'Peters'.

The problems of identification have occurred because there would have been at any time more than one claimant to the two titles 'Peter' and 'Beloved Disciple'. 'Peter' was within Roman Christianity; 'The Beloved Disciple' was within Christian Gnosticism. Hence, there have been re-readings of texts dealing with the Beloved Disciple, which have changed the details to include acceptable or exclude unacceptable claimants. No doubt the same process occurred with 'Peter'; there may well have been a variety of claimants to succession. At some point the Bishop of Rome succeeded in claiming the title for himself; but this is another story.[67]

We have seen that in the stray tradition in John 21: 4-14, dealing with the wondrous haul of 153 fish, the Beloved Disciple has been identified as Mary Magdalene by the disposition of the numbers. What might have been the purpose of this stray narrative identifying the Beloved Disciple as Mary? Probably it challenged other identifications in circulation as to the original Beloved Disciple. The addition put in a strong claim that the Beloved Disciple was Mary Magdalene.

Hence, the sequence of identifications seem to be:

Sign 7: The Cross and the Mother (19:26-30)

This was the original statement regarding a Beloved Disciple in the last section of the Book of Seven Signs. The Beloved Disciple was one of the three women and it could not be The Mother (Sophia) or the Sister (Eve). The obvious conclusion is that it was Mary Magdalene.

---

[67] This was precisely the problem with the Avignon papacy in the fourteenth century. At one stage there were popes in Rome and popes in Avignon. The question was: Who was 'Peter'? On this question see my book (2015), *Peter the Rock: What the Roman Papacy was and what it might become*, Spectrum Publications, Melbourne.

Independent Gnostic Treatise 4: Handing-Over of Jesus (13:1-32 and 18:1-14)

This composition circulated as a separate Treatise (perhaps before or perhaps later than the Book of Seven Signs). Again the Beloved Disciple is more arguably Mary Magdalene, who is presented in contrast to Peter, a Gnostic theme. Her role as identifying Judas, the one who hands-over, would fit with other Gnostic traditions.

Independent Gnostic Treatise 7: The Magdalene Vision (20:1-29)

The section on the Beloved Disciple (and Other Disciple) in the Magdalene Vision is a Roman insertion. The Disciple cannot be Mary Magdalene in this instance as she is simultaneously mentioned in the action. Most probably it is a Roman addition that identified John of Zebedee as the Beloved Disciple or Other Disciple. The tradition purports to show the superiority of Peter.

Stray Tradition 2: The Catch of 153 Fish (21:1-23)

This tradition claims that the Beloved Disciple is Mary Magdalene. But this cryptic identification need not mean that it was the identification in the original form of the story. The second part where Peter discusses the credentials of the Beloved Disciple would be presumed to refer likewise to Mary Magdalene (once again the Gnostic contrast of Magdalene and Peter) if the 153 and 'about 200' numeration were to be accepted.

Stray Tradition 3: Two Conclusions (21:24-25)

Even if this does refer to the Beloved Disciple, it is too indefinite for any identification.

In conclusion, we are faced with a number of Christian titles. There is first of all the Roman 'Peter'. The historical Peter may not have actually gone to Rome. However, the Roman gospel, following what it had received from the Jesus-Tradition, acclaimed him as the successor to Jesus. Therefore he must have become the mythical founder of Roman Christianity at some early stage. He was the Roman Apostle and his successors were the *apostoloi*. There was a *tropaion* or memorial built in Rome in his honour. Soon, the belief was that he was buried there. Successors to Peter (even if Peter had not been there) were elected. These were named a 'Peter' or 'Apostle'.

In Western Asia Minor, there had been the charismatic revival brought about by John of Patmos together with Gnostic foundations, some due to

Paul and some due to migrations from Palestine (among whom the Gnostic gospel – known to us as the gospel of John – was developing). The Book of Revelation, attributed to John of Patmos, had a widespread influence and Christians there began to look back to 'John'. Next, Roman Christianity arrived in Western Asia Minor and endeavoured to tone down Gnosticism and the more exuberant forms of apocalyptic thought; they also edited the gospel of John and probably gave it its title. 'The Elder' became the Roman name of the successors of John. Later Roman Christians, perceiving the pre-eminence of 'John' (John of Patmos), either deliberately or confusedly identified this 'John' with John of Zebedee, well known in their own tradition (which John of Patmos was not).

'The Beloved Disciple' was the next title. It was a Gnostic title and used to describe the Leader who had attained the fullness of *gnosis*. Arguably, the first claimant was Mary Magdalene, at least for some Gnostic groups. It would seem to be Mary Magdalene who was the Beloved Disciple in the Gnostic sections of the Gospel of John. This does not mean that the historical Mary Magdalene occupied a Gnostic office. She may have had a quite different history. Then, because of pressure from the Roman Church, John of Zebedee (known in the Synoptics but not in John) took over the role of Beloved Disciple. It was made clear by the Romans that the Beloved Disciple was submissive to Peter even if the two had to live side by side. Confusion reigned.

John of Patmos was identified with John of Zebedee as the author of the book of Revelation, the Gospel of John and the three Letters of John. He was a founder of Christianity but came third in the ranking of Peter, James and John.

Using the 'Beloved Disciple' and 'Peter' side by side was an attempt to bring harmony to developing communities formed from a merger of Christian Gnosticism and Roman Christianity. Likewise, using 'Peter' and 'Paul' side by side brought harmony to Pauline Christians and Petrine Roman Christians. In Rome, there must have been communities that looked to Peter and others who looked to Paul. There were two *tropaia* erected as memorials, one for each.

These complexities have done much to skew any attempt at writing a history of early Christianity.

NOTES

There is an enormous literature on the Gospel of John. Below is a small selection of influential books.

Anderson, Paul N., Felix Just, Tom Thatcher (2007), *John, Jesus, and History: Critical Appraisals of Critical Views*, Symposium Series 1 (44). Society of Biblical Literature: Atlanta.

Bauckham, Richard (2007), *The Testimony of the Beloved Disciple: Narrative, History, and Theology in the Gospel of John*. Baker: Grand Rapids.

Brown, Raymond E., two vols (1966 and 1970), *The Gospel According to John*, Anchor Bible Series, Doubleday: New York.

Brown, Raymond E. (1979), *The Community of the Beloved Disciple*, Paulist Press: New Jersey.

Bruce F. F. (2003), *The New Testament Documents: Are They Reliable?*, InterVarsity Press: Illinois.

Culpepper, R. Alan (1983), *Anatomy of the Fourth Gospel: A Study in Literary Design*, Fortress: Minneapolis.

Dodd, C. H. (1968), *The Interpretation of the Fourth Gospel*, Cambridge University Press: London.

Ehrman, Bart D. (2009), *Jesus Interrupted*, HarperOne: San Francisco.

Estes, Douglas (2008), *The Temporal Mechanics of the Fourth Gospel: A Theory of Hermeneutical Relativity in the Gospel of John (BIS 92)*, E. J. Brill: Leiden.

Funk, Robert W., The Jesus Seminar (1998), *The Acts of Jesus*. HarperSanFrancisco: San Francisco.

Hill, Charles E. (2004), *The Johannine Corpus in the Early Church* , Oxford University Press: New York.

Lindars, Barnabas (1990), *John*. Sheffield Academic Press, Manchester.

Maloney, F. (2005), *The Gospel of John*, Sacra Pagina Series, Michael Glazier: New York.

Robinson, John A. T. (1977), *Redating the New Testament*. SCM Press: London

Thatcher, Tom, ed. (2007), *What We Have Heard from the Beginning: The Past, Present and Future of Johannine Studies*, Baylor University Press: Waco.

On the specific question of the Beloved Disciple the following have extensive bibliographies:

Charlesworth, James H. (1995), *The Beloved Disciple: Whose Witness Validates the Gospel of John?*, Trinity Press: Valley Forge, Pennsylvania.

Baltz, Frederick W. (2010), *The Mystery of the Beloved Disciple: New Evidence, Complete Answer*, Infinity Publishing: Pennsylvania.

A more recent book contains matters of interest:

K. Linforth (2014), *The Beloved Disciple, Jacob the Brother of the Lord*, Vivid Publishing, Fremantle.

— 9 —
A FINAL SUMMARY OF THE GROWTH OF THE GOSPEL OF JOHN

WE WILL NOW ATTEMPT TO TRACE the path of the transmission of the text of the Gospel of John to its canonical form. This will be a summary of what has been done in this book. There will be some overlap with what has been covered earlier.

To do this, we must begin with a review of the stages of early Christianity as far as we can reconstruct them.

THE EARLY CHRISTIAN GROUPS

The Palestinian Jesus-movement Groups

The death of Jesus, a celebrated *zaddik* or saint, had stimulated followings in Palestine. Some of these can be traced. There was a Peter group, a James group, a Stephen group and doubtless others no longer recorded. They endeavoured to find meaning through their focus on Jesus. Meaning was translated into religious terminology as the coming of the Kingdom of God, a haven of peace and security, both social and religious, where they could fulfil the ideals that Judaism had given them.

From these early groups developed the Jesus-Tradition. This was amorphous and it consisted of sayings and deeds of Jesus, although its fluid form would have differed from place to place and, with the passage of time, quite different versions would have emerged. It broadly included the Sayings of Jesus either in oral or written form, a Greek version of the sayings in Thomas, collections of miracle stories, parables and proverbs, collections of pronouncement-stories, a Passion Narrative and post-death Visions Narrative. Birth narratives and an Empty Tomb tradition would have come later. Most probably the Jesus-Tradition contained both written and oral collections.

Jewish Proto-Gnosticism

The Gospel of John's text, however, began with groups of Gnostics in the Palestinian area who, also stimulated by the life of Jesus, claimed that Jesus had come as a divine Emanation from The Father. Their Jewish background would have been previously in Jewish Proto-Gnosticism, something like the form found in the *yahad* community of which the Dead Sea Scrolls speak. There would have been a number of these Jesus-movement groups, and even neighbouring groups would not have thought in exactly the same way. In fact the *Testimony of Truth* shows that there were bitter conflicts between the Gnostic groups themselves.

Looking at the Qumran model of such communities, it seems that the Jewish Gnostics were ascetics who eschewed materiality. The World, with its excesses of wealth and sex, was not the place for these visionaries. Some of these Jewish Gnostics were, however, unable to find full mediation in any form of Judaism and some simply moved their allegiance from standard Jewish Intermediaries (such as Moses or David/Enoch-returned-to-life, Melchizedek, the coming Messiahs) to Jesus. They became Christian Gnostics.

Christian Gnosticism

For these Christian Gnostics, Jesus was not a human. He was a Divine Being clothed in Flesh and that Flesh had to be divested, when Jesus would return to the heavenly realm, before the disciples could find their fulfilment.

These Gnostic groups looked back to a variety of successors of Jesus, named in the tradition. Certainly there was Mary Magdalene (known at least by some as the inaugural Beloved Disciple), but also Judas Iscariot, Philip, Peter and Thomas were acclaimed as leaders.

Within the circle of these Christian Gnostics there was access to the Jesus-Tradition. The Christian Gnostics manipulated the texts and traditions; they made use of current Gnostic writings and teachings in order to produce the following separate units, not necessarily circulating in the same locality:

Independent Gnostic Treatises

The Book of Seven Signs

Gnostic Discourses

At some stage these Christian Gnostic communities were put under pressure by the mainstream Jews and other Jesus-movements in Palestine. They seemed to have been forced out of the Palestinian area, whence they presumably originated, and into Western Asia Minor.

There they found churches already established by Paul. Paul had been a Gnostic and his Gnostic teaching, although certainly not identical to their own, was at least compatible. There would have been an easy and sympathetic relationship between the new arrivals and the Pauline churches.

Roman Christians

In Rome, a distinctive sect of the Jesus-movement had developed, Roman Christianity. It had been an offshoot from the Peter group, originally in Palestine. Within the confines of Rome, various traditions about Jesus were developed. They included the teaching that Peter was the vicar of Jesus. However, as the Roman Empire flourished so did the Roman Christians. Their particular teaching and practice became standard as the Roman power moved around the Mediterranean. At some time, Roman Christians appropriated Peter for themselves. He was not only the focus of their traditions; he had come to Rome and had consolidated the Christian community there. In fact, his memorial and tomb were there.

Mark's gospel is a summary and elaboration of this Roman teaching and practice. Matthew and Luke adapted this Roman Christianity for other centres in the Roman world outside Rome. The three Synoptics were all Roman gospels.

For convenience, let us repeat what we know of Roman Christianity, as it would have been incorporated into the Synoptics:

- An historical Jesus whose birth (in Matthew and Luke only) and ministry demonstrated that he was the expected Jewish Messiah.
- His death, physical resurrection and ascension (in Matthew and Luke) were affirmed by reliable witnesses.
- The choice of The Twelve.
- The appointment of Peter as the leader of The Twelve.
- The betrayal by the evil Judas.
- The trials of Jesus by Jews, although unwillingly condoned by Pilate.
- The blood-sacrifice of his factual death (this would require the eventual appointment of sacrificing priests).
- A sacramental system of Baptism and Eucharist, inaugurated historically by Jesus.
- The imminent coming of a Last Day, preceded by certain secret signs.

- The promise of the return of the Messiah, a Second Coming.
- The physical resurrection of all believers (Matthew: it had already begun).

Endemic to this entire presentation were two features: Roman Christian teaching and practice had all been foretold in the Hebrew Scriptures and it was factually historical and could be proved as such by reliable witnesses.

A complication in Rome was that some members of the Jesus-movement established by Paul had migrated to Rome. They extolled their own founder, Paul. From this group came the Acts of the Apostles. For some time, they were pacified by having Paul acknowledged as co-founder of the Roman Church and a memorial was built, also believed to be his tomb.

Christian Gnostics in Western Asia Minor and Roman Christians now had to share the same social space. This is Johannine Christianity. At this point we incorporate what has already been written about the Pauline Christian Gnostics, the Palestinian Gnostics and the apocalyptic zeal of John of Patmos. The end result was that Christians looked to the fiery prophet, John of Patmos, as a leader.

Into this complex situation Roman Christianity arrived.

Assimilation of Christian Gnostics and Roman Christians

There would have taken place a natural process of assimilation between the Christian Gnostics and the local Roman Christians in Western Asia Minor. The other groups in Palestine (such as the Peter group, the Hellenist group, the James the Just group) simply withered.

Assimilation would have meant that they held in common their adhesion to Jesus who had come into the World. The assimilation probably meant liturgical sharing when Baptism and the Eucharist became common sacraments, although the recipients understanding of them would have considerably differed.[68] The Gnostics would formerly have had their own sacraments. They would have acquired a new meaning as Roman Christianity celebrated their liturgy.

Next, there would have been a pooling of traditions regarding Jesus: the Gnostic understanding of the Jesus-Tradition would have been placed side by side with the Roman Christians' understanding of the Jesus-Tradition. The Gnostics' own writings and traditions, with their excessive spirituality

---

[68] This is not so different to Roman Catholics, Anglicans, Lutherans and other Christian churches today who each have a Eucharist but understand its significance differently. Occasionally there are (perhaps unauthorized) common celebrations.

and mysticism, presumably still had their natural attractiveness to resident Christians. These two lines of understanding fused.

What must have happened in this unusual situation is important to understand. We can analyse the process by referring once more, as we did in the Introduction, to human culture, the inherited way of human thinking, acting and valuing. What does culture, understood in this way, offer to the human being? The human individual has a need for order. To make sense of the universe, self and others, the individual within the group requires a direction, a purpose, a basic meaning. All cultural activity takes place in the context of the construction of a cultural 'world' of meanings. These constructed worlds, shaped according to perhaps significantly different configurations of values, power relationships and knowledge, achieve viability because they are supported by a group which, by its general acceptance of the culture, gives plausibility to such constructed worlds. The supportive group commits itself to its 'world' and defines its own roles and identities vis-à-vis it. The group members, committed to a culture's constructed world, makes sense of human existence through it.

Culture, every culture, offers this advantage to its adherents. In order to find meaning and direction, individuals and groups must accept and then adapt themselves to this cultural heritage of a constructed world. When the group has achieved this meaning and direction, it acts to retain its cultural heritage with the same tenacity as an individual displays in maintaining personal, physical life. Hence there is always an element of adherence and continuity in culture, together with a capacity to adapt and change.

Human cultures have often been compared. There are inevitable comparisons, so that some scholars have concluded that there are basic elements to every culture and to 'human nature'. This is the basis of the Natural Law theories. However, it needs to be said that such common factors considered to be universal are not inherited as such. There are certain general response capacities among humans (for example, protection of the young and helpless, abhorrence of murder and incest and, very importantly, a need for order in life) which give rise to the seeming facets of 'human nature'. The general response capacities of the human group, inherited certainly, are activated and directed in different ways by a particular culture. Because of these two factors there will be both diversity and similarity between human cultures.

As a result, there are two polar attitudes possible in respect to human culture and they become evident once culturally diverse groups cohabit. They exist at diverse ends of a continuum. We have already seen this theoretical perspective when dealing with the understanding of religion and its application to culture and religion.

We have also examined earlier the continuum from ethnocentrism to multiculturalism. Multiculturalism maintains that there have been and still are many cultures constructed by humans over space and time, all of which presumably give adequate order and meaning to their constituencies and activate the general response capacities of these constituencies in variant but yet acceptable ways (for example, the general response capacity towards sexual regulation in a cultural group can take the forms of monogamy, serial monogamy, polygamy, either acceptance or rejection of homosexuality; haphazard sexual relations would cause problems for humans). Multiculturalism encourages the preservation of a variety of cultures and their differences. It esteems and promotes the variant configurations of culturally different groups, including, for example, their different patterns of sexual activity, family structure and their languages.

In a multicultural society, a variety of relationships can exist between the dominant (frequently the majority, but not always) cultural group and the less-dominant cultural groups. Less-dominant cultures can be suppressed by the dominant group. But, if a culturally diverse society is governed by consensus rather than fascist coercion, a set of shared values could be evolved that would overarch culturally diverse groups. Under such a cultural 'umbrella', culturally diverse groups may retain certain core values, such as a distinct language or family tradition, while adhering to other values shared with others under the umbrella.[69]

Such a culturally diverse society would have to maintain a dynamic equilibrium between the overarching or shared values of the broad-based society, on the one hand, and the particular core values of its component groups on the other. The dominant group in the broad-based society would maintain its own set of values, many of which would percolate into the overarching framework. However, in a truly multicultural community, these shared values within the umbrella should not be regarded as the dominant group's own private domain, but as common to all individuals within the broad-based society.

If we apply this theory to the situation we have envisaged somewhere in Western Asia Minor perhaps in the earlier second century, then we can

---

[69] Hence, a Vietnamese group living in Australia, where knowledge and facility in the use of English is a core value of the cultural umbrella, would learn English but also would be encouraged to retain Vietnamese language and other Vietnamese core values.

presume the following sequence. The Palestinian Gnostics, who had formed themselves into small communities, were persecuted by both Jewish mainstream groups, for whom they represented a deviation from the Law of Moses, and by Palestinian Christian movement sects, for whom they represented a deviation from their constructed Literary Jesus. The Christian Gnostics were persecuted, forced out of the synagogues and were not welcomed in the Palestinian Jesus-movement groups. As a consequence they left Palestine and reassembled somewhere, presumably Western Asia Minor in the area of Ephesus.

They found some like-minded Christians, the descendants of Paul and his missionaries. But they also found the inroads of Roman Christianity as it made its inexorable road to the East.

Fleeing persecution, they brought with them their Gnostic beliefs, texts and practices. But these, in a new situation, had to be adapted. The Gnostic belief system would have been adapted to a point where both Gnostics and Roman Christians felt comfortable. Likewise, the sacramental system would have developed in practice and meaning to accommodate both groups.

We will now concentrate on the written texts. The literary creations of the Gnostic arrivals were edited according to the existing statements of the Roman Churches who relied, as did the Gnostics, on the Jesus-Tradition in its broadest form. This process would have required the inclusion of some Roman Christian traditions into the story of Gnostic Jesus. The Gnostic discourse as a whole needed a chronological context, to be settled in much the same context as the Roman understanding of the Jesus-Tradition, and it required the editing of the other materials to correct or supplement major theological tendencies that conflicted with what was current in the Roman presentation of Jesus. However, at the same stage, there was a desire to accept some of the spiritual flourish of the Christian Gnostic discourse. The 'umbrella' was working efficiently.

There were consistent corrections required in common Roman and Gnostic texts as regards other teachings and practice. These corrections took the form of additions to existing texts and insertions of new texts. They covered the following Roman Christian items:

- John the Baptist as the Forerunner of the Messiah.
- The role of Judas Iscariot, seen as a traitor in the Roman version, even if he was a Leader in some Gnostic traditions.
- The claim of Peter to be the successor to Jesus, and the claim of the Twelve to a pastoral leadership role. The Beloved Disciple was not the successor to Jesus.

- The recognition of Jesus' death as a bloody sacrifice for sins.

- The texts dealing with the institution and practice of Baptism as an initiation ritual and the Eucharist as a renewal of the Jesus sacrifice. (The Gnostics interpreted both as acknowledging stages of the *pneumatikos* towards full *gnosis*).

- The teaching in the texts regarding a Final Eschatology, with the end of this world, a judgement and an imminent return of the Messiah. (The Gnostics had an immediate eschatology, an immediate 'judgement', an immediate 'resurrection of the dead' and no return of Jesus but the sending of a Paraclete).

Accordingly, the Gnostic traditions that would have disregarded John the Baptist, that saw Judas as the privileged seer who assisted Jesus at his most fateful moment, that acknowledged the claim of the Beloved Disciple to be the successor of Jesus and lauded him, that validated the Gnostic sacraments, that proposed Immediate Eschatology had to be amended and sometimes muted.

The process of the assimilation and transmission can be followed for the four main successive situations that we have discovered: Jewish Gnostics, Gnostic Christians, Roman Christians in Asia Minor, the formation of the Johannine Churches. (The earlier Palestinian groups struggled to survive and eventually disappeared). The Johannine churches mark the formation of an 'umbrella', which is the Johannine religio-cultural and textual tradition. This list of religious groups can be summed up as follows:

1. Jewish Gnostic communities (Jewish texts circulated similar to some of the Dead Sea Scrolls and including others from the immediate pre-Christian period)

2. Christian Gnostics (Gnostic texts included: Hymn of the Word or *Logos*, the Book of Seven Signs, Independent Gnostic Treatises, Discourses – and doubtless much more)

3. The Roman form of Christianity in Asia Minor (parts of and editions of The Jesus-Tradition as it was used by Roman missionaries, but not the Synoptic tradition as eventually known in Rome itself)

4. Assimilation of the Christian Gnostics into the Roman form of Christianity in Asia Minor. (The controlling document would have been the developing 'Gospel of John', a combination of the above Gnostic material with expansions and correctives from the Roman

Jesus-Tradition and, very occasionally, correctives of the Gnostics into the Roman Christian tradition. This, in its various stages, became the common gospel of the expanded community in Asia Minor).

THE LITERARY COMPOSITION OF THE GOSPEL OF JOHN

Based on the historical reconstruction above, we are now able, at long last, to present a 'Gospel of John' with its component parts from the Gnostic Tradition and the expansions, corrections and added traditions from the Roman Jesus-Tradition. This was the Gospel accepted by Rome later as a canonical gospel.

First, we must envisage the life situation of separate Gnostic communities in the Palestinian area. They have derived from Jewish Gnosticism and have sacred writings that relate to Jesus, to whom they have directed their religious adhesion. Amongst other sacred writings, some no doubt lost forever, we are able to distinguish the Book of Seven Signs, perhaps heralded with a Hymn to the Word or Logos and a conclusion:

Independent Gnostic Treatise 1: The Hymn of the Word or *Logos* (1:1-18)

The Book of Seven Signs

Sign 1. Cana and The Mother (2:1-12)

Sign 2: The Cure of the Official's Son (4:43-54)

Sign 3: The Cure of the Crippled Man (5:1-18)

Sign 4: The Feeding of the 5000 (6:1-34)

Sign 5: The Cure of the Blind Man (9:1-41 and 10:19-21)

Sign 6: The Raising of Lazarus (11:1-57)

Sign 7: The Cross and the Mother (19:26-30)

Conclusion to Book of Signs (20:31-32)

In the second place, there were the seven Independent Gnostic Treatises that needed a home in the growing library of texts although the first, The Hymn of the Word or *Logos*, had probably already been included. These were inserted into the Book of Signs, in what were considered logical places for further instruction.

1. The Hymn of the Word or *Logos* (1:1-18)

2. Foretelling the Destruction of the Temple (2:13-25)

3. The Anointing by Mary (12:1-11)

4. Handing-Over of Jesus (13:1-32 and 18:1-14)

5. The Judgement of Jesus (18:28-19:16a)

6. The Crucifixion (19:16b-25)

7. The Magdalene Vision (20:1-29)

The form of this growing Gnostic gospel now took on this form:

Independent Gnostic Treatise 1: The Hymn of the Word or *Logos* (1:1-18)

The Book of Seven Signs (see Signs 1-7)

Sign 1. Cana and The Mother (2:1-12)

Independent Gnostic Treatise 2: Foretelling the Destruction of the Temple (2:13-25)

Sign 2: The Cure of the Official's Son (4:43-54)

Sign 3: The Cure of the Crippled Man (5:1-18)

Sign 4: The Feeding of the 5000 (6:1-34)

Sign 5: The Cure of the Blind Man (9:1-41 and 10:19-21)

Sign 6: Raising of Lazarus (11:1-57)

Independent Gnostic Treatise 3: Anointing by Mary (12:1-11)

Independent Gnostic Treatise 4: Handing-Over of Jesus (13:1-32 and 18:1-14)

Independent Gnostic Treatise 5: The Judgement of Jesus (18:28-19:16a)

Independent Gnostic Treatise 6: The Crucifixion (19:16b-25)

Sign 7: The Cross and the Mother (19:26-30)

Independent Gnostic Treatise 7: The Magdalene Vision (20:1-29)

Conclusion to the Book of Signs (20:30-31)

The next stage of development would have been the insertion of Gnostic Discourses into this extended Book of Seven Signs. They would have already circulated in a separate form (perhaps in a collection or collections):

1. Birth and Rebirth (3:1-21 and 31-36)

2. The Water of Life (4:4-42)

3. The Father and Son (5:19-47)

4. The Bread of Life (6:35-65)

5. Excerpts within a Tradition (7:1-52)

6. The Light of the World and Testimony (8:12-20)

7. Above and Below (8:21-30)

8. The Father and Abraham (8:31-59)

9. **The Good Shepherd (10:1-21)**

10. **The Works of the Father (10:22-42)**

11. **The Hour and Glory (12:19-50)**

12. **The Paraclete (13:33-14:31)**

13. **The True Vine (15:1-16:33)**

14. **The Prayer of Jesus (17:1-26)**

At some point these Discourses would have been seen as elaborating on the Seven Signs. Therefore they were interwoven with the Signs and the Treatises, sometimes with a clear appropriateness, sometimes not so. It is now clear that the Discourses were inserted as discrete blocks, as can be seen.

Sign 1, The Mother at Cana, which revealed Jesus as the Bridegroom who was the source of water and life, is related to Discourses 1 and 2. In the two Discourses, Jesus elaborates on the meaning of new birth and himself as the source of living Water. The Discourses are parallel, one involving a Monologue with a Jewish man, the other a Monologue with a Samaritan woman

Signs 2 and 3, which raised the issue of the Father and the Son, are followed by Discourse 3 on Father and Son. Jesus as the Giver of Life is explained in more detail.

Sign 4 was the core section of the Book of Seven Signs: Jesus has been sent to a new people to bring the Bread of Heaven. This Sign is then accompanied by Discourses 4-8. Discourse 4 is explicitly on the Bread of Heaven, but then other issues in the Gnostic debate are raised and explained in the attached Discourses 5-8.

In Sign 5 a blind man is given sight. Discourses 9 and 10 are attached to it. They are explanations of Jesus as the Good Shepherd who (as in the present instance) cares for his flock and protects it, and as The Son brings the *gnosis* of the Father into the World.

Sign 6, the raising of Lazarus, is followed by Discourses 11-14. This Sign of Lazarus is seen as leading to the Hour of Jesus. Discourses 11-13 point towards The Hour, dealing with the issues of the 'Little While' and the Paraclete, who will substitute for Jesus after his Glorification.

Discourse 14, The Prayer of Jesus, is the conclusion to the Discourses generally, prior to the climactic last Sign.

With the insertion of the Discourses as explanatory expansions, the Gospel of John now looked as follows:

Independent Gnostic Treatise 1: The Hymn of the Word or *Logos* (1:1-18)

The Book of Seven Signs (see Signs 1-7)

Sign 1. Cana and The Mother (2:1-12)

Independent Gnostic Treatise 2: Foretelling the Destruction of the Temple (2:13-25)

Gnostic Discourse 1: Birth and Rebirth (3:1-21 and 31-36)

Gnostic Discourse 2: The Water of Life (4:4-42)

Sign 2: The Cure of the Official's Son (4:43-54)

Sign 3: The Cure of the Crippled Man (5:1-18)

Gnostic Discourse 3: The Father and Son (5:19-47)

Sign 4: The Feeding of the 5000 (6:1-34)

Gnostic Discourse 4: The Bread of Life (6:35-65)

Gnostic Discourse 5: Excerpts within a Tradition (7:1-52)

Gnostic Discourse 6: The Light of the World and Testimony (8:12-20)

Gnostic Discourse 7: Above and Below (8:21-30)

Gnostic Discourse 8: The Father and Abraham (8:31-59)

Sign 5: The Cure of the Blind Man (9:1-41 and 10:19-21)

Gnostic Discourse 9: The Good Shepherd (10:1-21)

Gnostic Discourse 10: The Works of the Father (10:22-42)

Sign 6: Raising of Lazarus (11:1-57)

Independent Gnostic Treatise 3: Anointing by Mary (12:1-11)

Gnostic Discourse 11: The Hour and Glory (12:19-50)

Independent Gnostic Treatise 4: Handing-Over of Jesus (13:1-32 and 18:1-14)

Gnostic Discourse 12: The Paraclete (13:33-14:31)

Gnostic Discourse 13: The True Vine (15:1-16:33)

Gnostic Discourse 14: The Prayer of Jesus (17:1-26)

Independent Gnostic Treatise 5: The Judgement of Jesus (18:28-19:16a)

Independent Gnostic Treatise 6: The Crucifixion (19:16b-25)

Sign 7: The Cross and the Mother (19:26-30)

Independent Gnostic Treatise 7: The Magdalene Vision (20:1-29)

Conclusion to the Book of Signs (20:30-31)

The next important stage of gospel amalgamation presumes, as we have already seen, a new life situation – the pooling of traditions belonging to both the Gnostic group and the Roman Christians. The influence of the Roman Christian tradition took the form of expansions and corrections and larger insertions which were added into this Gnostic book to give it at least the semblance of a mainstream document. This resulted in the following Roman Church Insertions, forming an 'umbrella'.

1. John the Baptist (1:19-51 and 3:22-30 and 4:1-3)

2. Confession of Peter (6:66-71)

3. Entry into Jerusalem (12:12-19)

4. Peter's Denials and the Trial before the Sanhedrin (18:15-27)

5. The Burial (19:31-42)

The format of the gospel of John was by this time approaching its final stage:

Independent Gnostic Treatise 1: The Hymn of the Word or *Logos* (1:1-18)

Roman Christian Insertion 1: John the Baptist (1:19-51 and 3:22-30 and 4:1-3)

The Book of Seven Signs (see Signs 1-7)

Sign 1. Cana and The Mother (2:1-12)

Independent Gnostic Treatise 2: Foretelling the Destruction of the Temple (2:13-25)

Gnostic Discourse 1: Birth and Rebirth (3:1-21 and 31-36)

Gnostic Discourse 2: The Water of Life (4:4-42)

Sign 2: The Cure of the Official's Son (4:43-54)

Sign 3: The Cure of the Crippled Man (5:1-18)

Gnostic Discourse 3: The Father and Son (5:19-47)

Sign 4: The Feeding of the 5000 (6:1-34)

Gnostic Discourse 4: The Bread of Life (6:35-65)

Roman Christian Insertion 2: Confession of Peter (6:66-71)

Gnostic Discourse 5: Excerpts within a Tradition (7:1-52)

Gnostic Discourse 6: The Light of the World and Testimony (8:12-20)

Gnostic Discourse 7: Above and Below (8:21-30)

Gnostic Discourse 8: The Father and Abraham (8:31-59)

Sign 5: The Cure of the Blind Man (9:1-41 and 10:19-21)

Gnostic Discourse 9: The Good Shepherd (10: 1-21)

Gnostic Discourse 10: The Works of the Father (10:22-42)

Sign 6: Raising of Lazarus (11:1-57)

Independent Gnostic Treatise 3: Anointing by Mary (12:1-11)

Roman Christian Insertion 3: Entry into Jerusalem (12:12-19)

Gnostic Discourse 11: The Hour and Glory (12: 19-50)

Independent Gnostic Treatise 4: Handing-Over of Jesus (13:1-32 and 18:1-14)

Gnostic Discourse 12: The Paraclete (13:33-14:31)

Gnostic Discourse 13: The True Vine (15:1-16:33)

Gnostic Discourse 14: The Prayer of Jesus (17:1-26)

Roman Christian Insertion 4: Peter's Denials and the Trial before the Sanhedrin (18: 15-27)

Independent Gnostic Treatise 5: The Judgement of Jesus (18:28-19:16a)

Independent Gnostic Treatise 6: The Crucifixion (19:16b-25)

Sign 7: The Cross and the Mother (19:26-30)

Roman Christian Insertion 5: The Burial (19:31-42)

Independent Gnostic Treatise 7: The Magdalene Vision (20:1-29)

Conclusion to the Book of Signs (20:30-31)

At a later date still, the remaining three stray traditions were added. The Adulterous Woman was always outside the gospel structure and was only parked in John's text much later. The other two traditions were related to the Johannine text at the point at which assimilation was taking place, but they never formed part of the original literary work.

Stray Tradition 1: The Adulterous Woman (7:53-8:11)

Stray Tradition 2: The Catch of 153 Fish (21:1-23)

Stray Tradition 3: Two conclusions (21:24-25)

At this point in time, the Gospel of John, as it would be accepted into the official canon of the Roman Church, came into being. We will include Stray Tradition 1 in this final outline since that passage eventually was included in the canonical text.

Independent Gnostic Treatise 1: The Hymn of the Word or *Logos* (1:1-18)

Roman Christian Insertion 1: John the Baptist (1:19-51 and 3:22-30 and 4:1-3)

The Book of Seven Signs (see Signs 1-7)

Sign 1. Cana and The Mother (2:1-12)

Independent Gnostic Treatise 2: Foretelling the Destruction of the Temple (2:13-25)

Gnostic Discourse 1: Birth and Rebirth (3:1-21 and 31-36)

Gnostic Discourse 2: The Water of Life (4:4-42)

Sign 2: The Cure of the Official's Son (4:43-54)

Sign 3: The Cure of the Crippled Man (5:1-18)

Gnostic Discourse 3: The Father and Son (5:19-47)

Sign 4: The Feeding of the 5000 (6:1-34)

Gnostic Discourse 4: The Bread of Life (6:35-65)

Roman Christian Insertion 2: Confession of Peter (6:66-71)

Gnostic Discourse 5: Excerpts within a Tradition (7:1-52)

Stray Tradition 1: The Adulterous Woman (7:53-8:11)

Gnostic Discourse 6: The Light of the World and Testimony (8:12-20)

Gnostic Discourse 7: Above and Below (8:21-30)

Gnostic Discourse 8: The Father and Abraham (8:31-59)

Sign 5: The Cure of the Blind Man (9:1-41 and 10:19-21)

Gnostic Discourse 9: The Good Shepherd (10: 1-21)

Gnostic Discourse 10: The Works of The Father (10:22-42)

Sign 6: Raising of Lazarus (11:1-57)

Independent Gnostic Treatise 3: Anointing by Mary (12:1-11)

Roman Christian Insertion 3: Entry into Jerusalem (12:12-19)

Gnostic Discourse 11: The Hour and Glory (12:19-50)

Independent Gnostic Treatise 4: Handing-Over of Jesus (13:1-32 and 18:1-14)

Gnostic Discourse 12: The Paraclete (13:33-14:31)

Gnostic Discourse 13: The True Vine (15:1-16:33)

Gnostic Discourse 14: The Prayer of Jesus (17:1-26)

Roman Christian Insertion 4: Peter's Denials and the Trial before the Sanhedrin (18:15-27)

Independent Gnostic Treatise 5: The Judgement of Jesus (18:28-19:16a)

Independent Gnostic Treatise 6: The Crucifixion (19:16b-25)

Sign 7: The Cross and the Mother (19:26-30)

Roman Christian Insertion 5: The Burial (19:31-42)

Independent Gnostic Treatise 7: The Magdalene Vision (20:1-29)

Conclusion to the Book of Signs: (20: 30-31)

Stray Tradition 2: The Catch of 153 Fish (21:1-23)

Stray Tradition 3: Two conclusions (21:24-25)

When the material is read as an edited text with the addition of the Roman Insertions and corrections then the interpretation can be turned from a World that is inherently evil, from the possibility of immediate assimilation into Jesus, from a Jesus who did not actually die on the Cross but used this as a mechanism to divest himself of Flesh and be glorified, from an expectation that the Paraclete had come to replace Jesus, to another World that is basically good, to the expectation of a Final Judgement at the End of the World, to the expiation of Jesus' very real blood-sacrifice on the Cross, to an expectation that Jesus would return at the End of time.

This reworking has caused some non-sequiturs, as we have seen, and some contradictions in the text but we can certainly imagine that an 'umbrella' community accepted the final form of the gospel. We can presume that both Gnostics and Roman Christians felt satisfied with the end result. Doubtless, each group read it as they saw fit.

At once the modern reader is confronted with questions. Which of the two lines of seemingly incompatible interpretation within John is correct?

- Jesus only appeared to be human / Jesus was truly human, physically born of a Virgin.

- The life of Jesus was symbolic, revealing the Glory of the Father / the life of Jesus, including miracles and healings, was factual.

- Baptism is a sign of Gnostic initiation / the sacrament of Baptism is an initiation that incorporates the Christian into Christ.

- The sacrament of the Eucharist is a sign of spiritual advancement / the sacrament of the Eucharist is a sharing in a meal of the body and blood of Jesus.

- Jesus did not really die / Jesus died as a blood-sacrifice for sinful humans.

- Resurrection of the dead refers to those who have attained *gnosis* and become one with Jesus / the Resurrection was a physical event including an Empty Tomb and will be a future event including all the dead.

- Salvation is now / salvation is in the future after the Last Day when Jesus will have a Second Coming.

- Each Christian is responsible for their own salvation / Jesus left behind his successor Peter as leader of The Twelve who, through bishops, elders (priests) and deacons, would accept responsibility for the Christian community.

The answer is, of course: both lines are correct. Both are religious statements. The canonical version of John proposes the second of each of each of the above alternatives, even if a contrary opinion may raise its head. Whether one or other or neither depends on history is immaterial. The choice depends on the reader. We are here at the cutting-edge in this research where we can see the link between text, community and interpretation in early Christianity. Texts were created by communities. Communities changed, and interpretations changed and combined. Texts changed accordingly.

The literary critic and historian can do no more than propose reasonable hypotheses to cover the complexity of change in texts belonging to religious communities.

CONCLUSION

THIS BOOK IS THE RESULT OF literary criticism and the historical method applied to the canonical Gospel of John. Its conclusions would, we hope, be helpful to those who are interested in the history of early Christianity and in the literary disposition of the Christian writings which were selected to be the official guides of Roman Christianity.

While the role of the literary critic and historian is clear enough, and we hope that it has been properly utilized in this book, what can be said about the Christian believer of today (all of whom – East and West, Roman Catholic and Reformed, Pentecostal – are Roman Christians), and these findings, even though Christian faith has never been the focus of the book?

The time has come for such believers to become more sophisticated in their use of the literary gospels or to discontinue using them. First of all, it needs to be clearly understood that there were many early gospels; the Roman Church eventually chose four of them as canonical. It discarded the others. The 'others' have variously been seen as heretical or derivative by Roman authority.

Of course, most of today's Christians accept all four gospels, as the Roman Church has insisted they should do at least from the fourth century CE. Prior to then, a gospel text would be more limited in its circulation and appeal. Some Christians followed Matthew; some followed John. After all, in its final form the gospel of John can be said to complement the Synoptic Tradition, even if there are contradictions and inconsistencies. I suspect that most Roman Christians, having been first schooled in the facets of Roman Christian theology, later read the Synoptics and John accordingly. After all, John has been Romanized.

My own position would be that these mainstream believers should, however, recognize a number of things. The gospel of John is not the same in terminology and teaching as the three Synoptics, although we have seen the number of correctives applied to it. The gospel of John has always been on the edge of Gnosticism and at times Gnosticism is even at its centre. Its appeal will be more to those Christians who have a feeling for mysticism.

Indiscriminate exposure of mainstream Christians now to the Synoptics and now to John, without any reference to difference, cannot make sense. The four canonical gospels are not speaking exactly the same Christian message to the believers. For some of these mainstreamers this book might be helpful, but it would raise challenges.

However, many other Christians, over the centuries, have found that within the teachings of the four gospels, accepted indiscriminately as inspired texts, they can find ultimate meaning. For them, a passage of John's gospel can be explained by reference to a letter of Paul or the Book of Revelation; the Synoptics and John's gospel could not by definition be contradictory – they are inspired and inerrant; any seeming contradictions in teaching or narrative must be able to be reconciled. This book would be of little value to such.

But let us return to the religious pluralist who has happened to find a comfortable location in Christian commitment (while recognising, as a pluralist, the variety of other possible and genuine commitments).

There is nothing to stop such a pluralist Christian believer returning to an earlier non-canonical gospel, for example the *Gospel of Thomas*, or returning to an earlier form of the Gospel of John, for example the initial Gnostic complex. Thereby, these pluralist believers would remove themselves from mainstream Christianity (which is doggedly Roman Christian), but that is nothing novel. And such a pluralist could always go further. Pluralists might feel that the Christian system does not suit them and they may seek a new religious mechanism among the world religions, the new religious movements, the philosophies, all of which offer a coherent approach to living. These pluralists would find much of interest in the book. It might focus their minds.

But, in the end, it must be repeated, this book has been primarily about history and literary criticism. It has endeavoured to follow the transmission of the text of the Gospel of John. It has not proposed or even considered that the gospel of John might be inspired by God or be inerrant (difficult as these terms are to define). It has tried to show the sort of historical background that would explain consistently the textual meanderings that a literary critic can uncover.

Turning once again to the title of the book – *Jesus, his Mother, her Sister Mary and Mary Magdalene* – we see that the only answer to this conundrum is a Gnostic origin to the gospel of John. At the same time there is evidence in the Gospel of John that Jesus was human, he died a sacrificial death, that Peter was his successor, that there were The Twelve, that Baptism is a sacrament of initiation, that Eucharist is a sacrament of sharing in the sacrificial death of Jesus. Gnosticism was muted and over-written. That is the basis of the hypothesis underlying the book.

In conclusion, I would say that this study of the Gospel of John provides tremendous possibilities for the historian and particularly the historian of religion, to the literary critic and in particular the scholar engrossed in the Christian Scriptures as literature. It may even have something to say, as explained above, to certain Christian believers who are open to new possibilities.

BIBLIOGRAPHY

Akenson, D. (2000). *Saint Saul: A Skeleton Key to the Historical Jesus*, Oxford University Press: Oxford, New York.

Anderson, Paul N., Felix Just, Tom Thatcher (2007). *John, Jesus and History: Critical Appraisals of Crotical Views*, Symposium Series 1 (44), Society of Biblical Literature: Atlanta.

Appolonj-Ghetti B., Ferrua, A., Josi, E., Kirschbaum, E. (1951), 2 vols. *Esplorazioni sotto la Confessione di san Pietro in Vaticano*, Tipografia Poliglotta Vaticana: Rome.

Baigent, M. & Leigh, R. (1992). *The Dead Sea Scrolls Deception*, Corgi Books: London.

Baltz, Frederick W. (2010). *The Mystery of the Beloved Disciple: New Evidence, Complete Answer*, Infinity Publishing: Pennsylvania.

Barnes, T. D. (1984). *Early Christianity and the Roman Empire*, Variorum: London.

Bauckham, R. (2006). *Jesus and the Eyewitnesses*, William B. Eerdmans Publishing: Grand Rapids.

—— (2007). *The Testimony of the Beloved Disciple: Narrative, History, and Theology in the Gospel of John*. Baker: Grand Rapids.

Boxall, I., (2006). *The Revelation of Saint John*. Black's New Testament Commentary, Cambridge University Press: New York.

Brown, R. E. (1997). *Introduction to the New Testament*. Anchor Bible, Doubleday: New York.

—— & Meier, J. P. (1983). *Antioch and Rome: New Testament Cradles of Catholic Christianity*, Paulist Press: New York.

—— (1979). *The Community of the Beloved Disciple*. Paulist Press: New Jersey.

—— (2 vols, 1966 and 1970). *The Gospel According to John*. Anchor Bible Series, Doubleday: New York.

Bruce, F. F. (2003). *The New Testament Documents: Are They Reliable?* InterVarsity Press: Illinois.

Byrne R & McNary-Zak, B., eds (2009). *Resurrecting the Brother of Jesus: The James Ossuary Controversy and the Quest for Religious Relics*, University of South Carolina Press: Chapel Hill.

Charlesworth, James H. (1995). *The Beloved Disciple: Whose Witness Validates the Gospel of John?* Trinity Press: Valley Forge, Pennsylvania.

Crossan, J. & Reed, J. (2004). *In Search of Paul*, HarperSanFrancisco: New York.

Crotty R. (1996). *The Jesus Question: The Historical Search*, HarperCollins Religious: Melbourne.

—— (1996). 'James the Just in the History of Early Christianity'. *Australian Biblical Review*, 44, pp 42-52.

—— (2015). *Peter the Rock: What the Roman Papacy Was and What it Might Become*, Spectrum Publications: Melbourne.

—— (1995). 'The Role of Post Mortem Visions in the Jewish Intertestamental Literature', *Pacifica*, 8, pp. 1-8.

—— (1996a). *The Jesus Question: The historical search*, Harper-Collins: Melbourne.

—— (1996b). 'James the Just in the History of Early Christianity', *Australian Biblical Review* , 44, pp. 42-52.

—— (2001). *Roman Christianity: The Distancing of Jew and Christian*, CJCR Press: Cambridge.

—— (2003). *Beyond the Jesus Question; Confronting the Historical Jesus*, PostPressed: Flaxton, Qld.

—— (2012). *Three Revolutions. Three Drastic Changes in Biblical Interpretation*, ATF Press: Adelaide.

Culpepper, R. Alan (1983). *Anatomy of the Fourth Gospel: A Study in Literary Design*. Fortress: Minneapolis.

D'Costa, G. (1966). 'The impossibility of a pluralism view of religion', *Religious Studies*, 32, pp. 223-232.

Davies, P. (1992). *In Search of 'Ancient Israel'*, Sheffield Academic Press: London & New York.

—— (1998), *Scribes and Schools. The Canonisation of the Hebrew Scriptures*, Westminster John Knox Press: Louisville.

De Vaux, R. (1973), *Archaeology and the Dead Sea Scrolls*, OUP: London.

Dodd, C. H. (1968). *The Interpretation of the Fourth Gospel*. Cambridge University Press: London.

Ehrman, Bart D. (2009). *Jesus, Interrupted*. HarperOne: San Francisco.

Eisenman, R. (1983). *Maccabees, Zadokites, Christians and Qumran*, E. J. Brill: Leiden.

Estes, D. (2008). *The Temporal Mechanics of the Fourth Gospel: A Theory of Hermeneutical Relativity in the Gospel of John (BIS 92)*. E. J. Brill: Leiden.

Fitzmyer, J. (2009). *The Impact of the Dead Sea Scrolls*, Paulist Press: New York.

Franzmann, M. (2001). *Jesus in the Nag Hammadi Writings*, T. & T. Clark: Edinburgh.

—— (2011). "Gnostic Portraits of Jesus." In *The Blackwell Companion to Jesus*, ed. Delbert Burkett, pp. 160-175. Blackwell Publishing: London.

Funk, Robert W. and the Jesus Seminar (1998). *The Acts of Jesus*. HarperSanFrancisco: San Francisco.

Geertz, C (1984). 'Distinguished lecture: anti anti-relativism', *American Anthropologist*, 86, 263-278.

——. (1973). *The interpretation of cultures*, New York: Basic Books.

Golb, N. (1995). *Who Wrote the Dead Sea Scrolls? The Search for the Secret of Qumran*, BCA: London, New York, Sydney, Toronto.

Goodman, M. (1994). *Mission and Conversion: Proselytizing in the Religious History of the Roman Empire*, Clarendon Press: Oxford.

Guidobaldi, F. (1978). *Il complesso archeologico di San Clemente: Risultati degli scavi piu recenti e riesami dei resti architettonici*. 2 vols, Collegio San Clemente: Rome.

Hanson, F. A. (1979). 'Does God have a body? Truth, reality and cultural relativism.' *Man*, NS 14, 515-529.

Harari, Y. N. (2011). *Sapiens: A Brief History of Humankind*, London: Harvill Secker.

Harrington W. J. (1993). *Sacra Pagina: Revelation*, Michael Glazier: Delaware.

Hick, J. (1989). *An interpretation of religion: Human responses to the transcendent*, Macmillan: London.

Hill, C. E. (2004). *The Johannine Corpus in the Early Church*. Oxford University Press: New York.

Jeffers, J. (1991), *Conflict at Rome. Social Order and Hierarchy in Early Christianity*, Fortress Press: Minneapolis.

Kasser, R., Meyer, M. & Wurst, G., eds (2006). *The Gospel of Judas*, National Geographic: Washington.

King, K. (2003). *What is Gnosticism?* Harvard University Press: Harvard.

Krosney, H. (2006), *The Lost Gospel: The Quest for the Gospel of Judas Iscariot*, National Geographic: Washington.

Leon, H. (1960). *The Jews of Ancient Rome*, Jewish Publication Society of America: Philadelphia.

Limor, O. (1988), 'The Origins of a Tradition: King David's Tomb on Mount Zion', *Traditio* vol. 44, pp. 453-462

Lindars, B. (1990). *John*, Sheffield Academic Press: Manchester.

Linforth, K. (2014). *The Beloved Disciple: Jacob the Brother of the Lord*, Vivid Publishing: Fremantle.

Loughlin, G. (1987). 'Noumenon and phenomenon', *Religious Studies*, 23, 495-508.

Lumsden, C. & Wilson, E. (1981). *Genes, mind and culture*, Harvard University Press: Cambridge, Mass.

Maloney, F. (2005). *The Gospel of John*, Sacra Pagina Series, Michael Glazier: New York.

Martinez, F. G. and Tigchelaan, E. (1997-8). *The Dead Sea Scrolls* (2 vols), Brill: Leiden and Eerdmans: Grand Rapids.

Marvin, P. C. (2010). *Four Views on the Book of Revelation*. Zondervan: Grand Rapids.

Mounce, Robert H. (1998). *The Book of Revelation*. Eerdmans: Grand Rapids.

Murphy-O'Connor, J. (1994). 'The Cenacle and Community: The Background of Acts 2:44-45' in Coogan, M., Exum, J. & Stager L. (eds.), *Scripture and Other Artifacts: Essays on the Bible and Archaeology in honor of Philip J. King*, Westminster John Knox Press: Louisville.

Pagels, E. (1975). *The Gnostic Paul*, Fortress Press: Philadelphia.

—— (1979). *The Gnostic Gospels*, Weidenfeld & Nicholson: London.

—— (1988). *Adam, Eve and the Serpent*, Weidenfeld & Nicholson: London.

—— (1995). *The Origin of Satan*, Random House: New York.

Peterson, J. (1969). 'House-churches in Rome', *Vigiliae Christianae*, 23, pp. 264-272.

—— (1973). 'Some Titular Churches at Rome with traditional New Testament Connections', *Expository Times*, 84, pp. 277-279.

Pinkerfeld, J. (1960), '"David's Tomb": Notes on the History of the Building. Preliminary Report' in *Louis M. Rabinowitz Fund for the Exploration of Ancient Synagogues, Bulletin*, vol. 3, pp. 41-43.

Richardson, P. (1998). 'Augustan-Era Synagogues in Rome' in K. Donfried & P. Richardson (eds.), *Judaism and Christianity in First-Century Rome*, William B. Eerdmans: Grand Rapids and Cambridge, pp. 17-29.

Robinson, J. A. T. (1977). *Redating the New Testament*. SCM Press: London.

Robinson, J. M., ed. (1978), *The Nag Hammadi Library in English*, HarperSanFrancisco: San Francisco.

Schiffman, L.H. (2010). *Qumran and Jerusalem: Studies in the Dead Sea Scrolls and the History of Judaism*, William B. Eerdermans: Grand Rapids.

Schuller, E.M. (2006). *The Dead Sea Scrolls: What have we learned?* Westminster John Knox Press: New York.

Shanks, H. (1992). *Understanding the Dead Sea Scrolls*, Random House: New York.

Silver, L. (2006). *Challenging Nature: The Clash of Science and Spirituality at the New Frontiers of Life*, New York: HarperCollins.

Slingerland, D. (1989). 'Christus-Chrestus?' in A. Avery-Peck (ed.), *The Literature of Early Rabbinic Judaism: Issues in Talmudic Redaction and Interpretation*, University Press of America: Washington, pp. 133-144.

Smolicz, J. (1984). 'Multiculturalism and an overarching framework of values: Some educational responses to assimilation, interaction and separatism in ethnically plural societies', *European Journal of Education*, 2, 2-24.

—— (1988), 'Tradition, core values and intercultural development', *Ethnic and Racial Studies*, 11, 384-410.

Snyder, G. (1998), 'The Interaction of Jews with Non-Jews in Rome', in K. Donfried & P. Richardson (eds.), *Judaism and Christianity in First-Century Rome*, William B. Eerdmans: Grand Rapids and Cambridge, pp. 69-92.

Spiro, M. (1978). 'Culture and human nature', In G. Spindler (ed.), *The making of psychological anthropology*, University of California Press: Berkeley.

Starbird, M. (2005). *Mary Magdalene, Bride in Exile*, Bear & Co.: Vermont.

Strand, K. (1992). 'Peter and Paul in relationship to the episcopal succession in the Church at Rome', *Andrews University Seminary Studies*, 3, pp. 217-232.

Sweet, J. P. (1979, updated 1990). *Revelation*, SCM Press: London.

Taylor, J. (1993). *Christians and the Holy Places: The Myth of Jewish-Christian Origins*, Clarendon Press: Oxford.

Thatcher, T., ed. (2007). *What We Have Heard from the Beginning: The Past, Present and Future of Johannine Studies*. Baylor University Press: Waco.

Thompson, T. (2000). *The Bible in History: How writers create a past*, Pimlico: London.

—— & Verenna, T. (2012). *'Is this not the Carpenter?' The Question of the Historicity of the Figure of Jesus*, Acumen Publishing: Durham.

Vanderkam, J. (rev. ed. 2010). *The Dead Sea Scrolls Today*, William B. Eerdemans: Grand Rapids.

Vermes, G. (1997), *The Complete Dead Sea Scrolls in English*, Allen Lane Penguin: London.

Wall, R. W. (2011). *Revelation*, Baker Books: Ada, MI.

Walters, J. (1998). 'Romans, Jews and Christians: The Impact of the Romans on Jewish/Christian Relations in First-Century Rome' in K. Donfried & P. Richardson (eds.), *Judaism and Christianity in First-Century Rome*, William B. Eerdmans: Grand Rapids and Cambridge, pp. 175-195.

Westerholm, S., ed. (2014). *The Blackwell Companion to Paul*, Wiley Blackwell: Chichester.

Whiston, W., trans. (1987). *The Works of Josephus*, Hendrickson Publishers Inc.: Peabody, MA.

Wiefel, W. (1977). 'The Jewish Community in Ancient Rome and the Origins of Roman Christianity' in K. Donfried (ed), *The Romans Debate*, Augsburg Press: Minneapolis, pp. 100-119.

—— (1991). 'The Jewish Community in Rome' in K. Donfried (ed.), *The Romans Debate*, 2nd ed, Hendrickson: Peabody, Mass., pp.84-101.

Wills, G. (2006). *What Paul Meant*, Viking: New York.

Wilson, E.O. (2014). *The Meaning of Human Existence*, New York and London: Liveright Publishing Corporation.

Witherington III, Ben, (2003). *Revelation, The New Cambridge Bible Commentary*, Cambridge University Press; New York.

Yadin, Y. (1957). *The Message of the Scrolls*, Weidenfeld & Nicolson: London

Emeritus Professor Robert Crotty, STL (Rome),
SSL (Rome), MA (Melbourne), PhD (Adelaide),
Élève Titulaire de l'École Biblique (Jerusalem),
has studied history, Christian theology, biblical
studies and education in Australia, Rome and
Jerusalem.

He has since been a lecturer in Hebrew
language and Old Testament at Yarra Theological
Union in Melbourne, lecturer in Old Testament
at the United Faculty of Theology in Melbourne,
tutor in History and Classics at Melbourne
University, and Professor of Religion and
Education at the University of South Australia
and its predecessors. He is at present an Emeritus
Professor at the same University.

He has been appointed a Visiting Scholar
at the Centre for Hebrew and Jewish Studies at
Oxford five times, a Visiting Fellow at the Centre
for Jewish/Christian Relations at Cambridge and
Visiting Research Fellow in Education at the
University of Adelaide. He has written over thirty
books on religious and related topics.

Made in the USA
Columbia, SC
05 July 2025

60341388R00202